YAKITATE!! JAPAN
5
VIZ Media Edition

★The Story Thus Far★

Kazuma Azuma, a boy who possesses dough-friendly "Hands of the Sun," and the knowledgeable Kyosuke Kawachi were recruited by Pantasia Bakery scion Tsukino Azusagawa to work at the company's South Tokyo Branch.

Azuma and other new employees are embroiled in Pantasia Group's annual Rookie Tournament, a major event that could influence Tsukino's struggle to control Pantasia.

Azuma, who safely passed through the preliminaries, defeated Tsukino's little sister Mizuno in the first match of the main competition. In the second round, he won the fried-noodle-bread match against S.H. Hokou.

His next opponent is Mizuno's mysterious masked bread craftsman, Koala. What tricks does the massive marsupial have up his sleeve?

CONTENTS

Research Assistance/Bakery Consultant:
Koichi Uchimura.

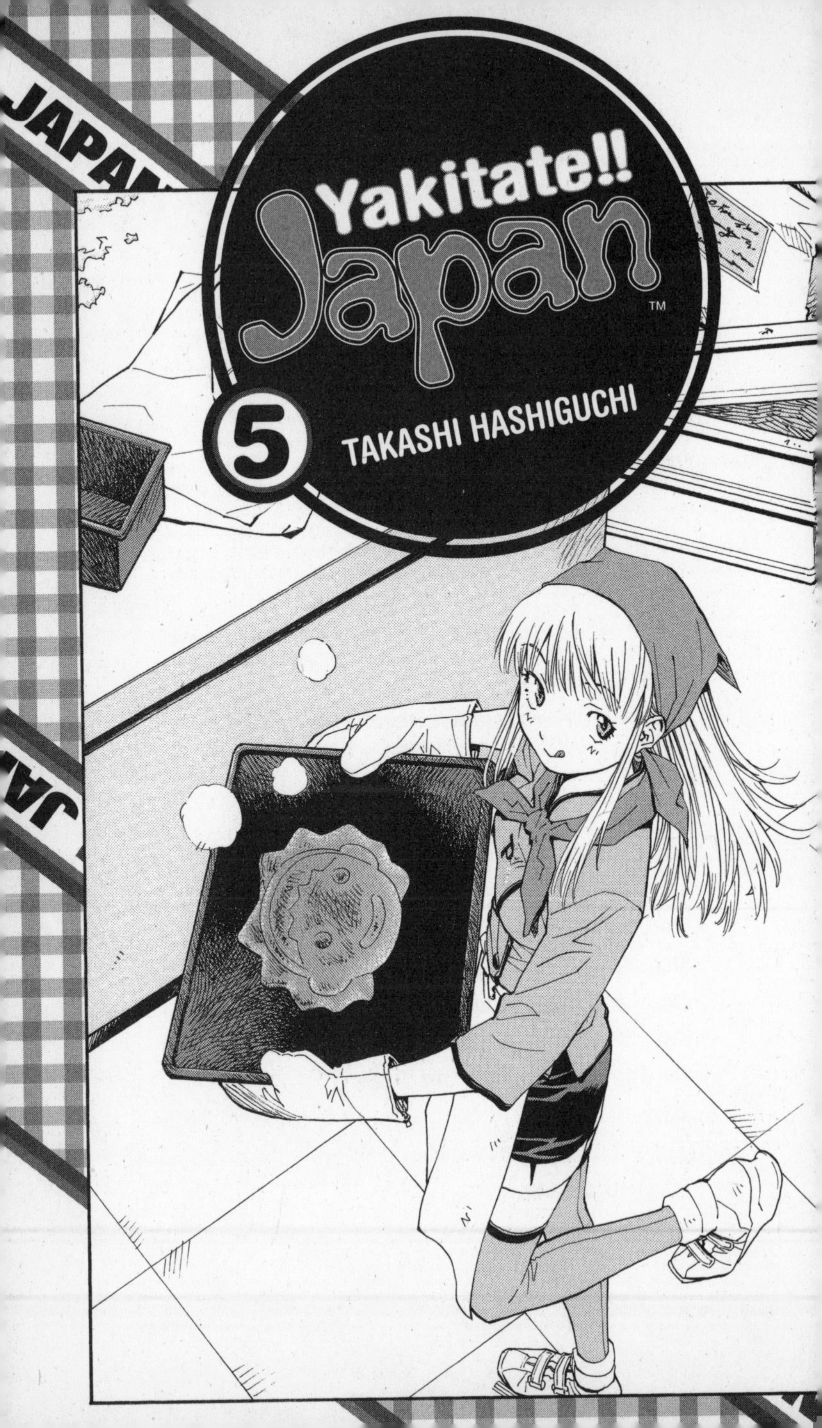
Yakitate!! Japan™
5
TAKASHI HASHIGUCHI
JAPAN

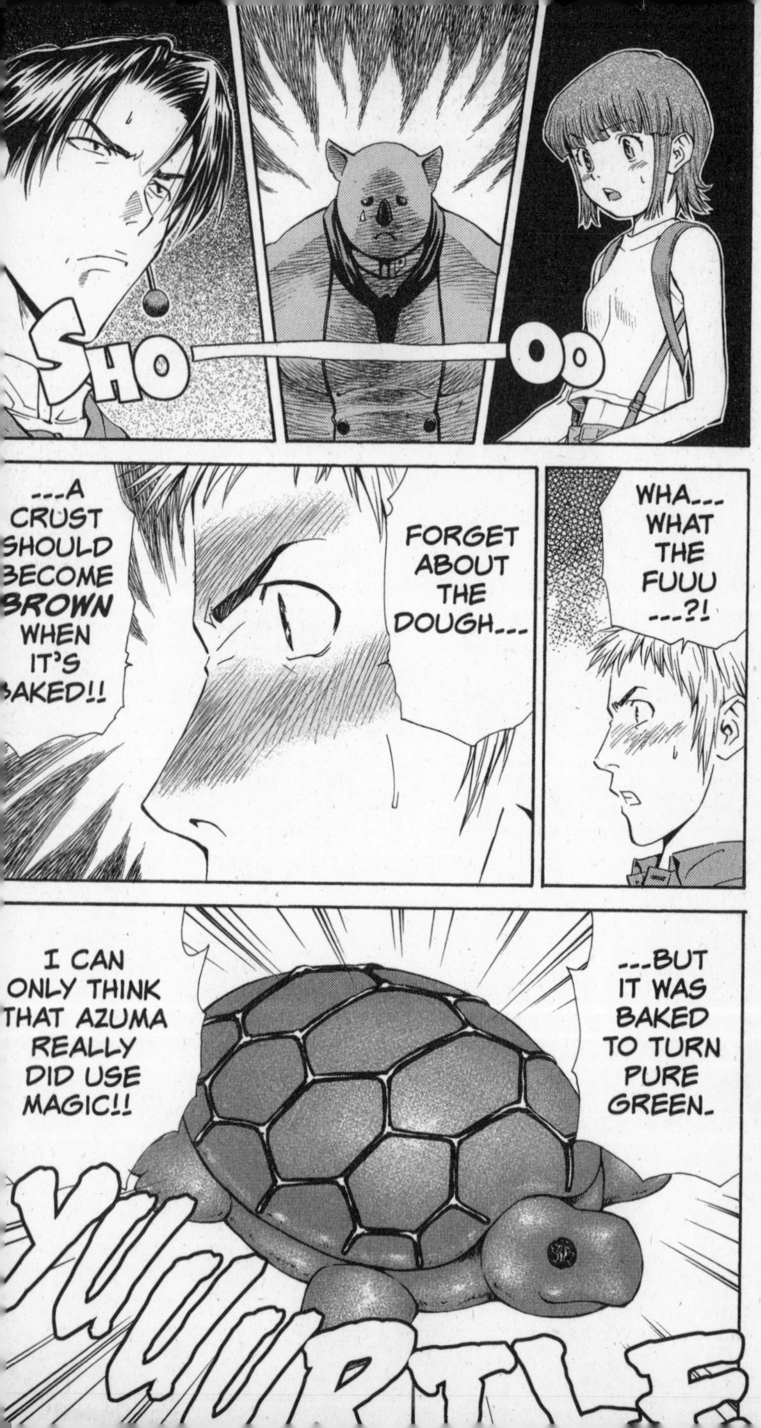
SHO OO
WHA... WHAT THE FUUU ...?!
FORGET ABOUT THE DOUGH...
...A CRUST SHOULD BECOME BROWN WHEN IT'S BAKED!!
...BUT IT WAS BAKED TO TURN PURE GREEN.
I CAN ONLY THINK THAT AZUMA REALLY DID USE MAGIC!!
YUUURTLE

Story 33:
Source of the Magic

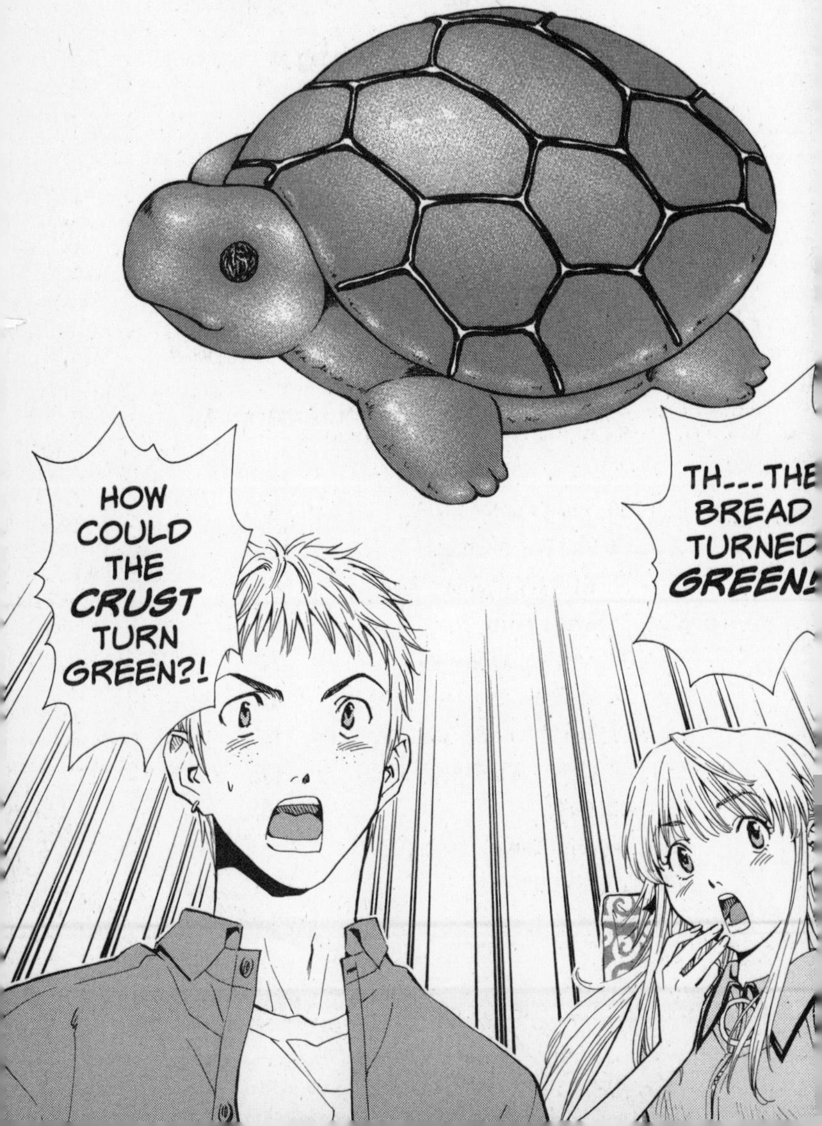
TH...THE BREAD TURNED GREEN!
HOW COULD THE CRUST TURN GREEN?!

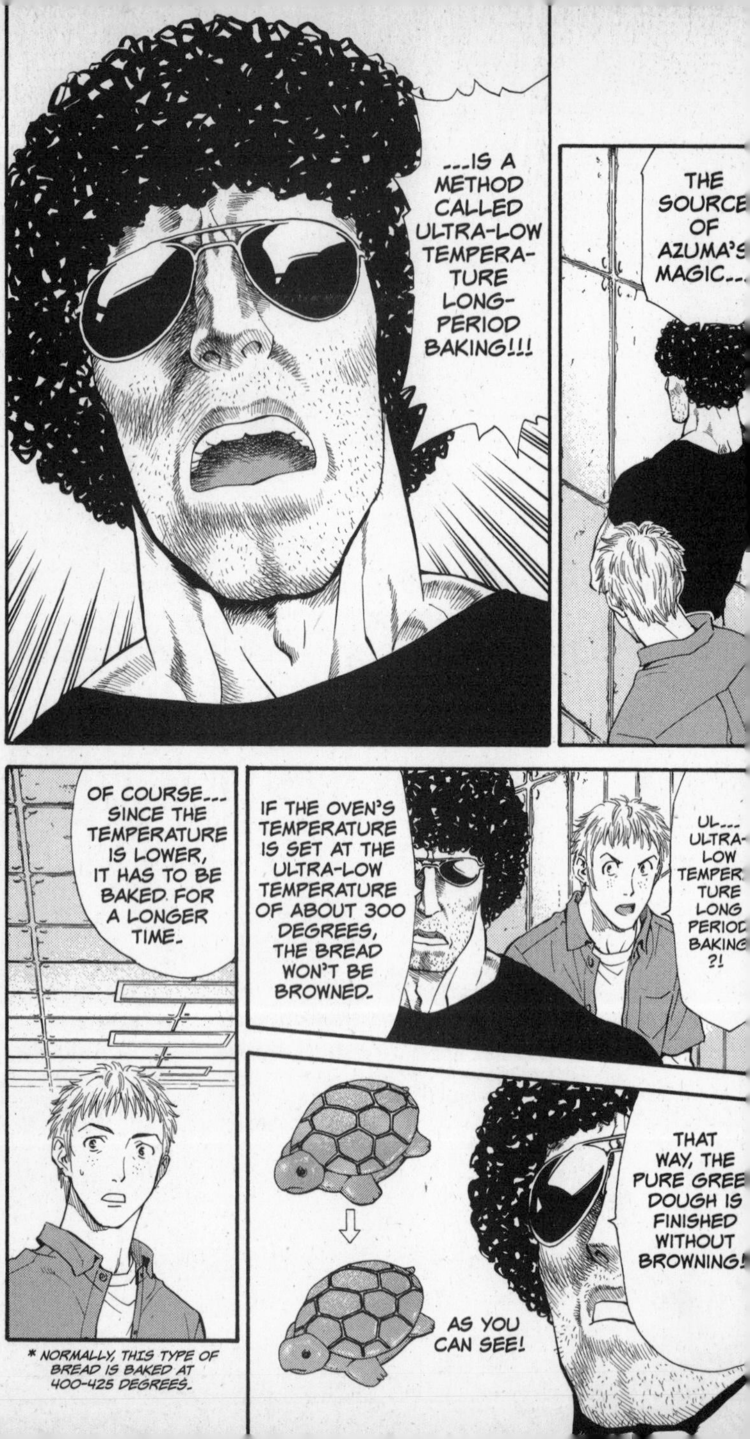
THE SOURCE OF AZUMA'S MAGIC...
...IS A METHOD CALLED ULTRA-LOW TEMPERATURE LONG-PERIOD BAKING!!!
UL... ULTRA-LOW TEMPERATURE LONG PERIOD BAKING ?!
IF THE OVEN'S TEMPERATURE IS SET AT THE ULTRA-LOW TEMPERATURE OF ABOUT 300 DEGREES, THE BREAD WON'T BE BROWNED.
THAT WAY, THE PURE GREEN DOUGH IS FINISHED WITHOUT BROWNING!
AS YOU CAN SEE!
OF COURSE... SINCE THE TEMPERATURE IS LOWER, IT HAS TO BE BAKED FOR A LONGER TIME.
* NORMALLY, THIS TYPE OF BREAD IS BAKED AT 400-425 DEGREES.

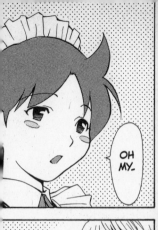

OH MY...

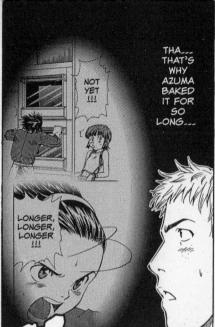

NOT YET !!!

THA... THAT'S WHY AZUMA BAKED IT FOR SO LONG...

LONGER, LONGER, LONGER !!!

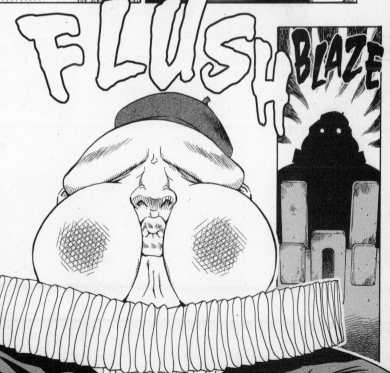

FLUSH

BLAZE

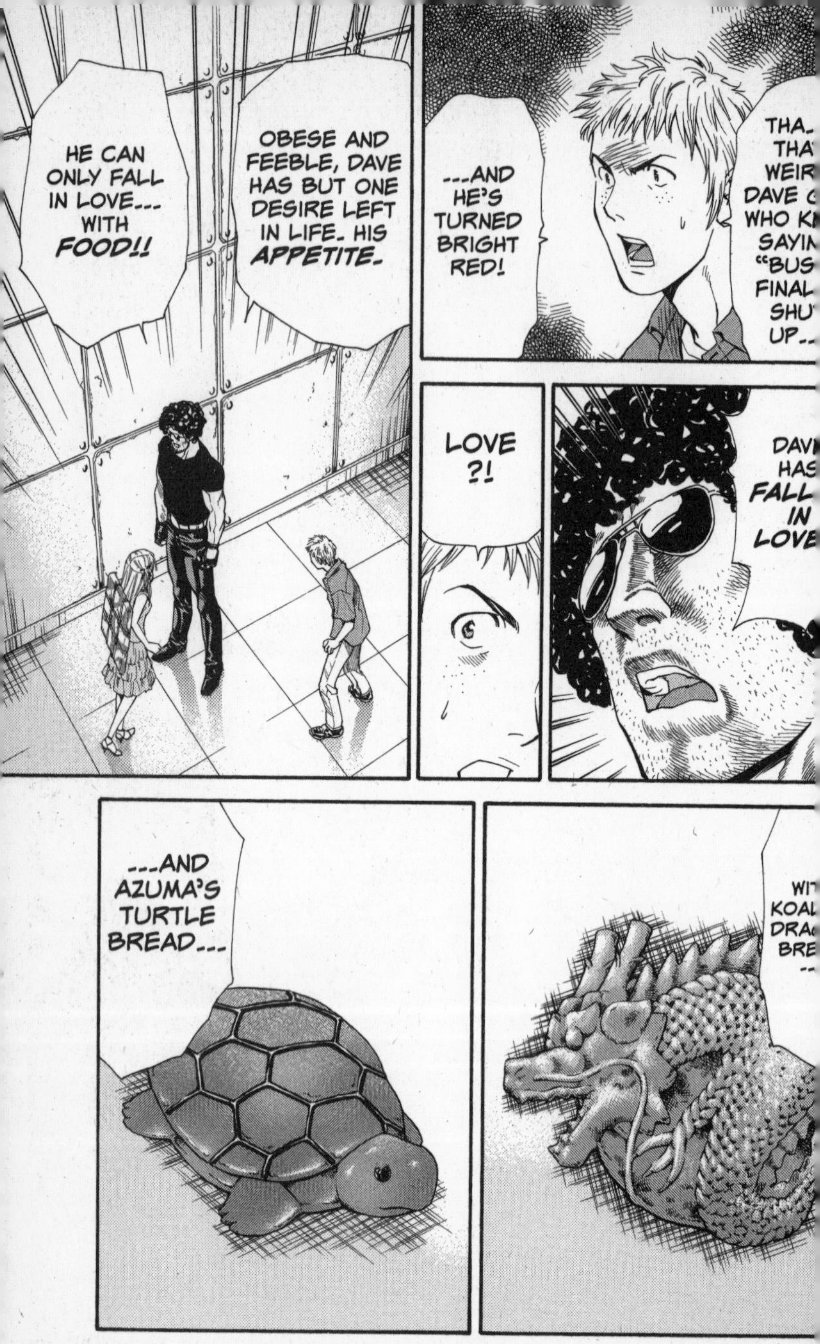
THA- THA WEIR DAVE WHO K SAYIN "BUS FINAL SHU UP--
---AND HE'S TURNED BRIGHT RED!
DAV HAS FALL IN LOVE
LOVE ?!
OBESE AND FEEBLE, DAVE HAS BUT ONE DESIRE LEFT IN LIFE. HIS APPETITE.
HE CAN ONLY FALL IN LOVE... WITH FOOD!!
WI KOAL DRA BRE --
---AND AZUMA'S TURTLE BREAD---

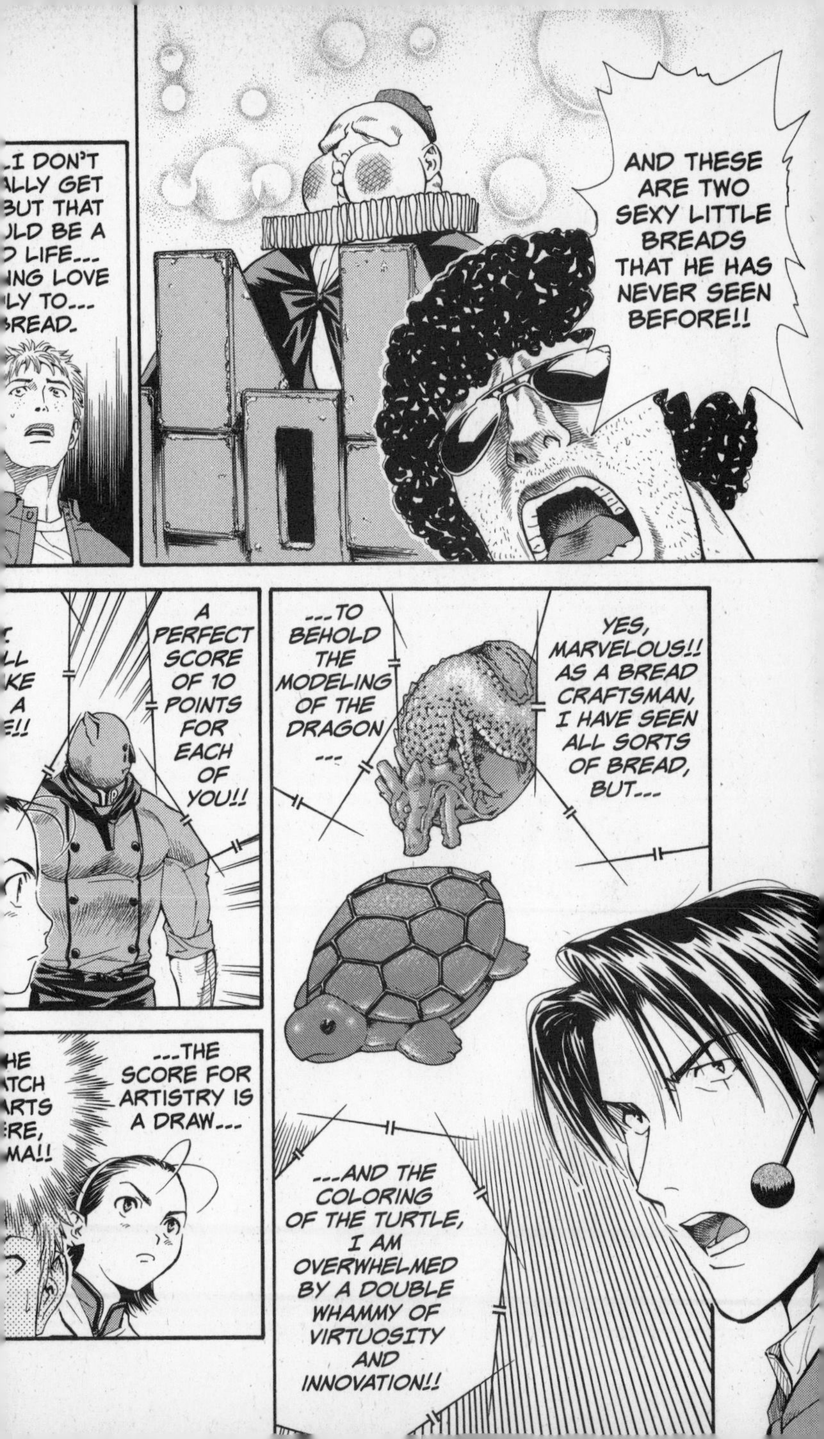
AND THESE ARE TWO SEXY LITTLE BREADS THAT HE HAS NEVER SEEN BEFORE!!
..I DON'T ALLY GET BUT THAT ULD BE A D LIFE... ING LOVE LY TO... READ.
YES, MARVELOUS!! AS A BREAD CRAFTSMAN, I HAVE SEEN ALL SORTS OF BREAD, BUT...
...TO BEHOLD THE MODELING OF THE DRAGON...
...AND THE COLORING OF THE TURTLE, I AM OVERWHELMED BY A DOUBLE WHAMMY OF VIRTUOSITY AND INNOVATION!!
A PERFECT SCORE OF 10 POINTS FOR EACH OF YOU!!
...THE SCORE FOR ARTISTRY IS A DRAW...
HE ATCH ARTS ERE, MA!!

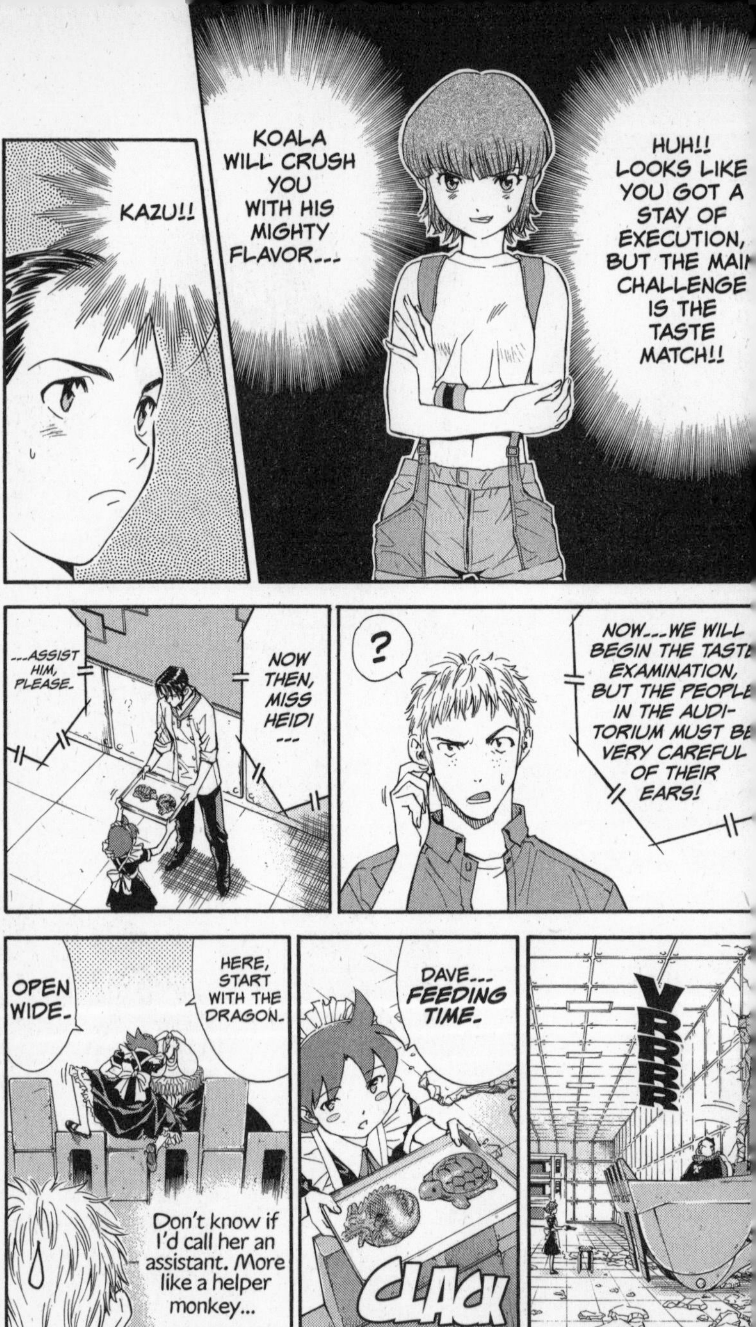
HUH!! LOOKS LIKE YOU GOT A STAY OF EXECUTION, BUT THE MAI CHALLENGE IS THE TASTE MATCH!!
KOALA WILL CRUSH YOU WITH HIS MIGHTY FLAVOR...
KAZU!!
NOW...WE WILL BEGIN THE TAST EXAMINATION, BUT THE PEOPL IN THE AUDI-TORIUM MUST B VERY CAREFUL OF THEIR EARS!
?
NOW THEN, MISS HEIDI ---
...ASSIST HIM, PLEASE.
YRRRR
DAVE... FEEDING TIME.
CLACK
HERE, START WITH THE DRAGON.
OPEN WIDE.
Don't know if I'd call her an assistant. More like a helper monkey...

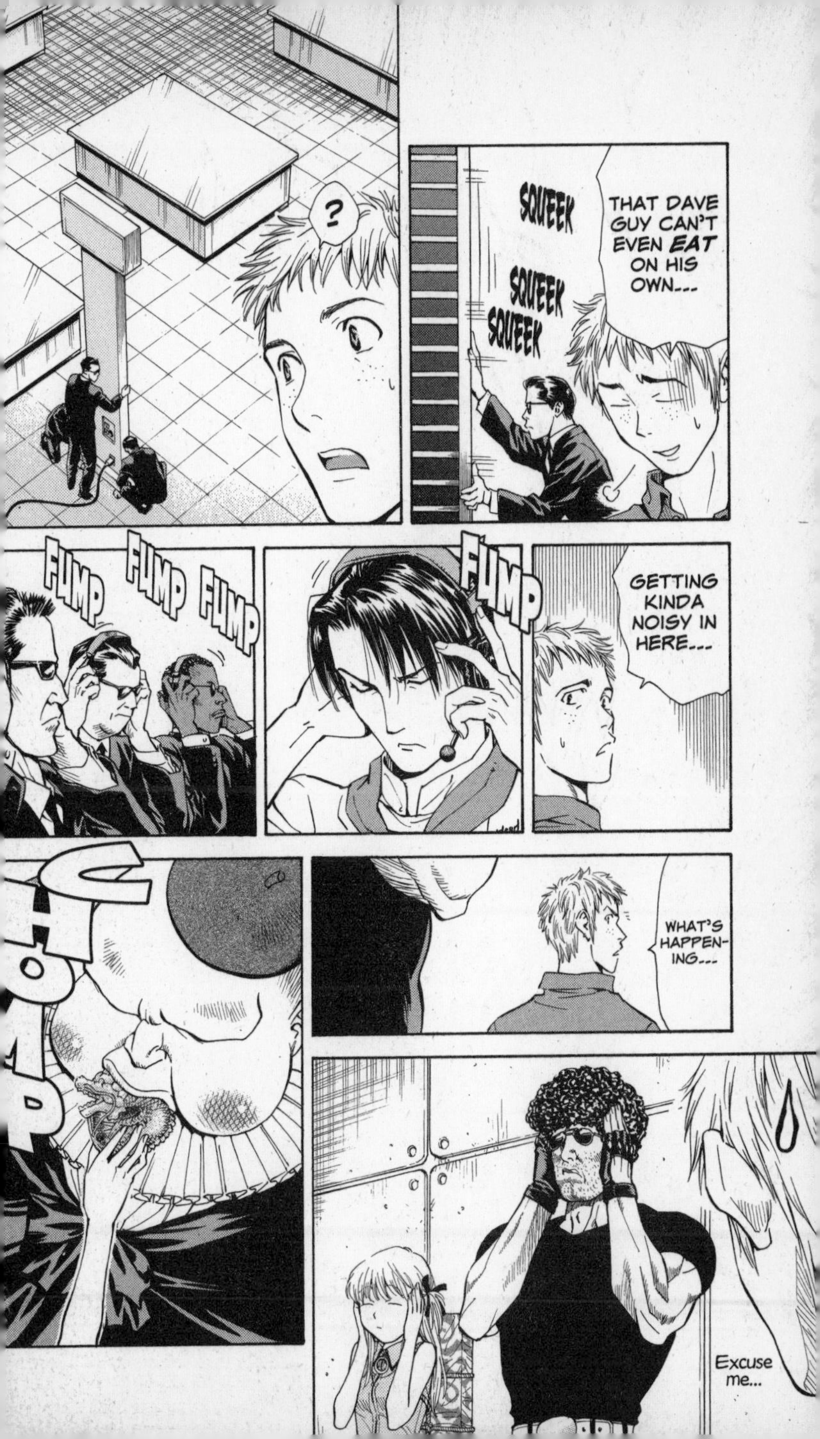
SQUEEK
SQUEEK
SQUEEK
THAT DAVE GUY CAN'T EVEN EAT ON HIS OWN...
?
GETTING KINDA NOISY IN HERE...
FUMP
FUMP
FUMP
FUMP
WHAT'S HAPPEN-ING...
Excuse me...
CHOMP

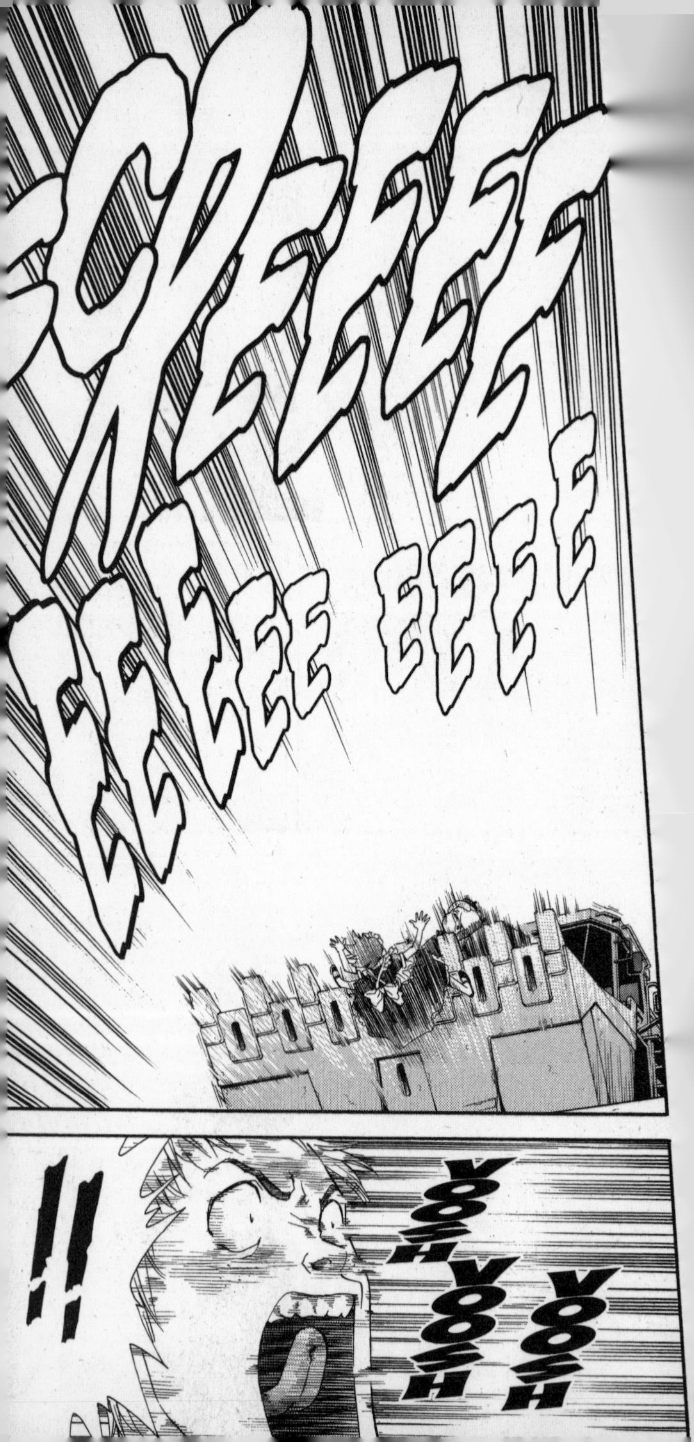
VOOSH
VOOSH
VOOSH
!!

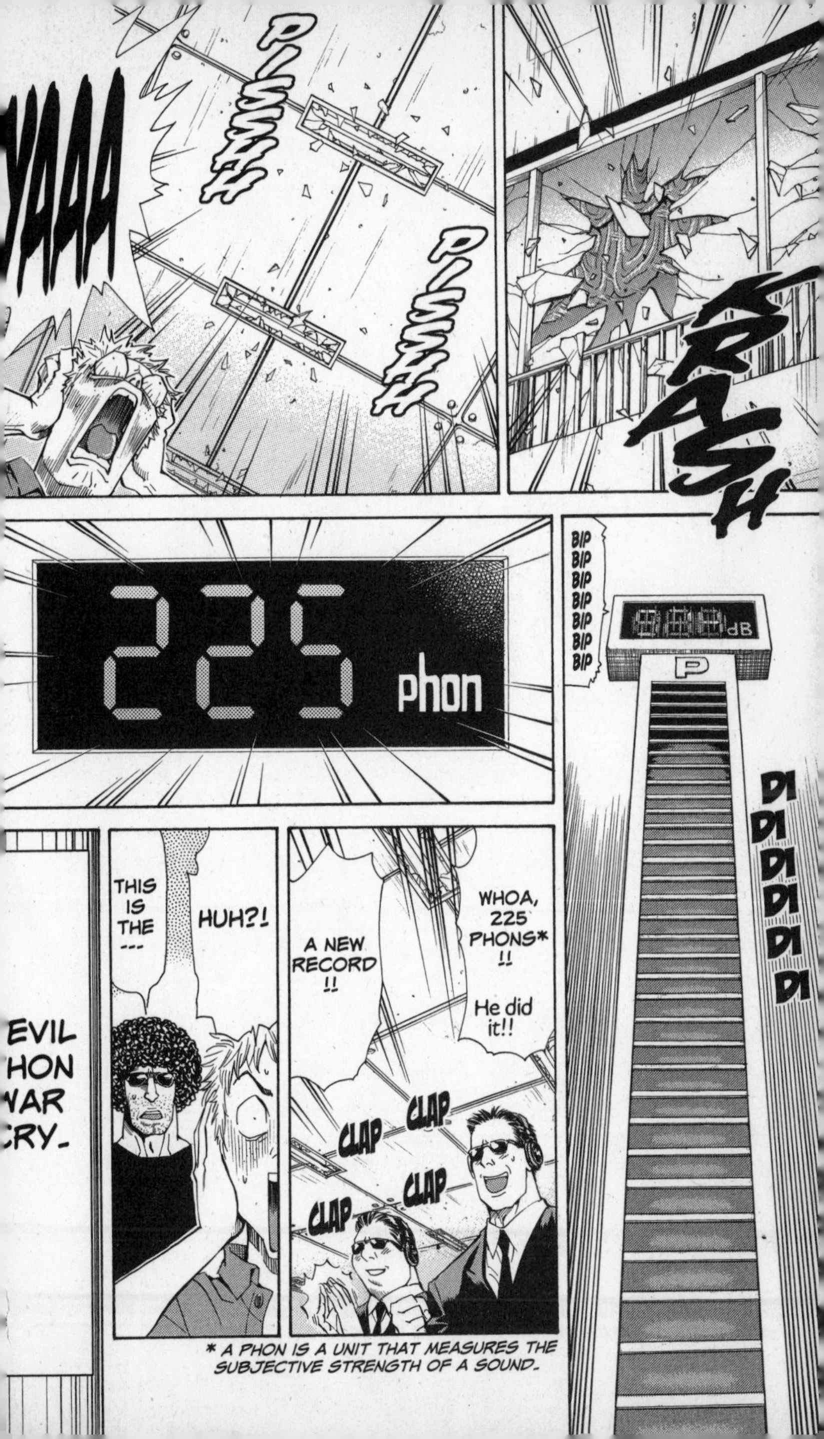
KRASH
PISHAH
PISHAH
YAAA
BIP BIP BIP BIP BIP BIP BIP
dB
P
DI DI DI DI DI DI
225 phon
WHOA, 225 PHONS* !!
He did it!!
A NEW RECORD !!
CLAP CLAP CLAP CLAP
HUH?!
THIS IS THE ---
EVIL
HON
VAR
CRY.
* A PHON IS A UNIT THAT MEASURES THE SUBJECTIVE STRENGTH OF A SOUND.

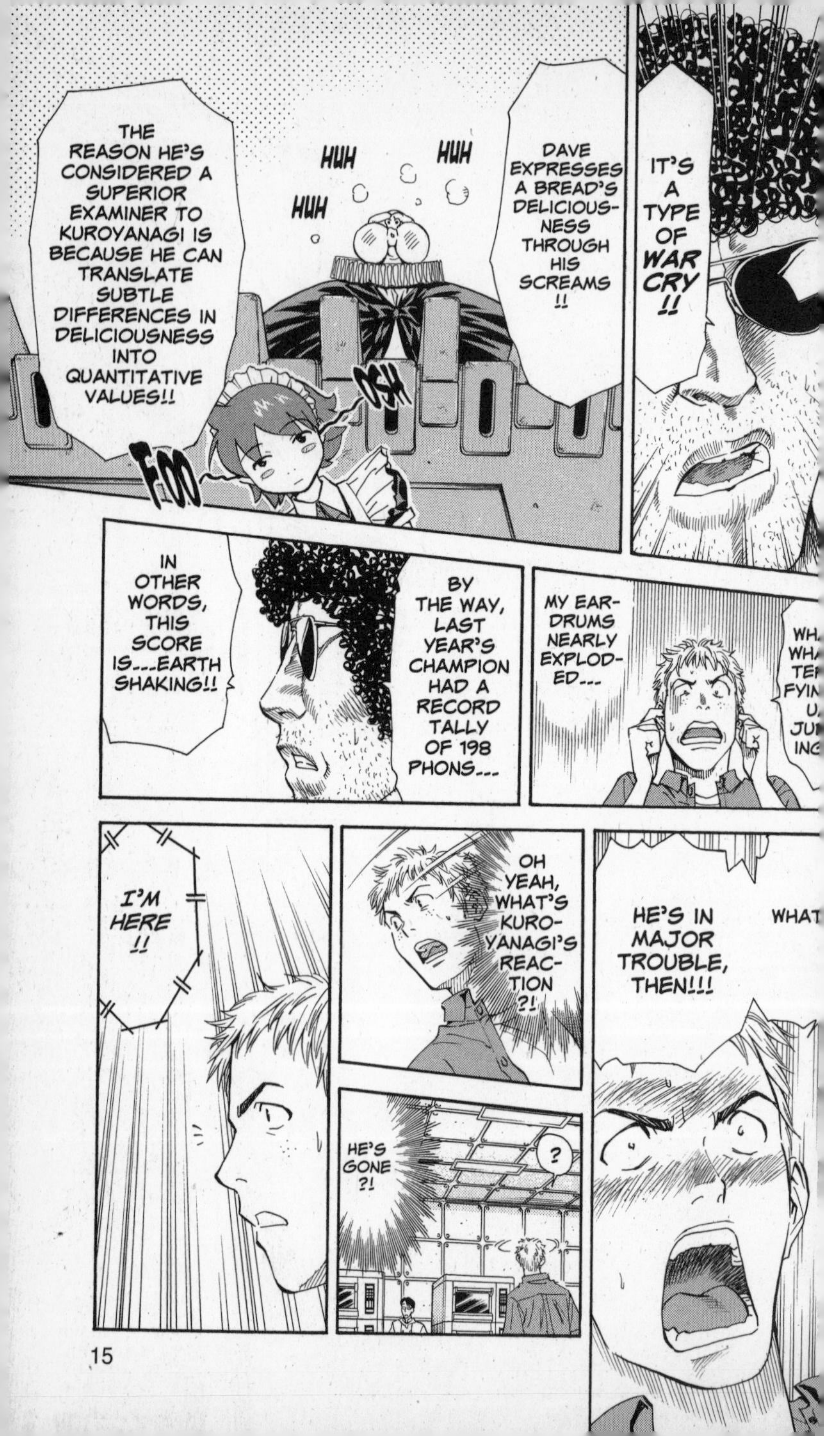
IT'S A TYPE OF WAR CRY!!
DAVE EXPRESSES A BREAD'S DELICIOUSNESS THROUGH HIS SCREAMS!!
HUH
HUH
HUH
OSH
FOO
THE REASON HE'S CONSIDERED A SUPERIOR EXAMINER TO KUROYANAGI IS BECAUSE HE CAN TRANSLATE SUBTLE DIFFERENCES IN DELICIOUSNESS INTO QUANTITATIVE VALUES!!
MY EAR-DRUMS NEARLY EXPLOD-ED...
BY THE WAY, LAST YEAR'S CHAMPION HAD A RECORD TALLY OF 198 PHONS...
IN OTHER WORDS, THIS SCORE IS...EARTH SHAKING!!
WHAT
HE'S IN MAJOR TROUBLE, THEN!!!
OH YEAH, WHAT'S KUROYANAGI'S REACTION?!
HE'S GONE?!
?
I'M HERE!!

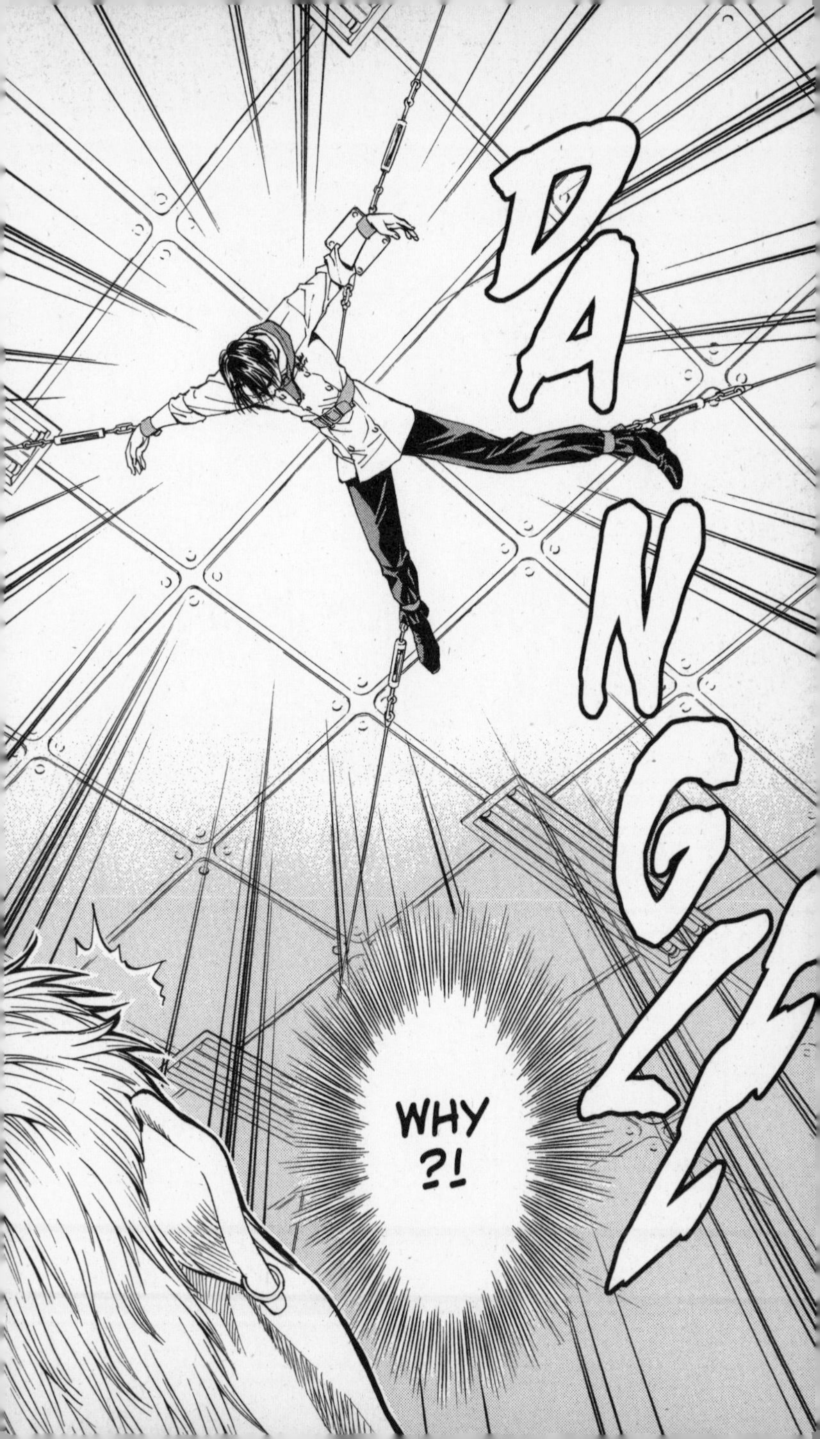
DANG!!
WHY ?!

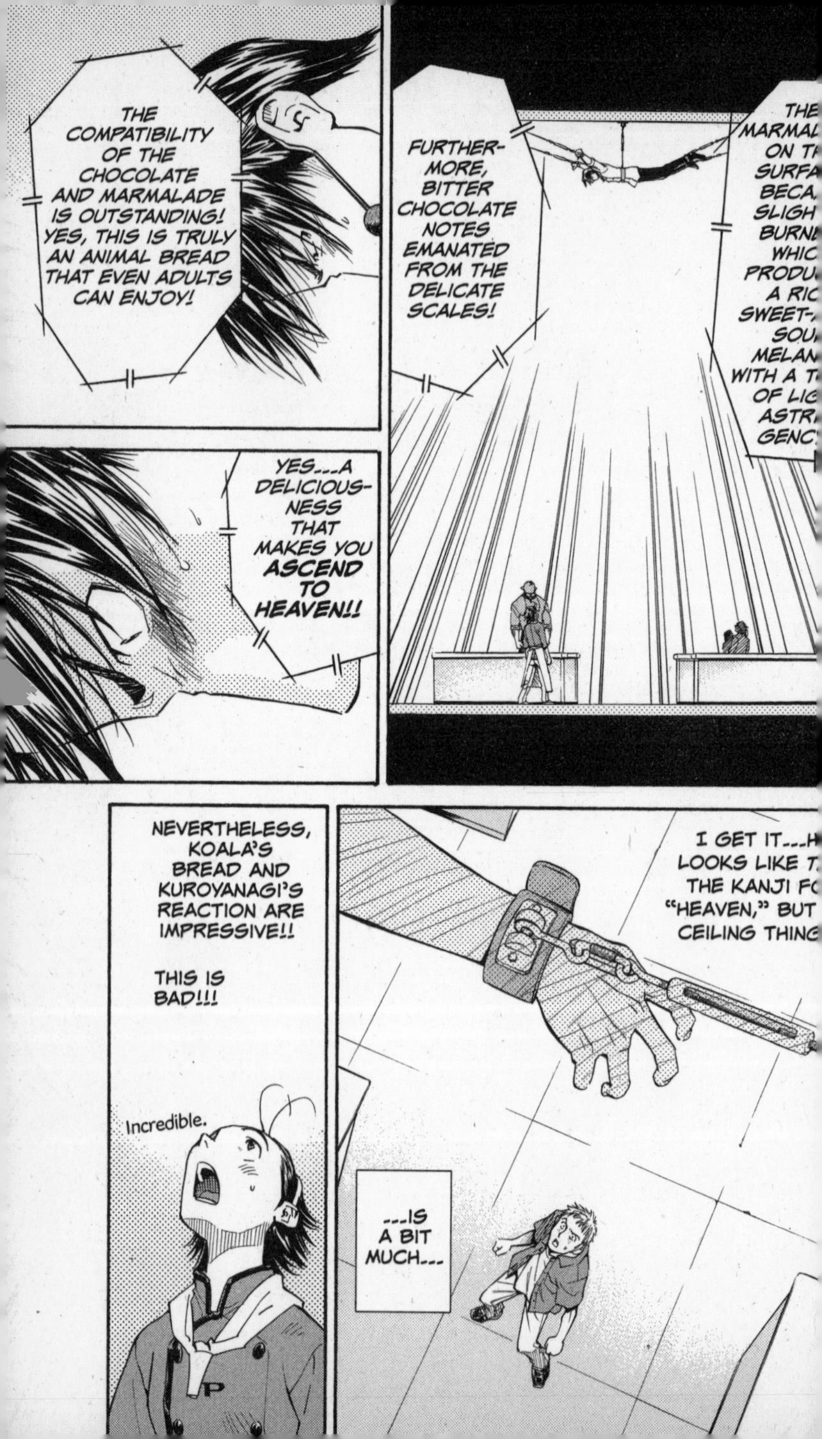
THE MARMAL ON T SURFA BECA SLIGH BURN WHIC PRODU A RIC SWEET- SOU MELAN WITH A T OF LIG ASTR GENC
FURTHER-MORE, BITTER CHOCOLATE NOTES EMANATED FROM THE DELICATE SCALES!
THE COMPATIBILITY OF THE CHOCOLATE AND MARMALADE IS OUTSTANDING! YES, THIS IS TRULY AN ANIMAL BREAD THAT EVEN ADULTS CAN ENJOY!
YES...A DELICIOUS-NESS THAT MAKES YOU ASCEND TO HEAVEN!!
I GET IT...H LOOKS LIKE T THE KANJI F "HEAVEN," BUT CEILING THING
...IS A BIT MUCH...
NEVERTHELESS, KOALA'S BREAD AND KUROYANAGI'S REACTION ARE IMPRESSIVE!!
THIS IS BAD!!!
Incredible.

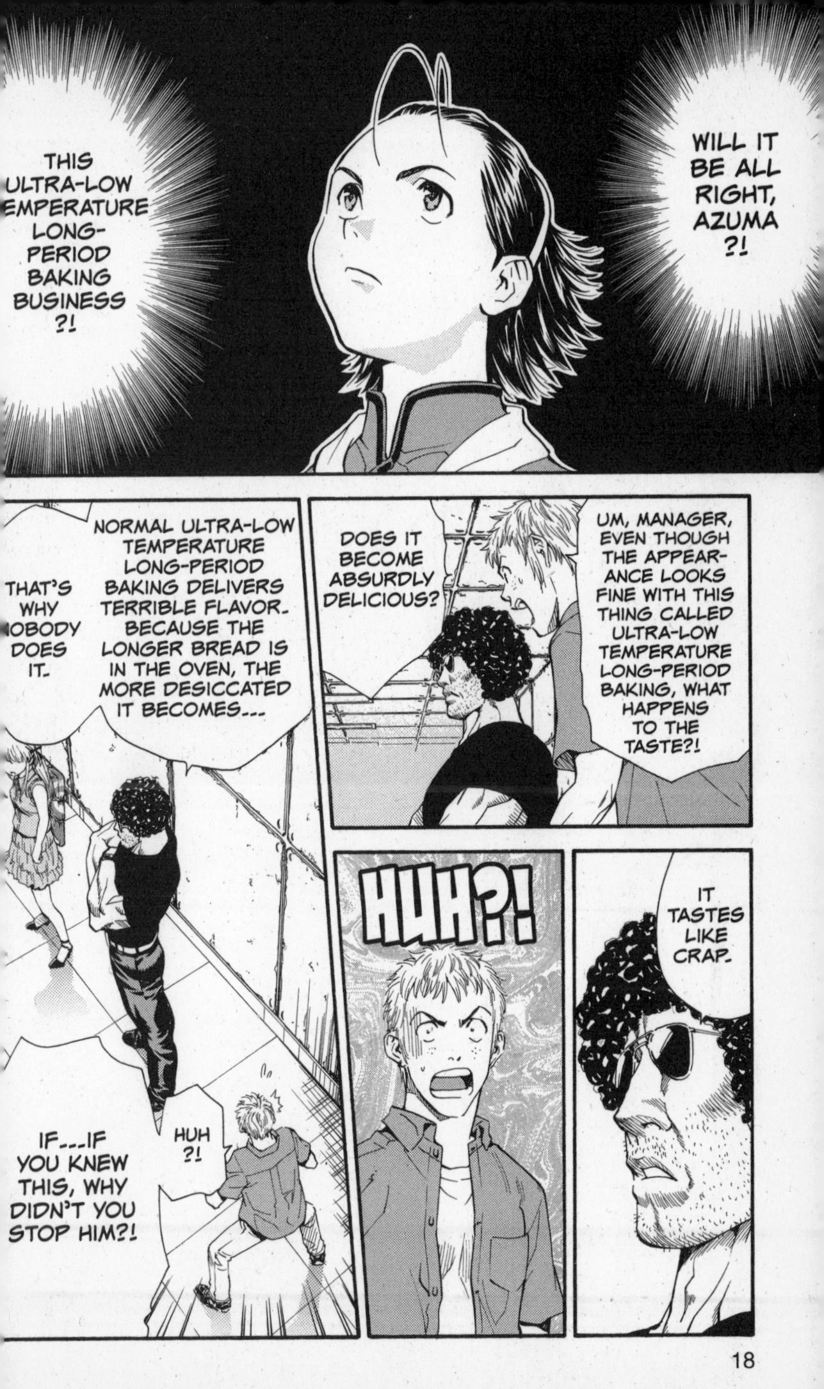

WILL IT BE ALL RIGHT, AZUMA?!
THIS ULTRA-LOW EMPERATURE LONG-PERIOD BAKING BUSINESS?!
UM, MANAGER, EVEN THOUGH THE APPEARANCE LOOKS FINE WITH THIS THING CALLED ULTRA-LOW TEMPERATURE LONG-PERIOD BAKING, WHAT HAPPENS TO THE TASTE?!
DOES IT BECOME ABSURDLY DELICIOUS?
IT TASTES LIKE CRAP.
HUH?!
NORMAL ULTRA-LOW TEMPERATURE LONG-PERIOD BAKING DELIVERS TERRIBLE FLAVOR. BECAUSE THE LONGER BREAD IS IN THE OVEN, THE MORE DESICCATED IT BECOMES...
THAT'S WHY IOBODY DOES IT.
HUH?!
IF...IF YOU KNEW THIS, WHY DIDN'T YOU STOP HIM?!

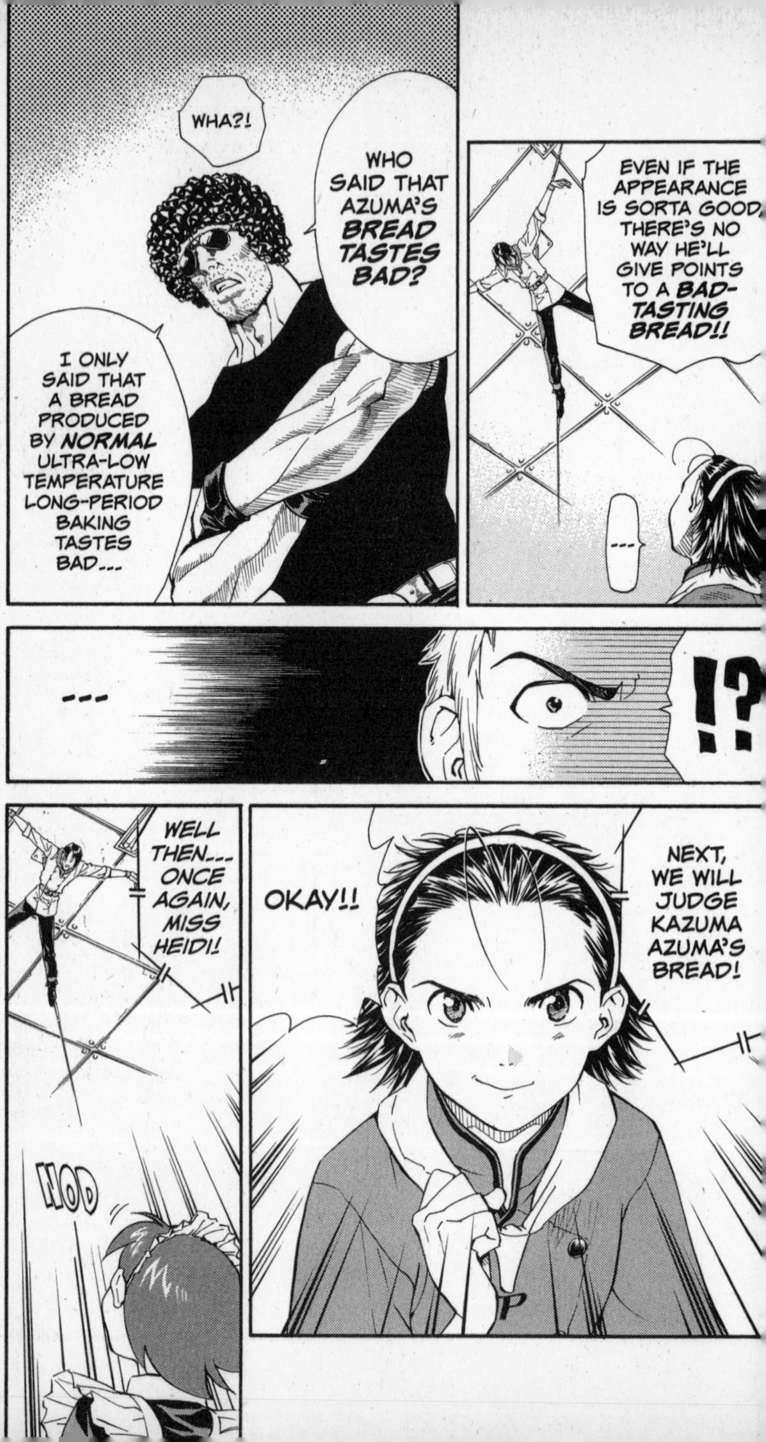
EVEN IF THE APPEARANCE IS SORTA GOOD, THERE'S NO WAY HE'LL GIVE POINTS TO A BAD-TASTING BREAD!!

WHA?!
WHO SAID THAT AZUMA'S BREAD TASTES BAD?
I ONLY SAID THAT A BREAD PRODUCED BY NORMAL ULTRA-LOW TEMPERATURE LONG-PERIOD BAKING TASTES BAD...
!?

NEXT, WE WILL JUDGE KAZUMA AZUMA'S BREAD!
OKAY!!
WELL THEN... ONCE AGAIN, MISS HEIDI!
NOD

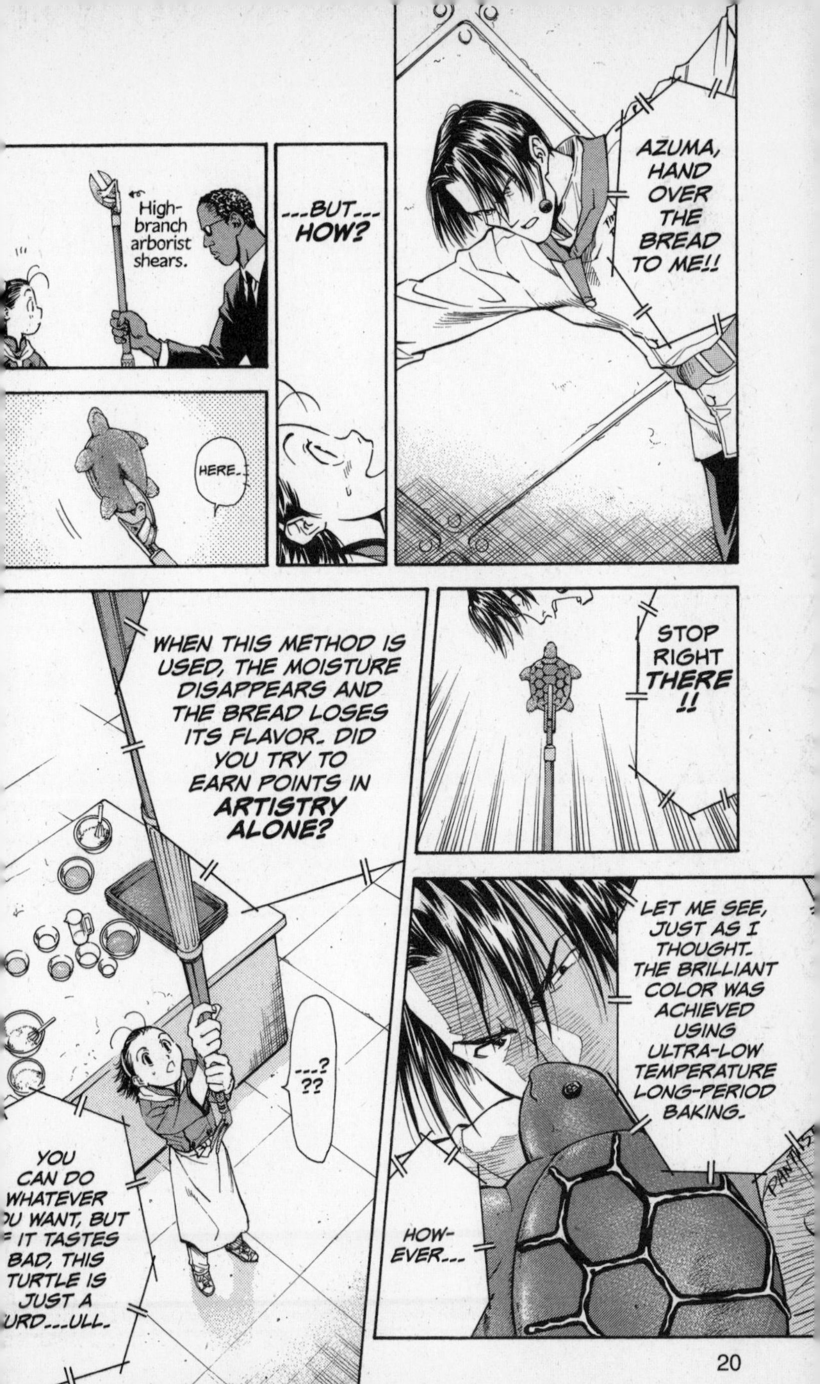
AZUMA, HAND OVER THE BREAD TO ME!!
...BUT... HOW?
High-branch arborist shears.
HERE...
STOP RIGHT THERE!!
LET ME SEE, JUST AS I THOUGHT. THE BRILLIANT COLOR WAS ACHIEVED USING ULTRA-LOW TEMPERATURE LONG-PERIOD BAKING.
HOW-EVER...
WHEN THIS METHOD IS USED, THE MOISTURE DISAPPEARS AND THE BREAD LOSES ITS FLAVOR. DID YOU TRY TO EARN POINTS IN ARTISTRY ALONE?
...? ??
YOU CAN DO WHATEVER OU WANT, BUT F IT TASTES BAD, THIS TURTLE IS JUST A URD...ULL.

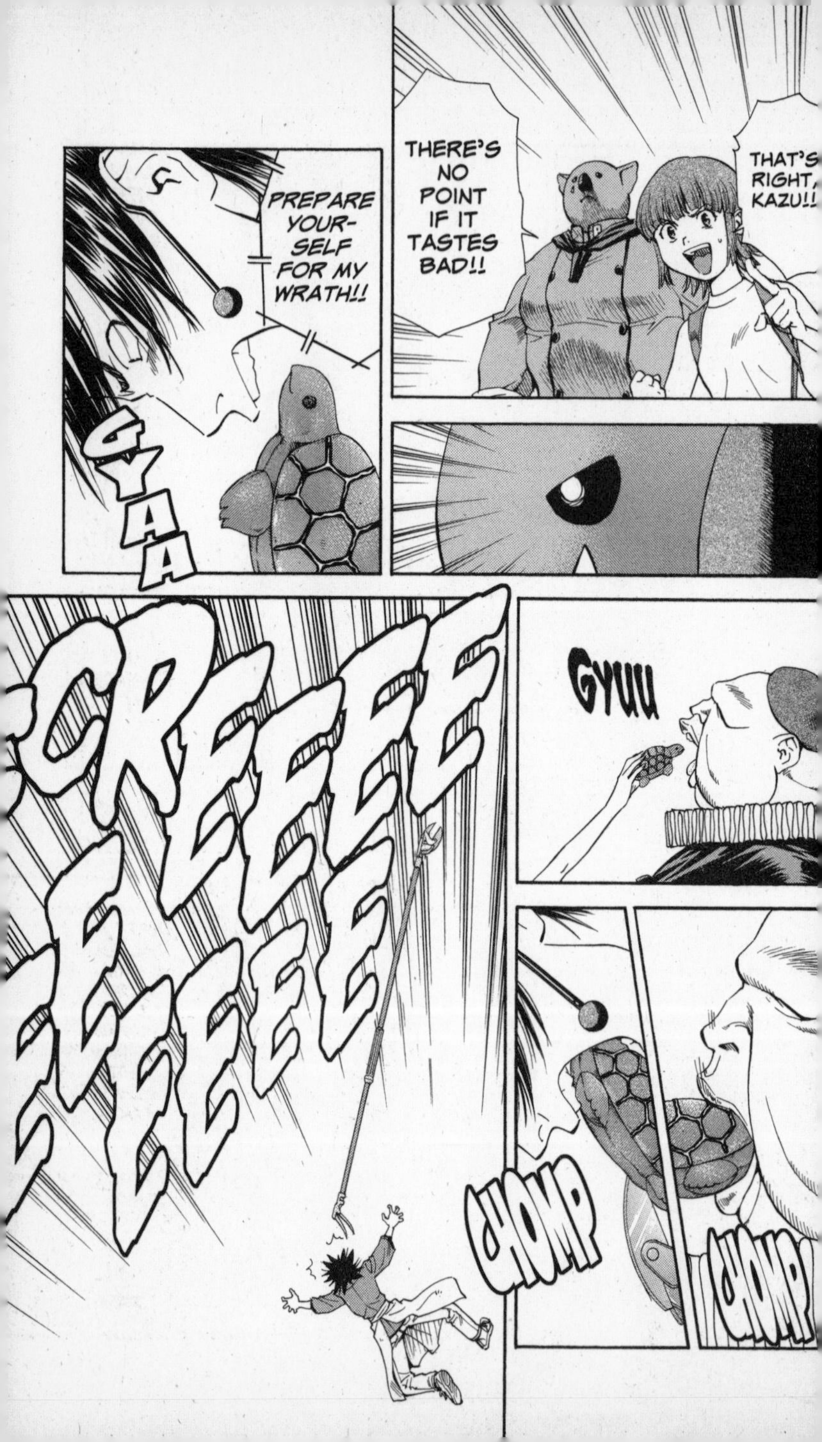

THAT'S RIGHT, KAZU!!
THERE'S NO POINT IF IT TASTES BAD!!
PREPARE YOURSELF FOR MY WRATH!!
GYAA
GYUU
CHOMP
CHOMP
CREEEEEEEEEE

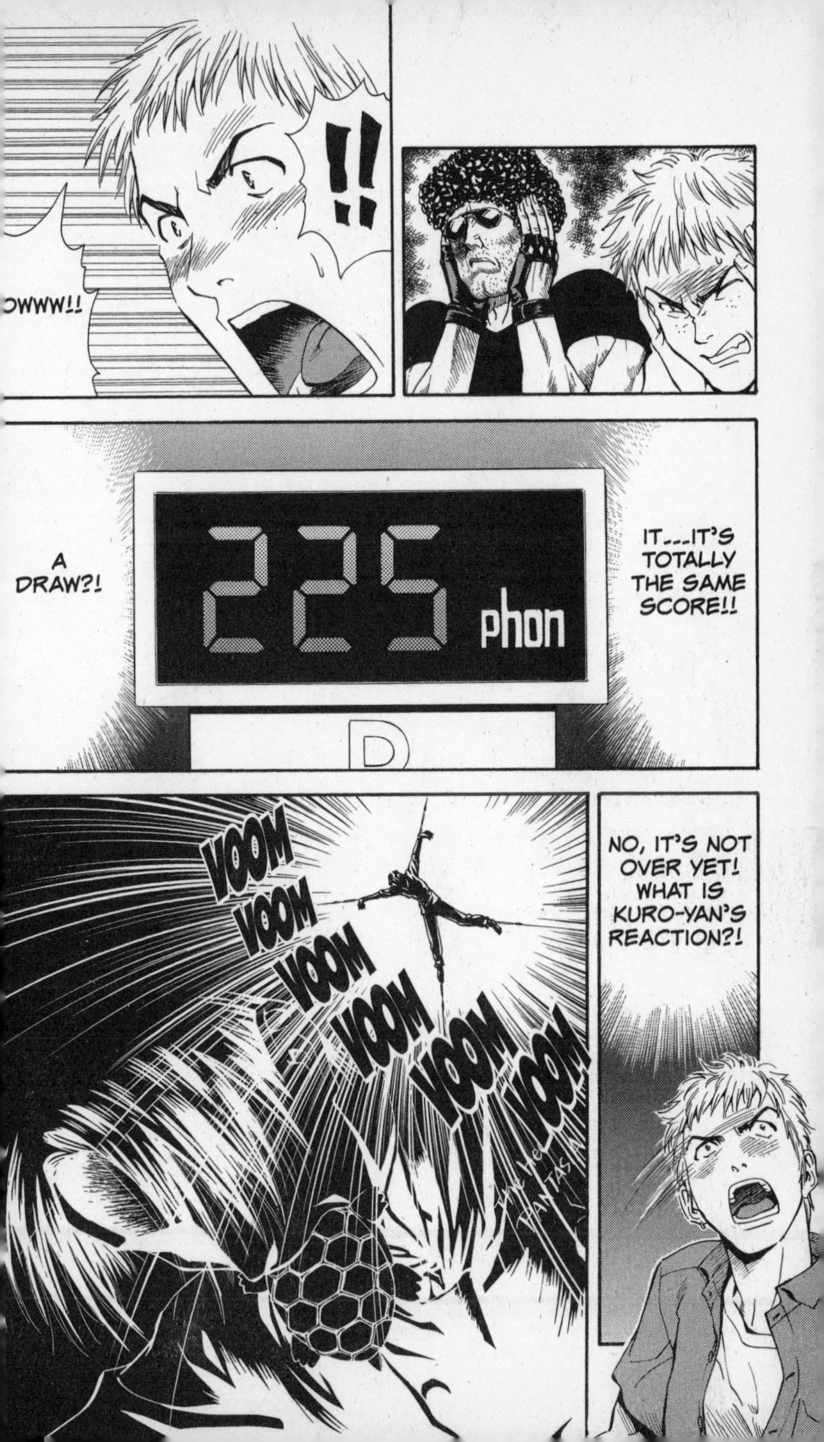
!!
OWWW!!
IT...IT'S TOTALLY THE SAME SCORE!!
225 phon
A DRAW?!
D
NO, IT'S NOT OVER YET! WHAT IS KURO-YAN'S REACTION?!
VOOM VOOM VOOM VOOM VOOM VOOM

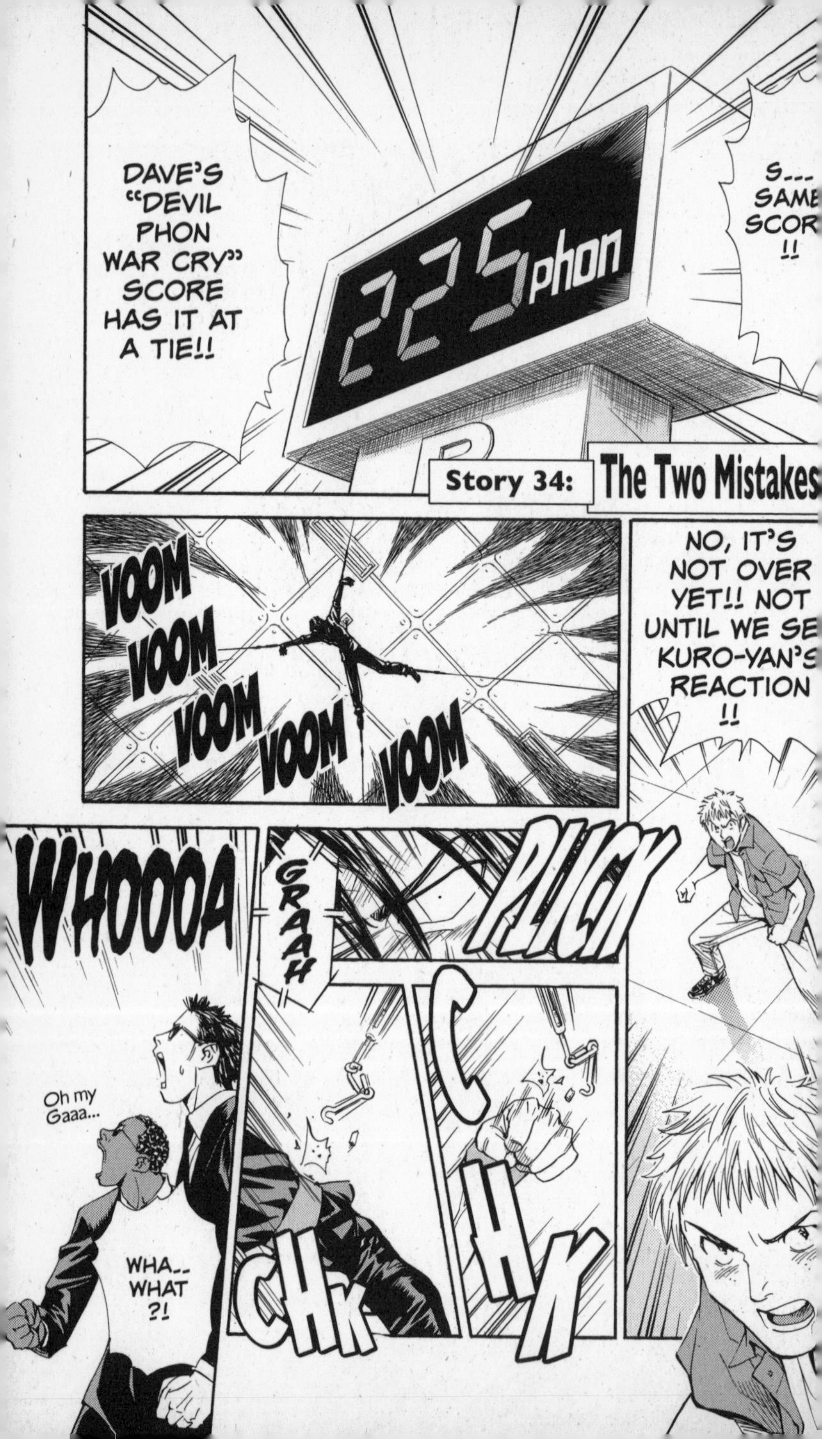
S... SAME SCORE!!
DAVE'S "DEVIL PHON WAR CRY" SCORE HAS IT AT A TIE!!
225 phon
Story 34: The Two Mistakes
NO, IT'S NOT OVER YET!! NOT UNTIL WE SEE KURO-YAN'S REACTION!!
VOOM VOOM VOOM VOOM VOOM
GRAAH
PLICK
CHK
CHK
WHOOOA
WHA... WHAT?!
Oh my Gaaa...

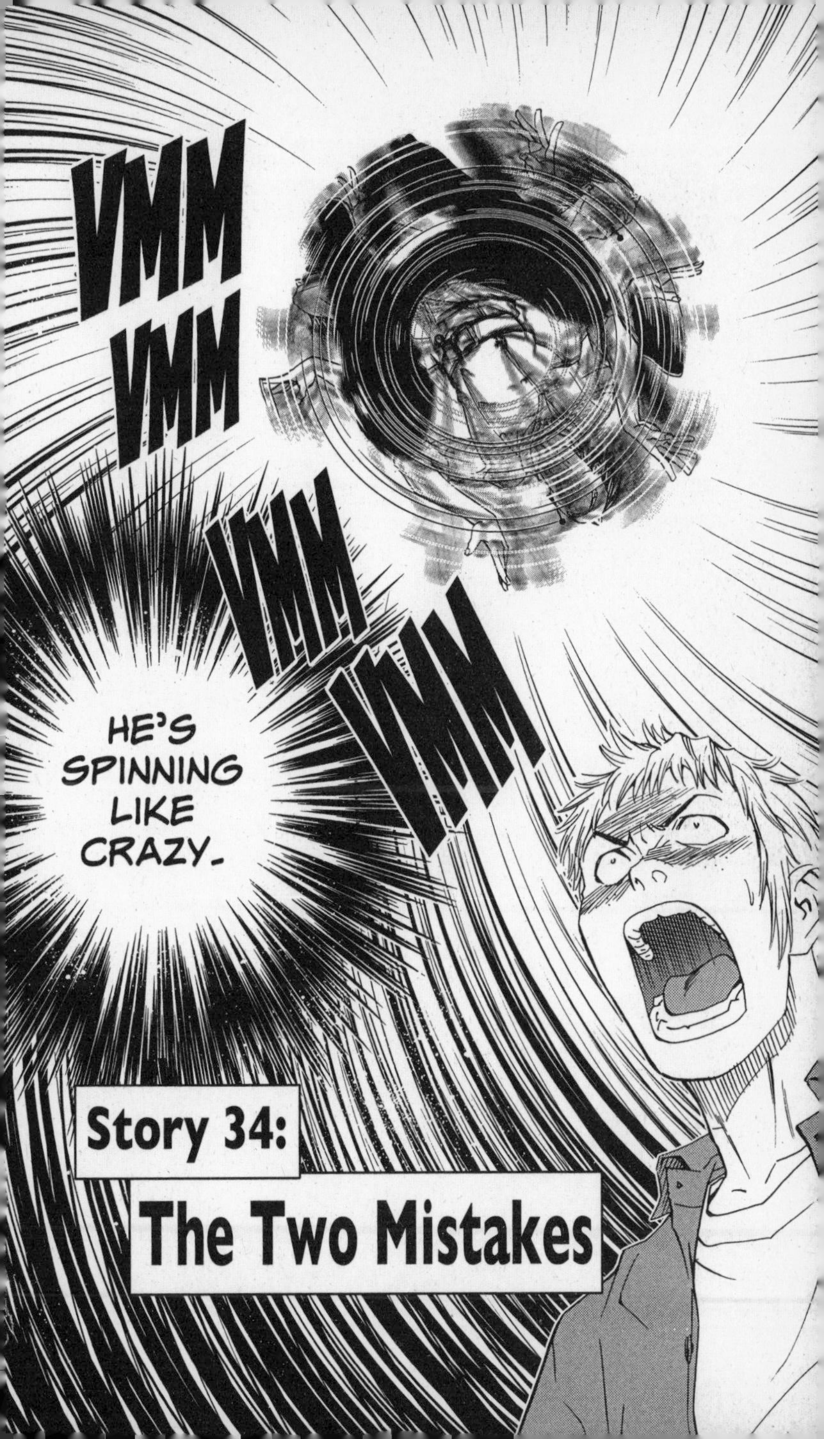
VMM VMM
VMM VMM
HE'S SPINNING LIKE CRAZY...
Story 34:
The Two Mistakes

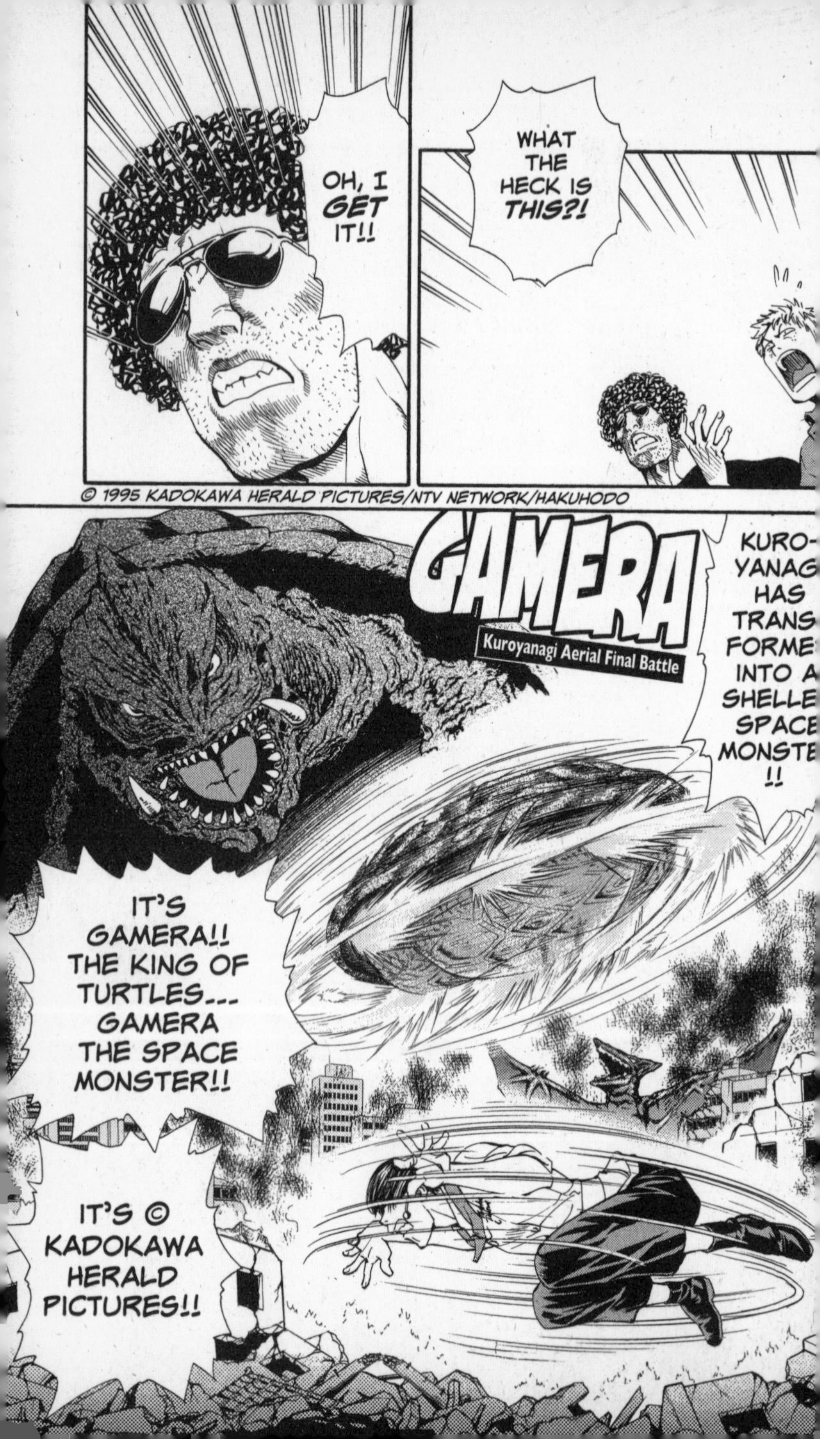
WHAT THE HECK IS *THIS?!*
OH, I *GET* IT!!
© 1995 KADOKAWA HERALD PICTURES/NTV NETWORK/HAKUHODO
KURO-YANAG HAS TRANS FORME INTO A SHELLE SPACE MONSTE !!
GAMERA
Kuroyanagi Aerial Final Battle
IT'S GAMERA!! THE KING OF TURTLES... GAMERA THE SPACE MONSTER!!
IT'S © KADOKAWA HERALD PICTURES!!

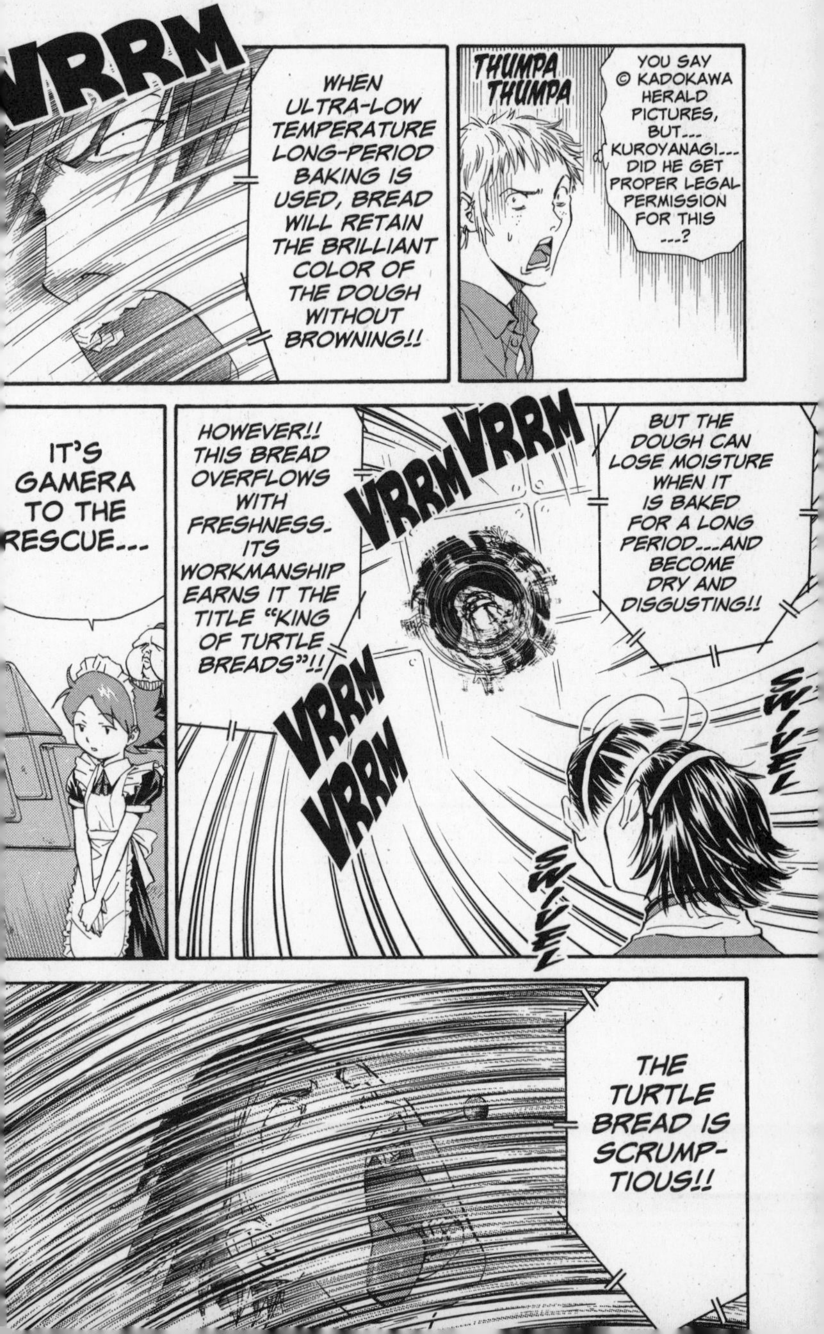
THUMPA THUMPA
YOU SAY © KADOKAWA HERALD PICTURES, BUT... KUROYANAGI... DID HE GET PROPER LEGAL PERMISSION FOR THIS ...?
VRRM
WHEN ULTRA-LOW TEMPERATURE LONG-PERIOD BAKING IS USED, BREAD WILL RETAIN THE BRILLIANT COLOR OF THE DOUGH WITHOUT BROWNING!!
BUT THE DOUGH CAN LOSE MOISTURE WHEN IT IS BAKED FOR A LONG PERIOD...AND BECOME DRY AND DISGUSTING!!
VRRM VRRM
HOWEVER!! THIS BREAD OVERFLOWS WITH FRESHNESS. ITS WORKMANSHIP EARNS IT THE TITLE "KING OF TURTLE BREADS"!!
VRRM VRRM
SWIVEL
SWIVEL
IT'S GAMERA TO THE RESCUE...
THE TURTLE BREAD IS SCRUMPTIOUS!!

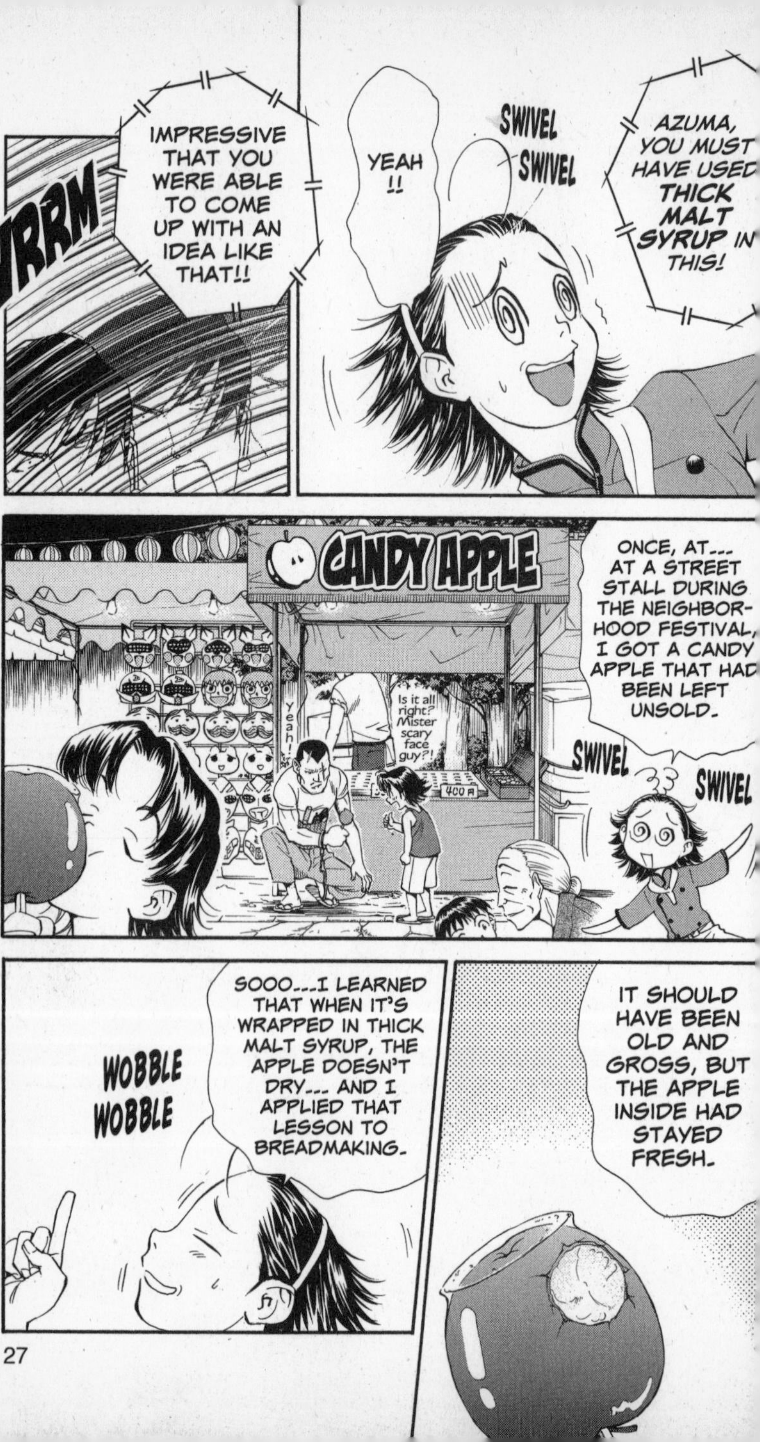
AZUMA, YOU MUST HAVE USED THICK MALT SYRUP IN THIS!
SWIVEL SWIVEL
YEAH!!
IMPRESSIVE THAT YOU WERE ABLE TO COME UP WITH AN IDEA LIKE THAT!!
VRRM
ONCE, AT... AT A STREET STALL DURING THE NEIGHBORHOOD FESTIVAL, I GOT A CANDY APPLE THAT HAD BEEN LEFT UNSOLD.
SWIVEL SWIVEL
CANDY APPLE
Is it all right? Mister scary face guy?!
Yeah!
400円
IT SHOULD HAVE BEEN OLD AND GROSS, BUT THE APPLE INSIDE HAD STAYED FRESH.
SOOO...I LEARNED THAT WHEN IT'S WRAPPED IN THICK MALT SYRUP, THE APPLE DOESN'T DRY... AND I APPLIED THAT LESSON TO BREADMAKING.
WOBBLE WOBBLE

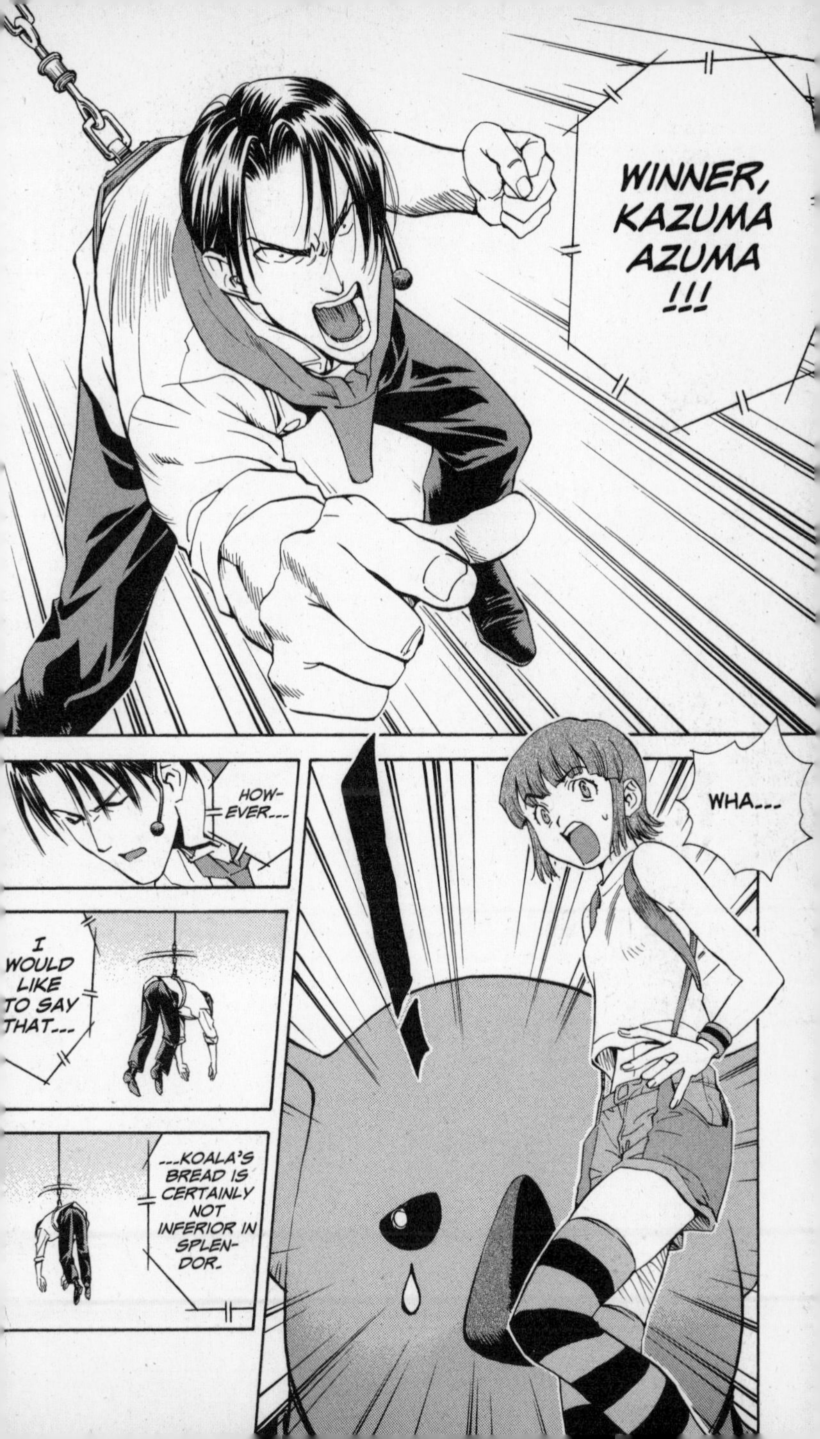
WINNER, KAZUMA AZUMA !!!
WHA...
HOW-EVER...
I WOULD LIKE TO SAY THAT...
...KOALA'S BREAD IS CERTAINLY NOT INFERIOR IN SPLEN-DOR.

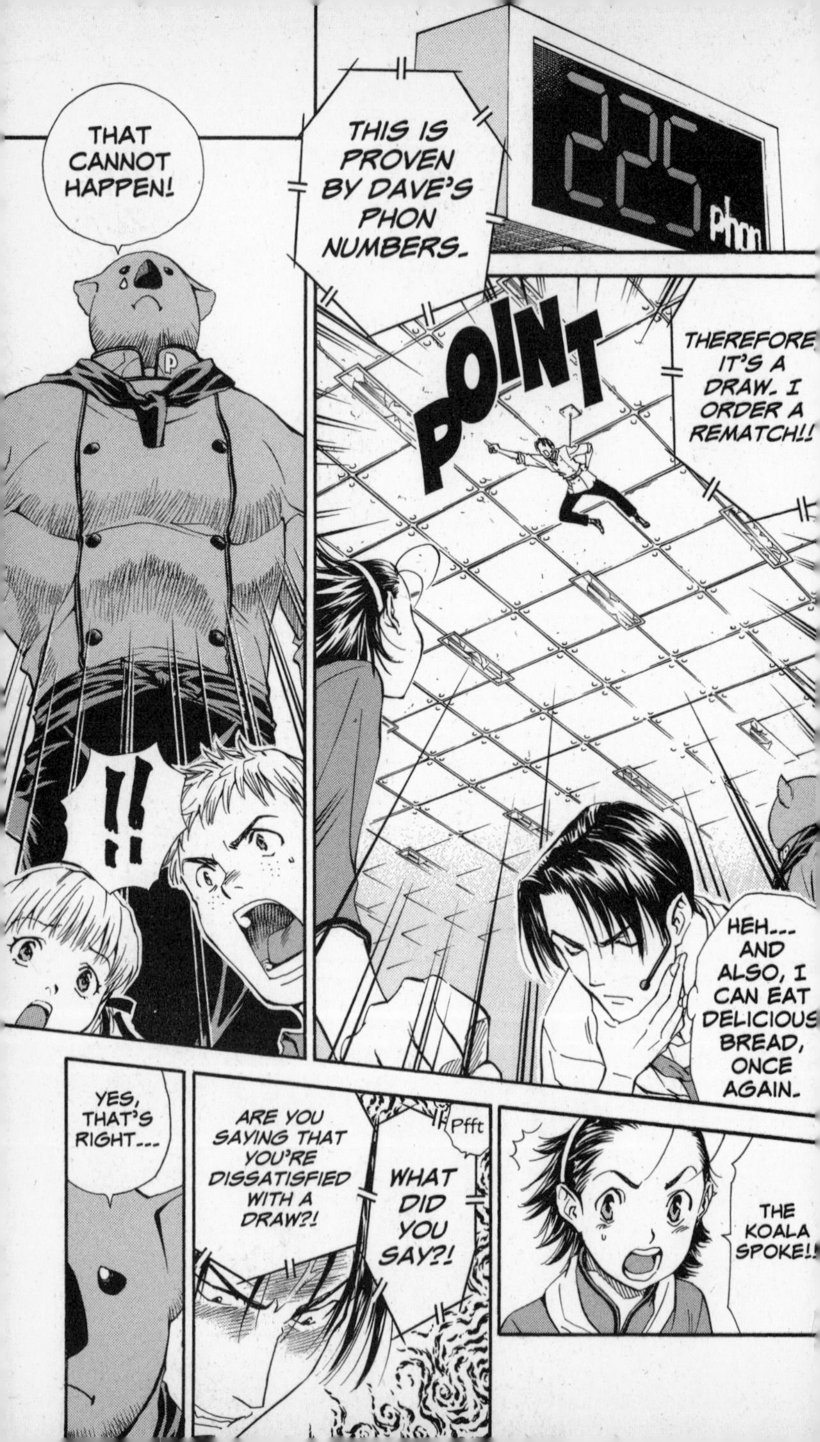

225 phon
THIS IS PROVEN BY DAVE'S PHON NUMBERS.
POINT
THEREFORE IT'S A DRAW. I ORDER A REMATCH!!
HEH... AND ALSO, I CAN EAT DELICIOUS BREAD, ONCE AGAIN.
THAT CANNOT HAPPEN!
!!
THE KOALA SPOKE!!
Pfft
WHAT DID YOU SAY?!
ARE YOU SAYING THAT YOU'RE DISSATISFIED WITH A DRAW?!
YES, THAT'S RIGHT...

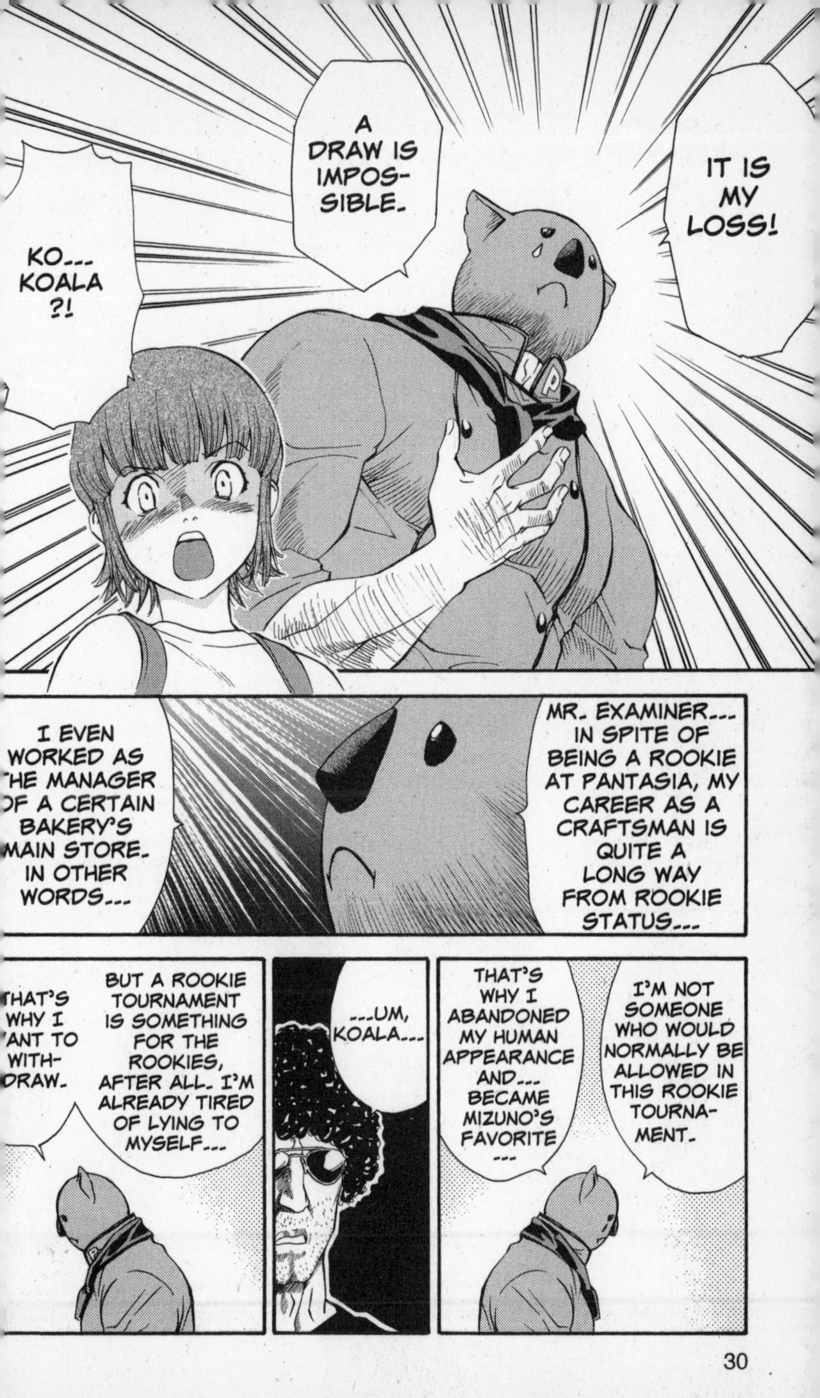
IT IS MY LOSS!
A DRAW IS IMPOSSIBLE.
KO... KOALA?!
MR. EXAMINER... IN SPITE OF BEING A ROOKIE AT PANTASIA, MY CAREER AS A CRAFTSMAN IS QUITE A LONG WAY FROM ROOKIE STATUS...
I EVEN WORKED AS THE MANAGER OF A CERTAIN BAKERY'S MAIN STORE. IN OTHER WORDS...
I'M NOT SOMEONE WHO WOULD NORMALLY BE ALLOWED IN THIS ROOKIE TOURNAMENT.
THAT'S WHY I ABANDONED MY HUMAN APPEARANCE AND... BECAME MIZUNO'S FAVORITE...
...UM, KOALA...
BUT A ROOKIE TOURNAMENT IS SOMETHING FOR THE ROOKIES, AFTER ALL. I'M ALREADY TIRED OF LYING TO MYSELF...
THAT'S WHY I WANT TO WITHDRAW.

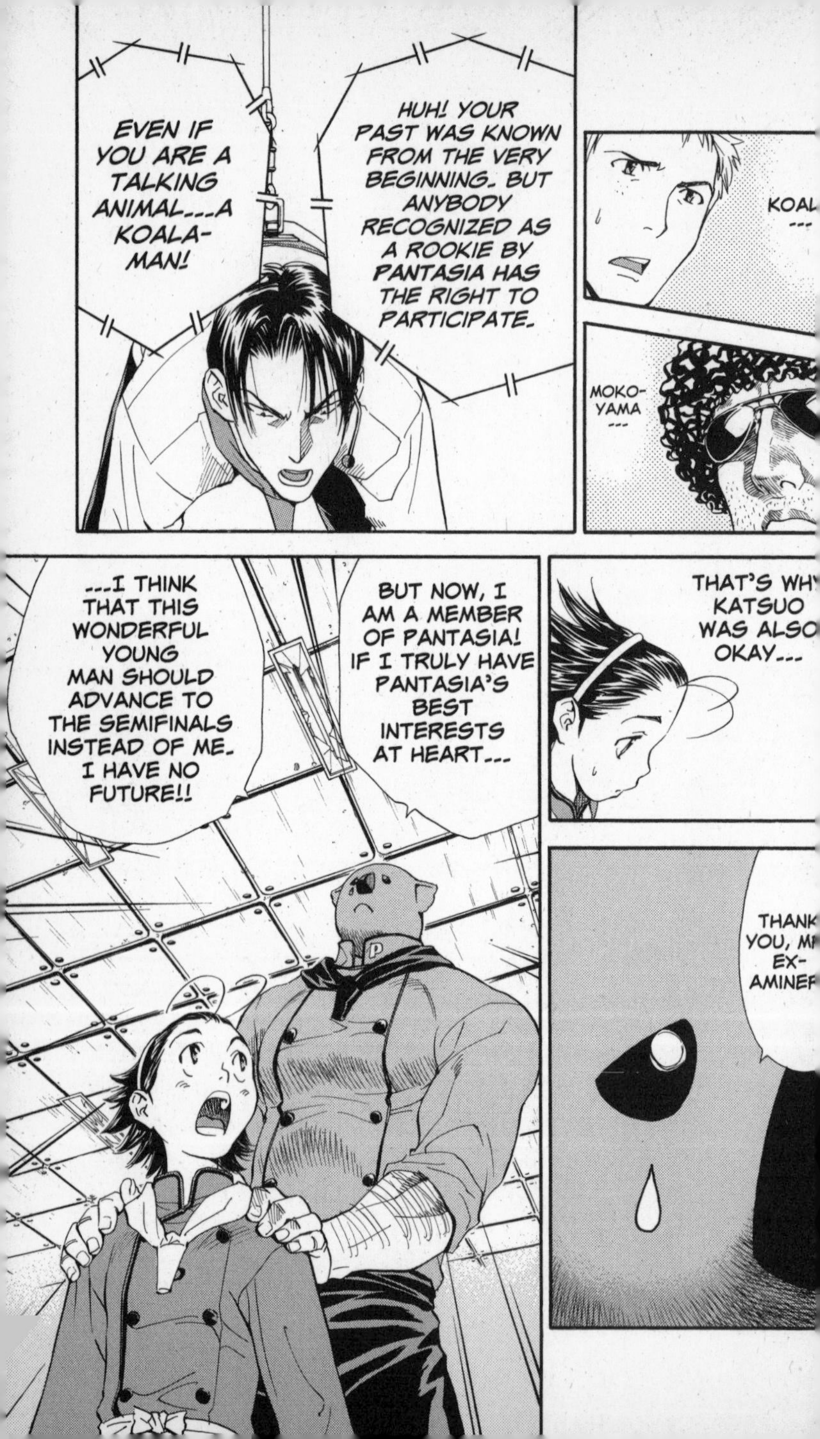
KOAL ---
MOKO-YAMA ---
HUH! YOUR PAST WAS KNOWN FROM THE VERY BEGINNING. BUT ANYBODY RECOGNIZED AS A ROOKIE BY PANTASIA HAS THE RIGHT TO PARTICIPATE.
EVEN IF YOU ARE A TALKING ANIMAL...A KOALA-MAN!
THAT'S WH KATSUO WAS ALSO OKAY...
THANK YOU, M EX-AMINE
BUT NOW, I AM A MEMBER OF PANTASIA! IF I TRULY HAVE PANTASIA'S BEST INTERESTS AT HEART...
...I THINK THAT THIS WONDERFUL YOUNG MAN SHOULD ADVANCE TO THE SEMIFINALS INSTEAD OF ME. I HAVE NO FUTURE!!

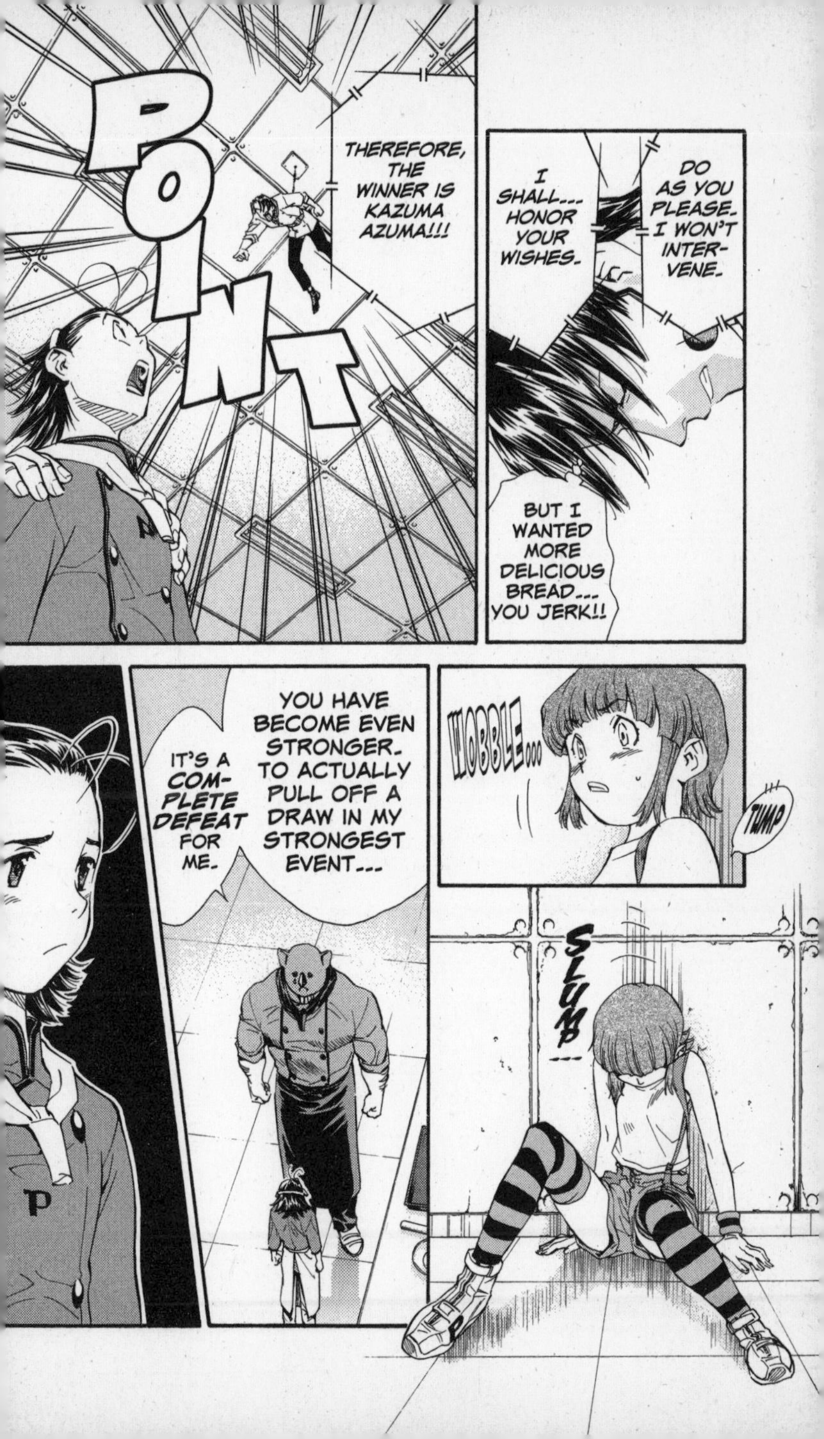
DO AS YOU PLEASE. I WON'T INTER-VENE.
I SHALL... HONOR YOUR WISHES.
BUT I WANTED MORE DELICIOUS BREAD... YOU JERK!!
THEREFORE, THE WINNER IS KAZUMA AZUMA!!!
POINT
TUMP
WOBBLE...
SLUMP...
YOU HAVE BECOME EVEN STRONGER. TO ACTUALLY PULL OFF A DRAW IN MY STRONGEST EVENT...
IT'S A COM-PLETE DEFEAT FOR ME.

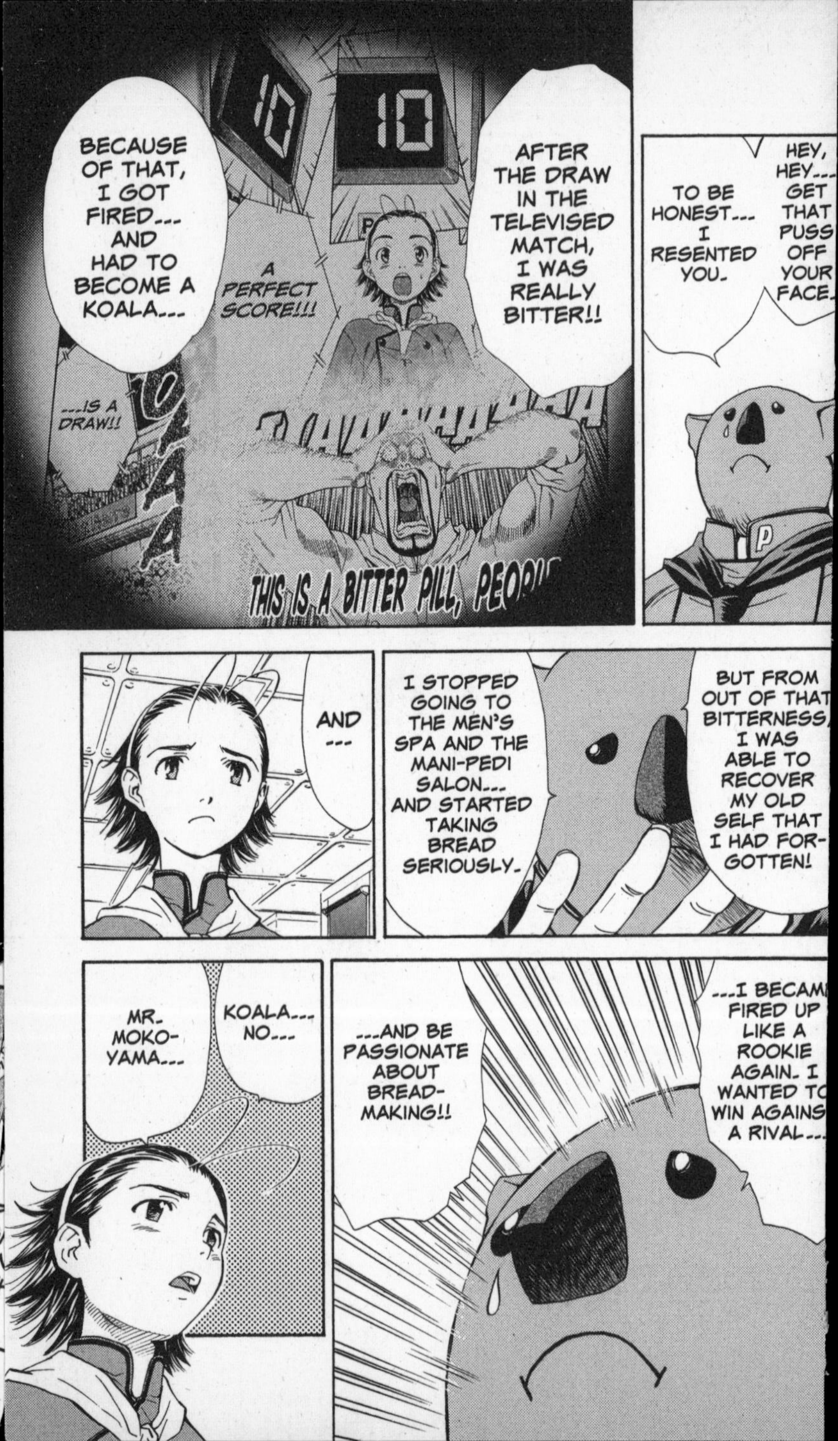
HEY, HEY... GET THAT PUSS OFF YOUR FACE.
TO BE HONEST... I RESENTED YOU.
AFTER THE DRAW IN THE TELEVISED MATCH, I WAS REALLY BITTER!!
BECAUSE OF THAT, I GOT FIRED... AND HAD TO BECOME A KOALA...
A PERFECT SCORE!!!
...IS A DRAW!!
THIS IS A BITTER PILL, PEOP
BUT FROM OUT OF THAT BITTERNESS, I WAS ABLE TO RECOVER MY OLD SELF THAT I HAD FOR-GOTTEN!
I STOPPED GOING TO THE MEN'S SPA AND THE MANI-PEDI SALON... AND STARTED TAKING BREAD SERIOUSLY.
AND ---
...I BECAM FIRED UP LIKE A ROOKIE AGAIN. I WANTED TO WIN AGAINS A RIVAL...
...AND BE PASSIONATE ABOUT BREAD-MAKING!!
KOALA... NO...
MR. MOKOYAMA...

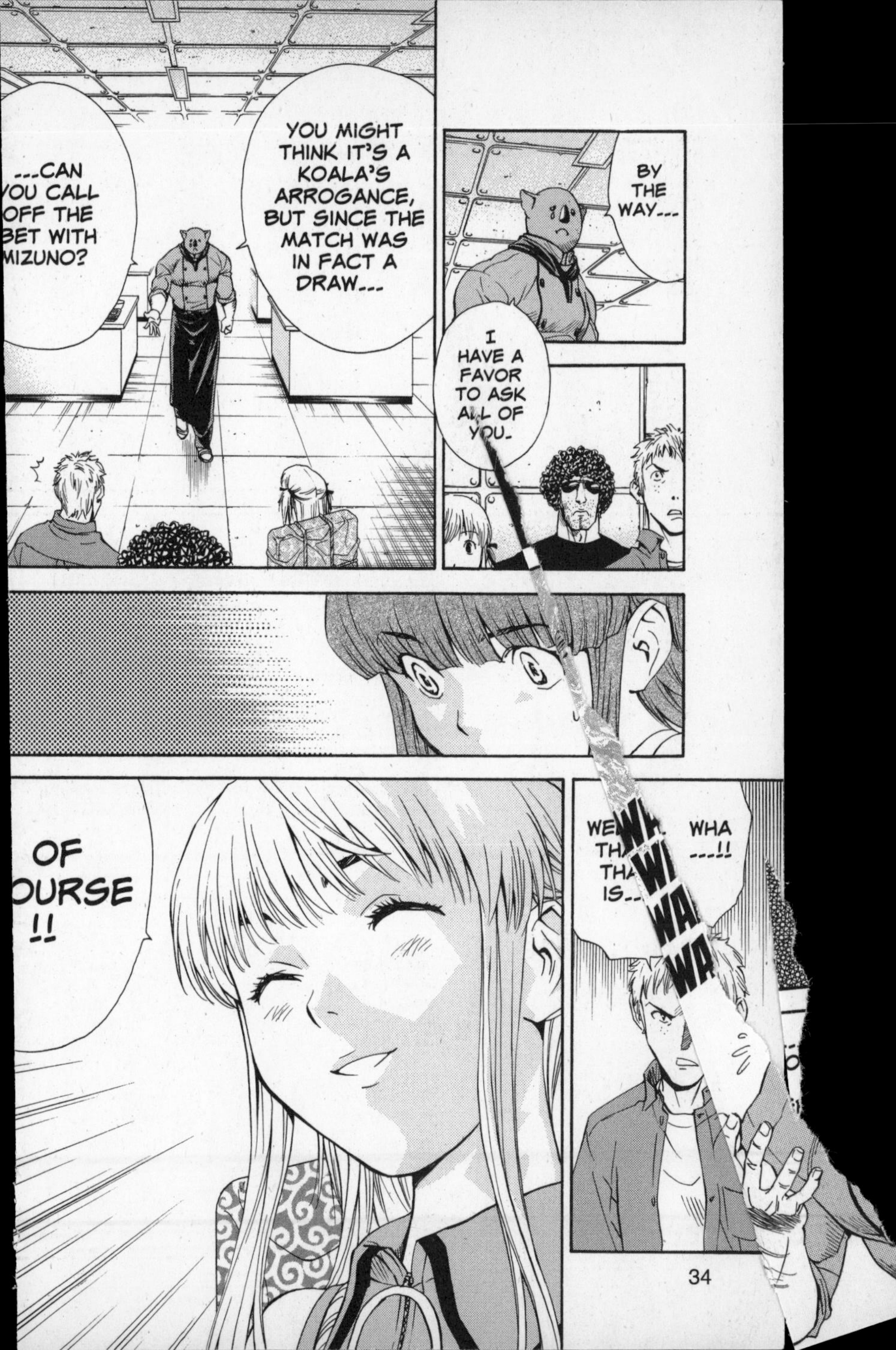
BY THE WAY...
I HAVE A FAVOR TO ASK ALL OF YOU.
YOU MIGHT THINK IT'S A KOALA'S ARROGANCE, BUT SINCE THE MATCH WAS IN FACT A DRAW...
...CAN OU CALL OFF THE ET WITH IZUNO?
WHA ---!!
WE THA THA IS...
WAWAWAWA
OF OURSE !!

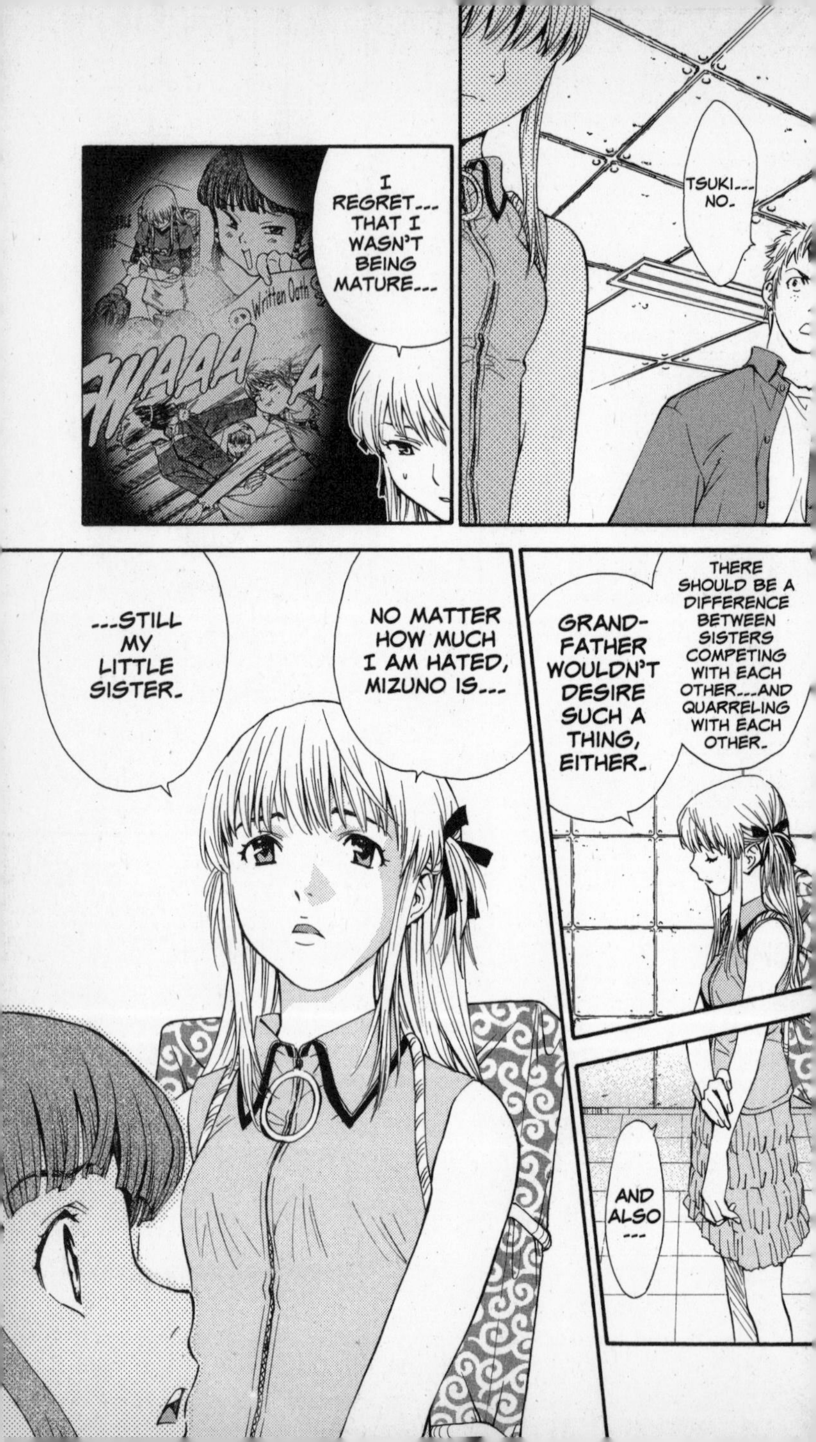
TSUKI... NO.
I REGRET... THAT I WASN'T BEING MATURE...
Written Oath
WAAAA A
THERE SHOULD BE A DIFFERENCE BETWEEN SISTERS COMPETING WITH EACH OTHER...AND QUARRELING WITH EACH OTHER.
GRAND-FATHER WOULDN'T DESIRE SUCH A THING, EITHER.
AND ALSO ---
NO MATTER HOW MUCH I AM HATED, MIZUNO IS...
...STILL MY LITTLE SISTER.

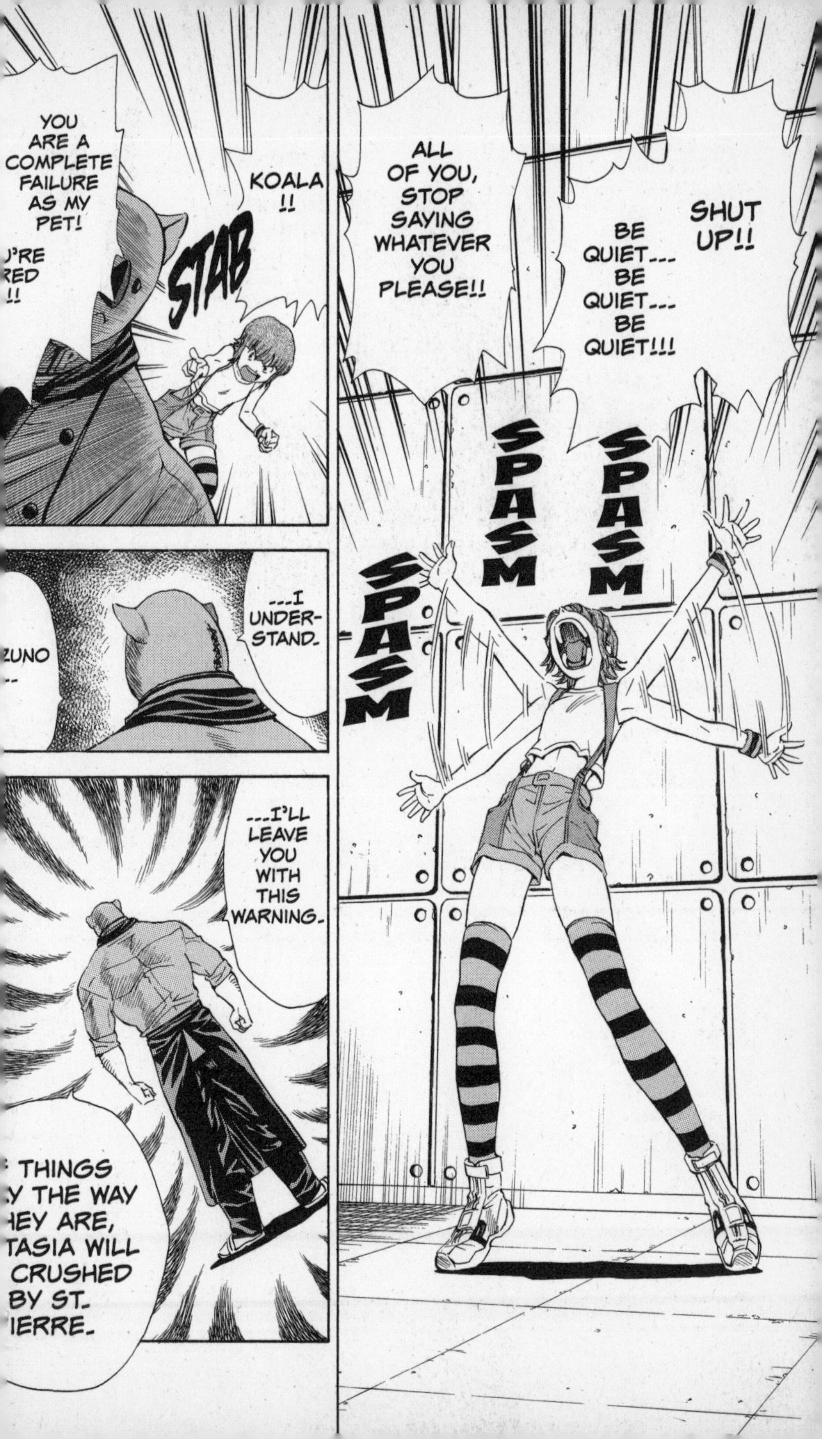
SHUT UP!!
BE QUIET... BE QUIET... BE QUIET!!!
ALL OF YOU, STOP SAYING WHATEVER YOU PLEASE!!
SPASM
SPASM
SPASM
KOALA!!
YOU ARE A COMPLETE FAILURE AS MY PET!
'RE RED !!
STAB
...I UNDERSTAND.
ZUNO
...I'LL LEAVE YOU WITH THIS WARNING.
THINGS Y THE WAY HEY ARE, TASIA WILL CRUSHED BY ST. IERRE.

Story 35: Katsuo's Counterattack

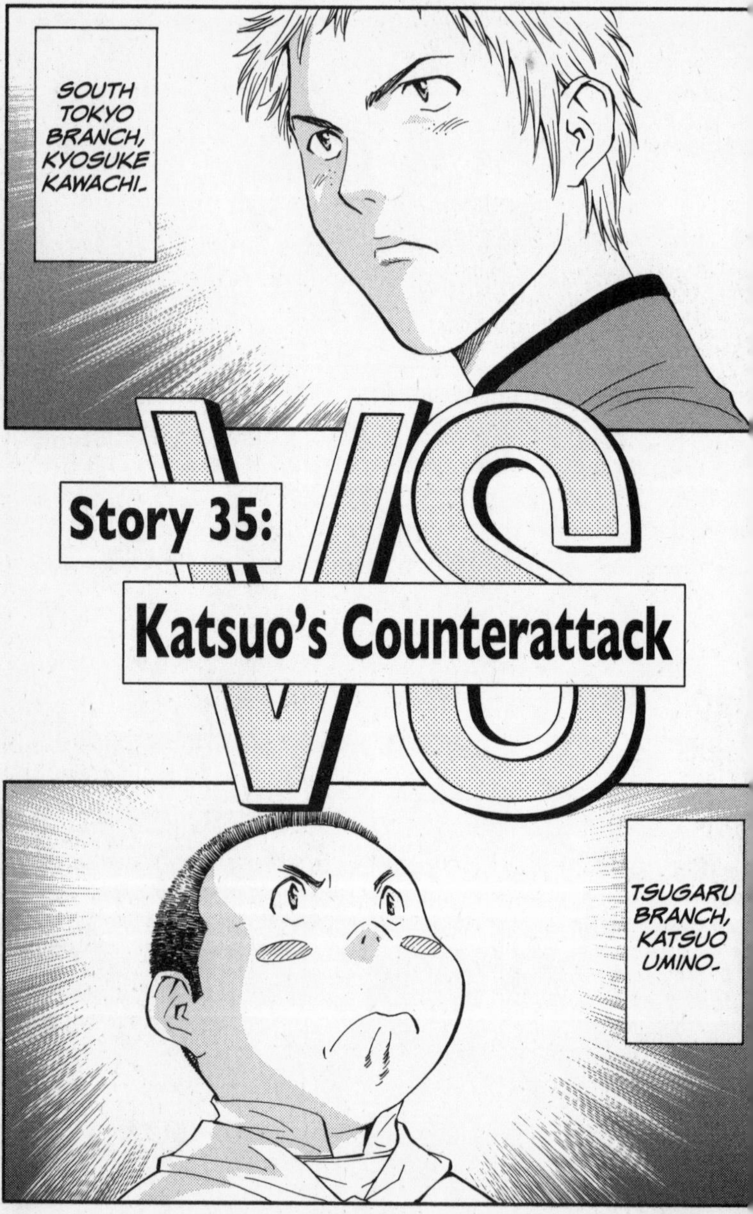
SOUTH TOKYO BRANCH, KYOSUKE KAWACHI...
VS
TSUGARU BRANCH, KATSUO UMINO...

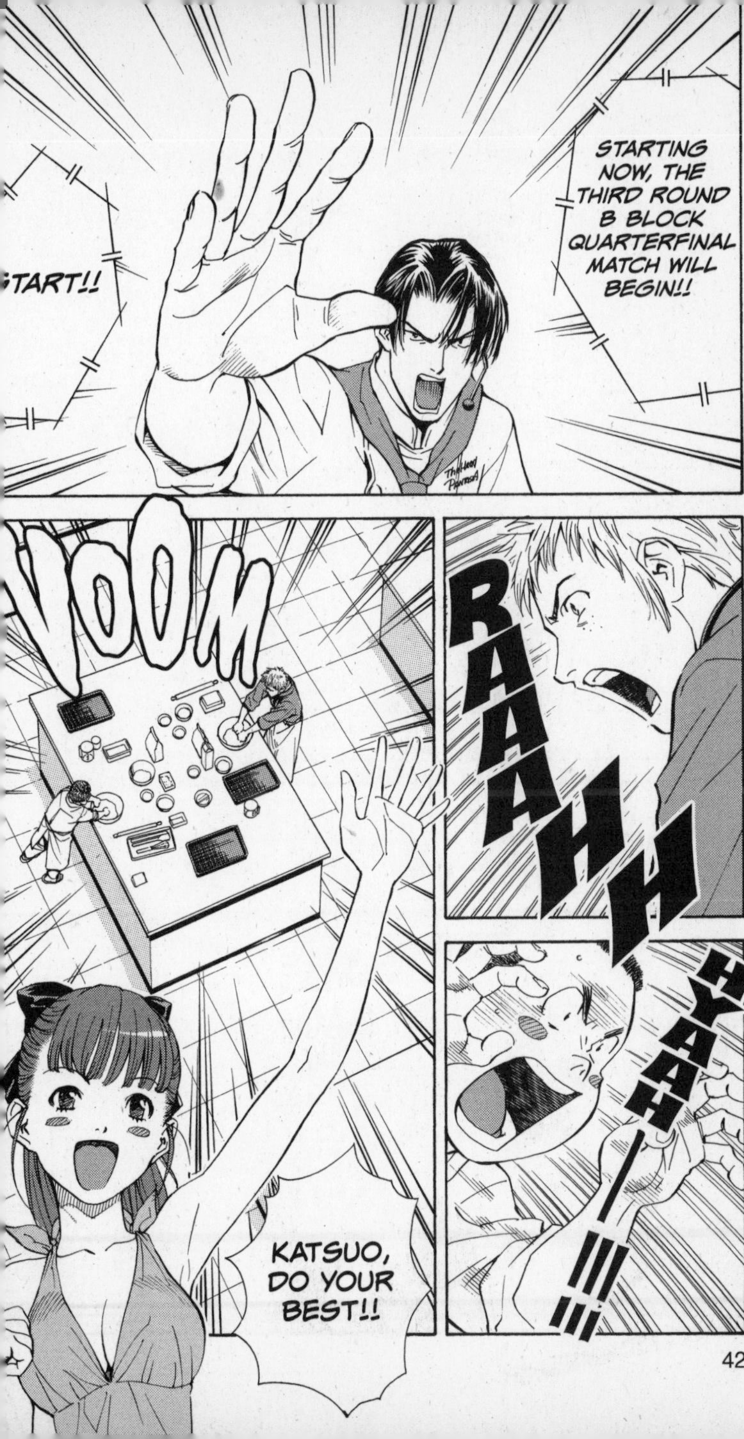
STARTING NOW, THE THIRD ROUND B BLOCK QUARTERFINAL MATCH WILL BEGIN!!
START!!
RAAHHH
HYAAAH!!!!
VOOM
KATSUO, DO YOUR BEST!!

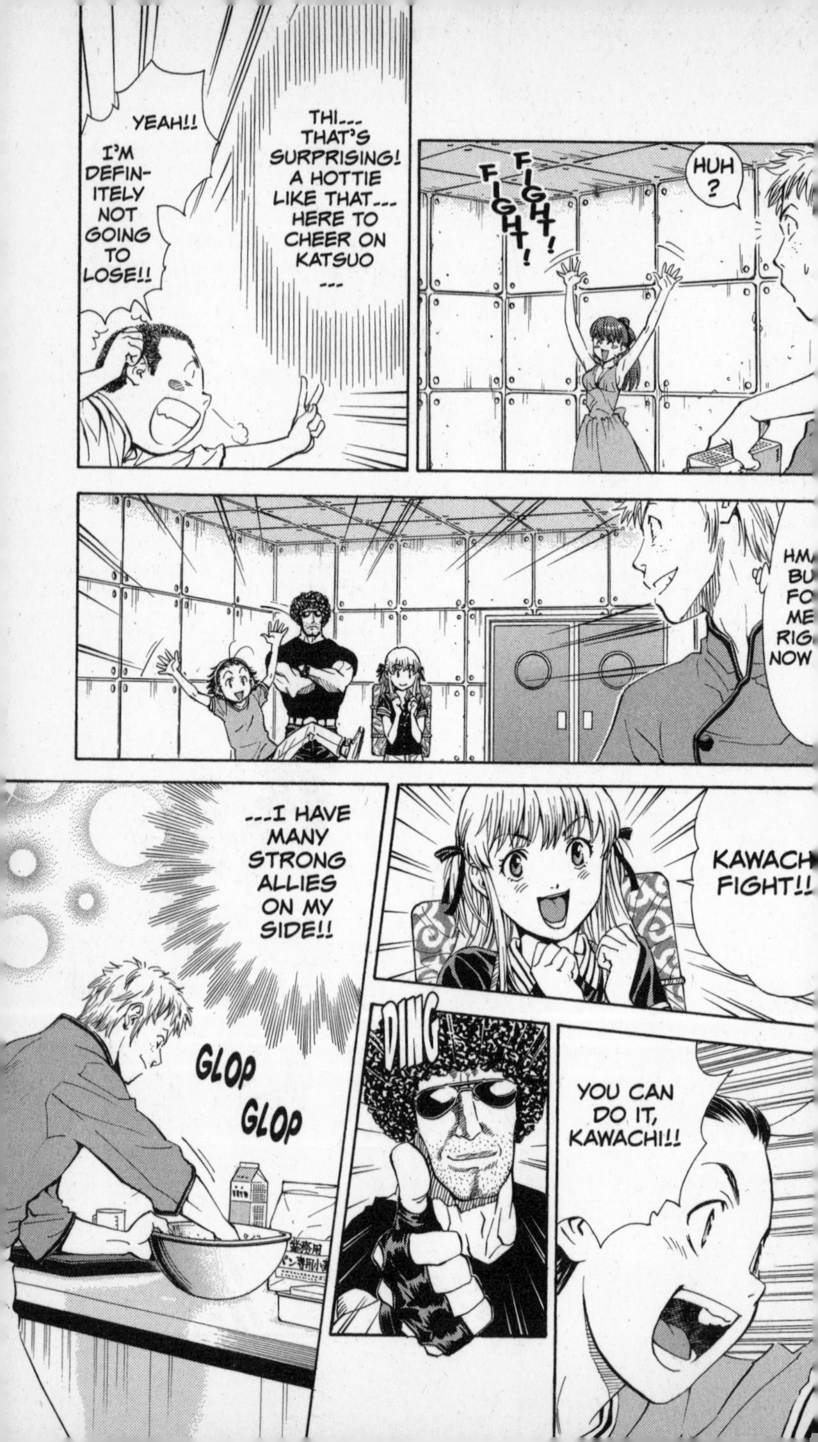
HUH?
FIGHT! FIGHT!
THI... THAT'S SURPRISING! A HOTTIE LIKE THAT... HERE TO CHEER ON KATSUO...
YEAH!! I'M DEFINITELY NOT GOING TO LOSE!!
HM BU FO ME RIG NOW
KAWACH FIGHT!!
YOU CAN DO IT, KAWACHI!!
DING
...I HAVE MANY STRONG ALLIES ON MY SIDE!!
GLOP
GLOP

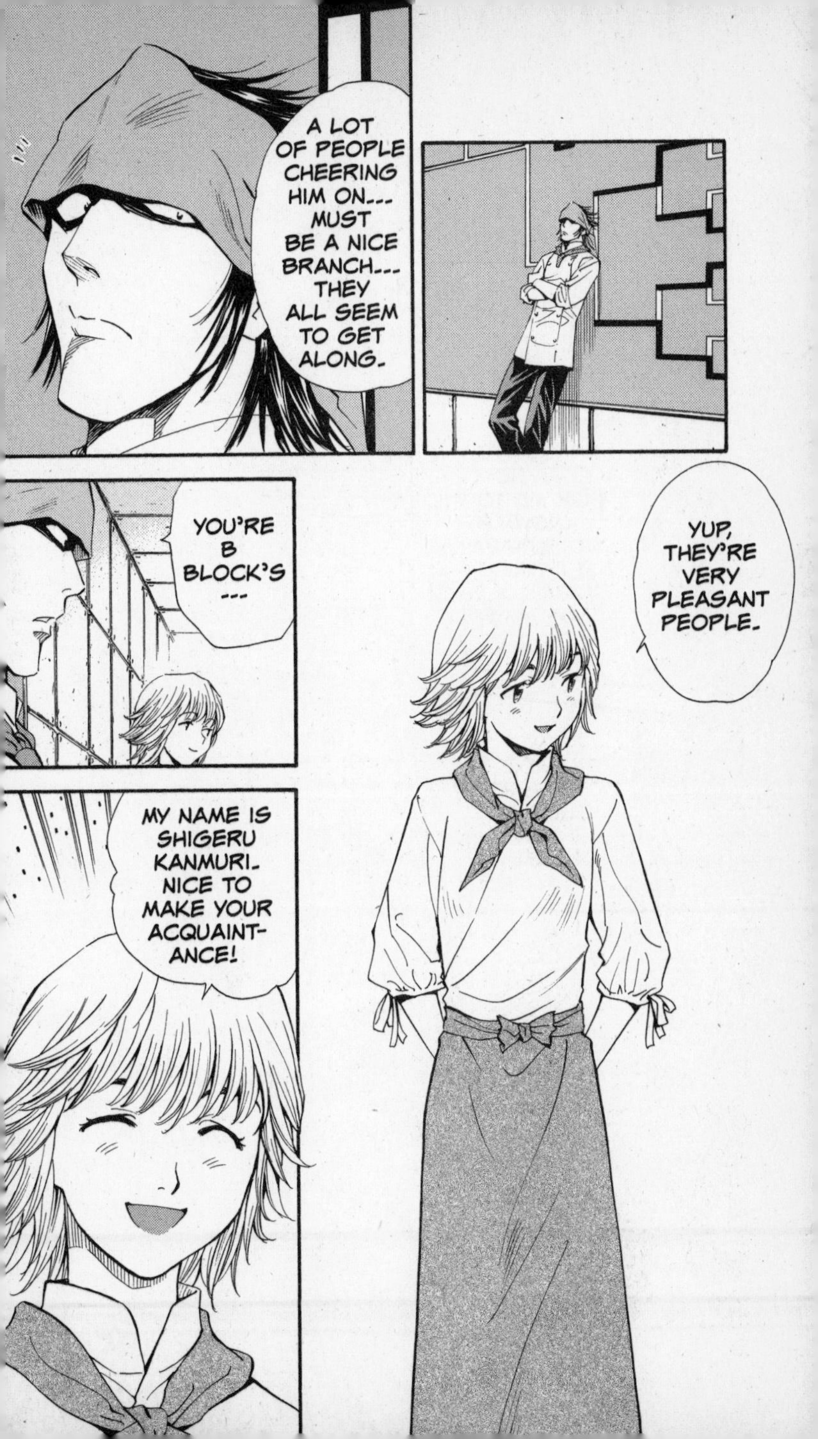
A LOT OF PEOPLE CHEERING HIM ON... MUST BE A NICE BRANCH... THEY ALL SEEM TO GET ALONG.
YUP, THEY'RE VERY PLEASANT PEOPLE.
YOU'RE B BLOCK'S...
MY NAME IS SHIGERU KANMURI. NICE TO MAKE YOUR ACQUAINT-ANCE!

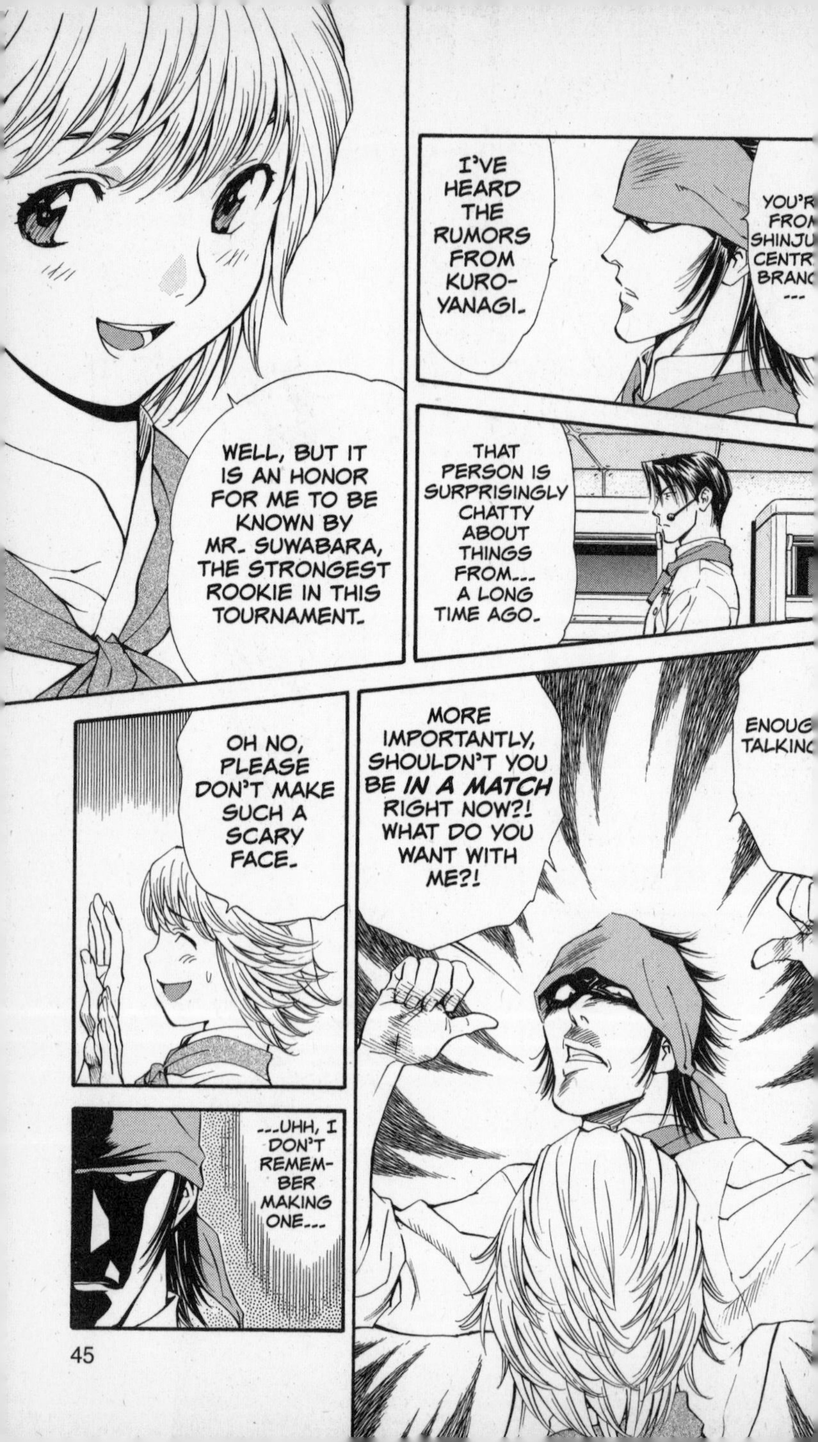
YOU'R FROM SHINJU CENTR BRANC ---
I'VE HEARD THE RUMORS FROM KURO-YANAGI.
THAT PERSON IS SURPRISINGLY CHATTY ABOUT THINGS FROM... A LONG TIME AGO.
WELL, BUT IT IS AN HONOR FOR ME TO BE KNOWN BY MR. SUWABARA, THE STRONGEST ROOKIE IN THIS TOURNAMENT.
ENOUG TALKINC
MORE IMPORTANTLY, SHOULDN'T YOU BE *IN A MATCH* RIGHT NOW?! WHAT DO YOU WANT WITH ME?!
OH NO, PLEASE DON'T MAKE SUCH A SCARY FACE.
...UHH, I DON'T REMEM-BER MAKING ONE...

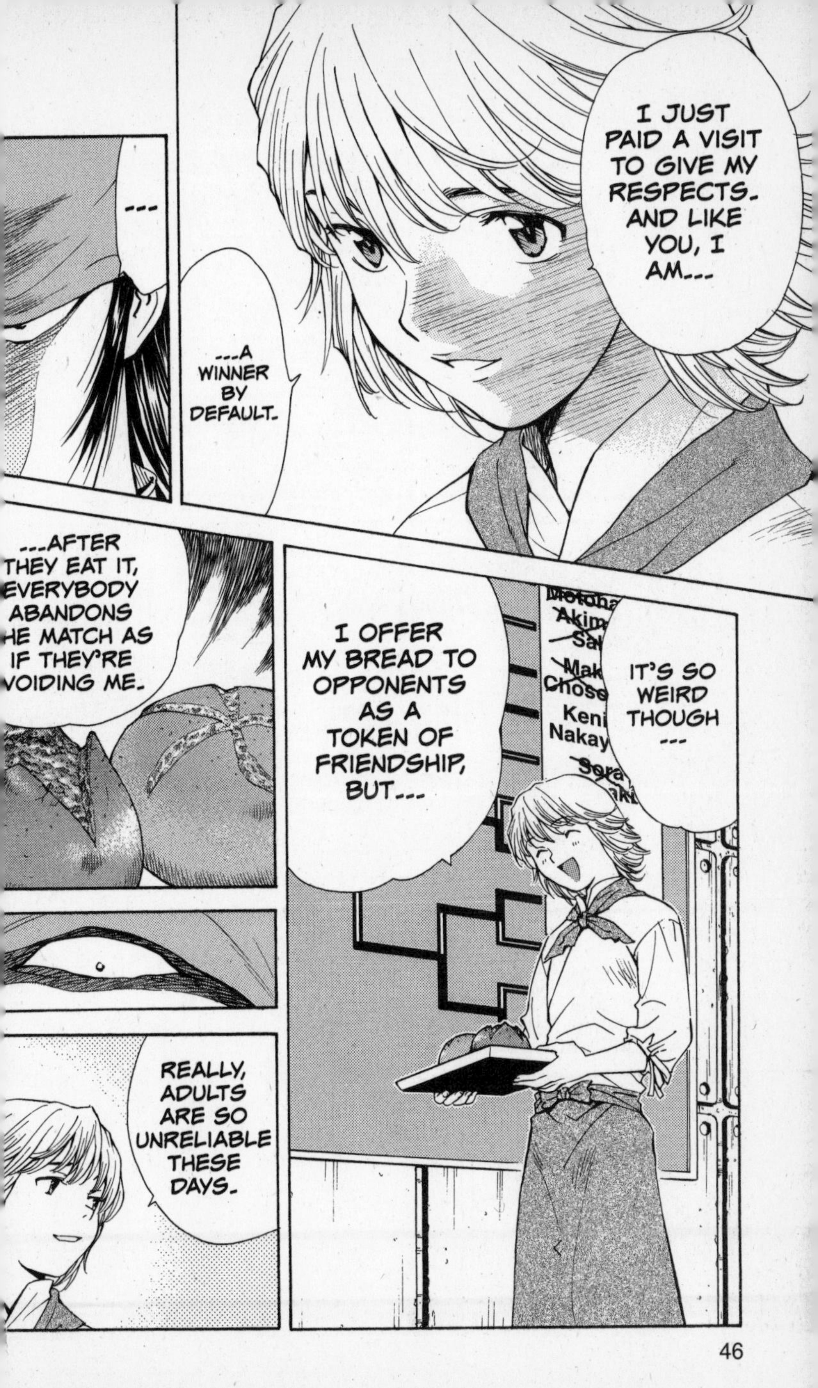
I JUST PAID A VISIT TO GIVE MY RESPECTS. AND LIKE YOU, I AM...
...A WINNER BY DEFAULT.
...
IT'S SO WEIRD THOUGH...
I OFFER MY BREAD TO OPPONENTS AS A TOKEN OF FRIENDSHIP, BUT...
...AFTER THEY EAT IT, EVERYBODY ABANDONS HE MATCH AS IF THEY'RE VOIDING ME.
REALLY, ADULTS ARE SO UNRELIABLE THESE DAYS.

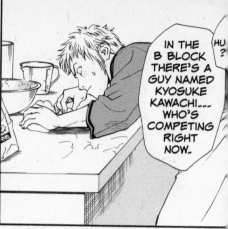

HU?
IN THE B BLOCK THERE'S A GUY NAMED KYOSUKE KAWACHI... WHO'S COMPETING RIGHT NOW.
EVEN *YOU* WON'T BE ABLE TO WIN BY DEFAULT NEXT TIME.
OH?!
THAT'S SOME KIND OF A JOKE, RIGHT?!
IF YOU SAY IT WITH THAT KIND OF SCARY FACE, I MIGHT THINK THAT YOU'RE BEING SERIOUS.
I DON'T MAKE JOKES.
THIS IS MY NORMAL FACE.
I'LL PRESENT THIS AS A TOKEN OF FRIEND-SHIP...
...THEN, I'M OFF!
HMPF.
I DON'T LIKE THAT GUY...
YET...

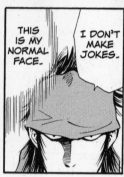

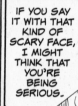

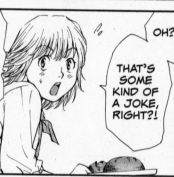

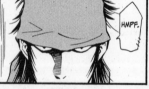

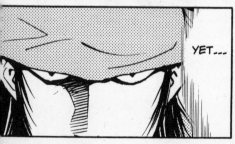

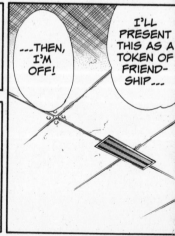

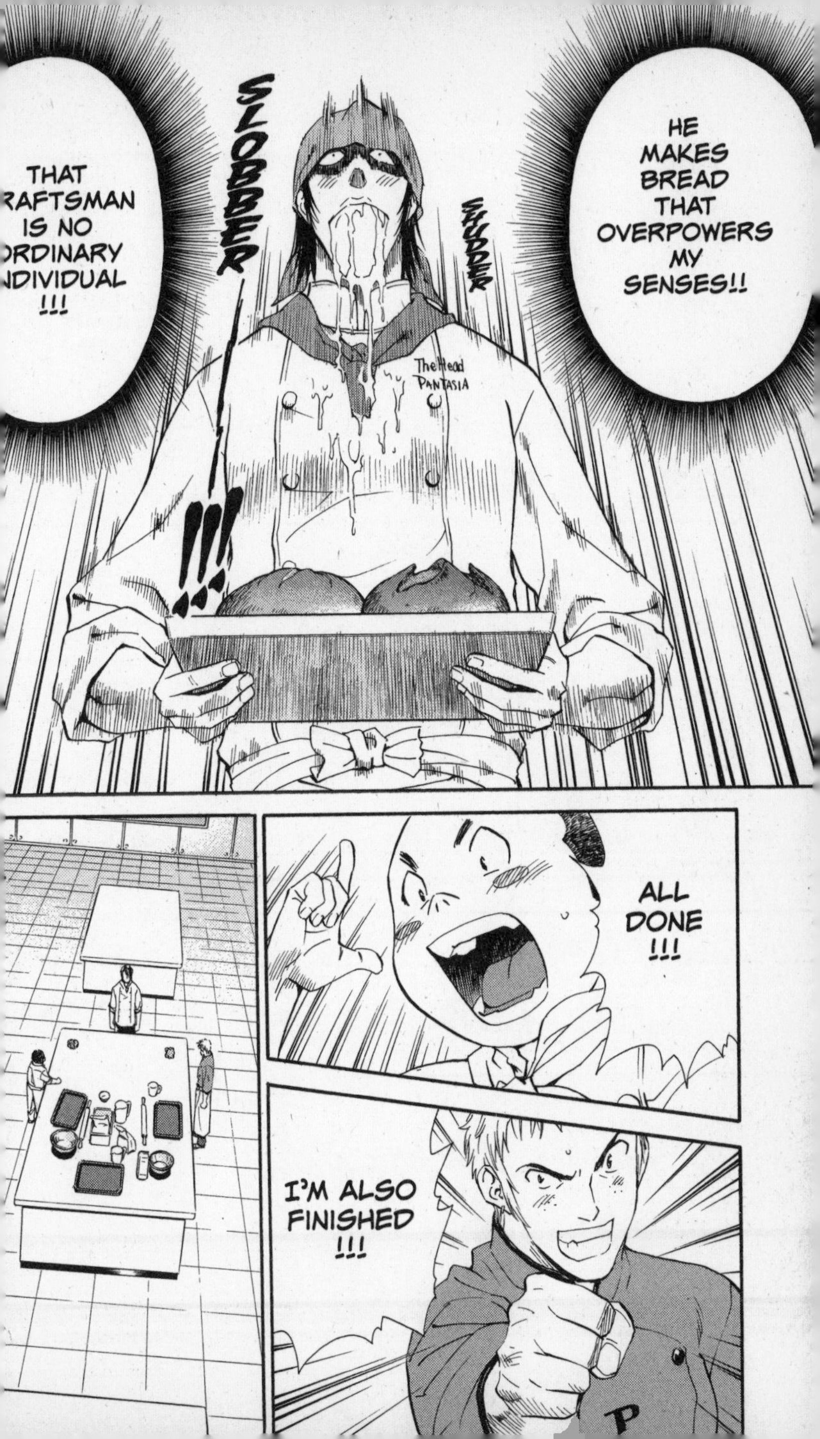
HE MAKES BREAD THAT OVERPOWERS MY SENSES!!
SHUDDER
SLOBBER
THAT RAFTSMAN IS NO RDINARY NDIVIDUAL !!!
The Head PANTASIA
ALL DONE !!!
I'M ALSO FINISHED !!!

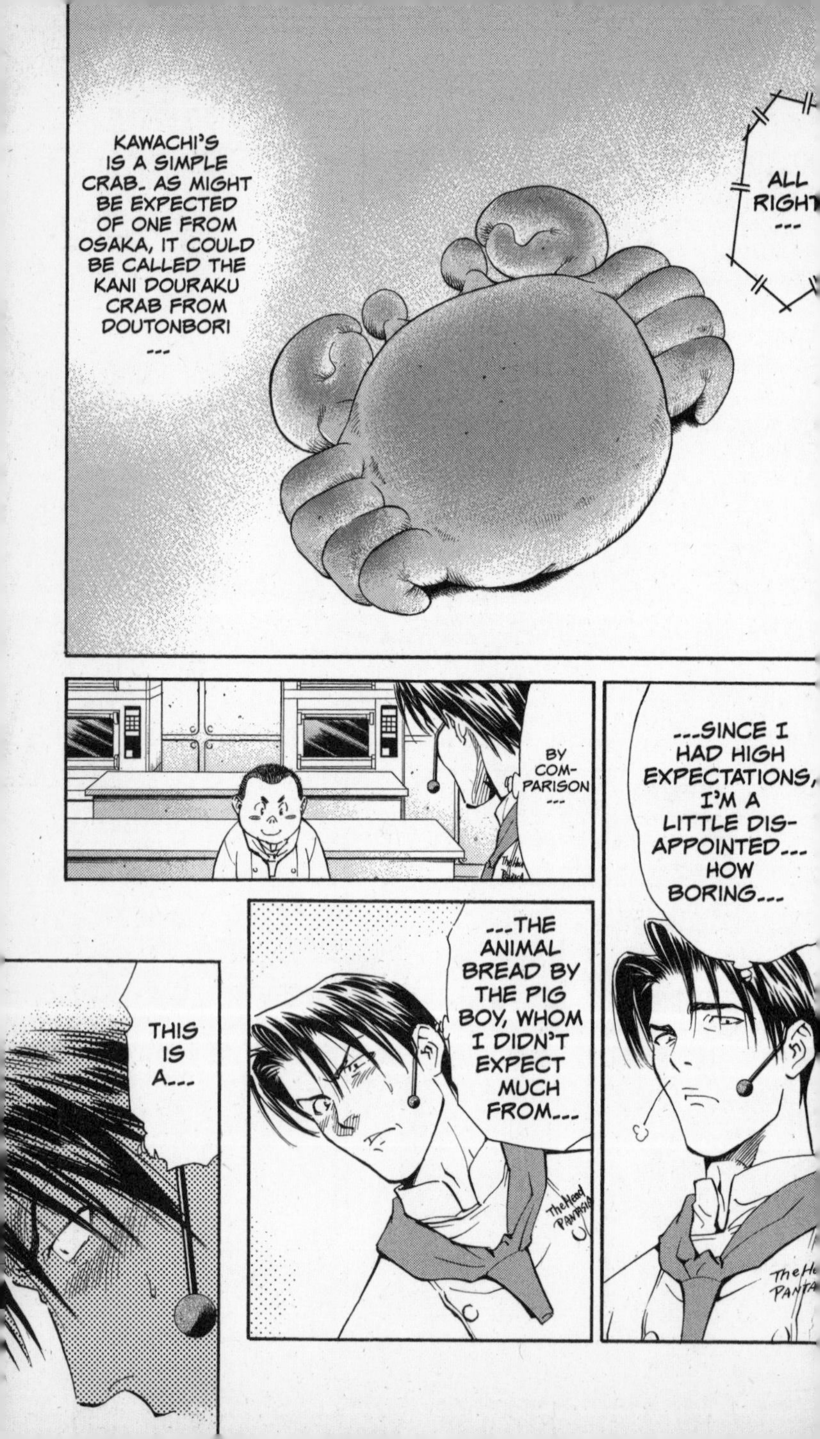
ALL RIGHT---
KAWACHI'S IS A SIMPLE CRAB. AS MIGHT BE EXPECTED OF ONE FROM OSAKA, IT COULD BE CALLED THE KANI DOURAKU CRAB FROM DOUTONBORI ---
---SINCE I HAD HIGH EXPECTATIONS, I'M A LITTLE DIS-APPOINTED... HOW BORING...
BY COM-PARISON ---
---THE ANIMAL BREAD BY THE PIG BOY, WHOM I DIDN'T EXPECT MUCH FROM...
THIS IS A---

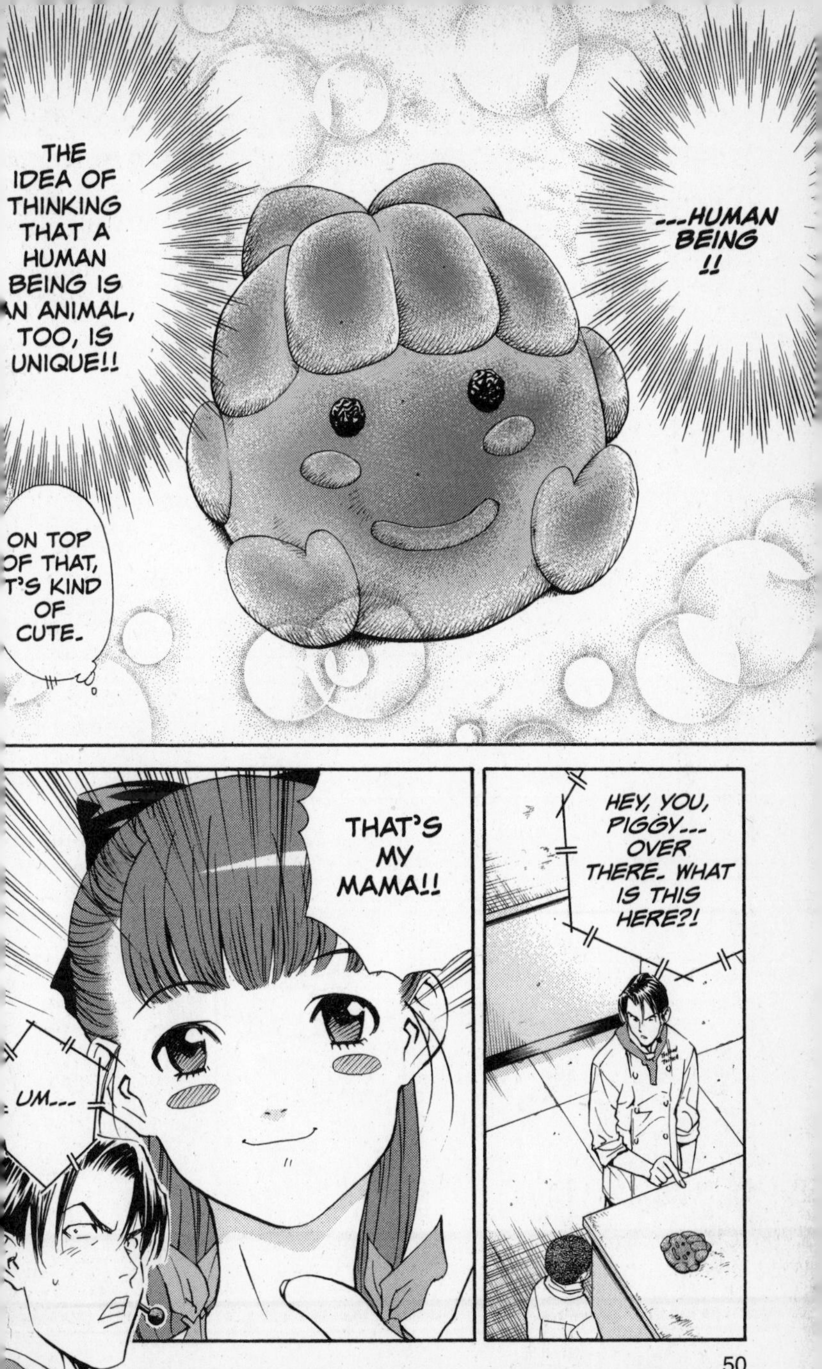
---HUMAN BEING !!
THE IDEA OF THINKING THAT A HUMAN BEING IS AN ANIMAL, TOO, IS UNIQUE!!
ON TOP OF THAT, IT'S KIND OF CUTE.
HEY, YOU, PIGGY... OVER THERE. WHAT IS THIS HERE?!
THAT'S MY MAMA!!
UM...

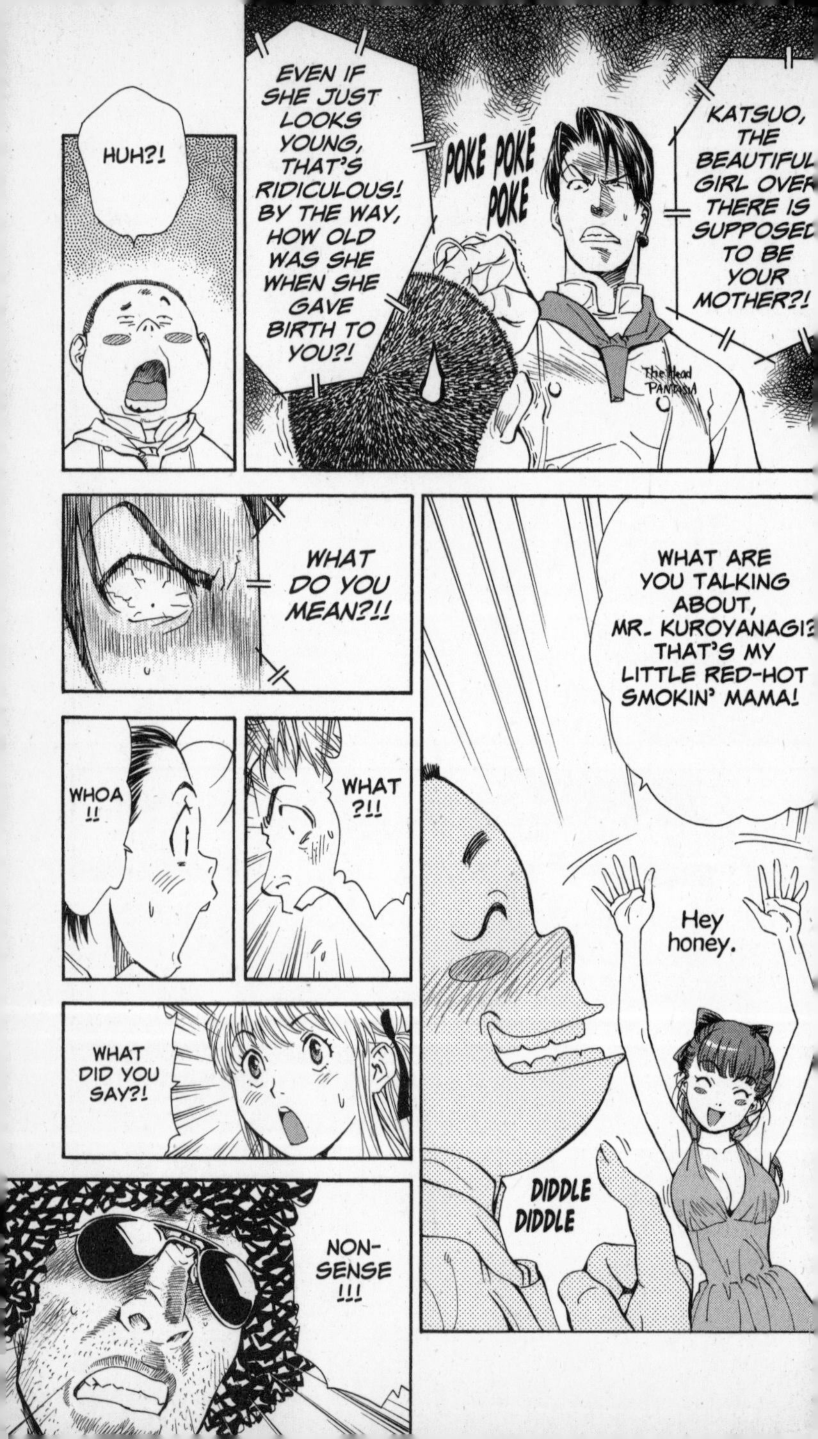
KATSUO, THE BEAUTIFUL GIRL OVER THERE IS SUPPOSED TO BE YOUR MOTHER?!
POKE POKE POKE
EVEN IF SHE JUST LOOKS YOUNG, THAT'S RIDICULOUS! BY THE WAY, HOW OLD WAS SHE WHEN SHE GAVE BIRTH TO YOU?!
HUH?!
WHAT ARE YOU TALKING ABOUT, MR. KUROYANAGI? THAT'S MY LITTLE RED-HOT SMOKIN' MAMA!
Hey honey.
DIDDLE DIDDLE
WHAT DO YOU MEAN?!!
WHAT ?!!
WHOA !!
WHAT DID YOU SAY?!
NON-SENSE !!!

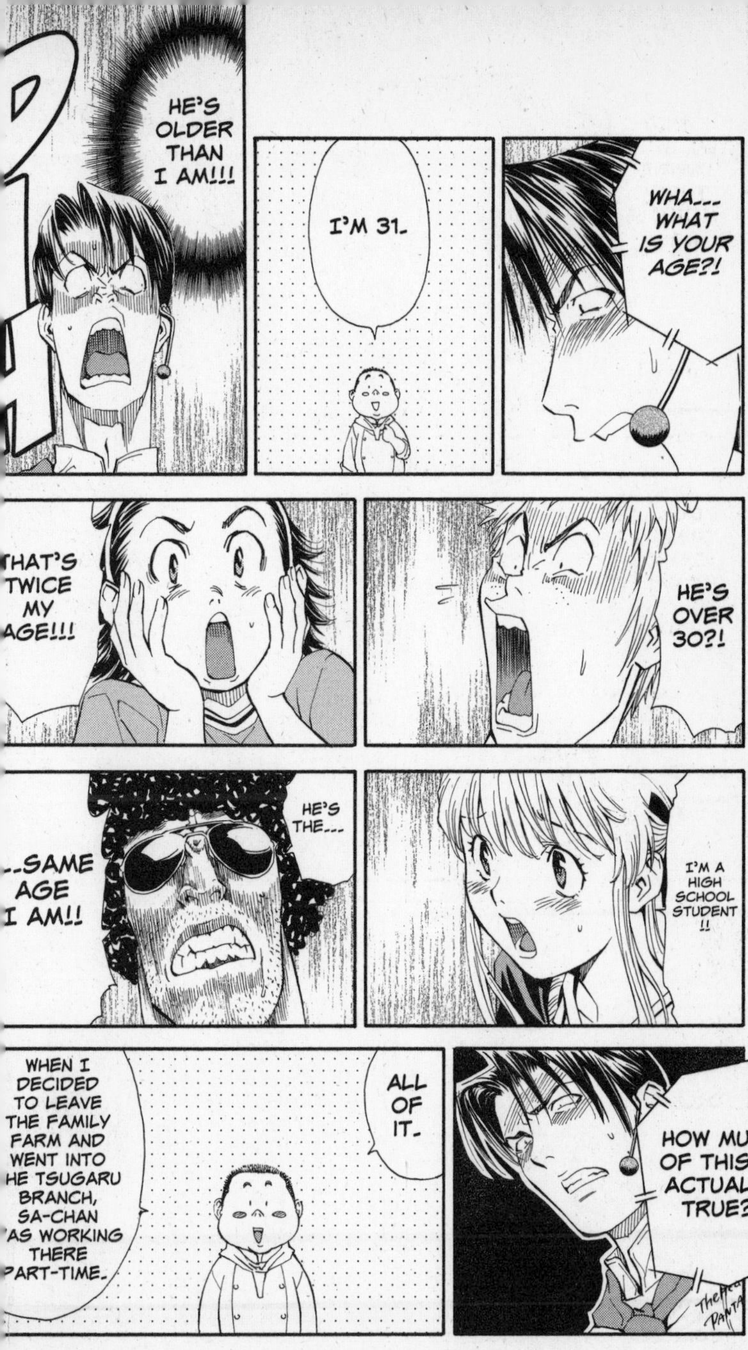
WHA... WHAT IS YOUR AGE?!
I'M 31.
HE'S OLDER THAN I AM!!!
HE'S OVER 30?!
THAT'S TWICE MY AGE!!!
I'M A HIGH SCHOOL STUDENT !!
HE'S THE...
...SAME AGE I AM!!
HOW MUCH OF THIS IS ACTUALLY TRUE?!
ALL OF IT.
WHEN I DECIDED TO LEAVE THE FAMILY FARM AND WENT INTO HE TSUGARU BRANCH, SA-CHAN AS WORKING THERE PART-TIME.

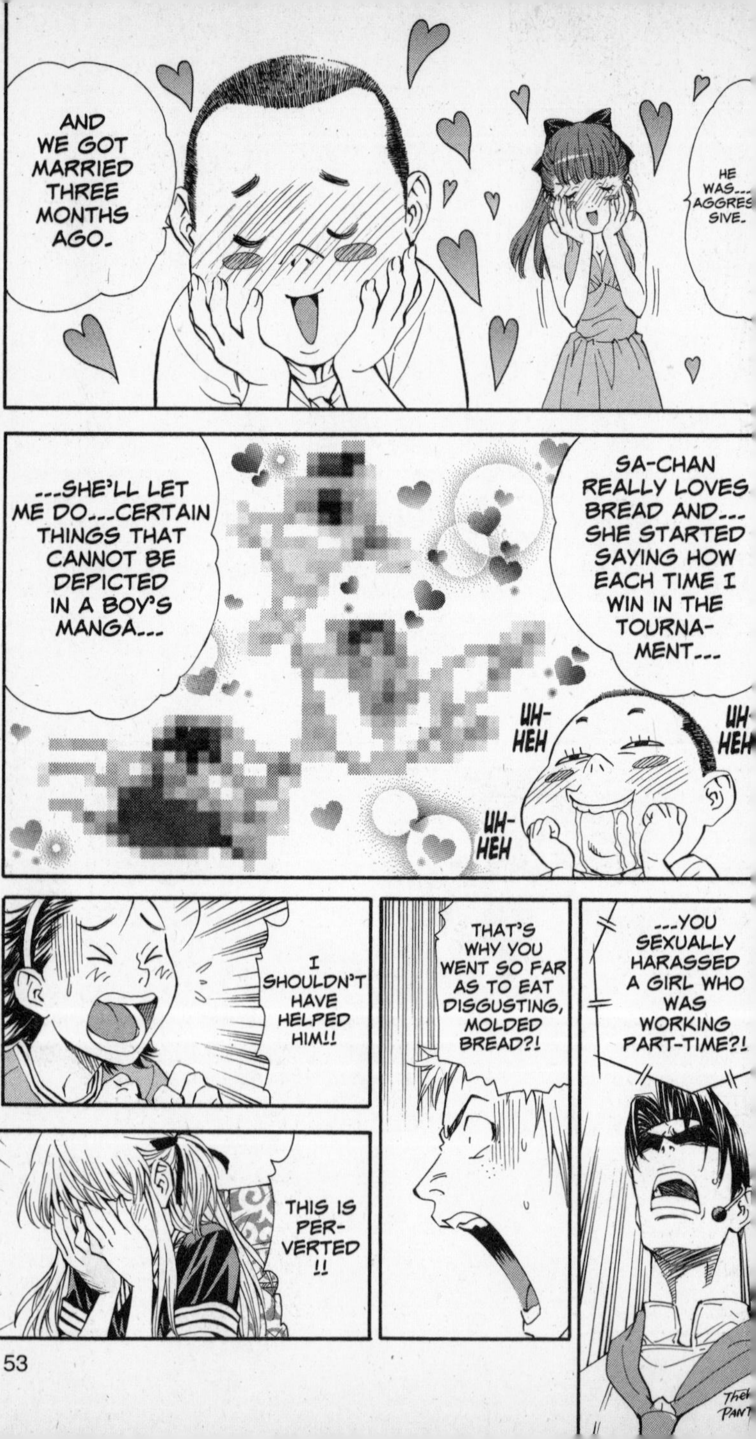
HE WAS... AGGRESSIVE.
AND WE GOT MARRIED THREE MONTHS AGO.
SA-CHAN REALLY LOVES BREAD AND... SHE STARTED SAYING HOW EACH TIME I WIN IN THE TOURNAMENT...
UH-HEH
UH-HEH
UH-HEH
...SHE'LL LET ME DO...CERTAIN THINGS THAT CANNOT BE DEPICTED IN A BOY'S MANGA...
...YOU SEXUALLY HARASSED A GIRL WHO WAS WORKING PART-TIME?!
THAT'S WHY YOU WENT SO FAR AS TO EAT DISGUSTING, MOLDED BREAD?!
I SHOULDN'T HAVE HELPED HIM!!
THIS IS PERVERTED!!

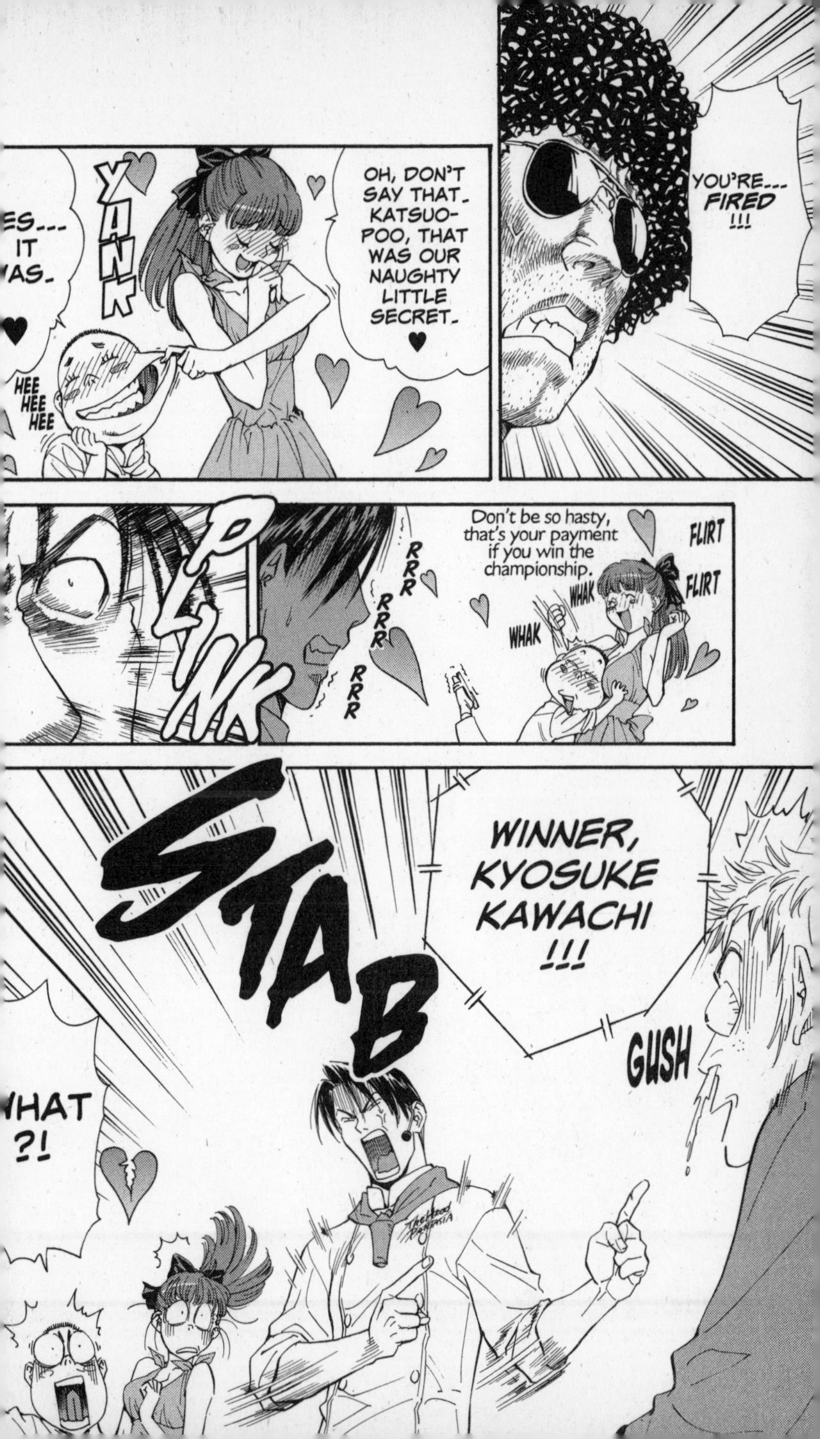
YOU'RE... FIRED !!!
OH, DON'T SAY THAT... KATSUO-POO, THAT WAS OUR NAUGHTY LITTLE SECRET... ♥
YANK
ES... IT AS... ♥
HEE HEE HEE
Don't be so hasty, that's your payment if you win the championship.
FLIRT
FLIRT
WHAK
WHAK
RRR
RRR
RRR
PLINK
WINNER, KYOSUKE KAWACHI !!!
GUSH
STAB
HAT ?!

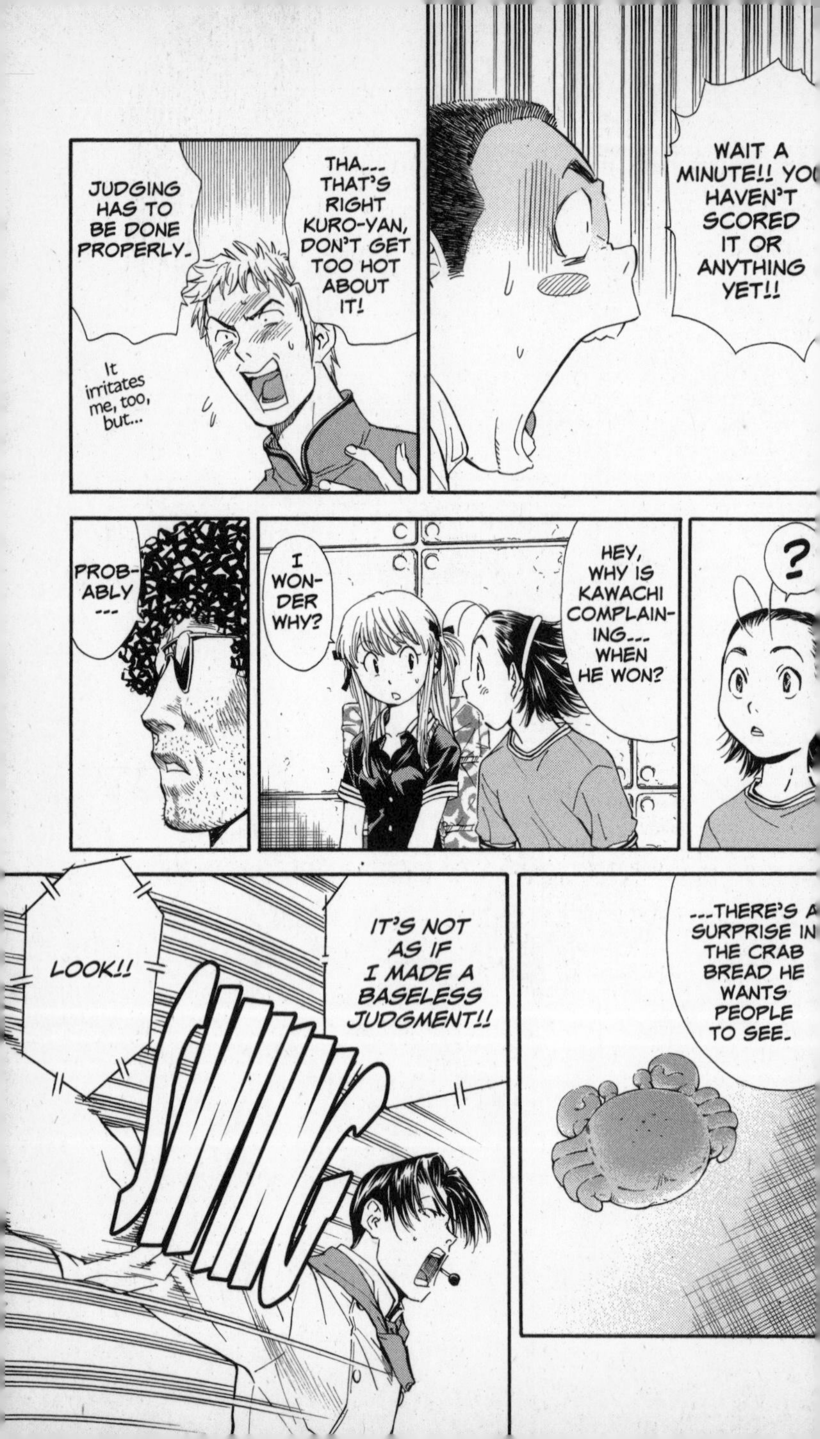
WAIT A MINUTE!! YO HAVEN'T SCORED IT OR ANYTHING YET!!
THA... THAT'S RIGHT KURO-YAN, DON'T GET TOO HOT ABOUT IT!
JUDGING HAS TO BE DONE PROPERLY.
It irritates me, too, but...
?
HEY, WHY IS KAWACHI COMPLAINING... WHEN HE WON?
I WONDER WHY?
PROBABLY...
...THERE'S A SURPRISE IN THE CRAB BREAD HE WANTS PEOPLE TO SEE.
IT'S NOT AS IF I MADE A BASELESS JUDGMENT!!
LOOK!!

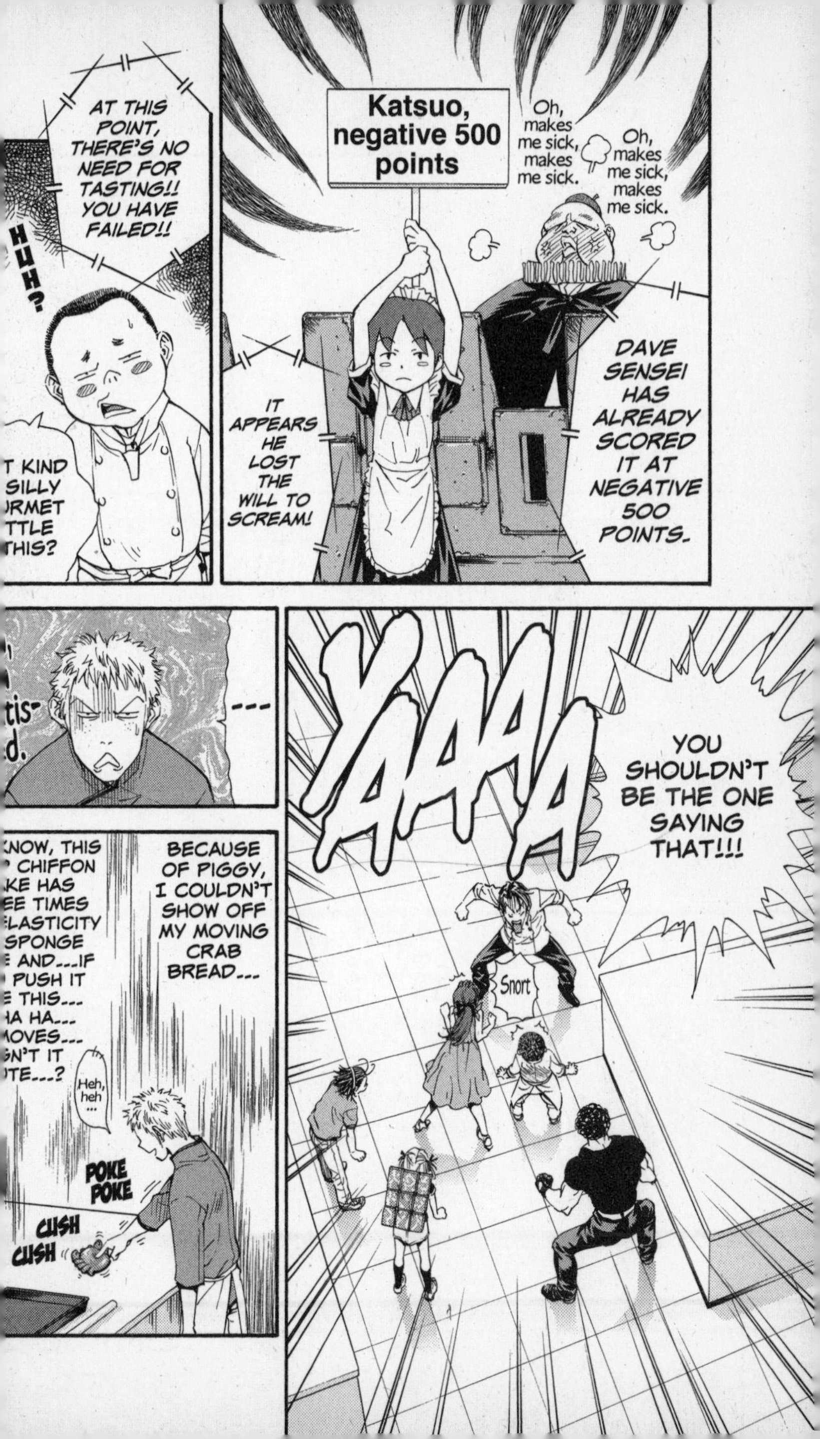
Katsuo, negative 500 points
Oh, makes me sick, makes me sick.
Oh, makes me sick, makes me sick.
DAVE SENSEI HAS ALREADY SCORED IT AT NEGATIVE 500 POINTS.
IT APPEARS HE LOST THE WILL TO SCREAM!
AT THIS POINT, THERE'S NO NEED FOR TASTING!! YOU HAVE FAILED!!
HUH?
T KIND SILLY RMET TTLE THIS?
YAAA
YOU SHOULDN'T BE THE ONE SAYING THAT!!!
Snort
tis- d.

BECAUSE OF PIGGY, I COULDN'T SHOW OFF MY MOVING CRAB BREAD...
KNOW, THIS CHIFFON KE HAS EE TIMES ELASTICITY SPONGE E AND...IF PUSH IT E THIS... HA HA... MOVES... N'T IT TE...?
Heh, heh ...
POKE POKE
CUSH CUSH

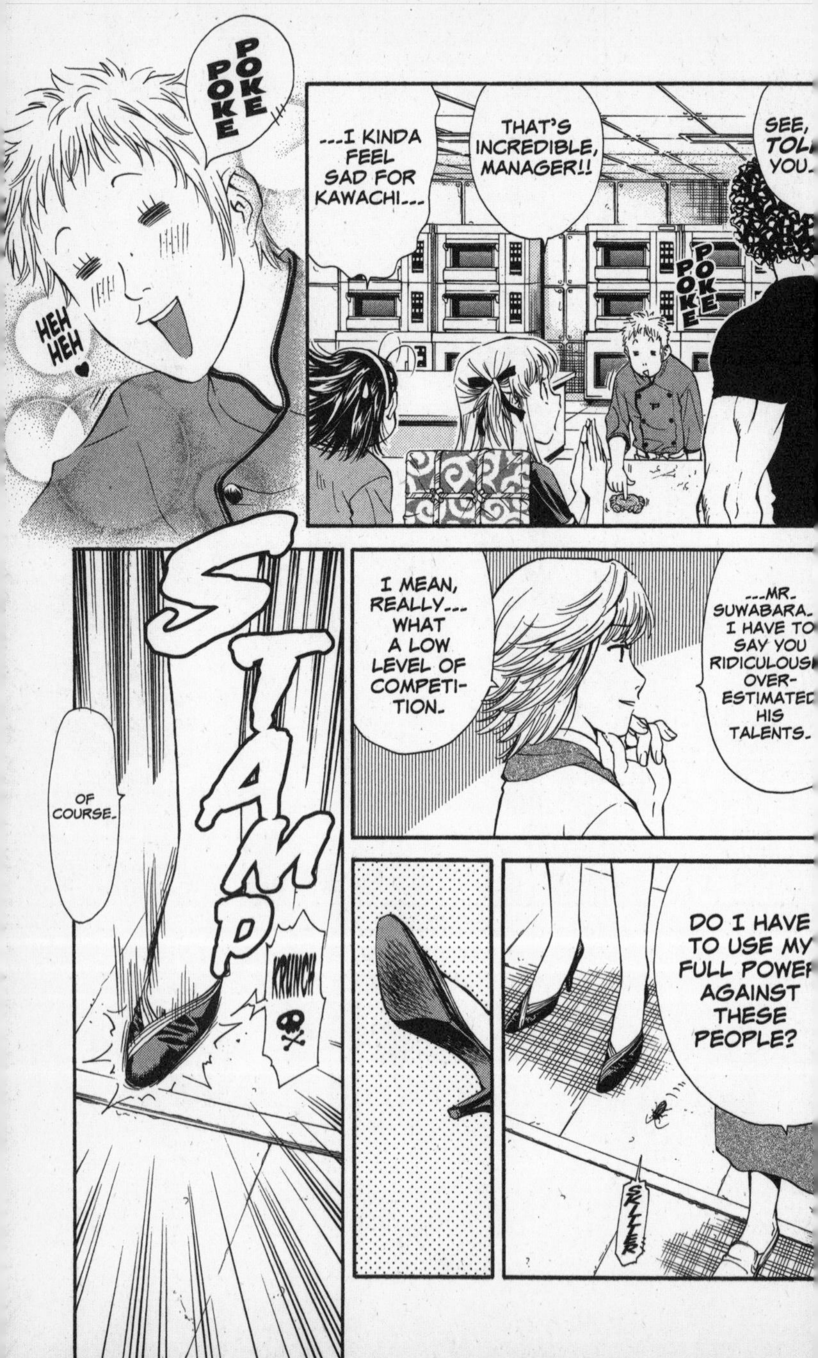
SEE, TOL YOU..
THAT'S INCREDIBLE, MANAGER!!
POKE POKE
...I KINDA FEEL SAD FOR KAWACHI...
POKE POKE
HEH HEH ♥
...MR. SUWABARA.. I HAVE TO SAY YOU RIDICULOUS OVER-ESTIMATED HIS TALENTS..
I MEAN, REALLY... WHAT A LOW LEVEL OF COMPETITION.
DO I HAVE TO USE MY FULL POWE AGAINST THESE PEOPLE?
SKITTER
STAMP
KRUNCH
OF COURSE.

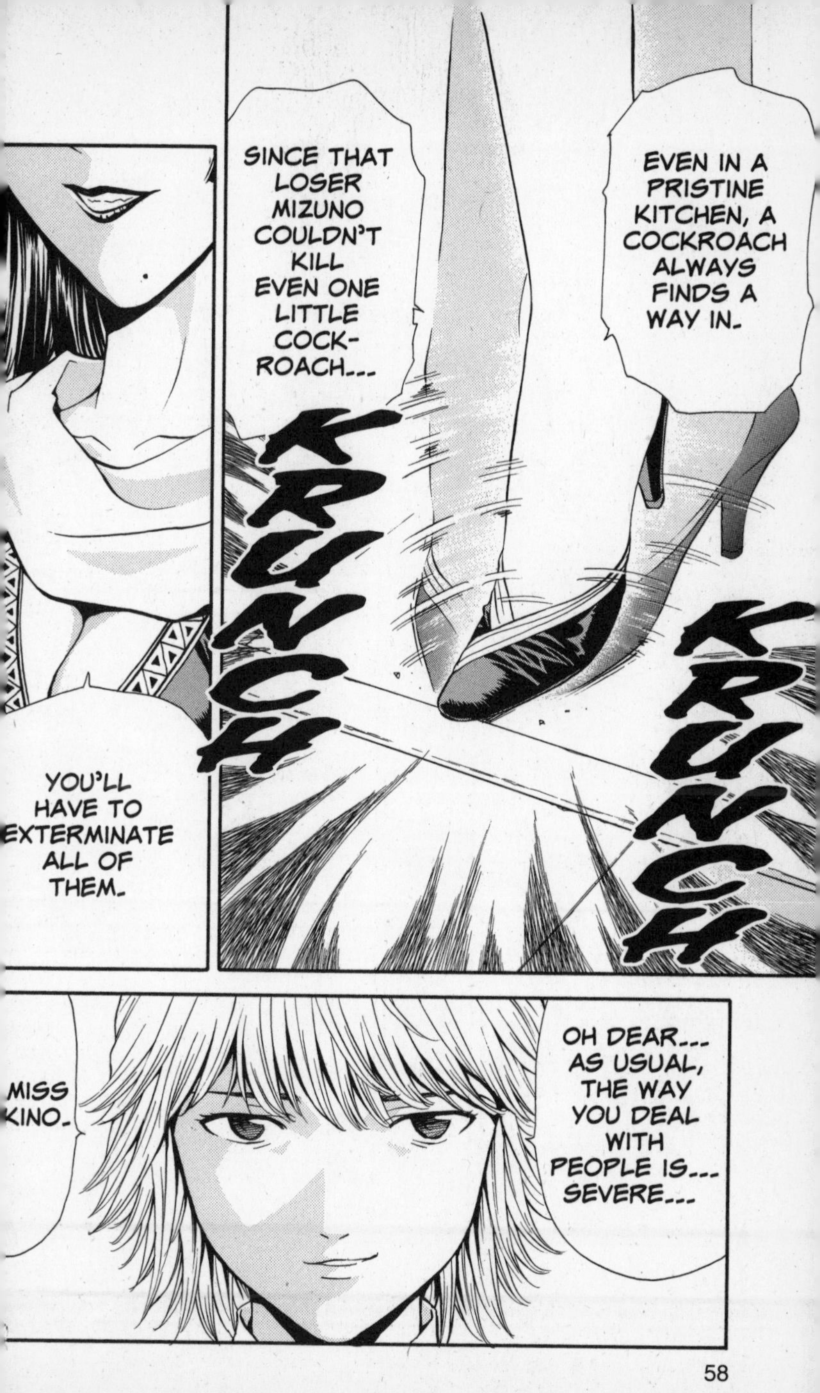
EVEN IN A PRISTINE KITCHEN, A COCKROACH ALWAYS FINDS A WAY IN.
SINCE THAT LOSER MIZUNO COULDN'T KILL EVEN ONE LITTLE COCK-ROACH...
KRUNCH
KRUNCH
YOU'LL HAVE TO EXTERMINATE ALL OF THEM.
OH DEAR... AS USUAL, THE WAY YOU DEAL WITH PEOPLE IS... SEVERE...
MISS KINO.

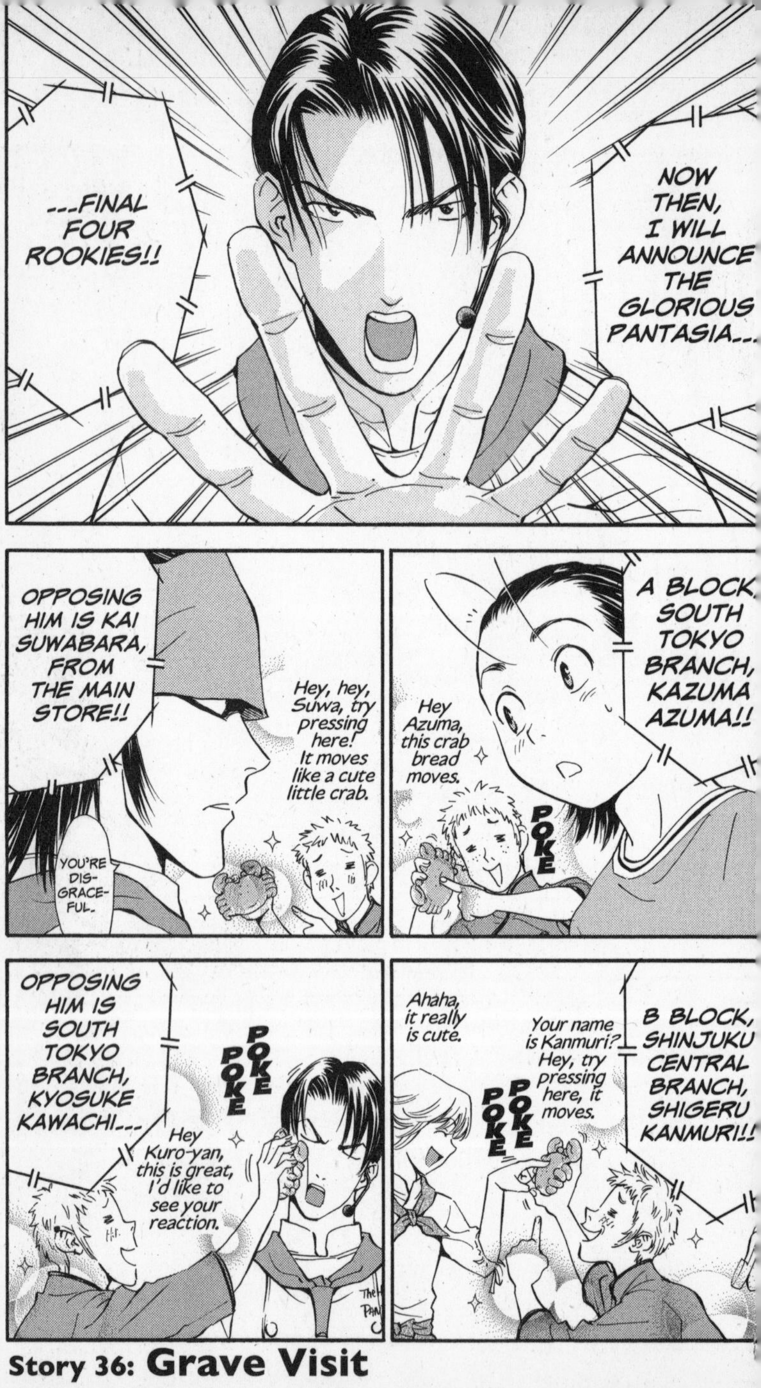
NOW THEN, I WILL ANNOUNCE THE GLORIOUS PANTASIA...
---FINAL FOUR ROOKIES!!
A BLOCK, SOUTH TOKYO BRANCH, KAZUMA AZUMA!!
Hey Azuma, this crab bread moves.
POKE
OPPOSING HIM IS KAI SUWABARA, FROM THE MAIN STORE!!
Hey, hey, Suwa, try pressing here! It moves like a cute little crab.
YOU'RE DISGRACEFUL.
B BLOCK, SHINJUKU CENTRAL BRANCH, SHIGERU KANMURI!!
Your name is Kanmuri? Hey, try pressing here, it moves.
POKE POKE
Ahaha, it really is cute.
OPPOSING HIM IS SOUTH TOKYO BRANCH, KYOSUKE KAWACHI...
POKE POKE
Hey Kuro-yan, this is great, I'd like to see your reaction.

Story 36: Grave Visit

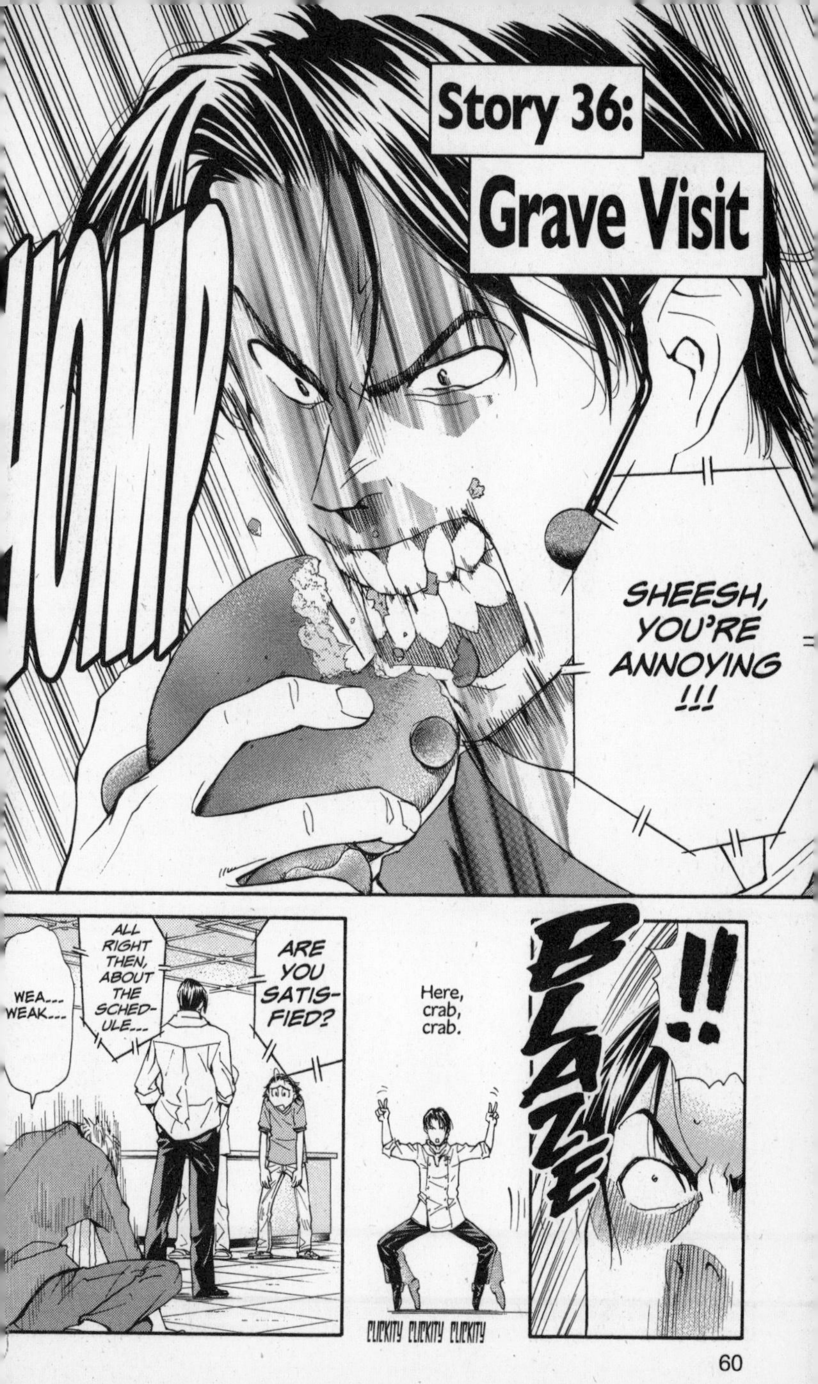
Story 36:
Grave Visit
SHEESH, YOU'RE ANNOYING !!!
BLAZE !!
Here, crab, crab.
CLICKITY CLICKITY CLICKITY
ARE YOU SATIS-FIED?
ALL RIGHT THEN, ABOUT THE SCHED-ULE...
WEA... WEAK...

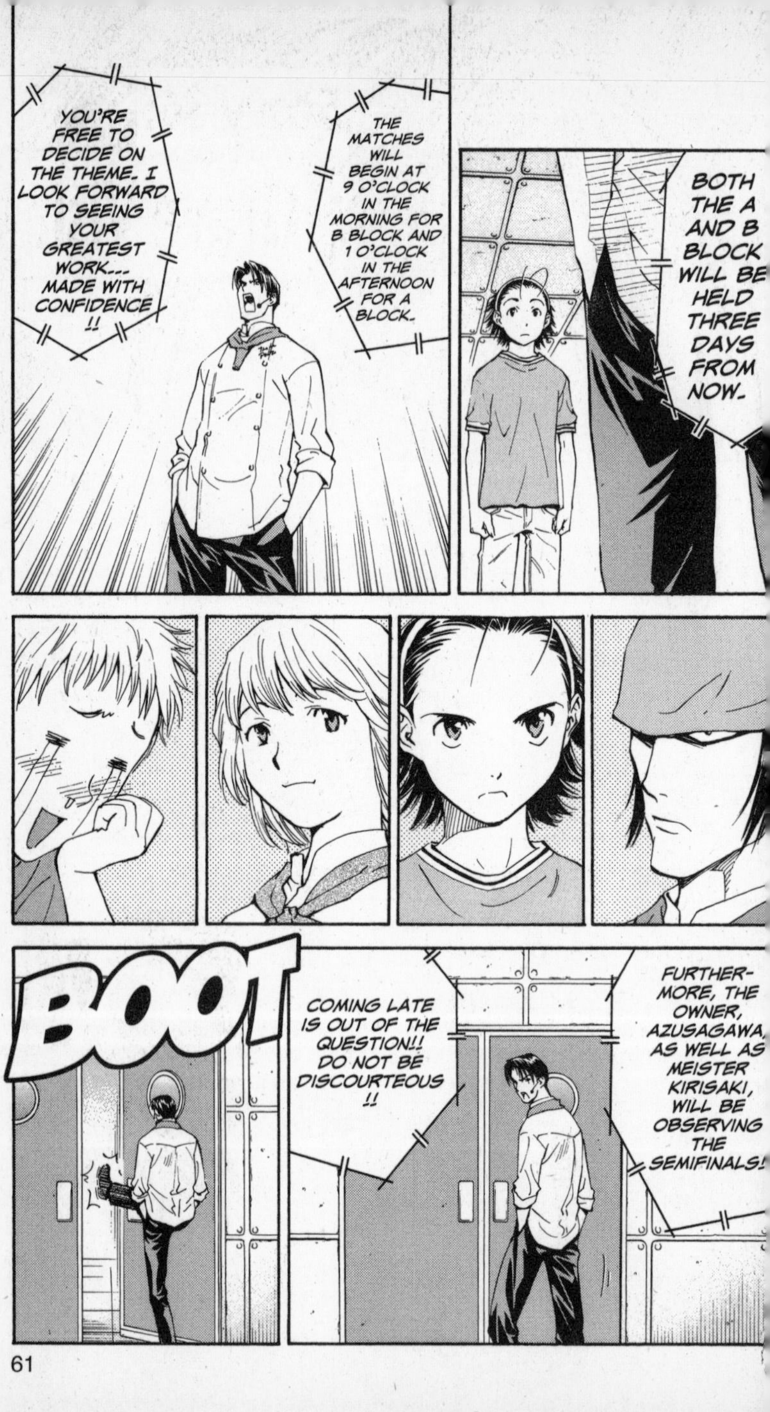
BOTH THE A AND B BLOCK WILL BE HELD THREE DAYS FROM NOW.
THE MATCHES WILL BEGIN AT 9 O'CLOCK IN THE MORNING FOR B BLOCK AND 1 O'CLOCK IN THE AFTERNOON FOR A BLOCK.
YOU'RE FREE TO DECIDE ON THE THEME. I LOOK FORWARD TO SEEING YOUR GREATEST WORK... MADE WITH CONFIDENCE!!
FURTHER-MORE, THE OWNER, AZUSAGAWA, AS WELL AS MEISTER KIRISAKI, WILL BE OBSERVING THE SEMIFINALS!
COMING LATE IS OUT OF THE QUESTION!! DO NOT BE DISCOURTEOUS!!
BOOT

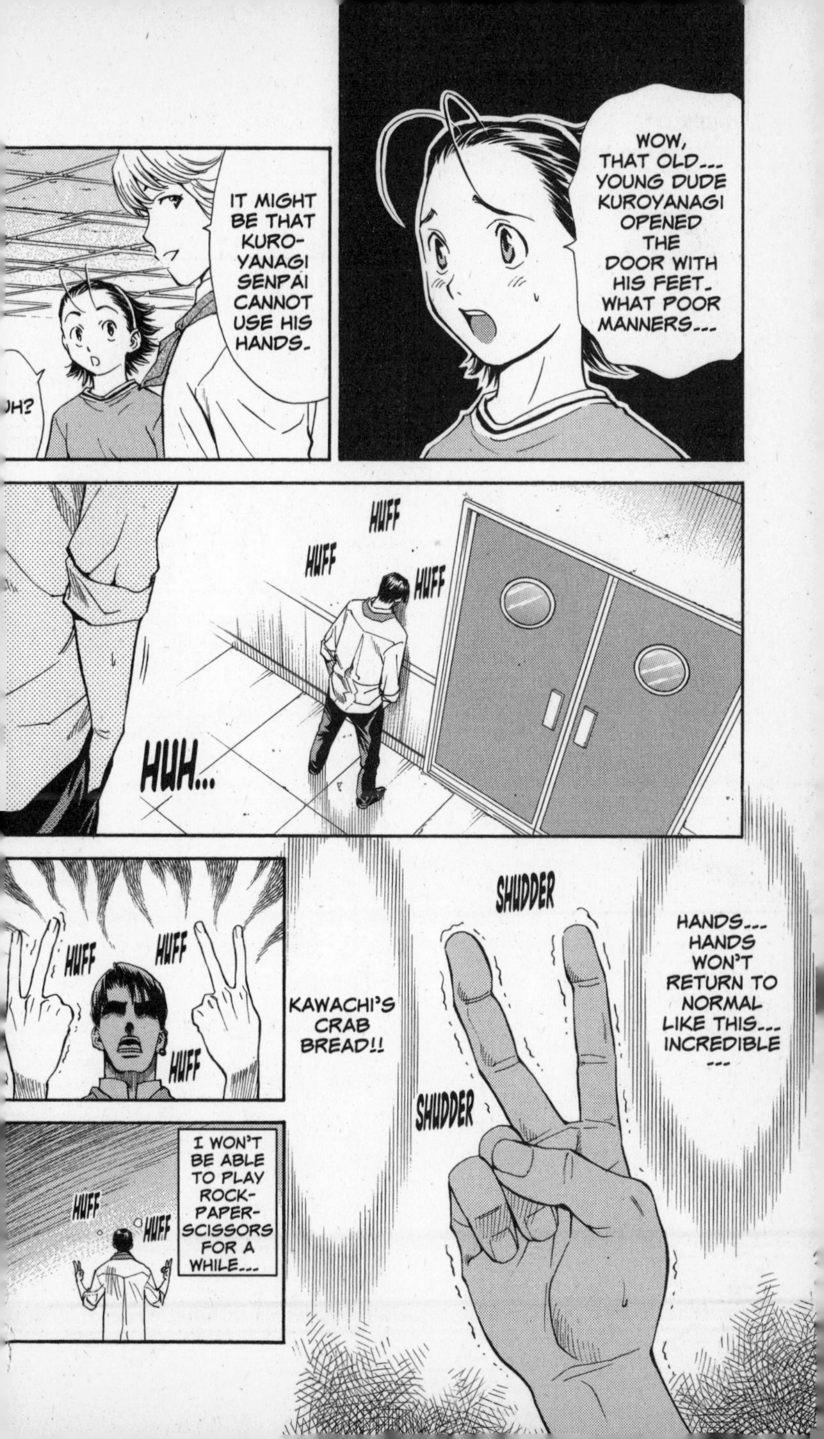

WOW, THAT OLD... YOUNG DUDE KUROYANAGI OPENED THE DOOR WITH HIS FEET. WHAT POOR MANNERS...
IT MIGHT BE THAT KURO-YANAGI SENPAI CANNOT USE HIS HANDS.
UH?
HUFF
HUFF
HUFF
HUH...
HANDS... HANDS WON'T RETURN TO NORMAL LIKE THIS... INCREDIBLE...
SHUDDER
KAWACHI'S CRAB BREAD!!
SHUDDER
HUFF
HUFF
HUFF
I WON'T BE ABLE TO PLAY ROCK-PAPER-SCISSORS FOR A WHILE...
HUFF
HUFF

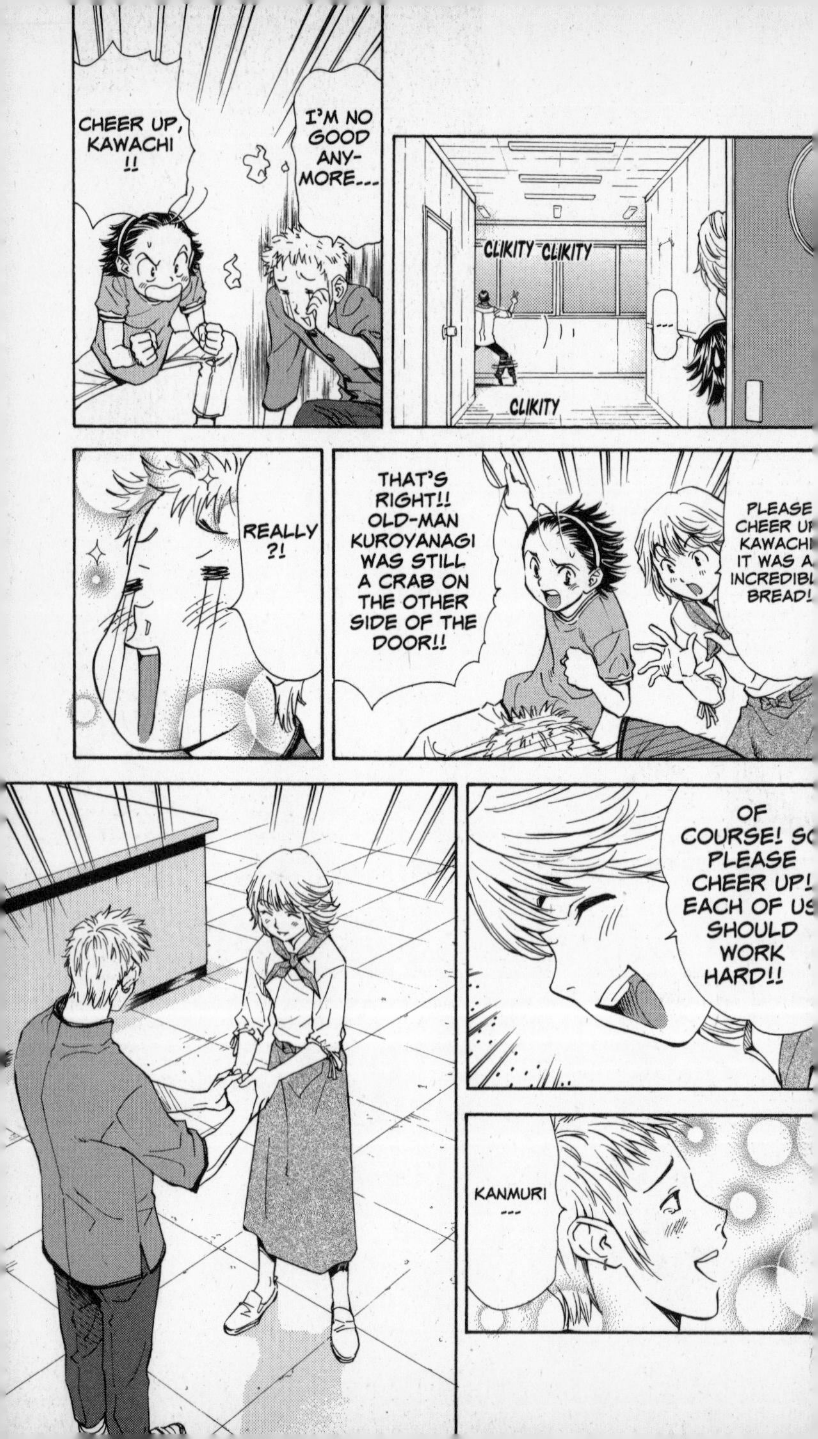
CLIKITY CLIKITY
...
CLIKITY
I'M NO GOOD ANYMORE...
CHEER UP, KAWACHI!!
PLEASE CHEER UP KAWACHI IT WAS A INCREDIBL BREAD!
THAT'S RIGHT!! OLD-MAN KUROYANAGI WAS STILL A CRAB ON THE OTHER SIDE OF THE DOOR!!
REALLY?!
OF COURSE! SO PLEASE CHEER UP! EACH OF US SHOULD WORK HARD!!
KANMURI...

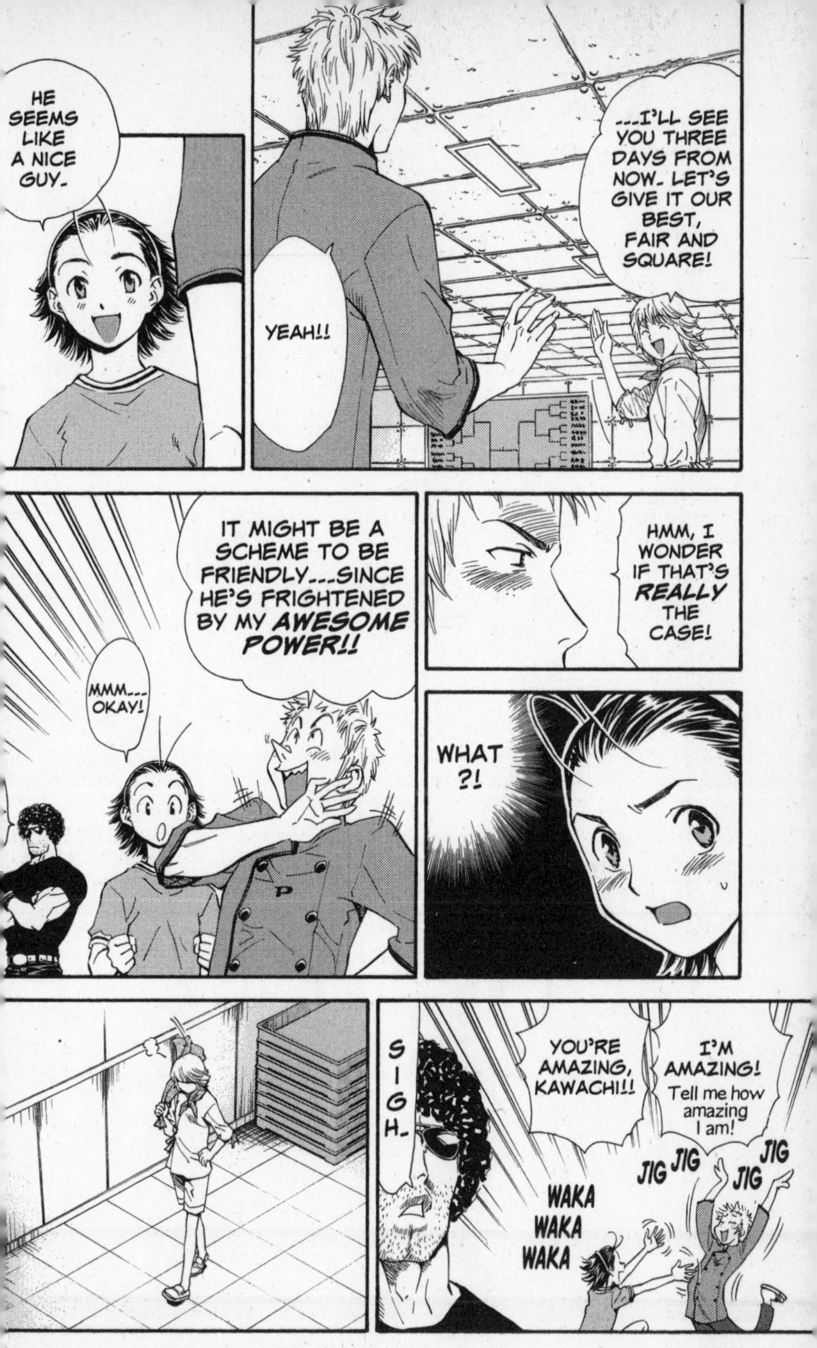
...I'LL SEE YOU THREE DAYS FROM NOW. LET'S GIVE IT OUR BEST, FAIR AND SQUARE!
YEAH!!
HE SEEMS LIKE A NICE GUY.
HMM, I WONDER IF THAT'S *REALLY* THE CASE!
WHAT?!
IT MIGHT BE A SCHEME TO BE FRIENDLY...SINCE HE'S FRIGHTENED BY MY ***AWESOME POWER!!***
MMM... OKAY!
I'M AMAZING! Tell me how amazing I am!
YOU'RE AMAZING, KAWACHI!!
JIG JIG JIG JIG
SIGH.
WAKA WAKA WAKA

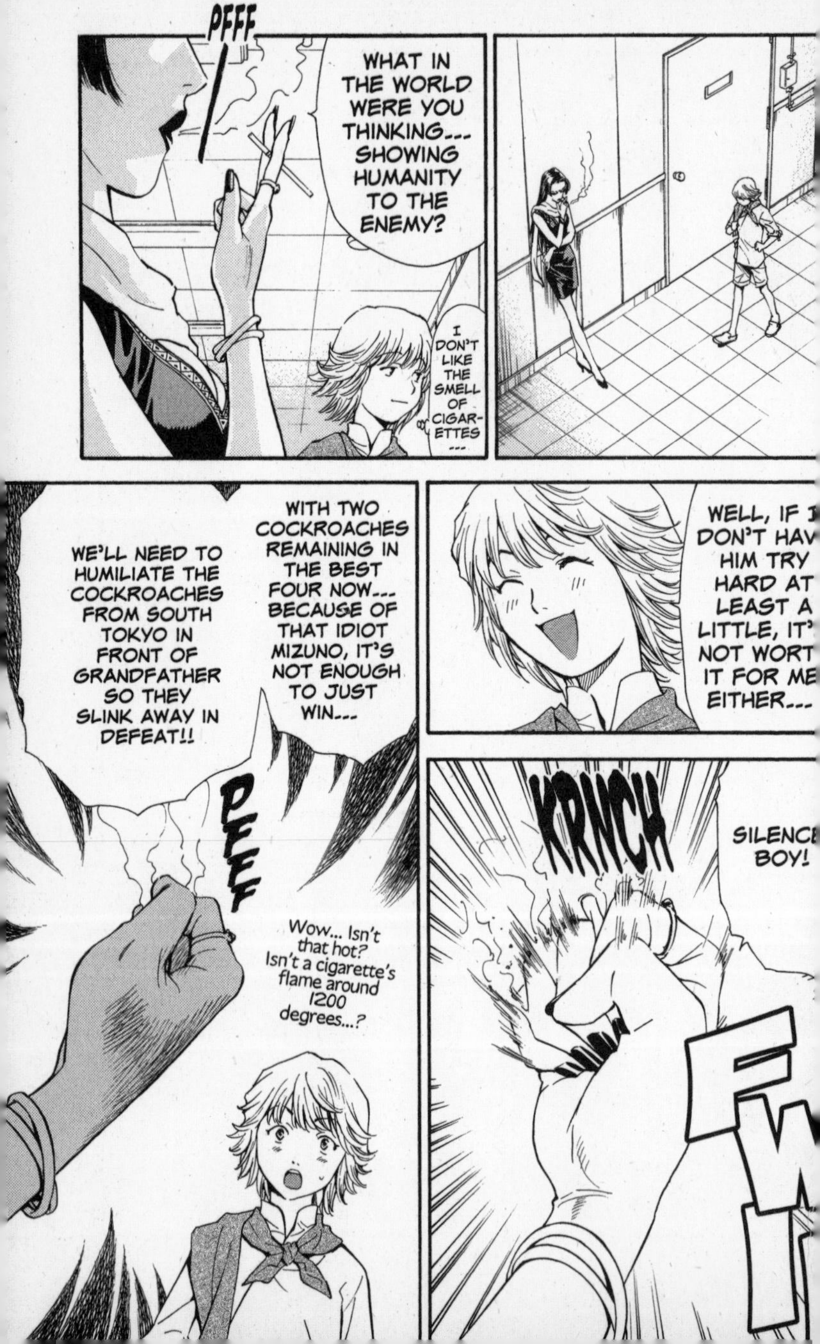
WHAT IN THE WORLD WERE YOU THINKING... SHOWING HUMANITY TO THE ENEMY?
PFFF
I DON'T LIKE THE SMELL OF CIGAR-ETTES...
WELL, IF I DON'T HAV HIM TRY HARD AT LEAST A LITTLE, IT' NOT WORT IT FOR ME EITHER...
KRNCH
SILENC BOY!
WITH TWO COCKROACHES REMAINING IN THE BEST FOUR NOW... BECAUSE OF THAT IDIOT MIZUNO, IT'S NOT ENOUGH TO JUST WIN...
WE'LL NEED TO HUMILIATE THE COCKROACHES FROM SOUTH TOKYO IN FRONT OF GRANDFATHER SO THEY SLINK AWAY IN DEFEAT!!
PFFF
Wow... Isn't that hot? Isn't a cigarette's flame around 1200 degrees...?

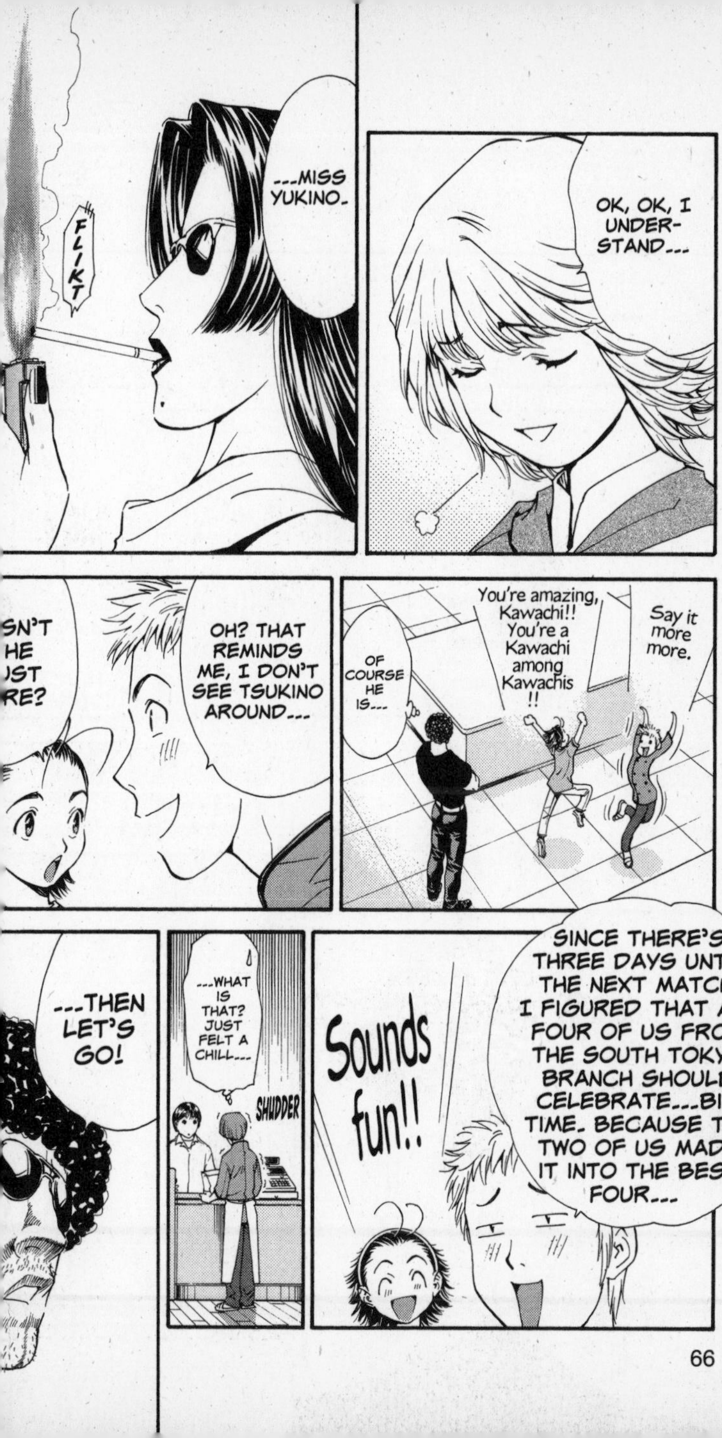
OK, OK, I UNDERSTAND...
...MISS YUKINO.
FLIKT
You're amazing, Kawachi!! You're a Kawachi among Kawachis!!
Say it more more.
OF COURSE HE IS...
OH? THAT REMINDS ME, I DON'T SEE TSUKINO AROUND...
SN'T HE JST RE?
SINCE THERE'S THREE DAYS UNTIL THE NEXT MATCH, I FIGURED THAT ALL FOUR OF US FROM THE SOUTH TOKYO BRANCH SHOULD CELEBRATE...BIG TIME. BECAUSE THE TWO OF US MADE IT INTO THE BEST FOUR...
Sounds fun!!
...WHAT IS THAT? JUST FELT A CHILL...
SHUDDER
...THEN LET'S GO!

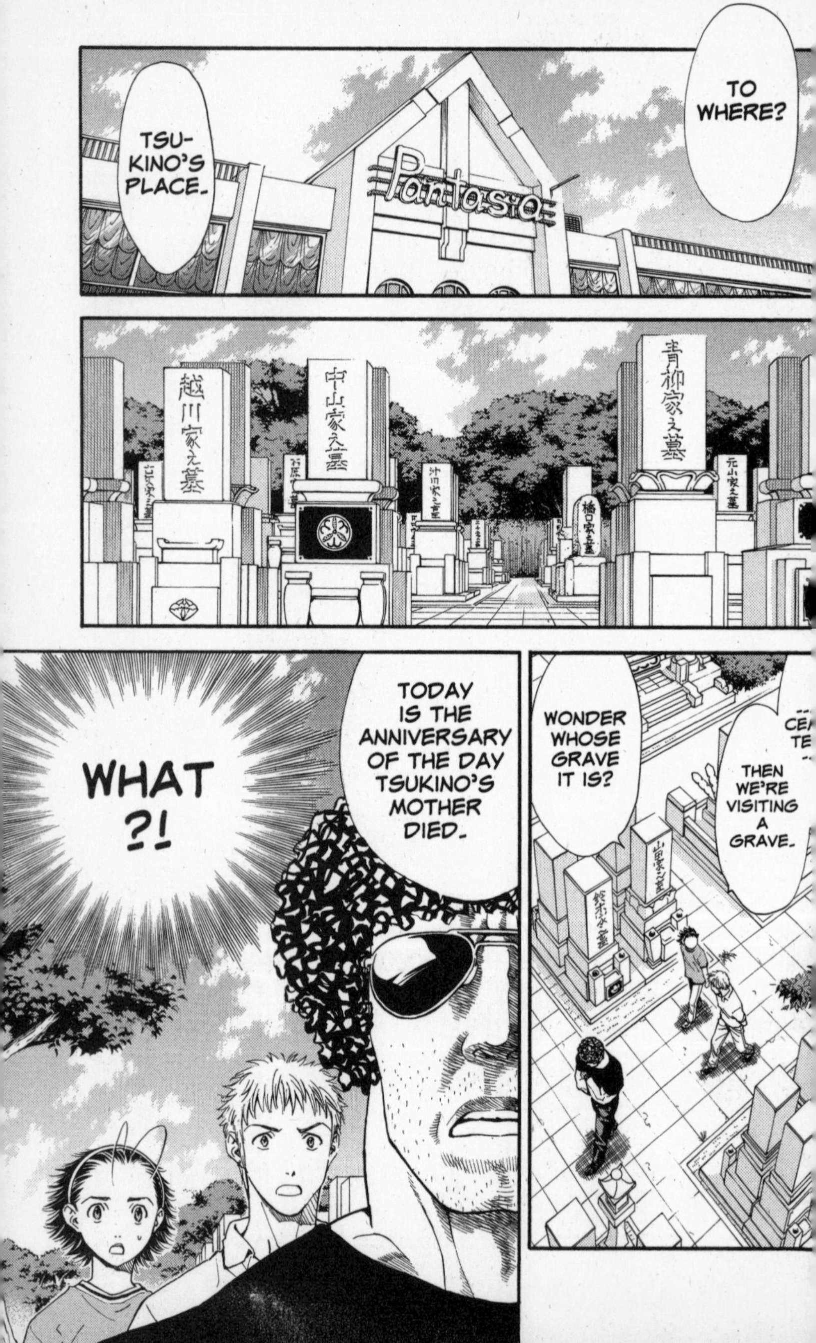
TO WHERE?
TSU-KINO'S PLACE.
Pantasia
青柳家之墓
中山家之墓
越川家之墓
THEN WE'RE VISITING A GRAVE.
WONDER WHOSE GRAVE IT IS?
TODAY IS THE ANNIVERSARY OF THE DAY TSUKINO'S MOTHER DIED.
WHAT ?!

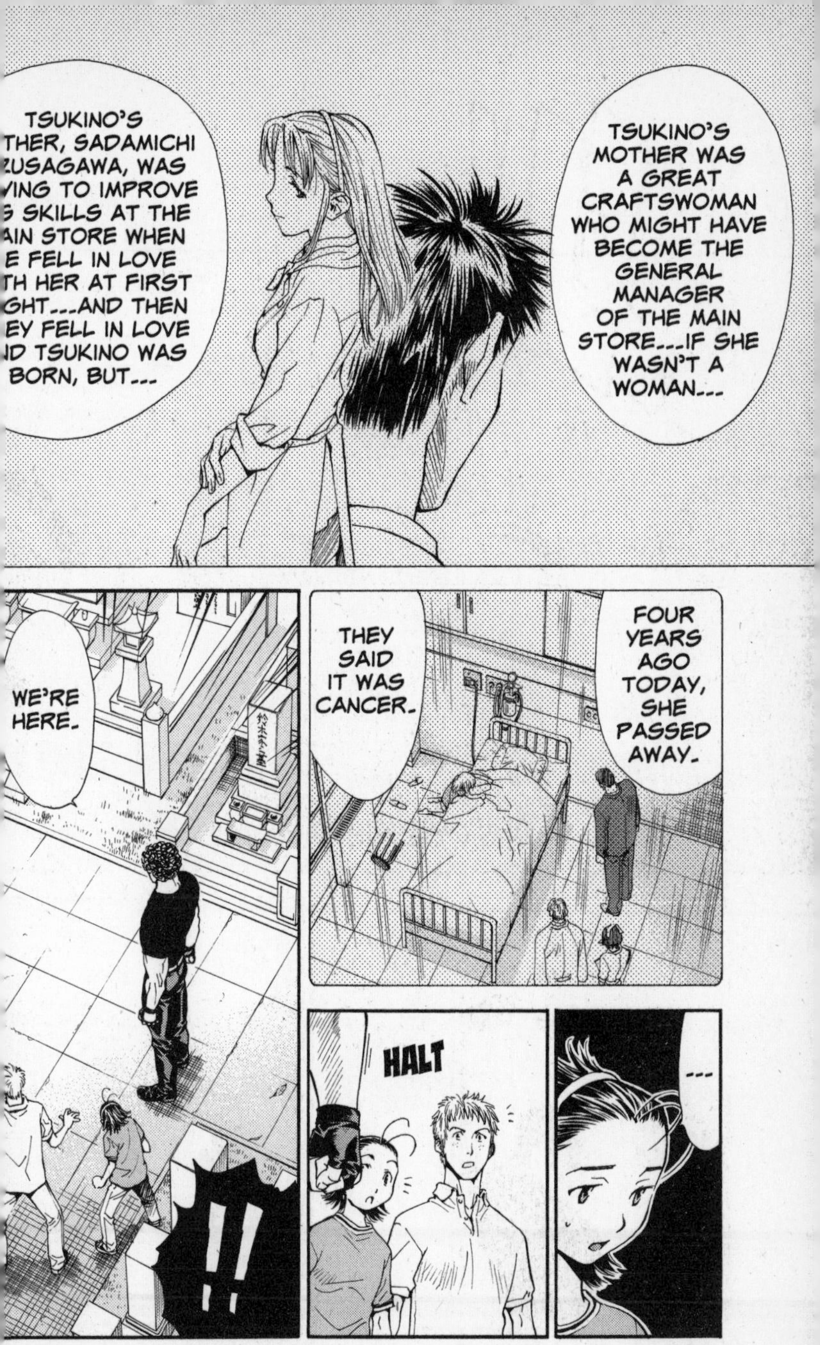
TSUKINO'S MOTHER WAS A GREAT CRAFTSWOMAN WHO MIGHT HAVE BECOME THE GENERAL MANAGER OF THE MAIN STORE...IF SHE WASN'T A WOMAN...
TSUKINO'S THER, SADAMICHI ZUSAGAWA, WAS YING TO IMPROVE S SKILLS AT THE AIN STORE WHEN E FELL IN LOVE TH HER AT FIRST GHT...AND THEN EY FELL IN LOVE D TSUKINO WAS BORN, BUT...
FOUR YEARS AGO TODAY, SHE PASSED AWAY.
THEY SAID IT WAS CANCER.
...
HALT
WE'RE HERE.
!!

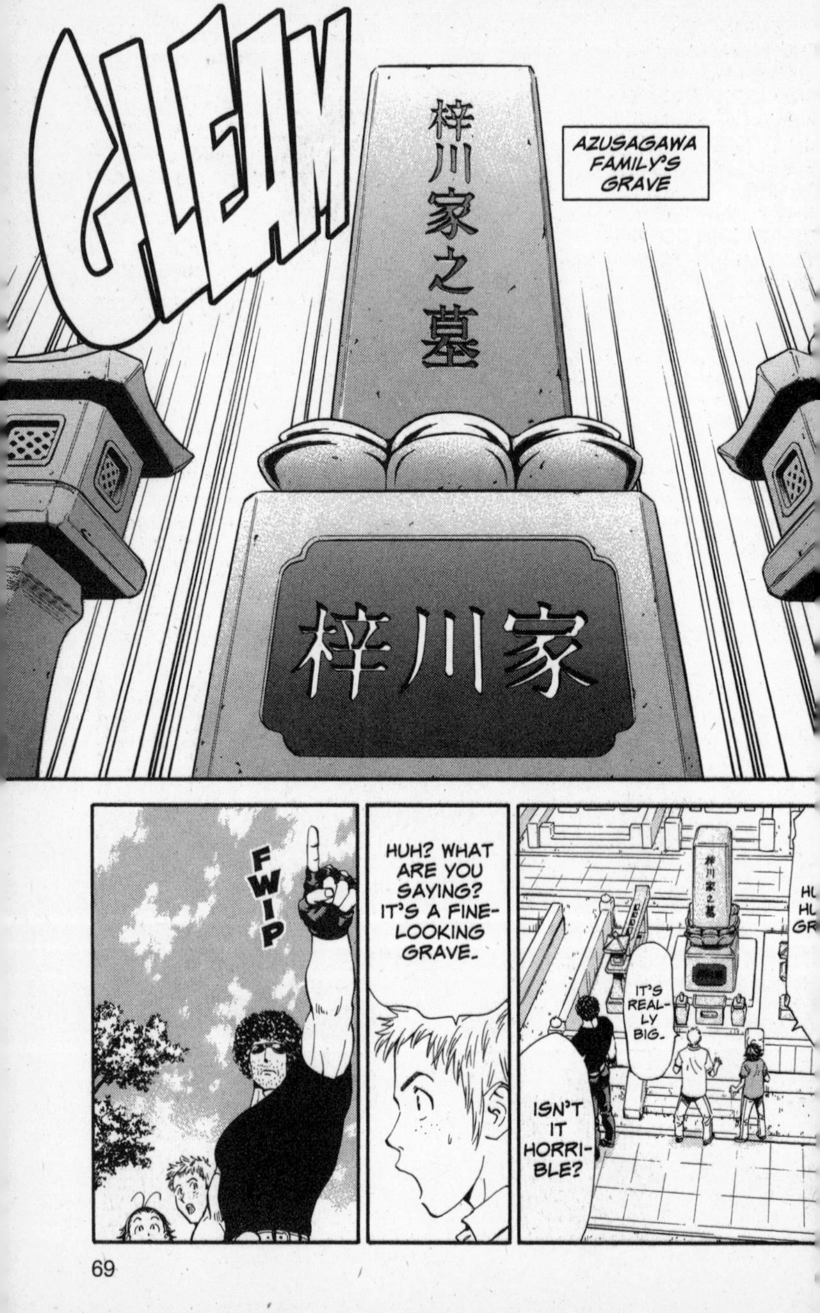
GLEAM
梓川家之墓
AZUSAGAWA FAMILY'S GRAVE
梓川家
梓川家之墓
IT'S REAL-LY BIG.
ISN'T IT HORRI-BLE?
HUH? WHAT ARE YOU SAYING? IT'S A FINE-LOOKING GRAVE.
FWIP

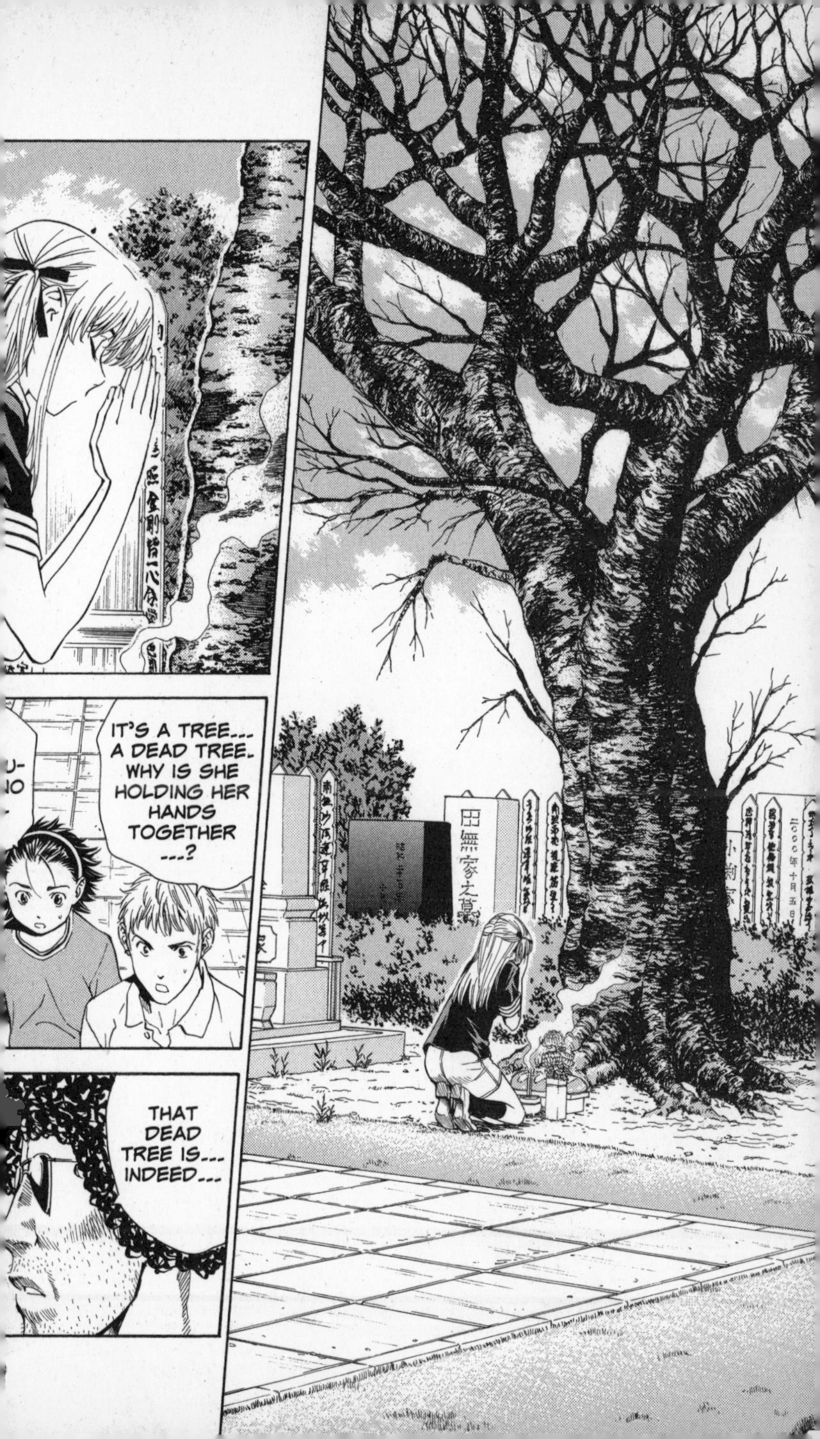
田無家之墓
IT'S A TREE... A DEAD TREE. WHY IS SHE HOLDING HER HANDS TOGETHER...?
THAT DEAD TREE IS... INDEED...

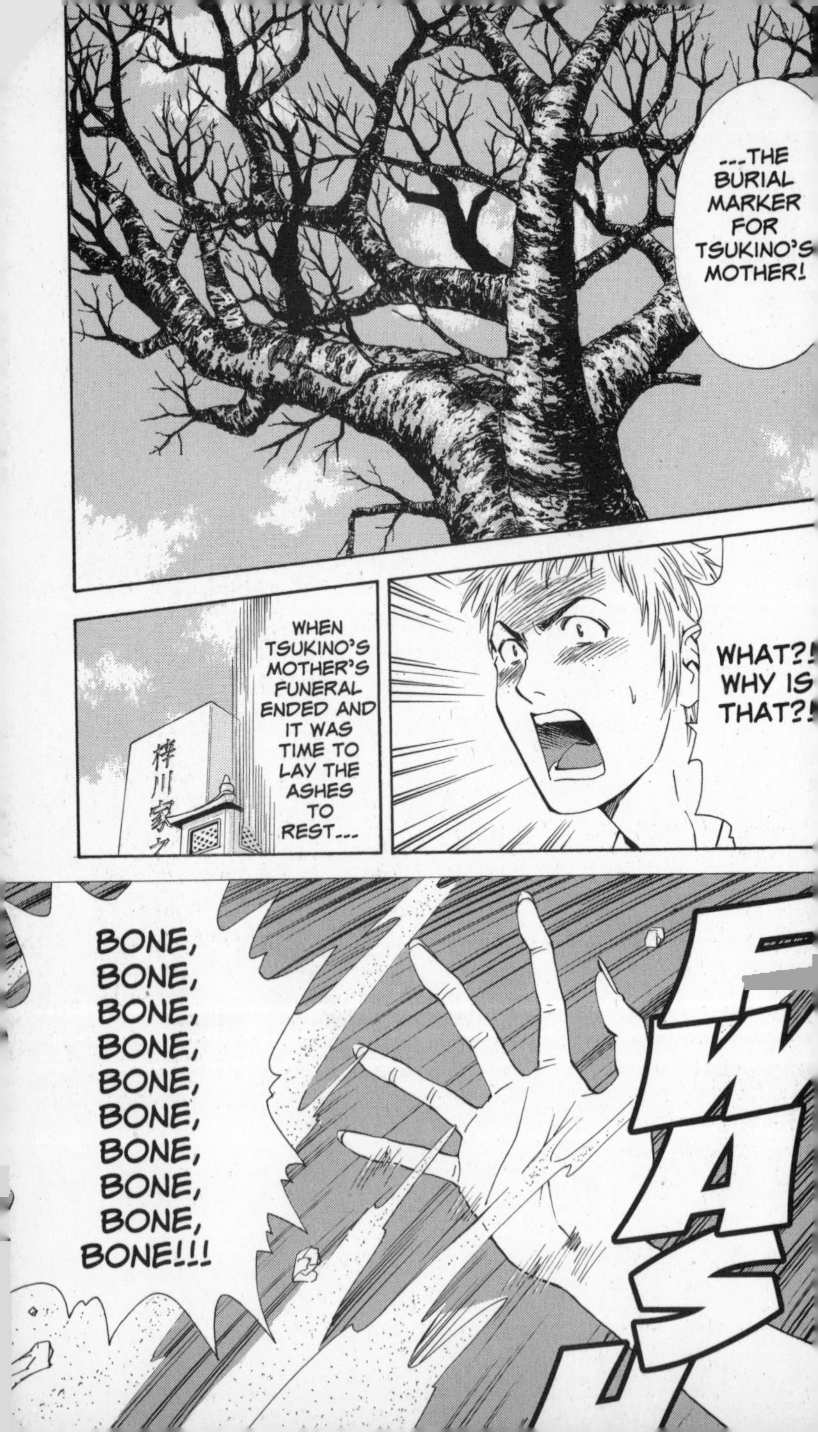
---THE BURIAL MARKER FOR TSUKINO'S MOTHER!
WHAT?! WHY IS THAT?!
WHEN TSUKINO'S MOTHER'S FUNERAL ENDED AND IT WAS TIME TO LAY THE ASHES TO REST---
BONE, BONE, BONE, BONE, BONE, BONE, BONE, BONE, BONE, BONE!!!

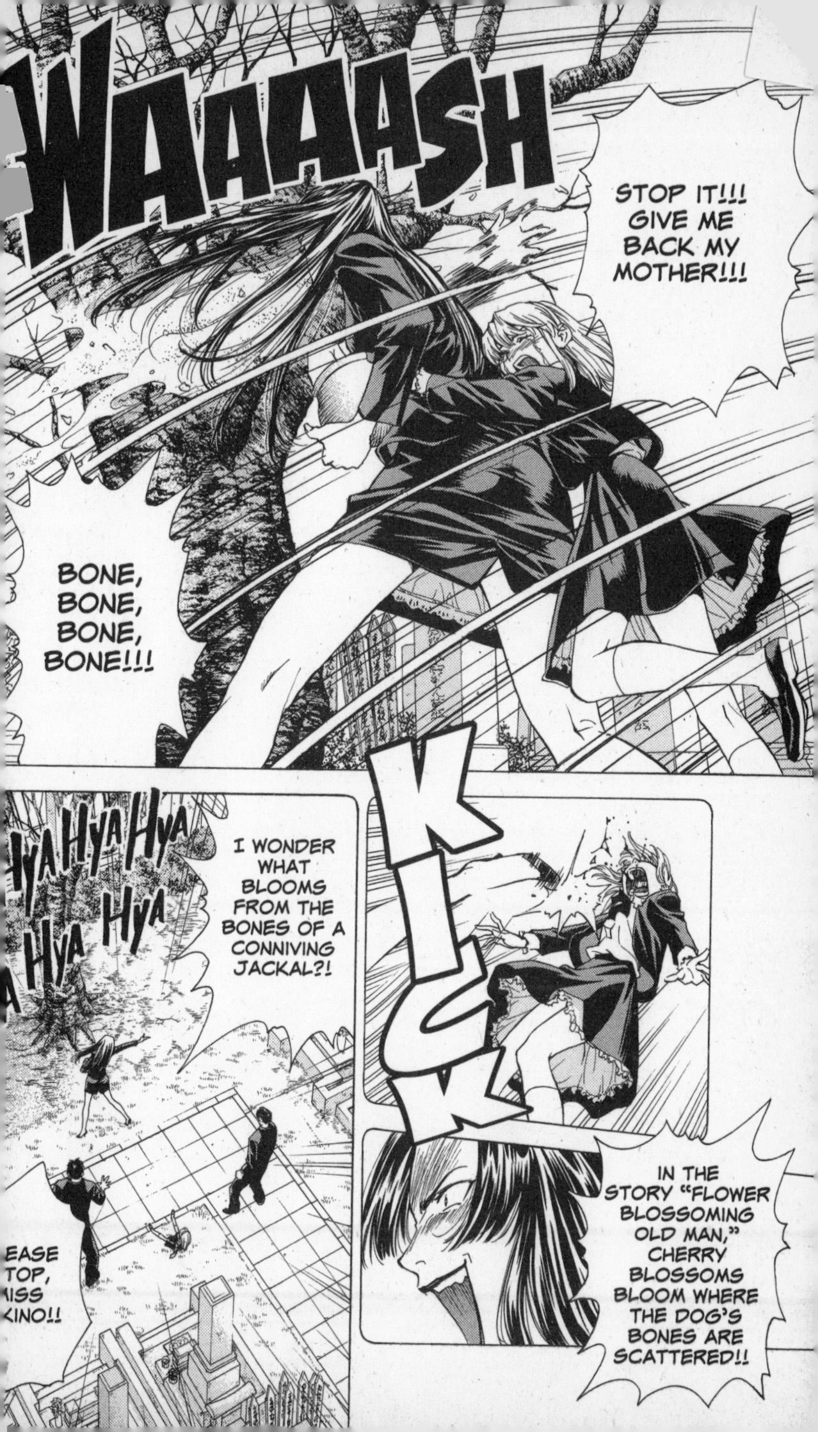
STOP IT!!! GIVE ME BACK MY MOTHER!!!
WAAASH
BONE, BONE, BONE, BONE!!!
KICK
IN THE STORY "FLOWER BLOSSOMING OLD MAN," CHERRY BLOSSOMS BLOOM WHERE THE DOG'S BONES ARE SCATTERED!!
I WONDER WHAT BLOOMS FROM THE BONES OF A CONNIVING JACKAL?!
Hya Hya Hya Hya Hya
EASE TOP, ISS KINO!!

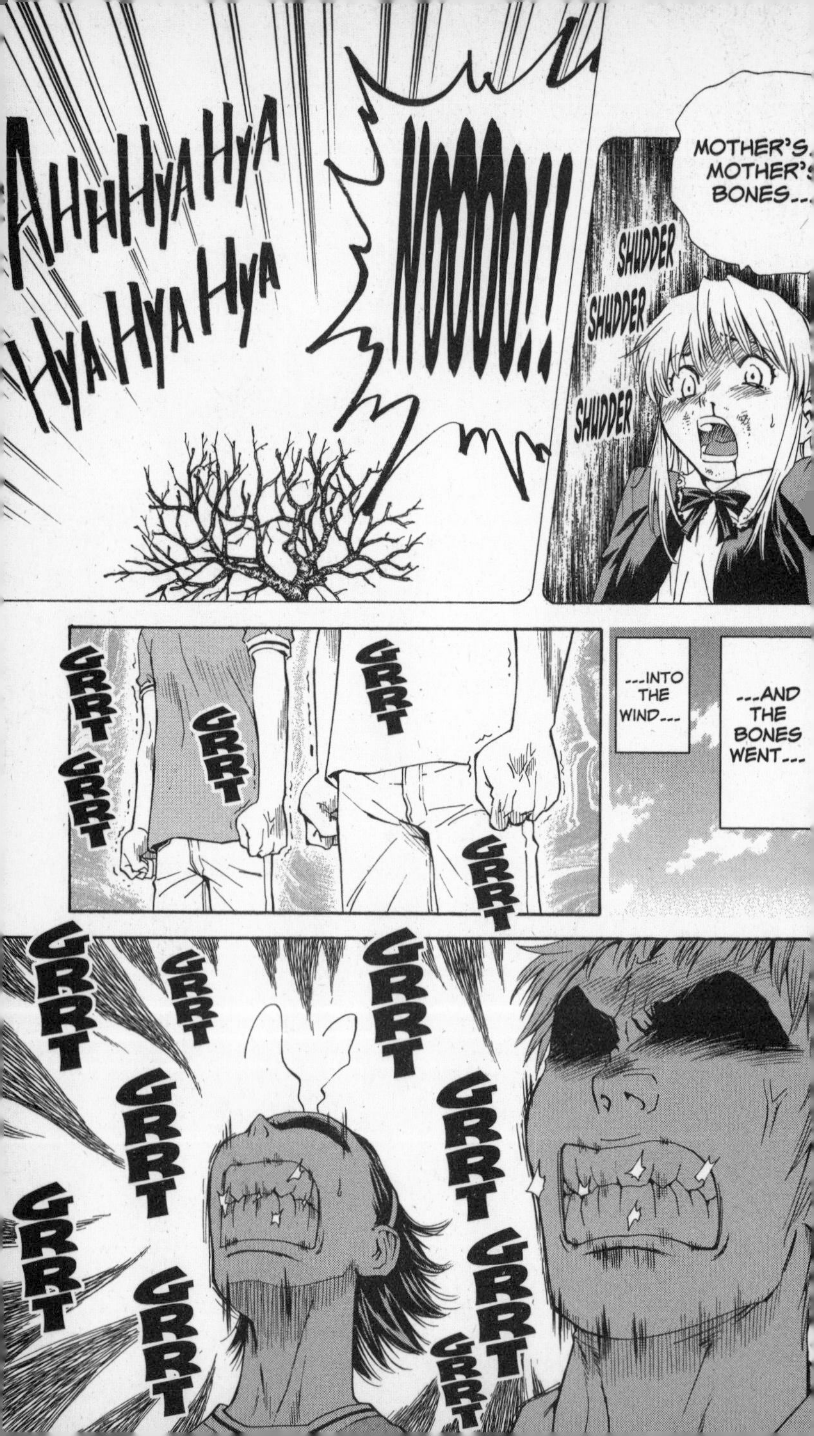
MOTHER'S... MOTHER'S BONES...
SHUDDER
SHUDDER
SHUDDER
NOOOO!!
AHHHYAHYA HYAHYAHYA
...AND THE BONES WENT...
...INTO THE WIND...
GRRT
GRRT
GRRT GRRT
GRRT
GRRT
GRRT
GRRT
GRRT
GRRT
GRRT GRRT
GRRT
GRRT

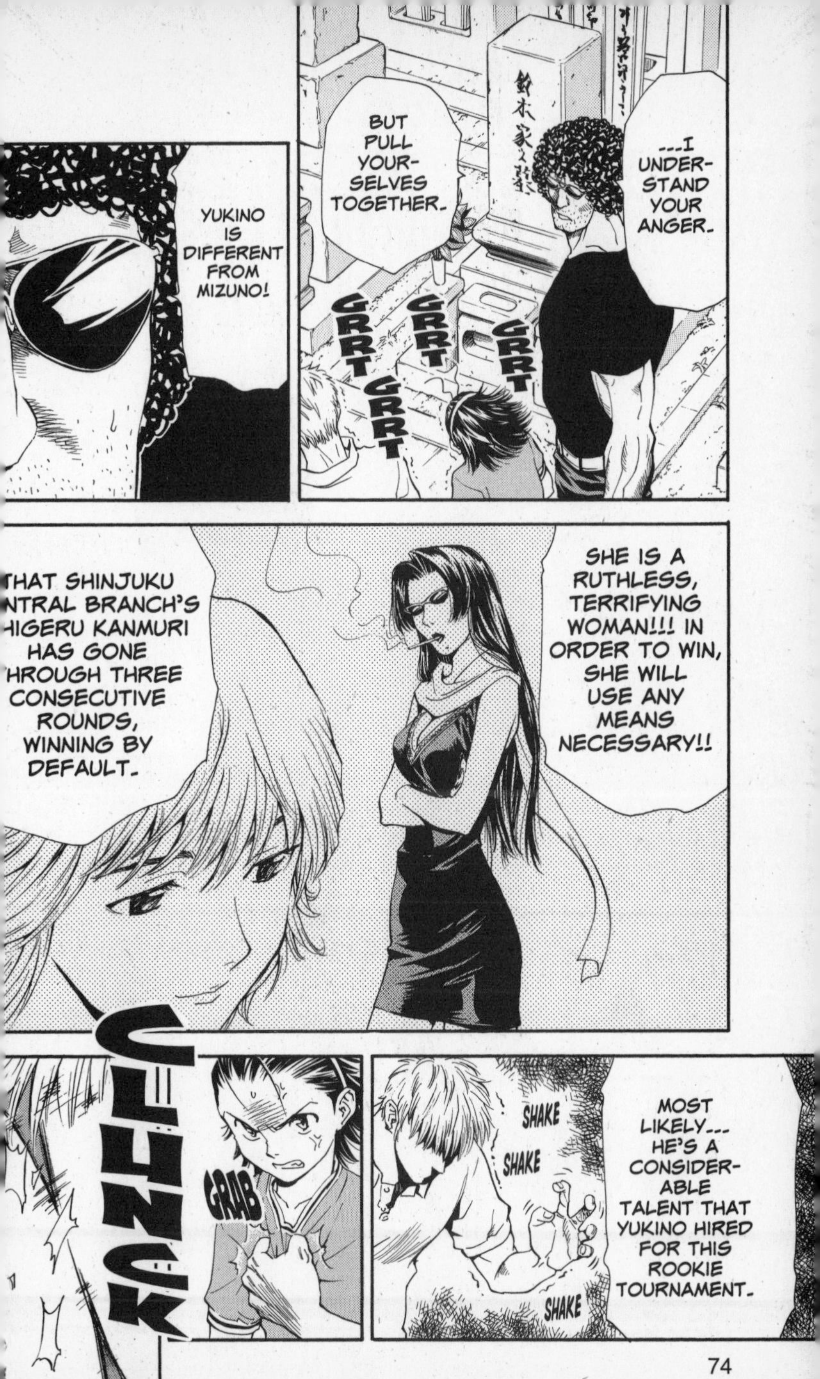

...I UNDERSTAND YOUR ANGER.
BUT PULL YOURSELVES TOGETHER.
GRRT GRRT GRRT GRRT
YUKINO IS DIFFERENT FROM MIZUNO!
SHE IS A RUTHLESS, TERRIFYING WOMAN!!! IN ORDER TO WIN, SHE WILL USE ANY MEANS NECESSARY!!
THAT SHINJUKU NTRAL BRANCH'S HIGERU KANMURI HAS GONE HROUGH THREE CONSECUTIVE ROUNDS, WINNING BY DEFAULT.
MOST LIKELY... HE'S A CONSIDERABLE TALENT THAT YUKINO HIRED FOR THIS ROOKIE TOURNAMENT.
SHAKE SHAKE SHAKE
GRAB
CLUNCK

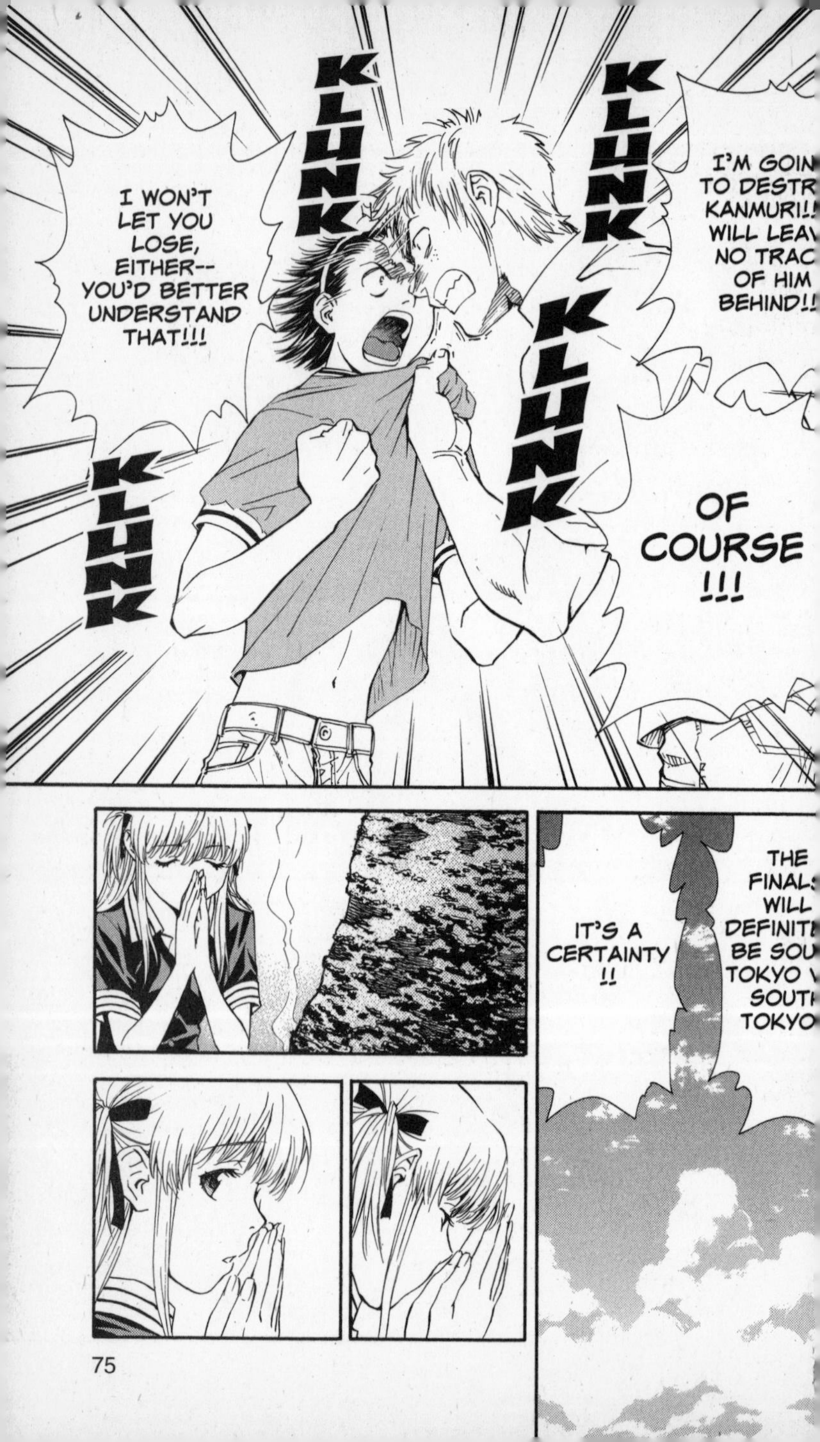
I'M GOIN
TO DESTR
KANMURI!!
WILL LEAV
NO TRAC
OF HIM
BEHIND!!
KLUNK
KLUNK
KLUNK
I WON'T LET YOU LOSE, EITHER-- YOU'D BETTER UNDERSTAND THAT!!!
KLUNK
OF COURSE !!!
THE FINALS WILL DEFINIT BE SOU TOKYO SOUT TOKYO
IT'S A CERTAINTY !!

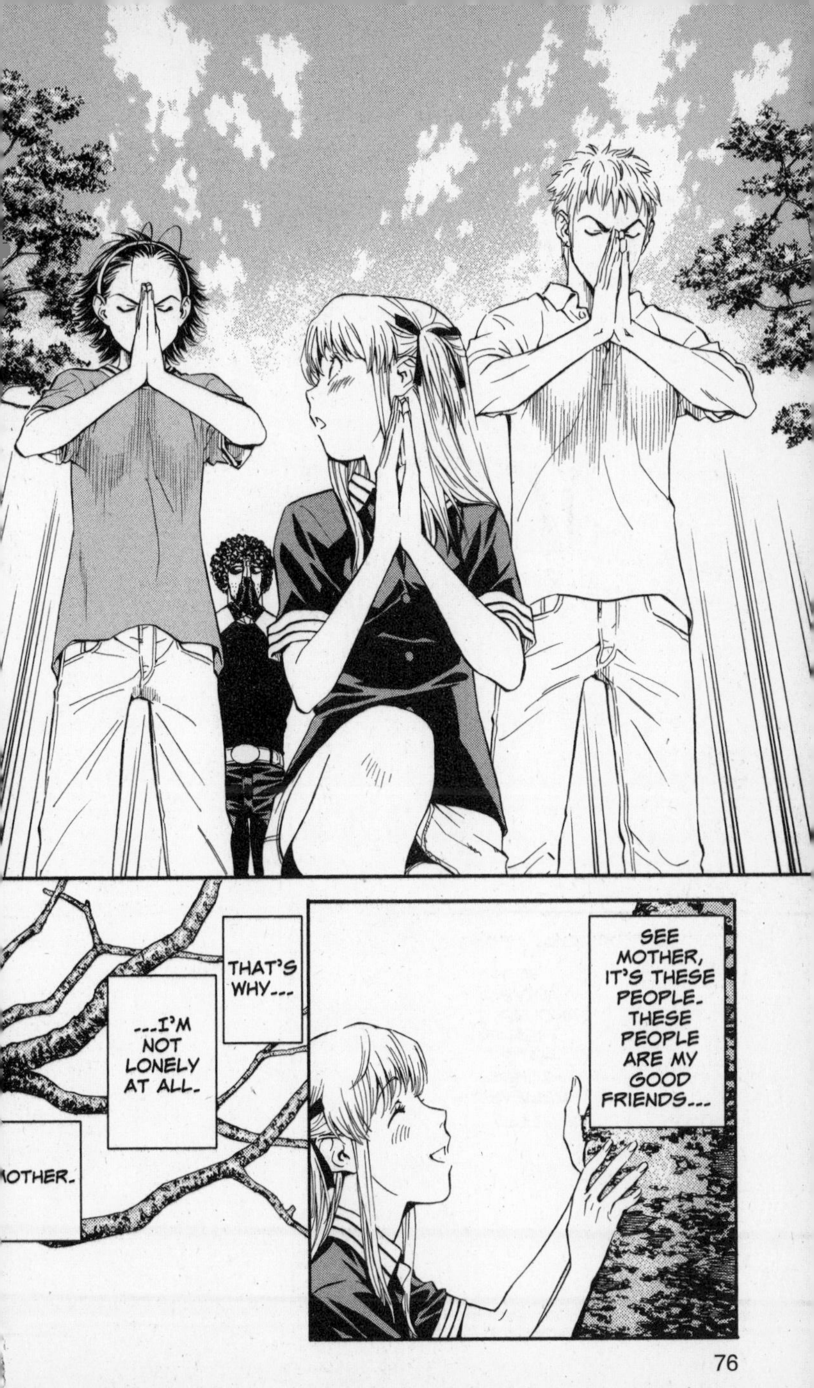
SEE MOTHER, IT'S THESE PEOPLE. THESE PEOPLE ARE MY GOOD FRIENDS...
THAT'S WHY...
...I'M NOT LONELY AT ALL.
OTHER.

Story 37: Kuroyanagi Senpai?

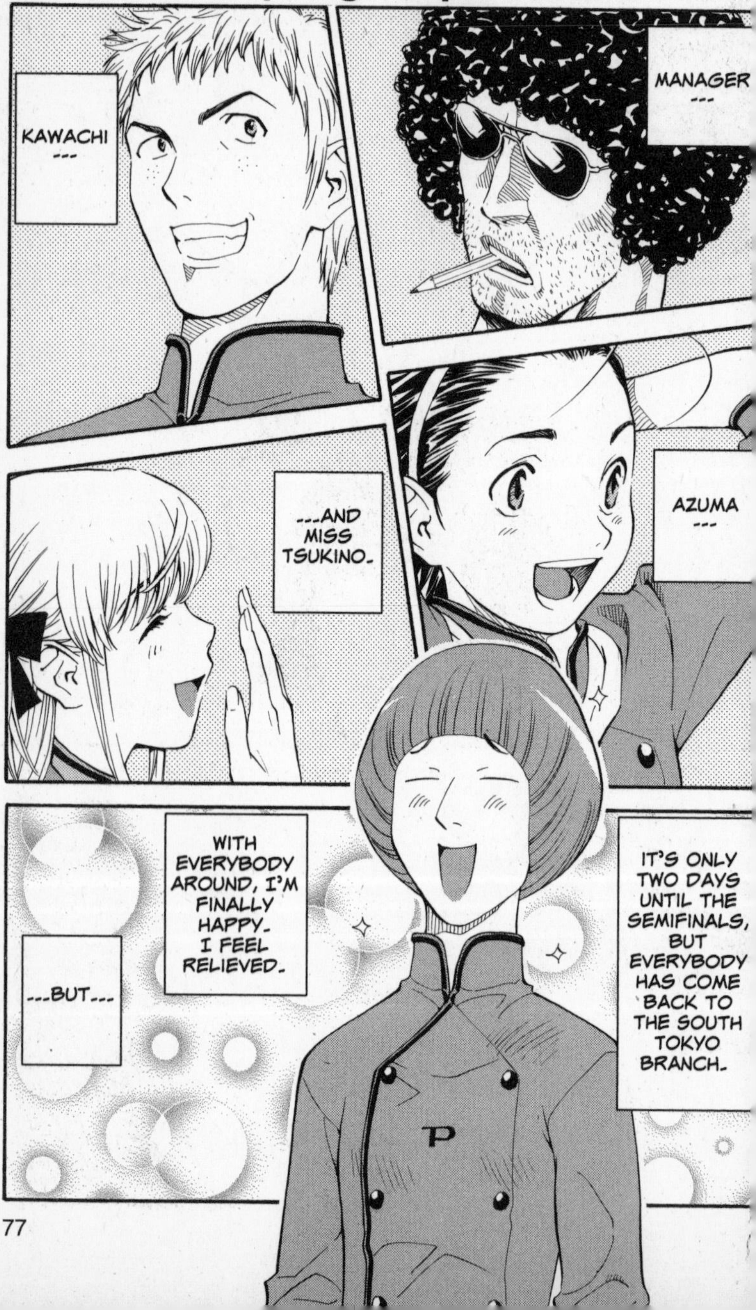
MANAGER---
KAWACHI---
AZUMA---
---AND MISS TSUKINO.
IT'S ONLY TWO DAYS UNTIL THE SEMIFINALS, BUT EVERYBODY HAS COME BACK TO THE SOUTH TOKYO BRANCH.
WITH EVERYBODY AROUND, I'M FINALLY HAPPY. I FEEL RELIEVED.
---BUT---
P

Story 37: Kuroyanagi Senpai?

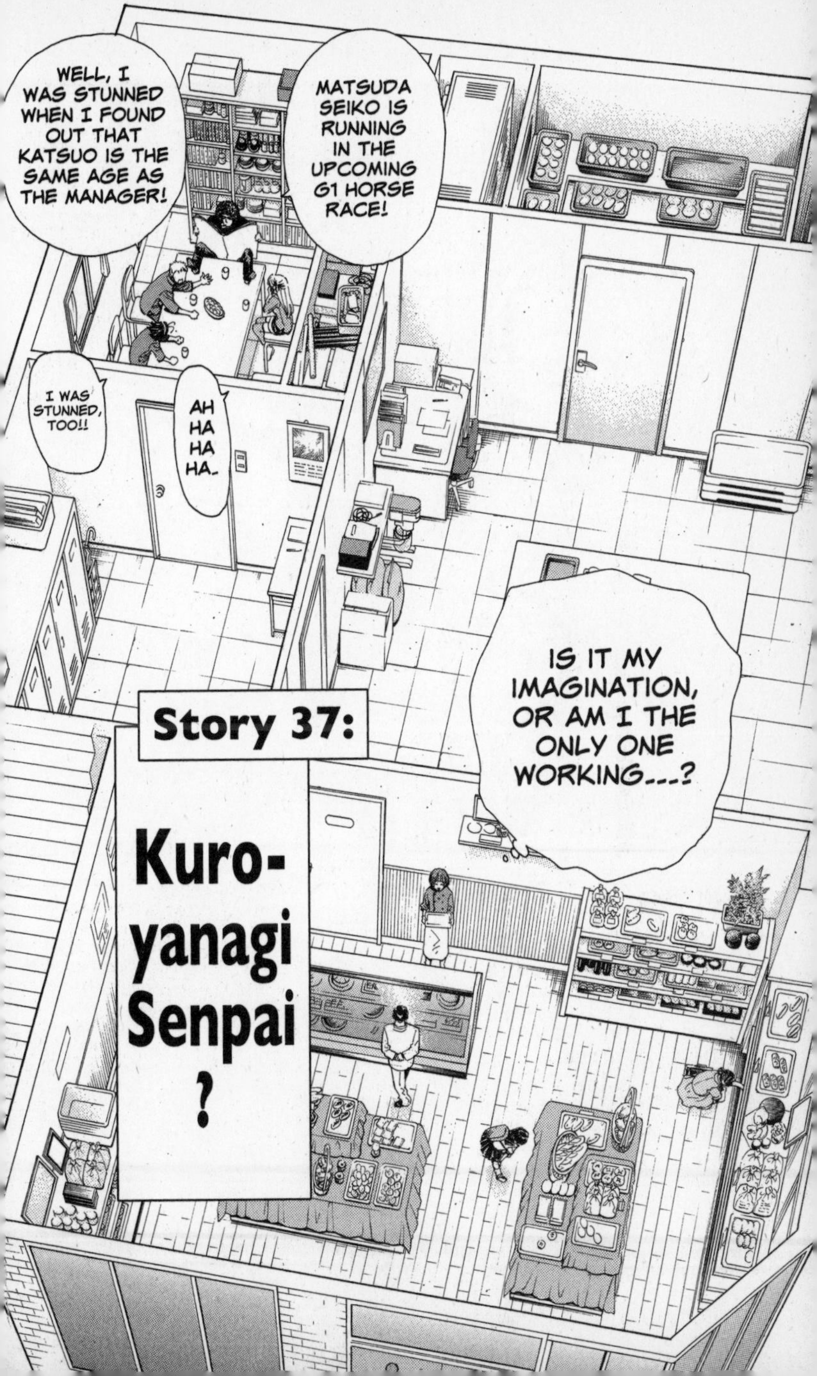
MATSUDA SEIKO IS RUNNING IN THE UPCOMING G1 HORSE RACE!
WELL, I WAS STUNNED WHEN I FOUND OUT THAT KATSUO IS THE SAME AGE AS THE MANAGER!
AH HA HA HA...
I WAS STUNNED, TOO!!
IS IT MY IMAGINATION, OR AM I THE ONLY ONE WORKING...?

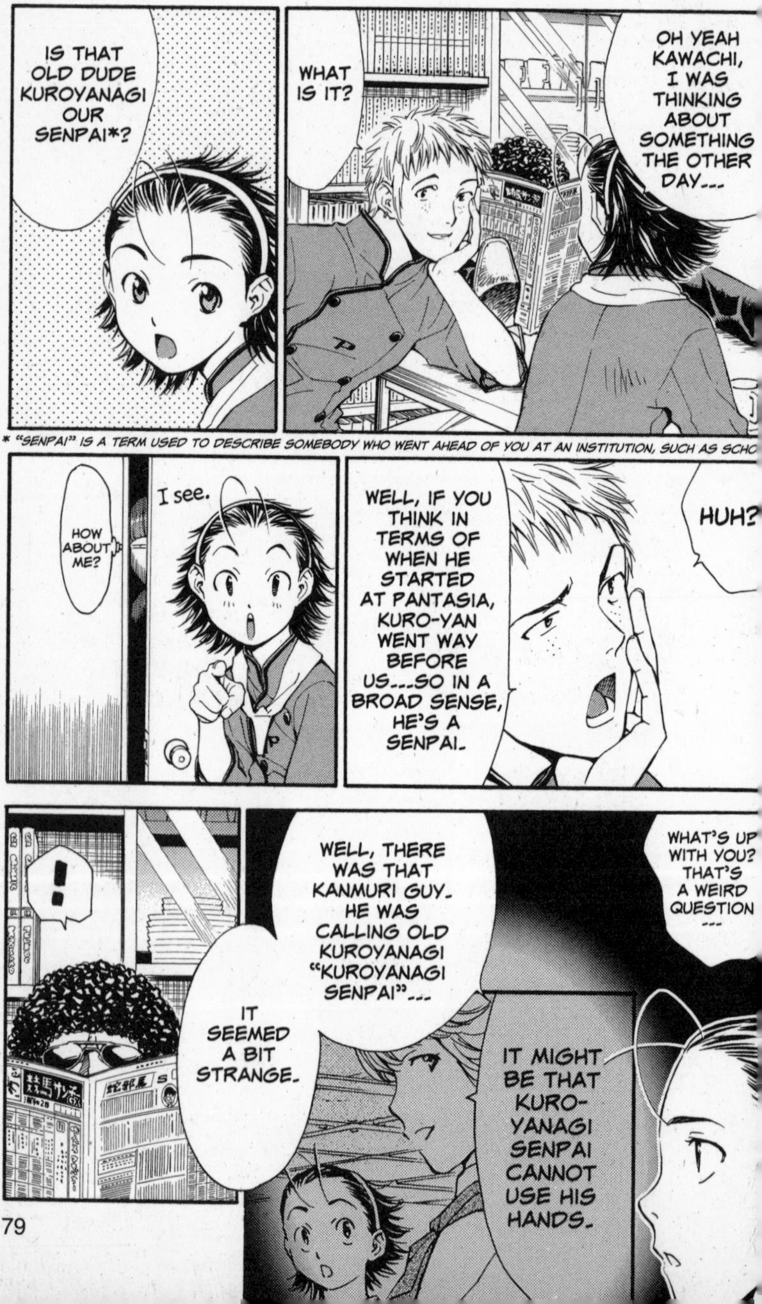
OH YEAH KAWACHI, I WAS THINKING ABOUT SOMETHING THE OTHER DAY...
WHAT IS IT?
IS THAT OLD DUDE KUROYANAGI OUR SENPAI*?
HUH?
WELL, IF YOU THINK IN TERMS OF WHEN HE STARTED AT PANTASIA, KURO-YAN WENT WAY BEFORE US...SO IN A BROAD SENSE, HE'S A SENPAI.
I see.
HOW ABOUT ME?
WHAT'S UP WITH YOU? THAT'S A WEIRD QUESTION...
WELL, THERE WAS THAT KANMURI GUY. HE WAS CALLING OLD KUROYANAGI "KUROYANAGI SENPAI"...
IT SEEMED A BIT STRANGE.
IT MIGHT BE THAT KURO-YANAGI SENPAI CANNOT USE HIS HANDS.
!

* "SENPAI" IS A TERM USED TO DESCRIBE SOMEBODY WHO WENT AHEAD OF YOU AT AN INSTITUTION, SUCH AS SCHO

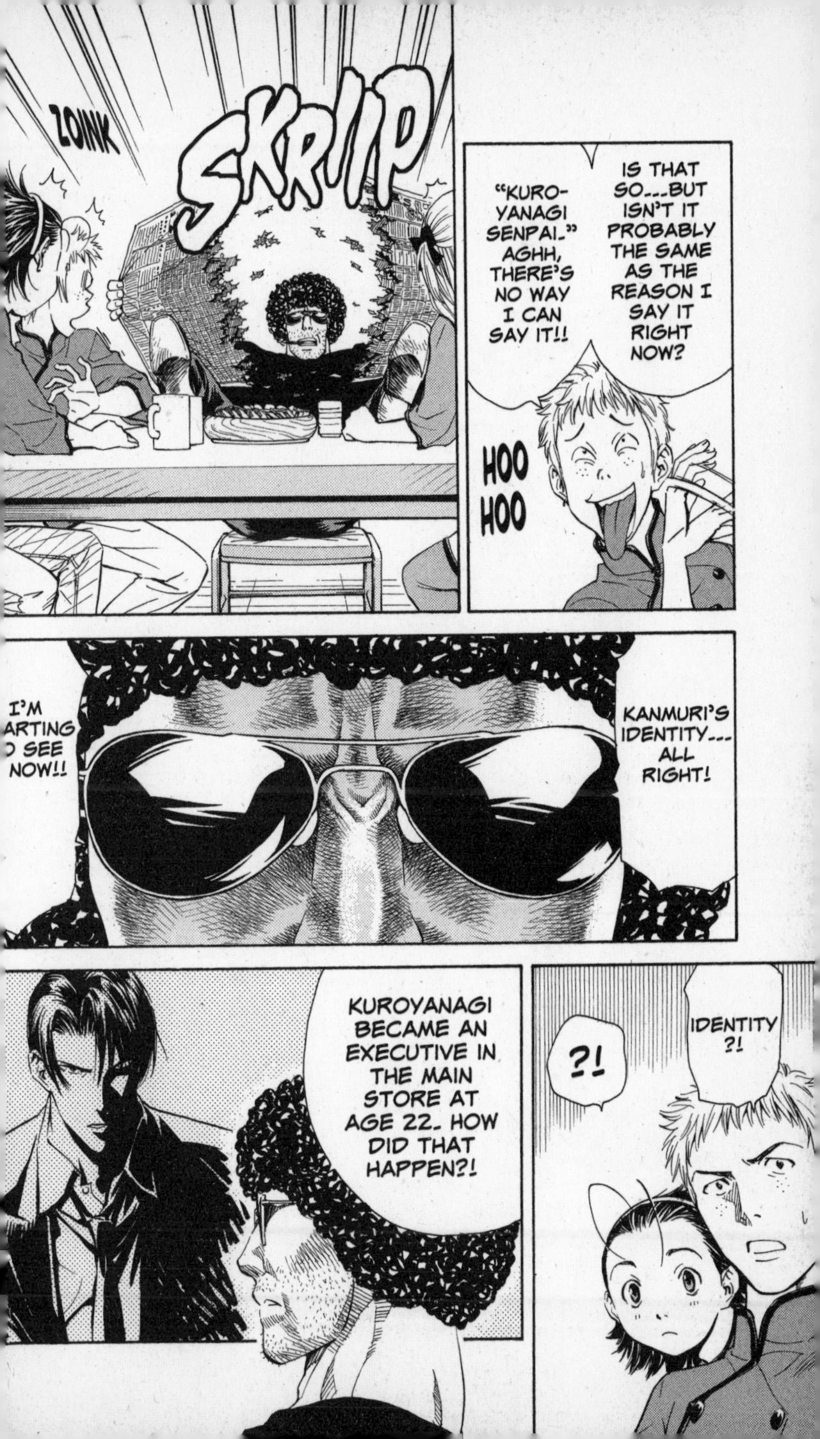
IS THAT SO...BUT ISN'T IT PROBABLY THE SAME AS THE REASON I SAY IT RIGHT NOW?
"KURO-YANAGI SENPAI." AGHH, THERE'S NO WAY I CAN SAY IT!!
HOO HOO
SKRIP
ZOINK
KANMURI'S IDENTITY... ALL RIGHT!
I'M ARTING SEE NOW!!
IDENTITY?!
?!
KUROYANAGI BECAME AN EXECUTIVE IN THE MAIN STORE AT AGE 22. HOW DID THAT HAPPEN?!

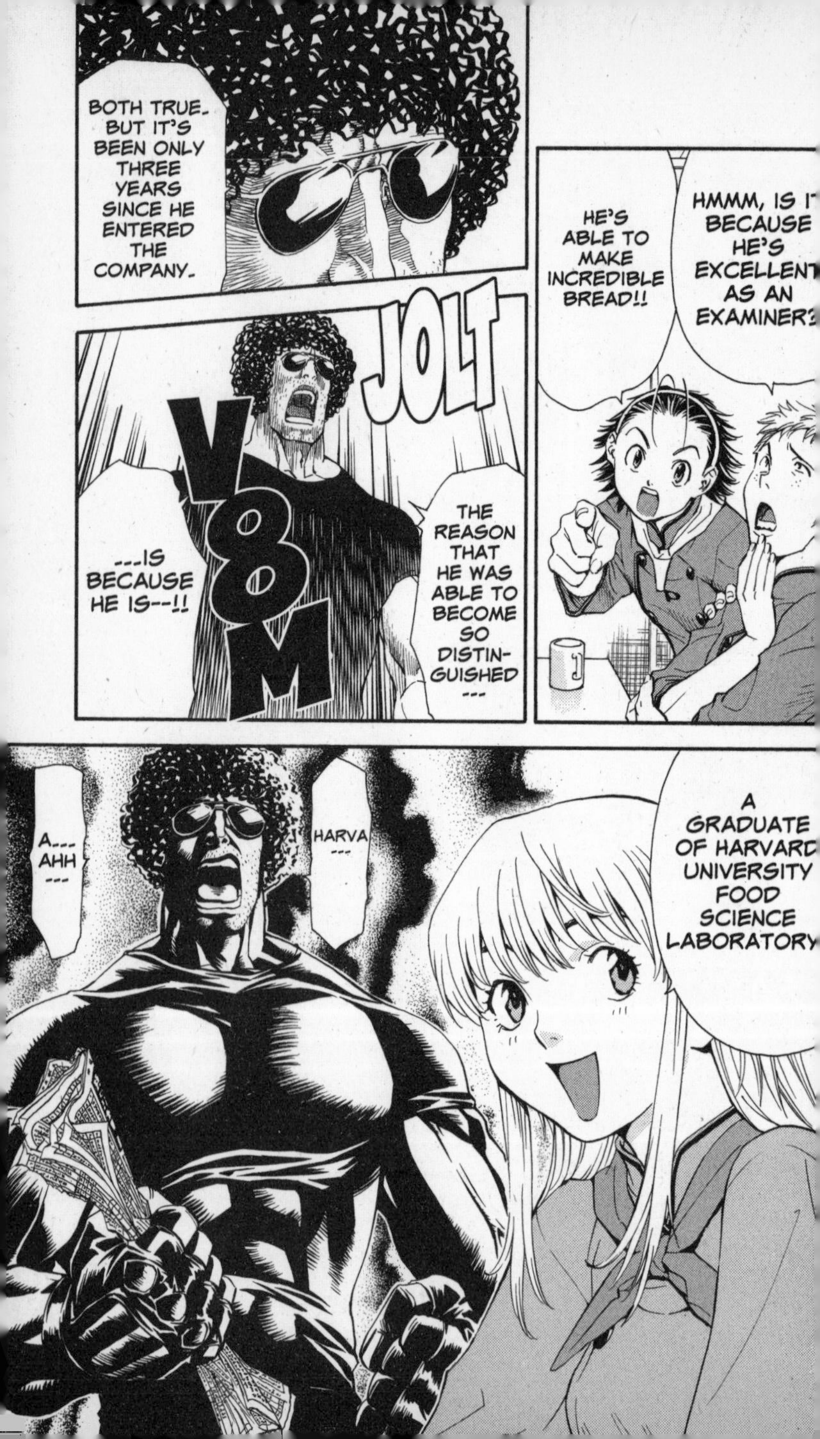
HMMM, IS I
BECAUSE HE'S EXCELLEN AS AN EXAMINER?
HE'S ABLE TO MAKE INCREDIBLE BREAD!!
BOTH TRUE. BUT IT'S BEEN ONLY THREE YEARS SINCE HE ENTERED THE COMPANY.
JOLT
V8M
THE REASON THAT HE WAS ABLE TO BECOME SO DISTIN-GUISHED ---
---IS BECAUSE HE IS--!!
A GRADUATE OF HARVARD UNIVERSITY FOOD SCIENCE LABORATORY
HARVA ---
A--- AHH ---

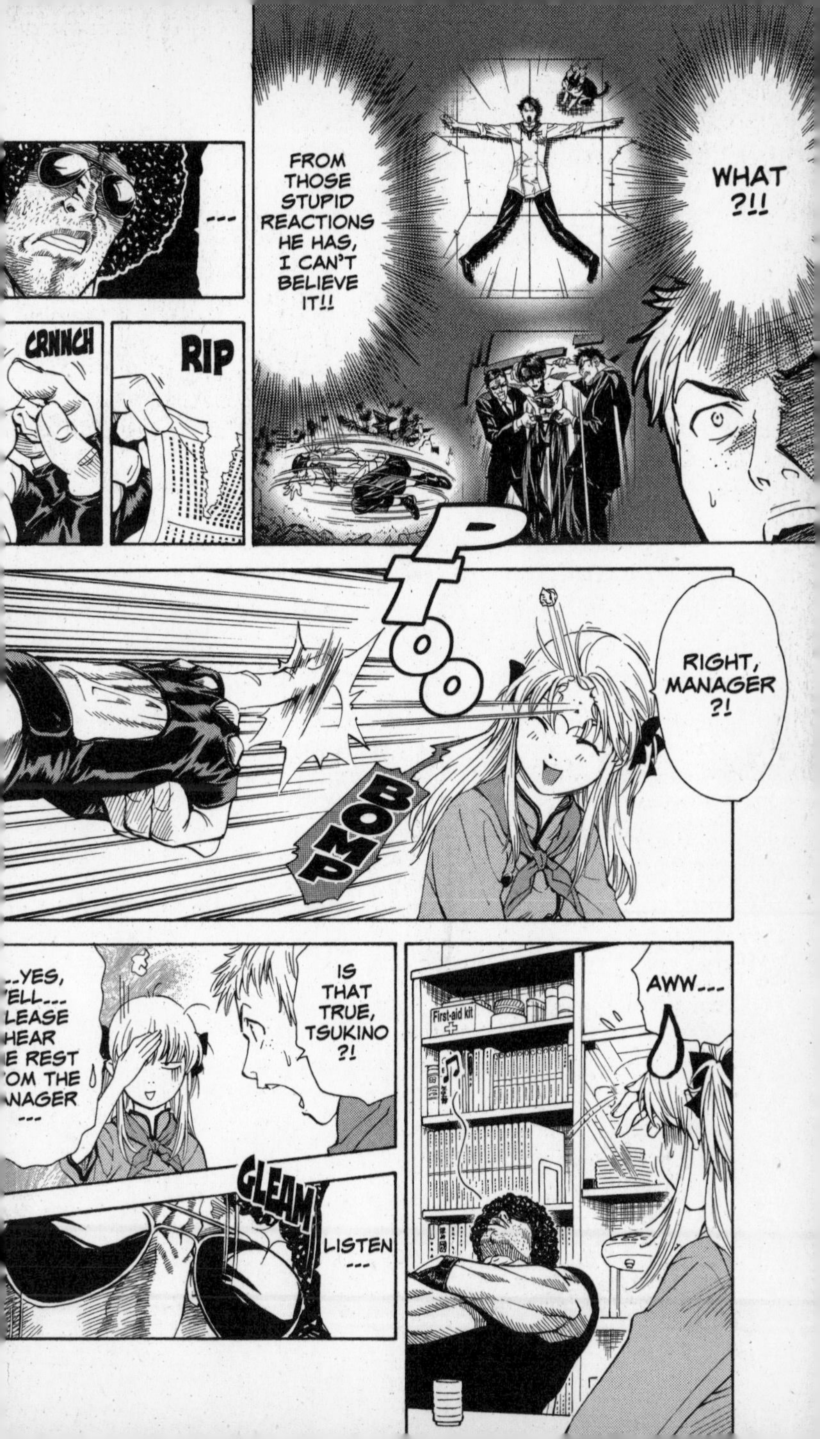
WHAT ?!!
FROM THOSE STUPID REACTIONS HE HAS, I CAN'T BELIEVE IT!!

RIP
CRNNCH
RIGHT, MANAGER ?!
PTOO
BOMP
AWW---
IS THAT TRUE, TSUKINO ?!
--YES, ELL--- LEASE HEAR E REST OM THE NAGER ---
GLEAM
LISTEN ---

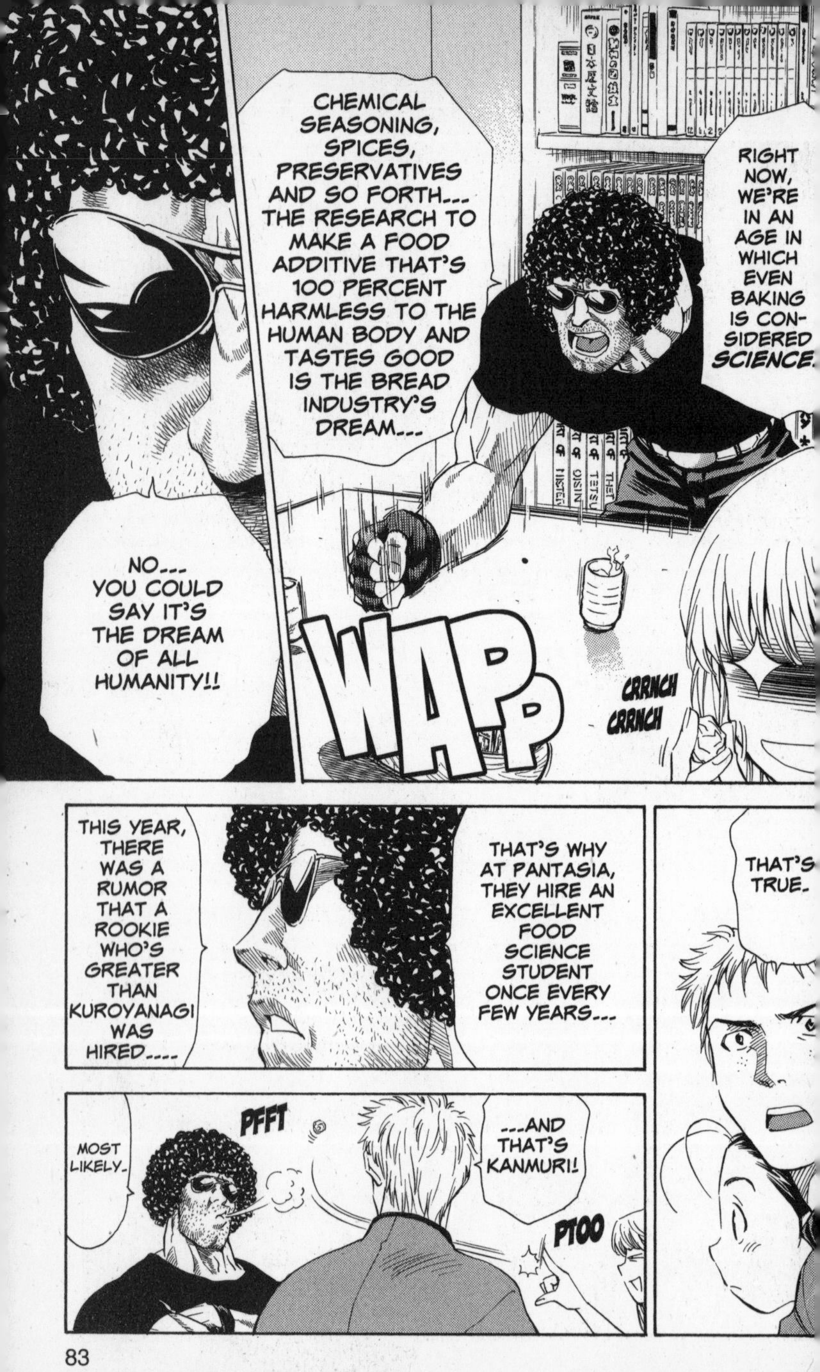
RIGHT NOW, WE'RE IN AN AGE IN WHICH EVEN BAKING IS CON-SIDERED SCIENCE.
CHEMICAL SEASONING, SPICES, PRESERVATIVES AND SO FORTH... THE RESEARCH TO MAKE A FOOD ADDITIVE THAT'S 100 PERCENT HARMLESS TO THE HUMAN BODY AND TASTES GOOD IS THE BREAD INDUSTRY'S DREAM...
WAPP
CRRNCH
CRRNCH
NO... YOU COULD SAY IT'S THE DREAM OF ALL HUMANITY!!
THAT'S TRUE.
THAT'S WHY AT PANTASIA, THEY HIRE AN EXCELLENT FOOD SCIENCE STUDENT ONCE EVERY FEW YEARS...
THIS YEAR, THERE WAS A RUMOR THAT A ROOKIE WHO'S GREATER THAN KUROYANAGI WAS HIRED....
...AND THAT'S KANMURI!
PTOO
PFFT
MOST LIKELY.

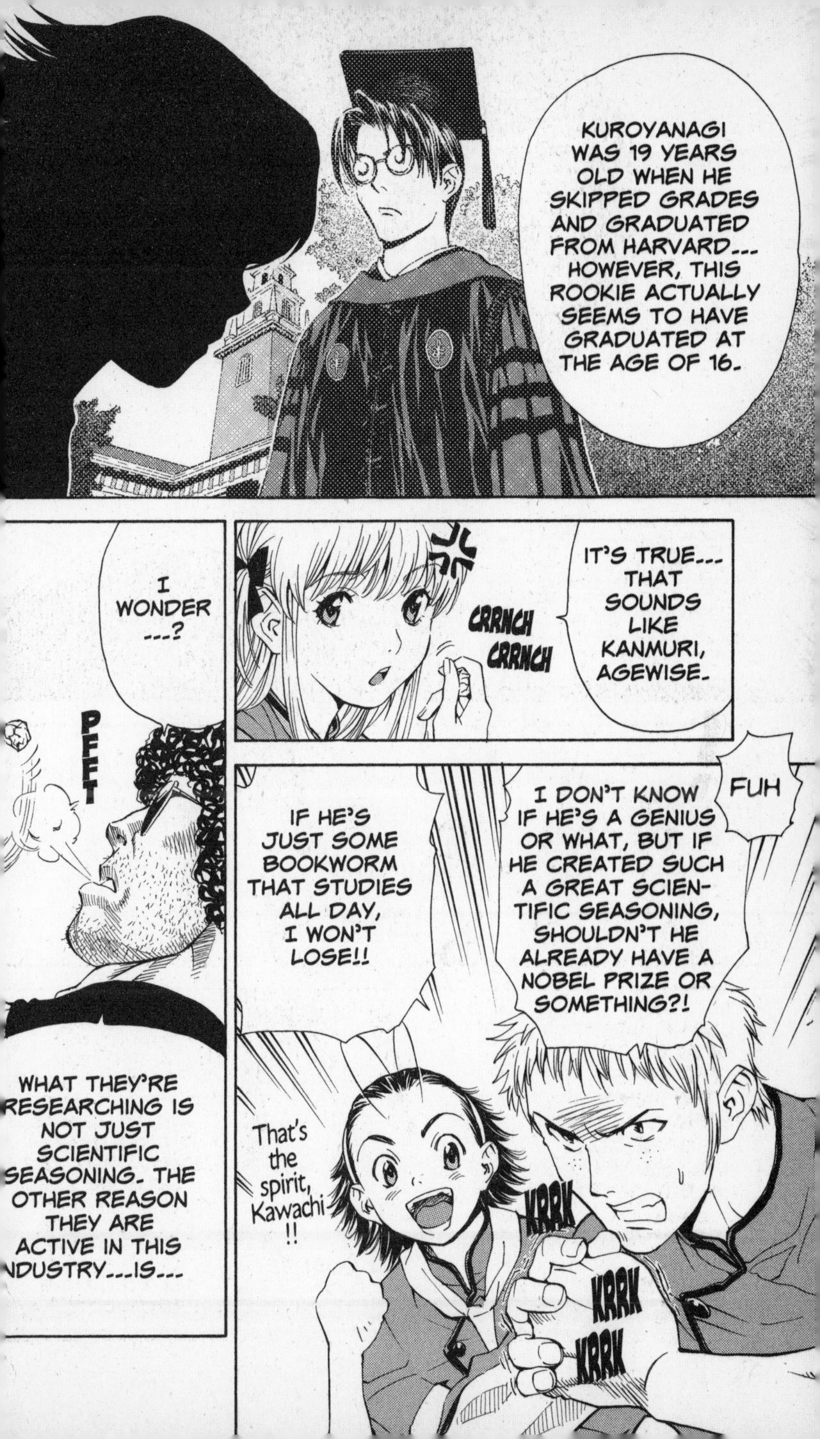
KUROYANAGI WAS 19 YEARS OLD WHEN HE SKIPPED GRADES AND GRADUATED FROM HARVARD... HOWEVER, THIS ROOKIE ACTUALLY SEEMS TO HAVE GRADUATED AT THE AGE OF 16.
IT'S TRUE... THAT SOUNDS LIKE KANMURI, AGEWISE.
CRRNCH CRRNCH
FUH
I DON'T KNOW IF HE'S A GENIUS OR WHAT, BUT IF HE CREATED SUCH A GREAT SCIENTIFIC SEASONING, SHOULDN'T HE ALREADY HAVE A NOBEL PRIZE OR SOMETHING?!
IF HE'S JUST SOME BOOKWORM THAT STUDIES ALL DAY, I WON'T LOSE!!
That's the spirit, Kawachi!!
KRRK KRRK KRRK
I WONDER...?
PFFT
WHAT THEY'RE RESEARCHING IS NOT JUST SCIENTIFIC SEASONING. THE OTHER REASON THEY ARE ACTIVE IN THIS INDUSTRY...IS...

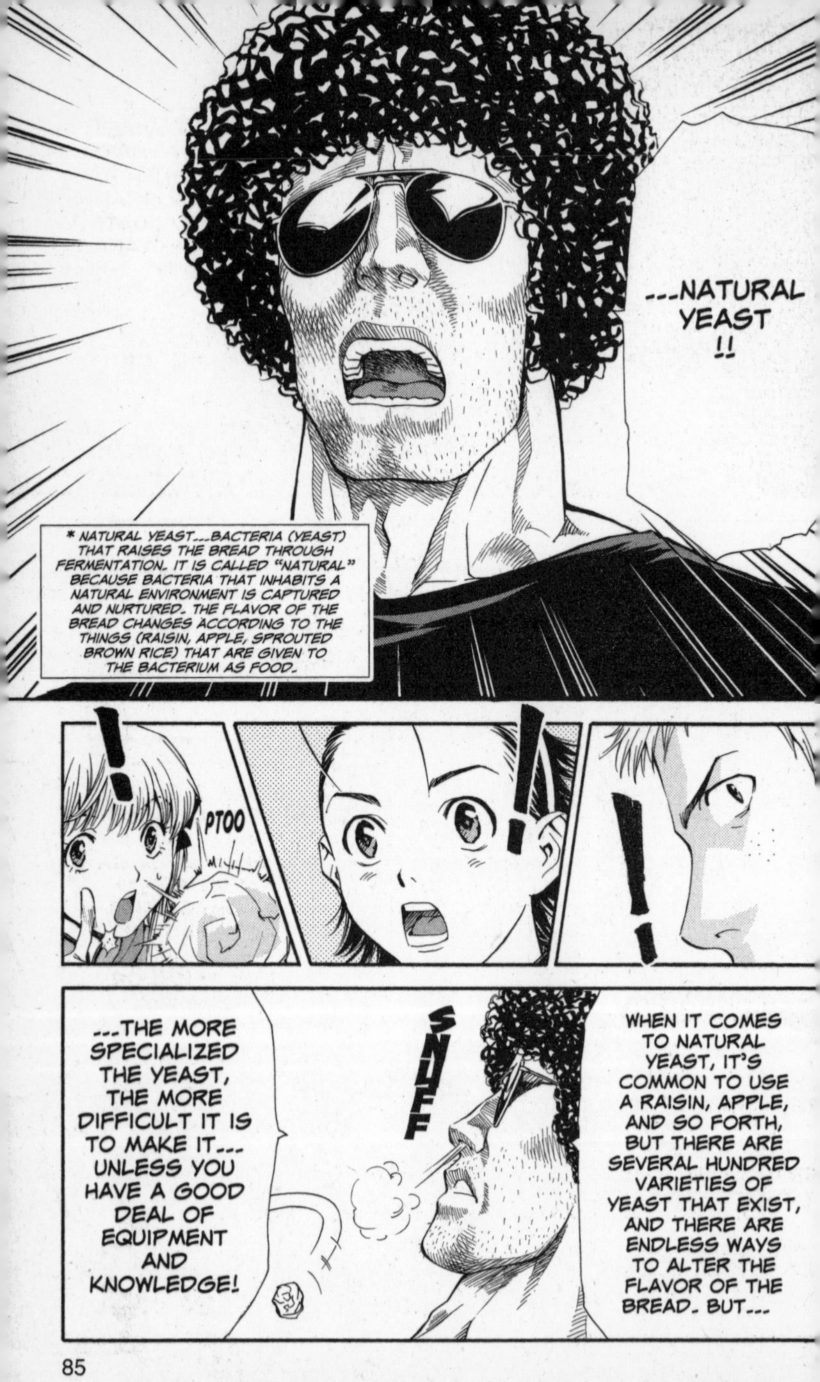
---NATURAL YEAST !!
* NATURAL YEAST---BACTERIA (YEAST) THAT RAISES THE BREAD THROUGH FERMENTATION. IT IS CALLED "NATURAL" BECAUSE BACTERIA THAT INHABITS A NATURAL ENVIRONMENT IS CAPTURED AND NURTURED. THE FLAVOR OF THE BREAD CHANGES ACCORDING TO THE THINGS (RAISIN, APPLE, SPROUTED BROWN RICE) THAT ARE GIVEN TO THE BACTERIUM AS FOOD.
!
!
!
PTOO
WHEN IT COMES TO NATURAL YEAST, IT'S COMMON TO USE A RAISIN, APPLE, AND SO FORTH, BUT THERE ARE SEVERAL HUNDRED VARIETIES OF YEAST THAT EXIST, AND THERE ARE ENDLESS WAYS TO ALTER THE FLAVOR OF THE BREAD. BUT---
SNUFF
---THE MORE SPECIALIZED THE YEAST, THE MORE DIFFICULT IT IS TO MAKE IT--- UNLESS YOU HAVE A GOOD DEAL OF EQUIPMENT AND KNOWLEDGE!

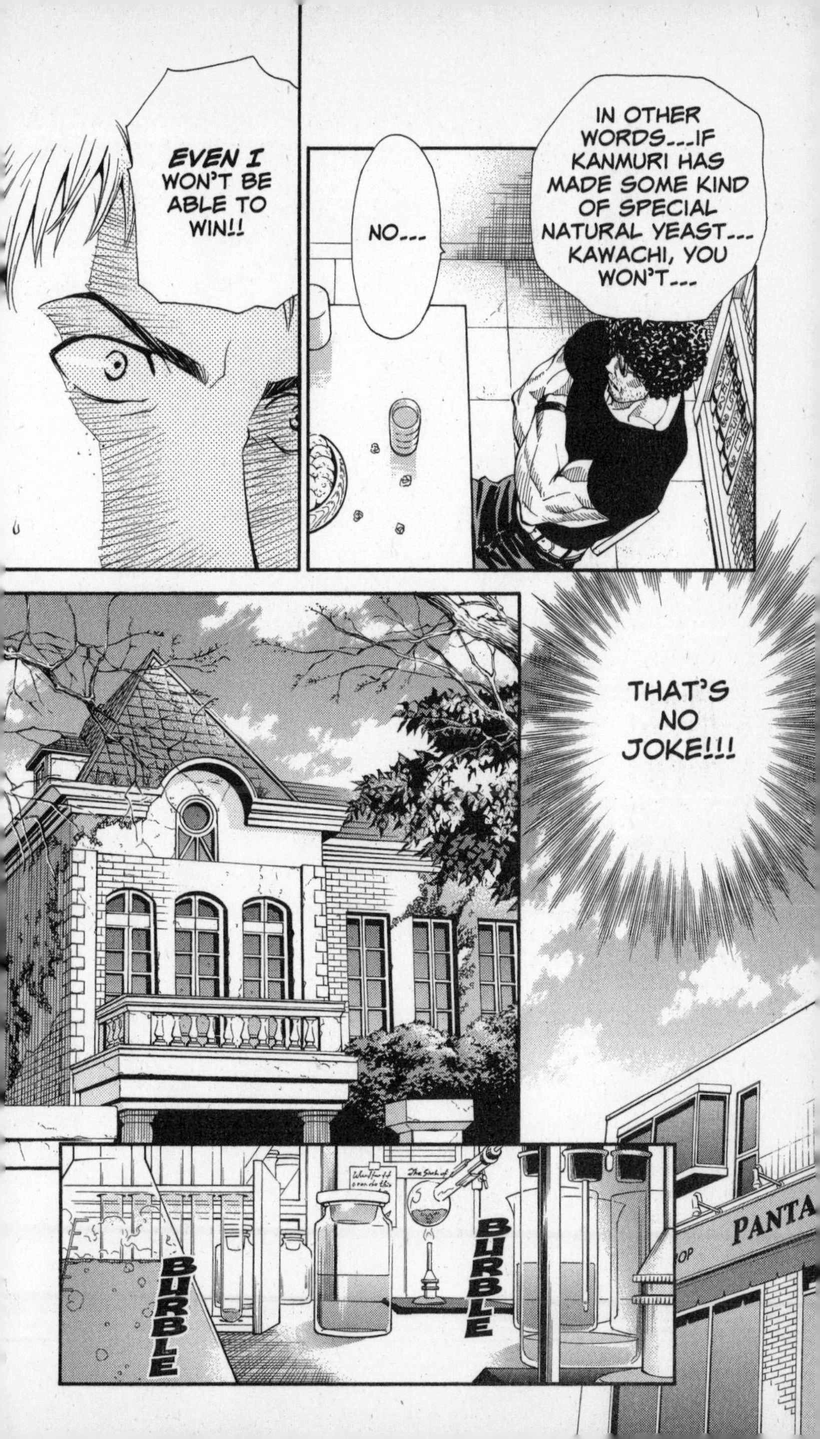
IN OTHER WORDS...IF KANMURI HAS MADE SOME KIND OF SPECIAL NATURAL YEAST... KAWACHI, YOU WON'T...
NO...
EVEN I WON'T BE ABLE TO WIN!!
THAT'S NO JOKE!!!
PANTA
BURBLE
BURBLE

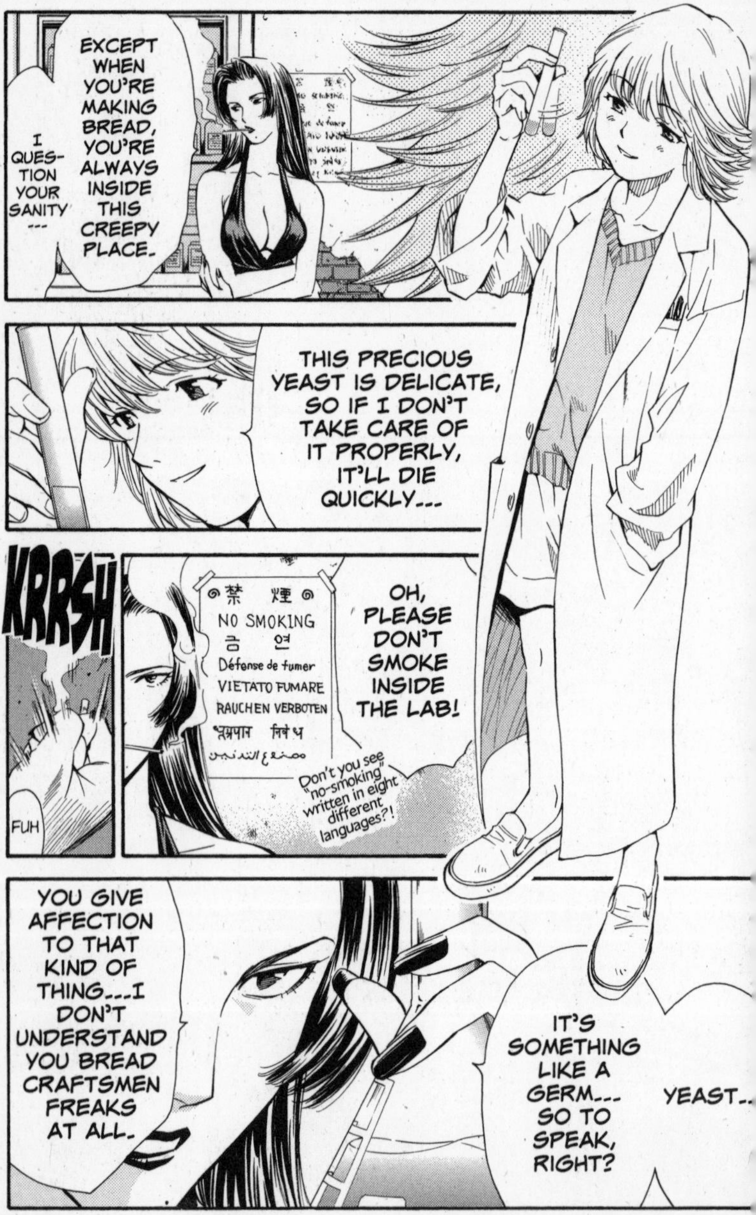
EXCEPT WHEN YOU'RE MAKING BREAD, YOU'RE ALWAYS INSIDE THIS CREEPY PLACE.
I QUES- TION YOUR SANITY ---
THIS PRECIOUS YEAST IS DELICATE, SO IF I DON'T TAKE CARE OF IT PROPERLY, IT'LL DIE QUICKLY---
OH, PLEASE DON'T SMOKE INSIDE THE LAB!
禁 煙
NO SMOKING
금 연
Défense de fumer
VIETATO FUMARE
RAUCHEN VERBOTEN
धूम्रपान निषेध
ممنوع التدخين
Don't you see "no-smoking" written in eight different languages?!
KRRSH
FUH
YEAST--
IT'S SOMETHING LIKE A GERM--- SO TO SPEAK, RIGHT?
YOU GIVE AFFECTION TO THAT KIND OF THING---I DON'T UNDERSTAND YOU BREAD CRAFTSMEN FREAKS AT ALL.

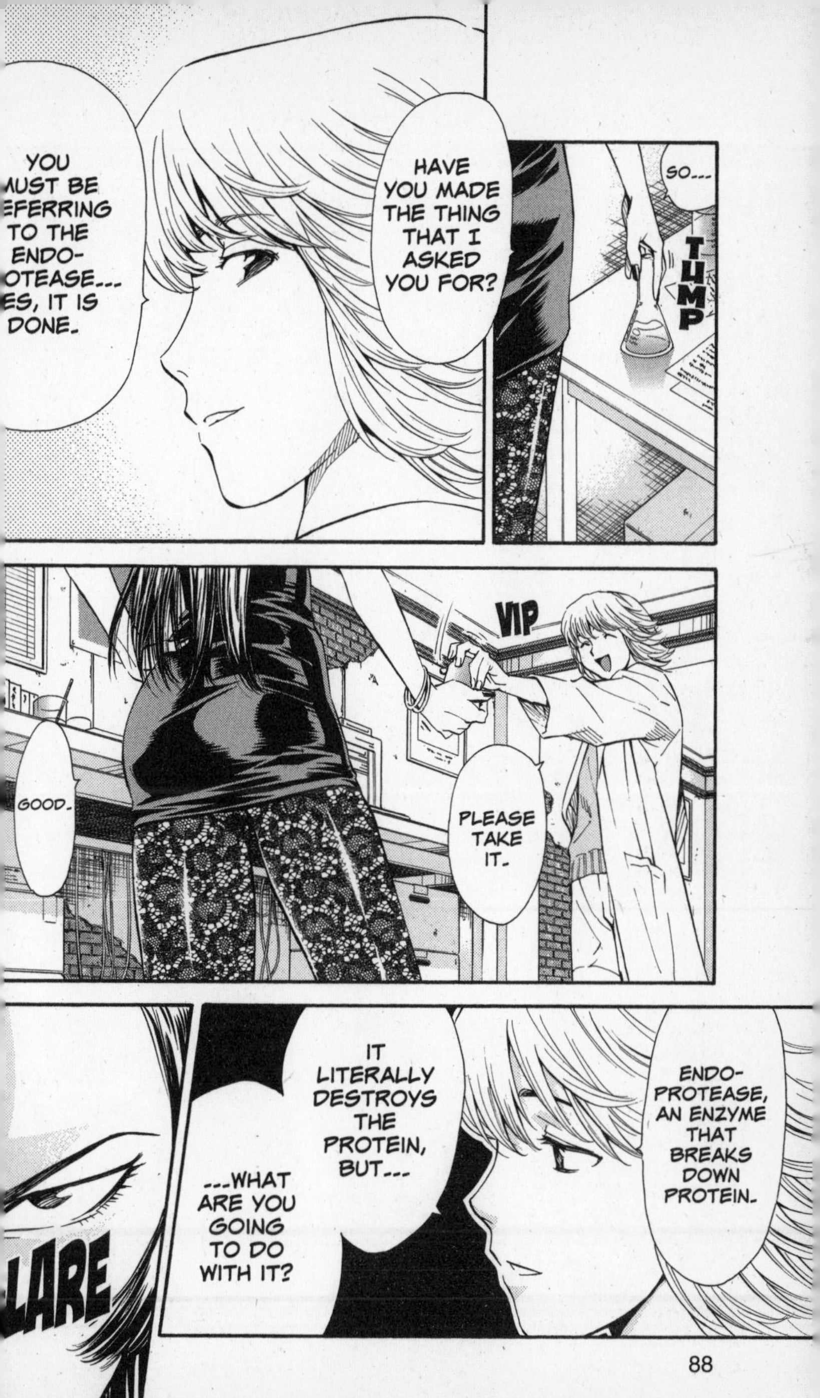
SO...
TUMP
HAVE YOU MADE THE THING THAT I ASKED YOU FOR?
YOU MUST BE EFERRING TO THE ENDO-OTEASE... ES, IT IS DONE.
VIP
PLEASE TAKE IT.
GOOD.
ENDO-PROTEASE, AN ENZYME THAT BREAKS DOWN PROTEIN.
IT LITERALLY DESTROYS THE PROTEIN, BUT...
...WHAT ARE YOU GOING TO DO WITH IT?
LARE

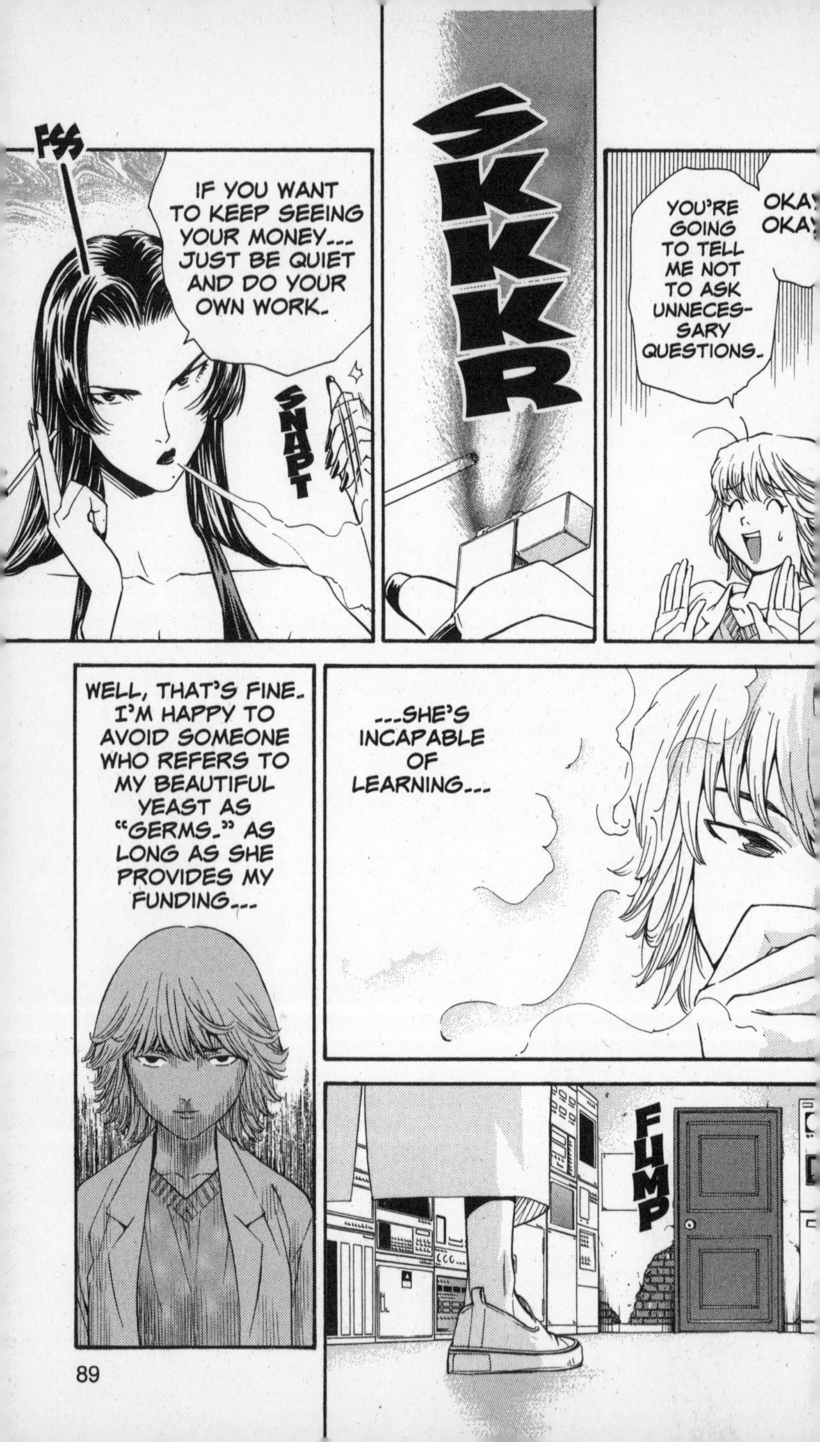

YOU'RE GOING TO TELL ME NOT TO ASK UNNECES-SARY QUESTIONS.
OKA OKA
SKKR
FSS
IF YOU WANT TO KEEP SEEING YOUR MONEY... JUST BE QUIET AND DO YOUR OWN WORK.
SNAPT
...SHE'S INCAPABLE OF LEARNING...
FUMP
WELL, THAT'S FINE. I'M HAPPY TO AVOID SOMEONE WHO REFERS TO MY BEAUTIFUL YEAST AS "GERMS." AS LONG AS SHE PROVIDES MY FUNDING...

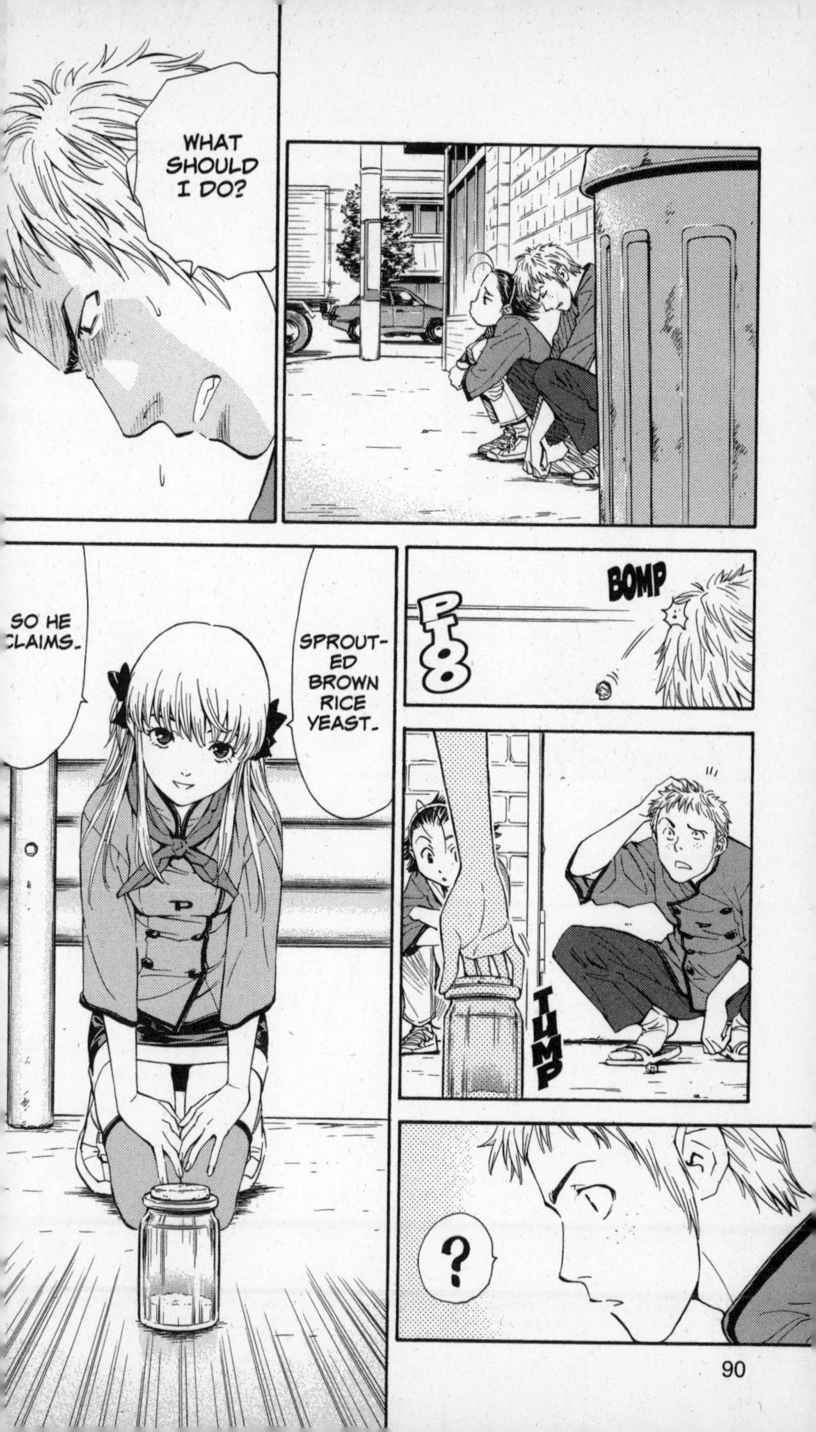
WHAT SHOULD I DO?
BOMP
TUMP
?
SPROUTED-ED BROWN RICE YEAST...
SO HE CLAIMS...

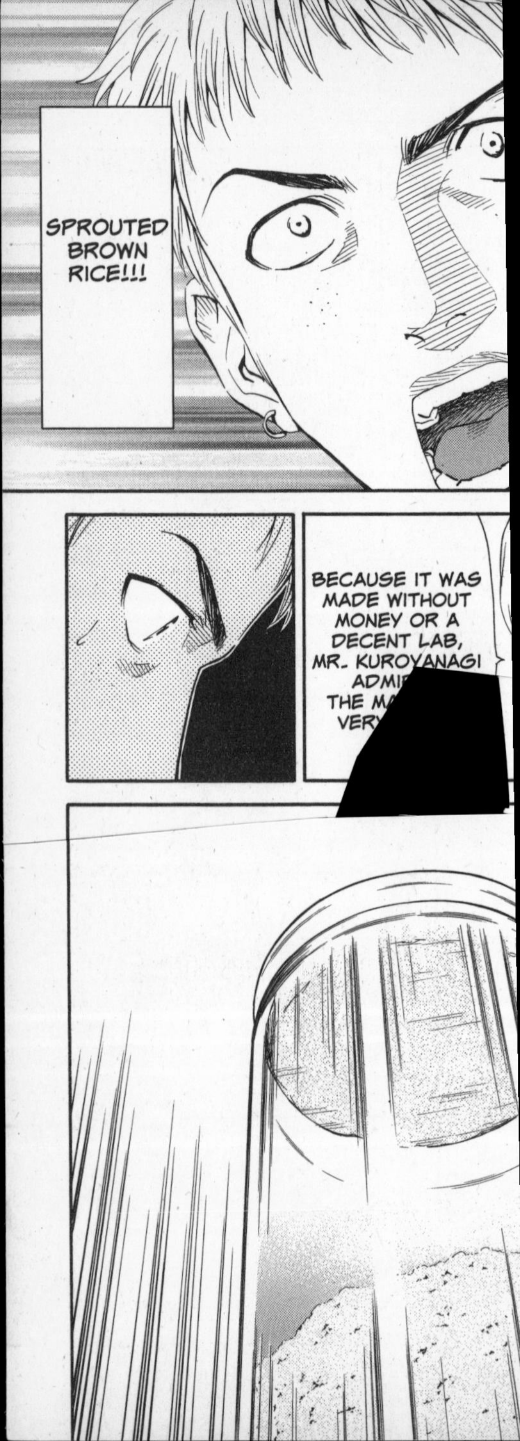
SPROUTED BROWN RICE!!!
BECAUSE IT WAS MADE WITHOUT MONEY OR A DECENT LAB, MR. KUROYANAGI ADMI[redacted] THE MA[redacted] VERY[redacted]

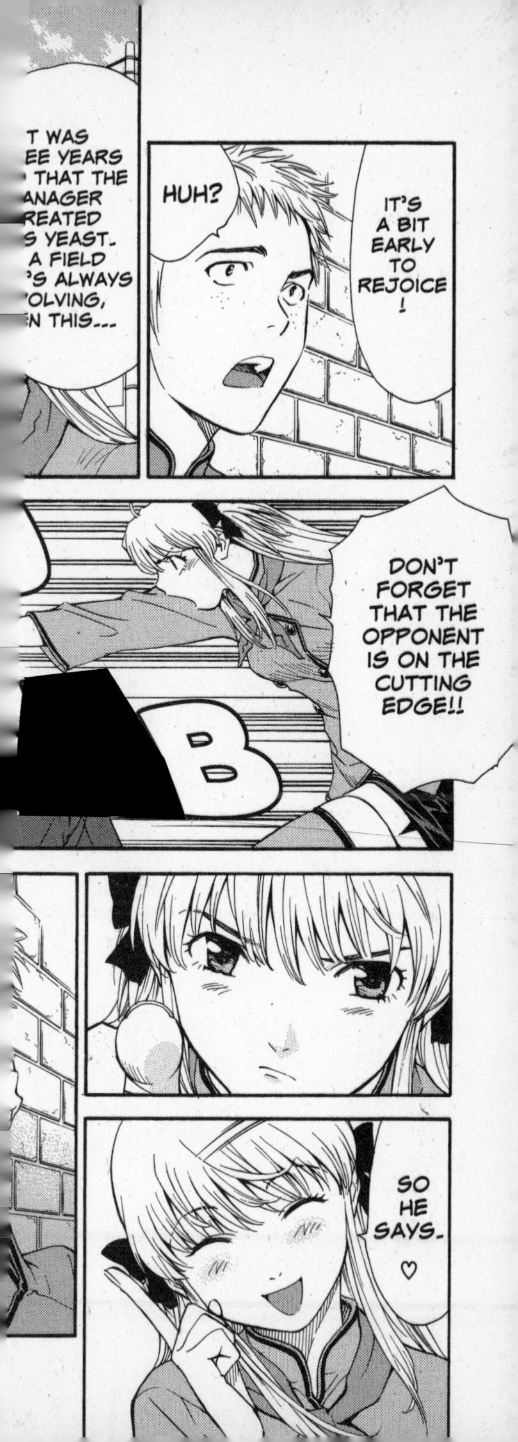
IT'S A BIT EARLY TO REJOICE!
HUH?
T WAS EE YEARS THAT THE ANAGER REATED S YEAST. A FIELD 'S ALWAYS OLVING, N THIS...
DON'T FORGET THAT THE OPPONENT IS ON THE CUTTING EDGE!!
B
SO HE SAYS. ♡

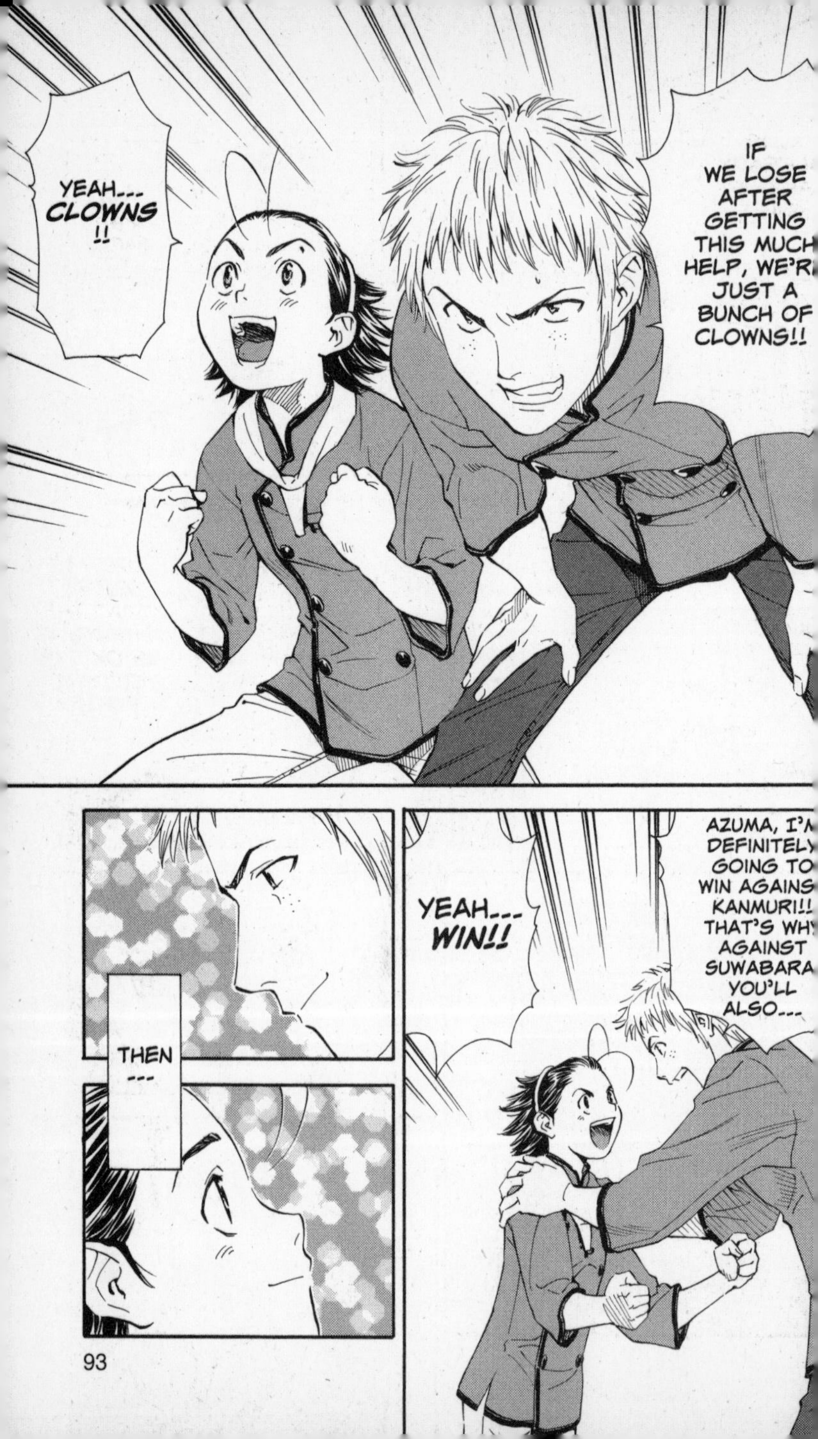
IF WE LOSE AFTER GETTING THIS MUCH HELP, WE'RE JUST A BUNCH OF CLOWNS!!
YEAH... CLOWNS!!
AZUMA, I'M DEFINITELY GOING TO WIN AGAINST KANMURI!! THAT'S WHY AGAINST SUWABARA YOU'LL ALSO...
YEAH... WIN!!
THEN...

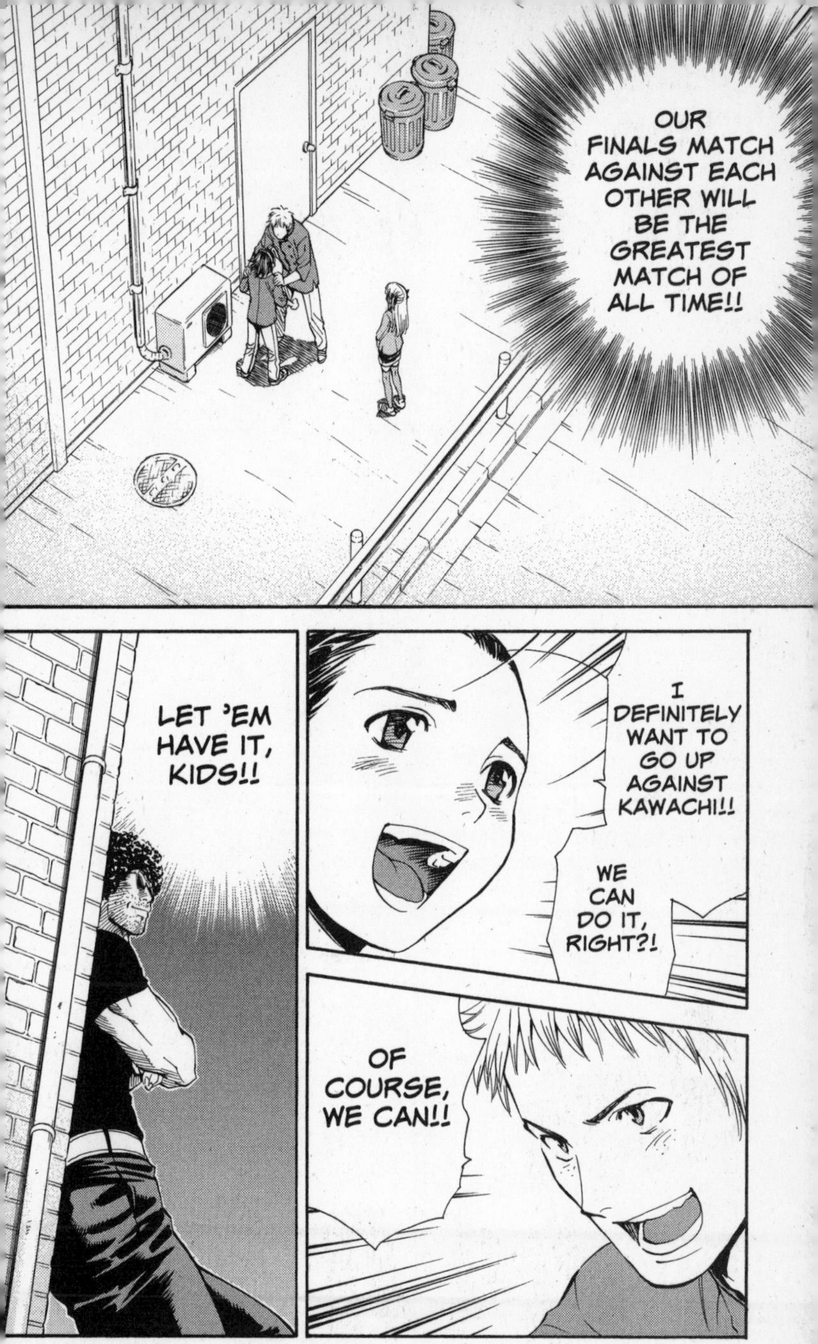
OUR FINALS MATCH AGAINST EACH OTHER WILL BE THE GREATEST MATCH OF ALL TIME!!
I DEFINITELY WANT TO GO UP AGAINST KAWACHI!!
WE CAN DO IT, RIGHT?!
OF COURSE, WE CAN!!
LET 'EM HAVE IT, KIDS!!

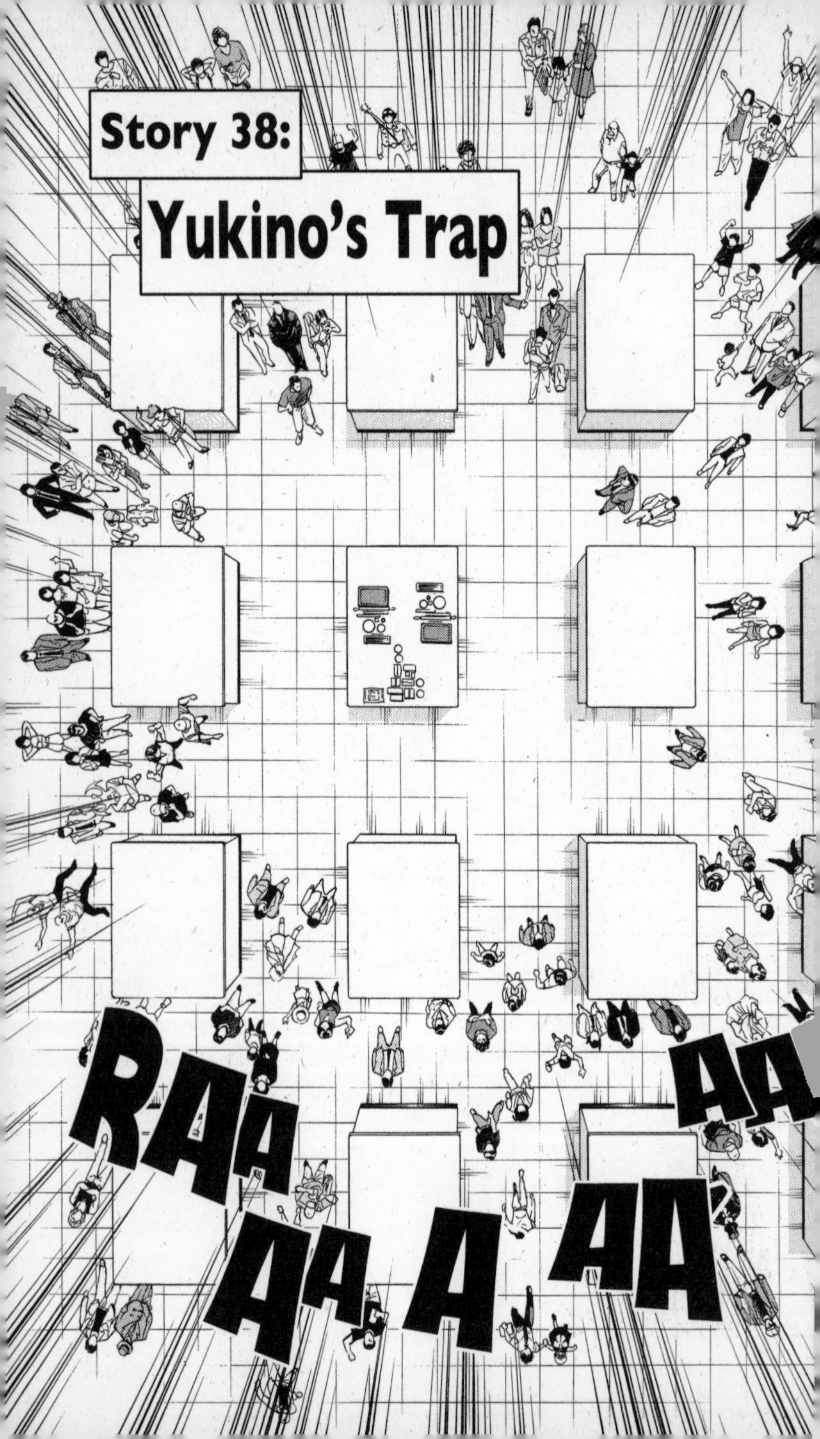
Story 38:
Yukino's Trap
RAAAAAAAAA

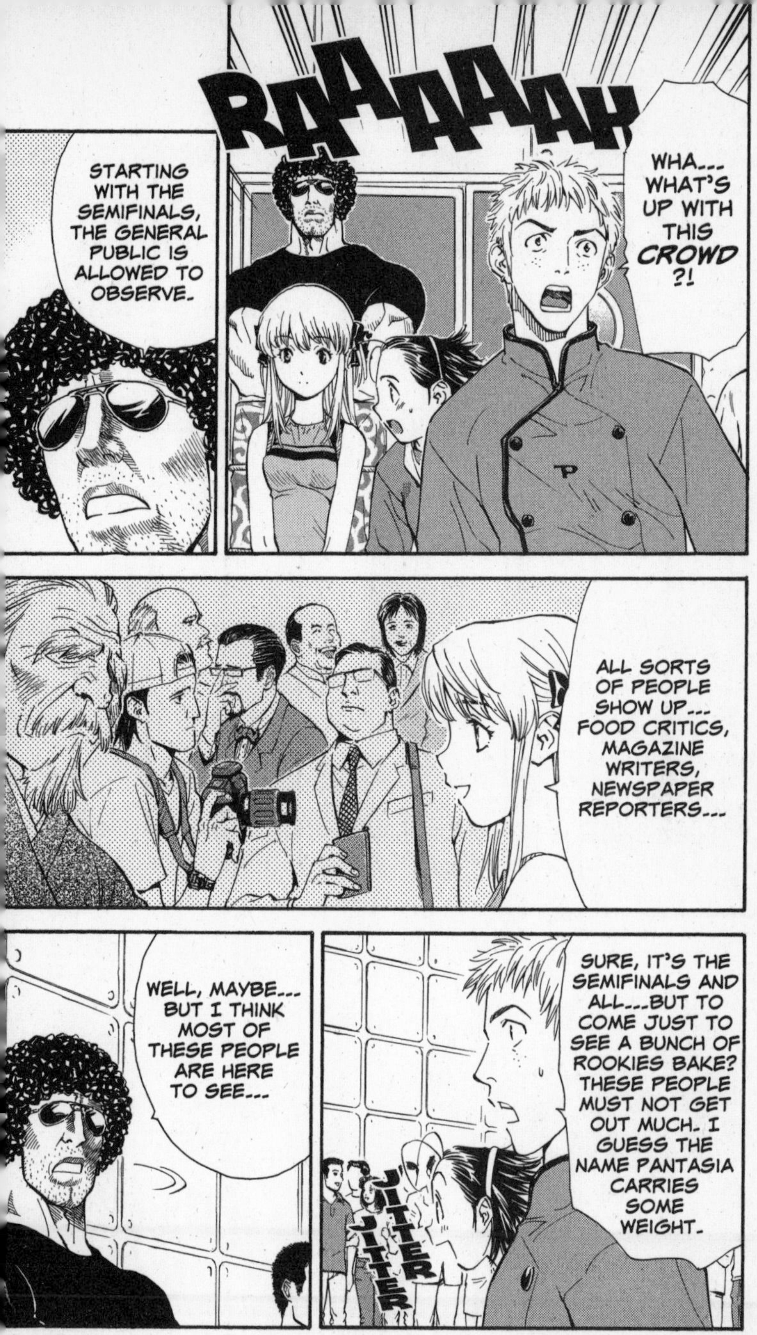
RAAAAAH
WHA... WHAT'S UP WITH THIS *CROWD* ?!
STARTING WITH THE SEMIFINALS, THE GENERAL PUBLIC IS ALLOWED TO OBSERVE.
ALL SORTS OF PEOPLE SHOW UP... FOOD CRITICS, MAGAZINE WRITERS, NEWSPAPER REPORTERS...
SURE, IT'S THE SEMIFINALS AND ALL...BUT TO COME JUST TO SEE A BUNCH OF ROOKIES BAKE? THESE PEOPLE MUST NOT GET OUT MUCH. I GUESS THE NAME PANTASIA CARRIES SOME WEIGHT.
JITTER JITTER
WELL, MAYBE... BUT I THINK MOST OF THESE PEOPLE ARE HERE TO SEE...

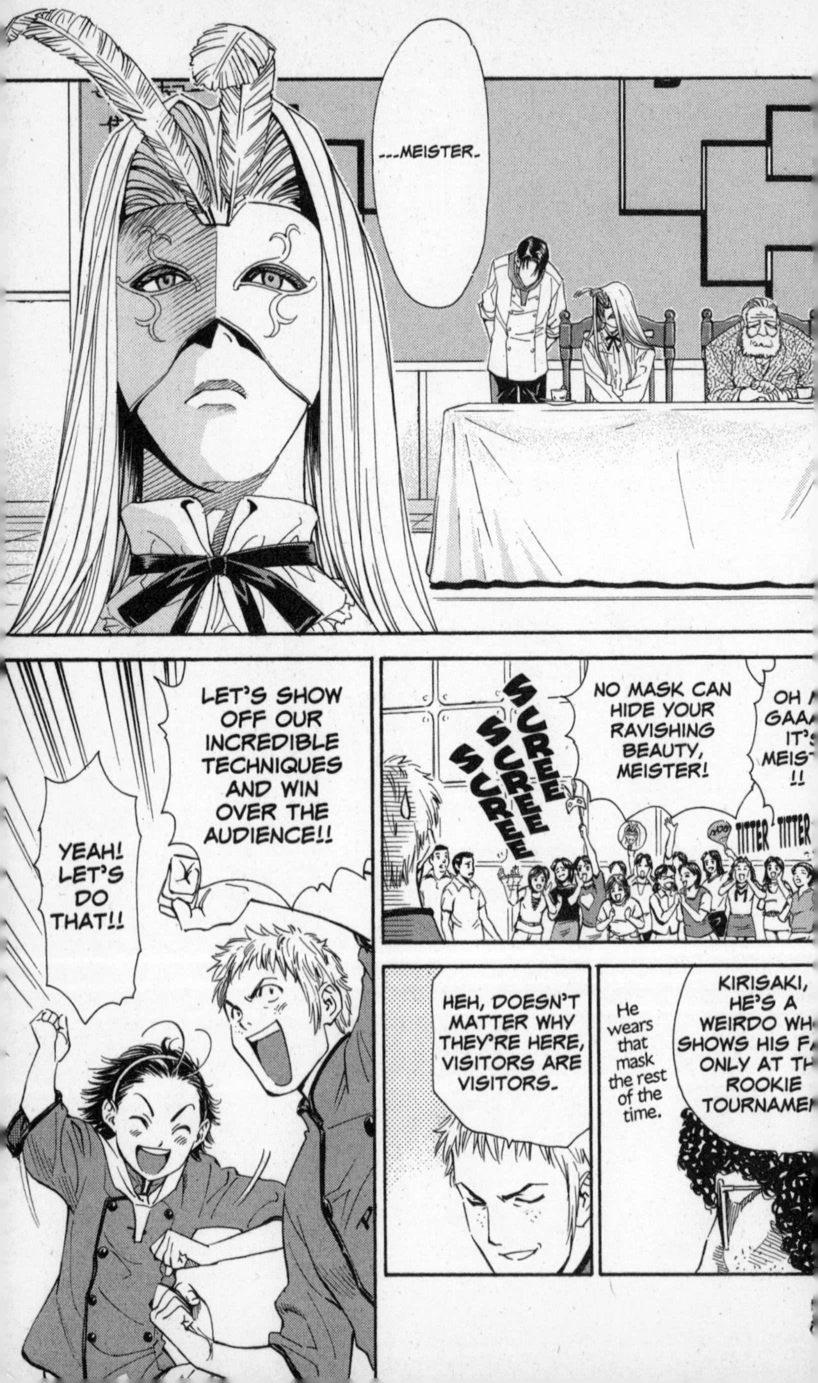
---MEISTER.
OH A GAAA IT'S MEIS !!
NO MASK CAN HIDE YOUR RAVISHING BEAUTY, MEISTER!
SUREE SUREE SUREE
TITTER TITTER
KIRISAKI, HE'S A WEIRDO WH SHOWS HIS FA ONLY AT TH ROOKIE TOURNAME
He wears that mask the rest of the time.
HEH, DOESN'T MATTER WHY THEY'RE HERE, VISITORS ARE VISITORS.
LET'S SHOW OFF OUR INCREDIBLE TECHNIQUES AND WIN OVER THE AUDIENCE!!
YEAH! LET'S DO THAT!!

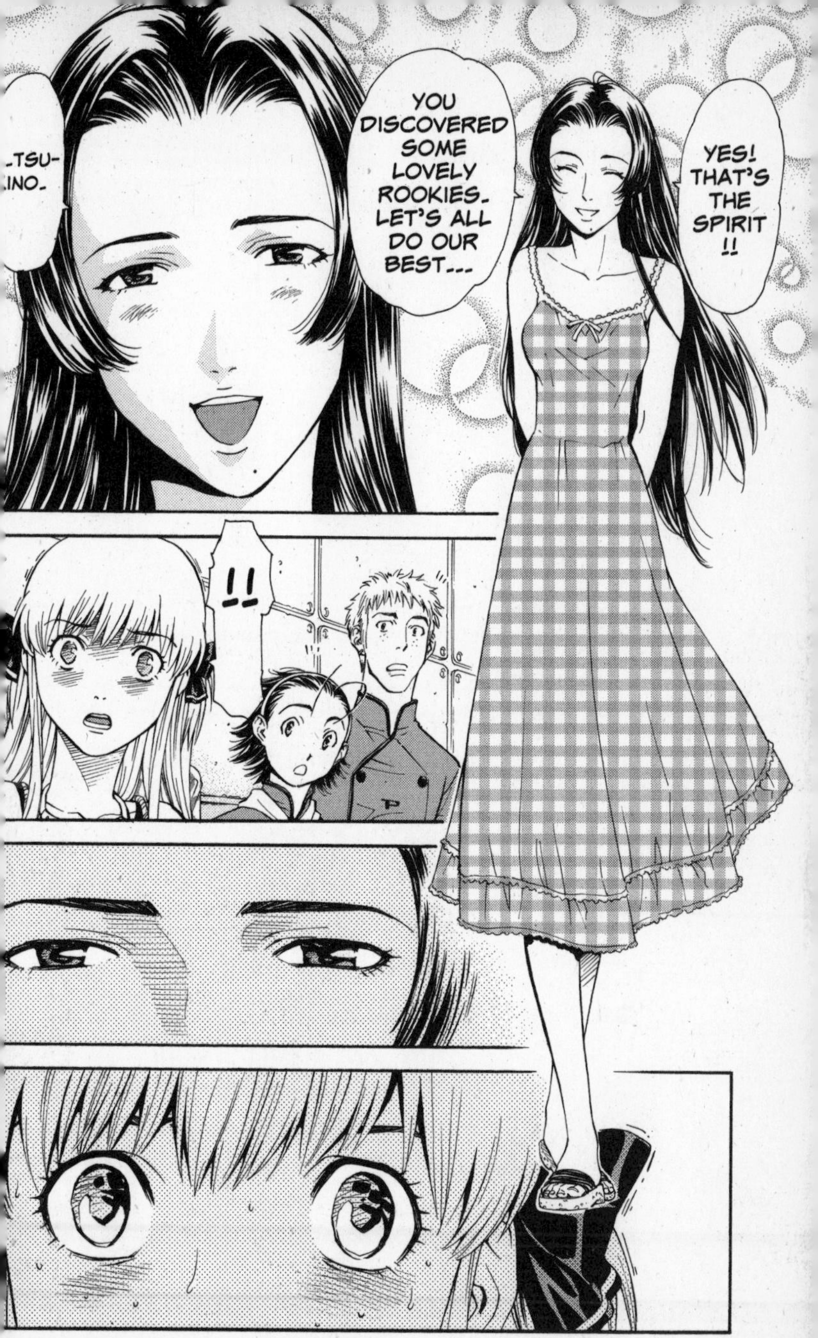
YES! THAT'S THE SPIRIT !!
YOU DISCOVERED SOME LOVELY ROOKIES. LET'S ALL DO OUR BEST...
TSU- INO.
!!

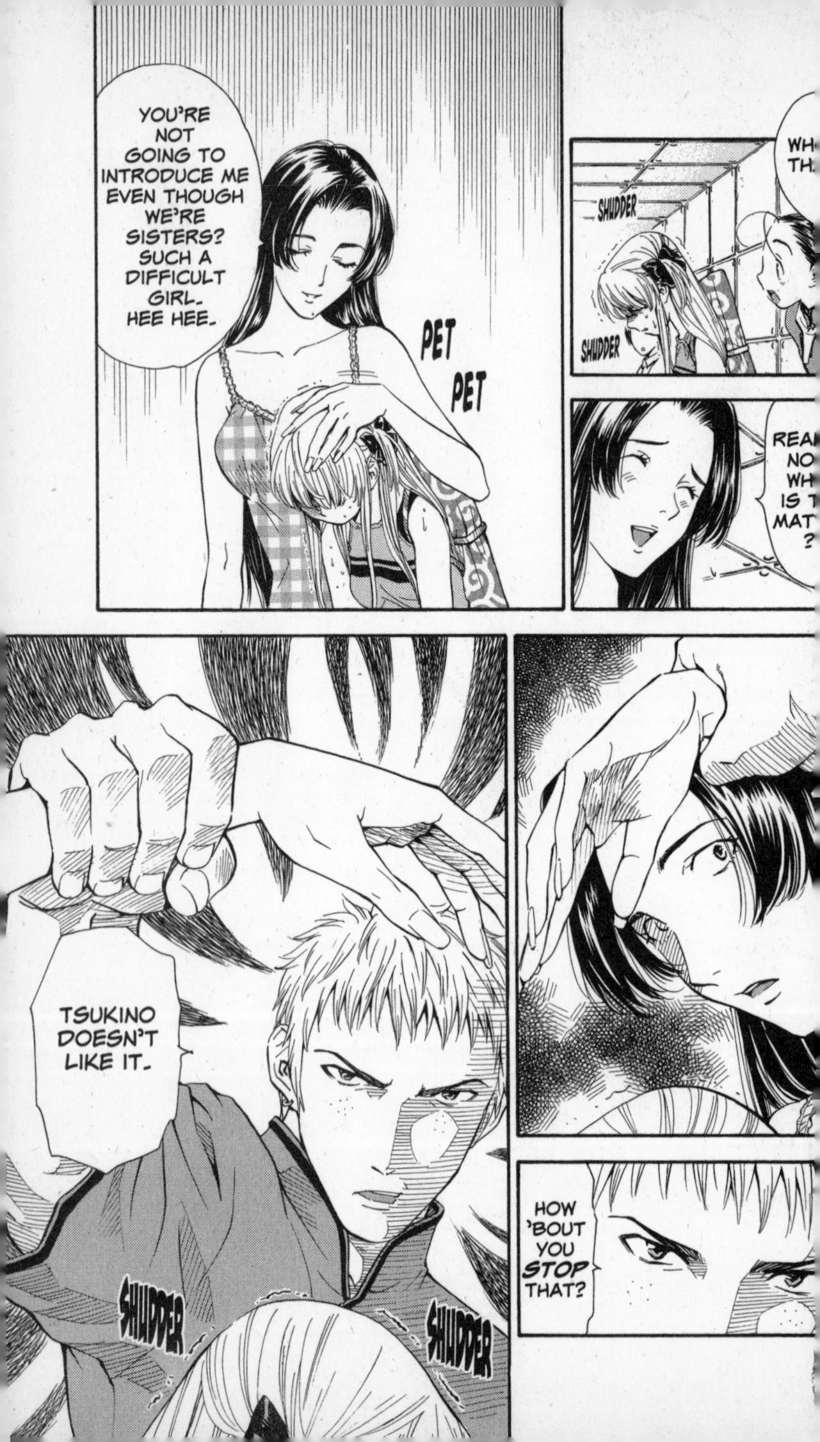
WH
TH
SHUDDER
SHUDDER
REA NO WH IS T MAT ?
YOU'RE NOT GOING TO INTRODUCE ME EVEN THOUGH WE'RE SISTERS? SUCH A DIFFICULT GIRL. HEE HEE.
PET
PET
HOW 'BOUT YOU *STOP* THAT?
TSUKINO DOESN'T LIKE IT.
SHUDDER
SHUDDER

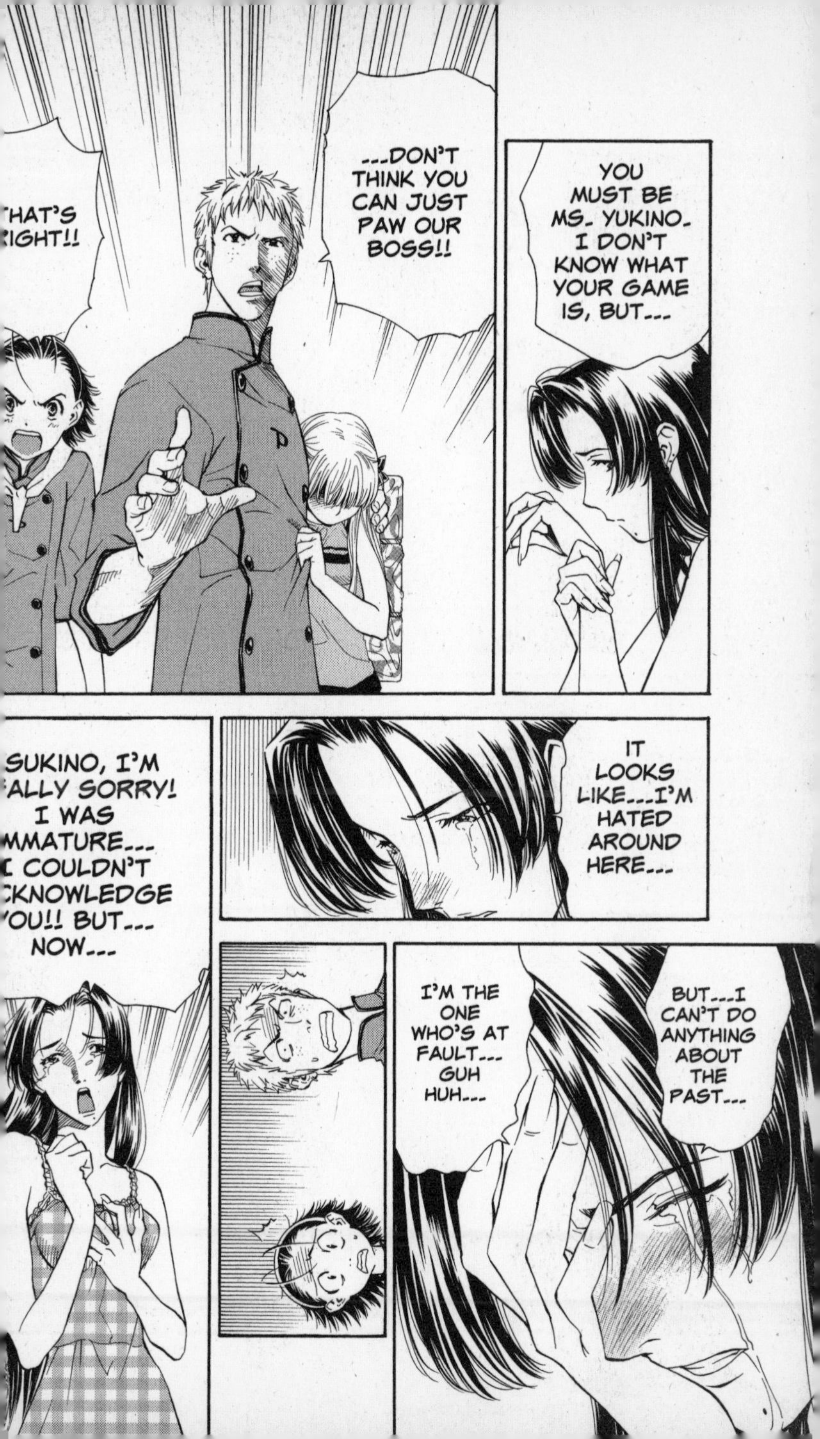
YOU MUST BE MS. YUKINO. I DON'T KNOW WHAT YOUR GAME IS, BUT...
...DON'T THINK YOU CAN JUST PAW OUR BOSS!!
HAT'S IGHT!!
IT LOOKS LIKE...I'M HATED AROUND HERE...
BUT...I CAN'T DO ANYTHING ABOUT THE PAST...
I'M THE ONE WHO'S AT FAULT... GUH HUH...
SUKINO, I'M ALLY SORRY! I WAS MMATURE... COULDN'T CKNOWLEDGE OU!! BUT... NOW...

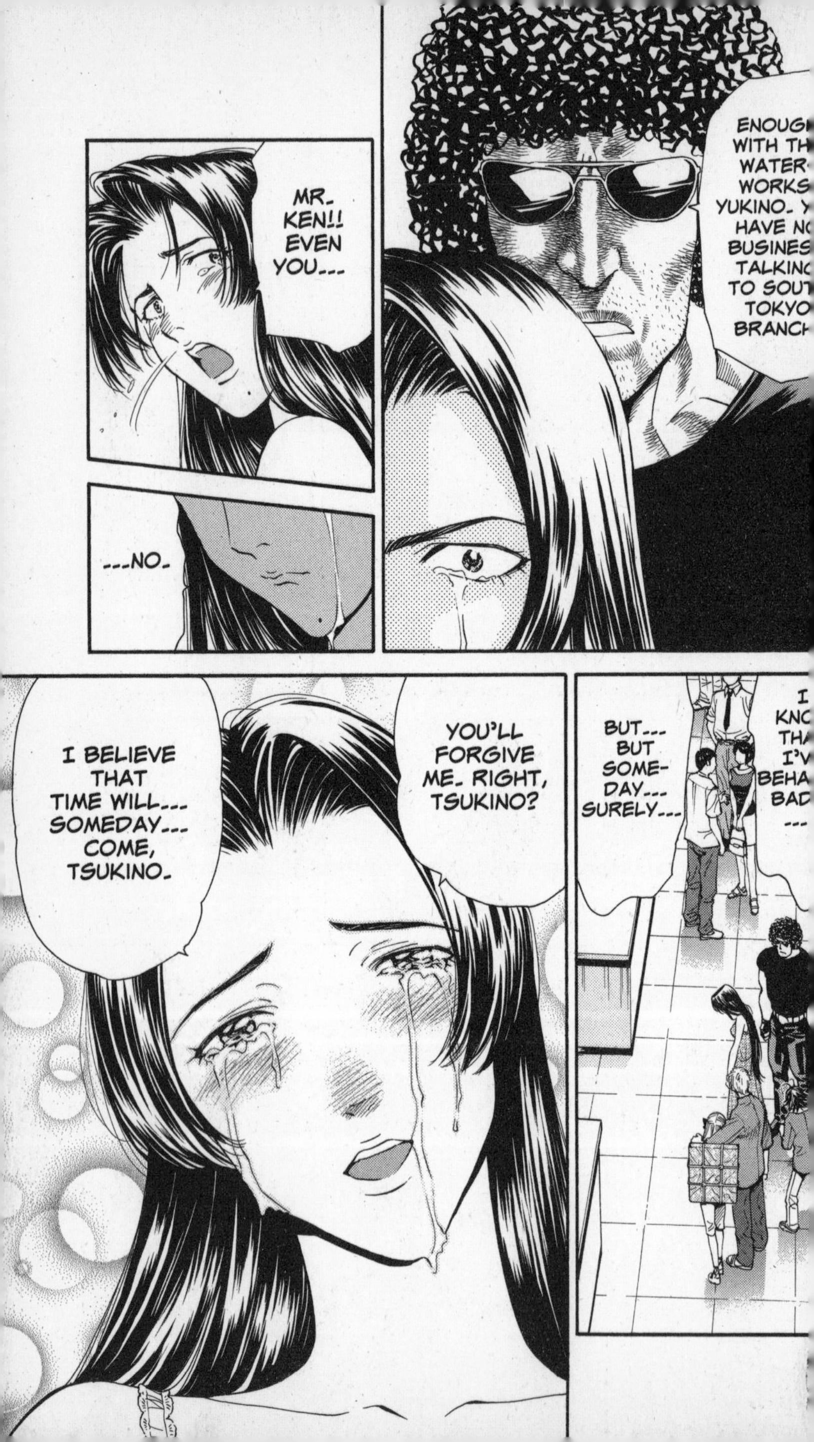
ENOUG WITH TH WATER- WORKS YUKINO. Y HAVE NO BUSINES TALKING TO SOUT TOKYO BRANCH
MR. KEN!! EVEN YOU...
...NO.
I KNO THA I'V BEHA BAD ...
BUT... BUT SOME-DAY... SURELY...
YOU'LL FORGIVE ME. RIGHT, TSUKINO?
I BELIEVE THAT TIME WILL... SOMEDAY... COME, TSUKINO.

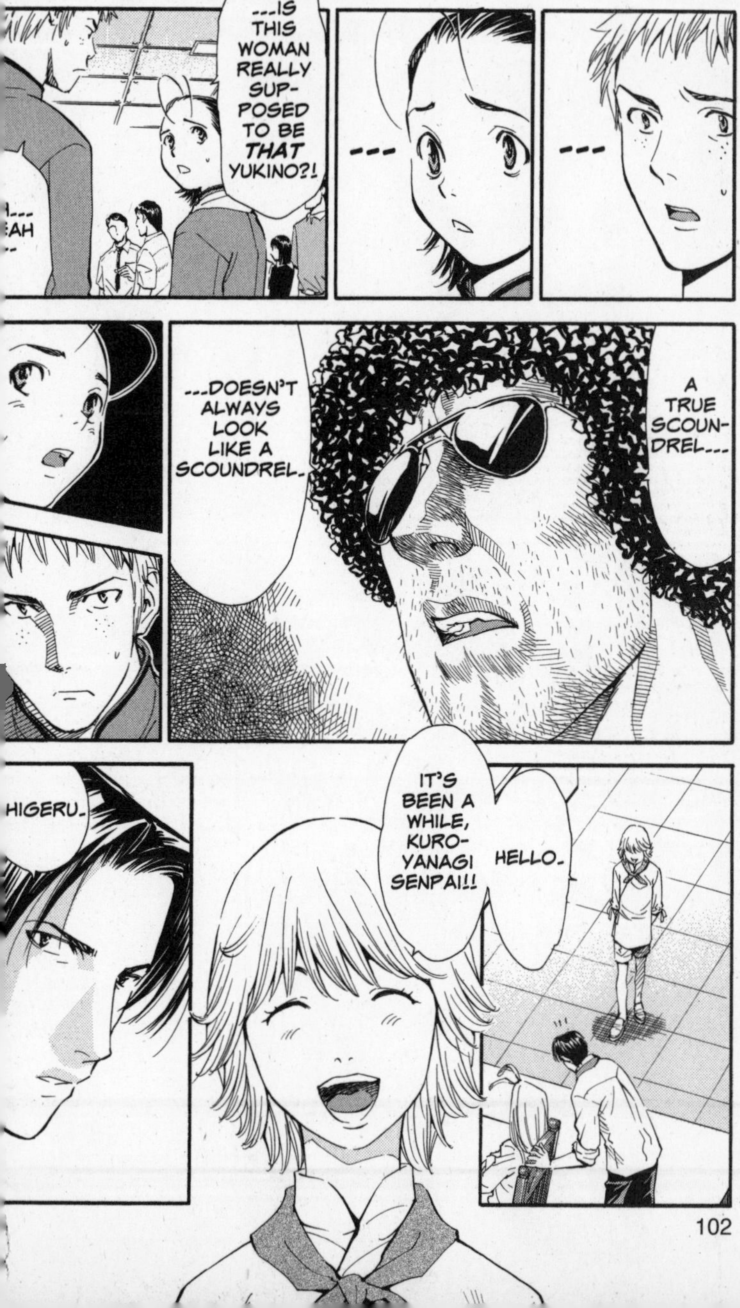

---IS THIS WOMAN REALLY SUPPOSED TO BE *THAT* YUKINO?!
H---
EAH
--
A TRUE SCOUNDREL---
---DOESN'T ALWAYS LOOK LIKE A SCOUNDREL.
HELLO.
IT'S BEEN A WHILE, KURO-YANAGI SENPAI!!
HIGERU.

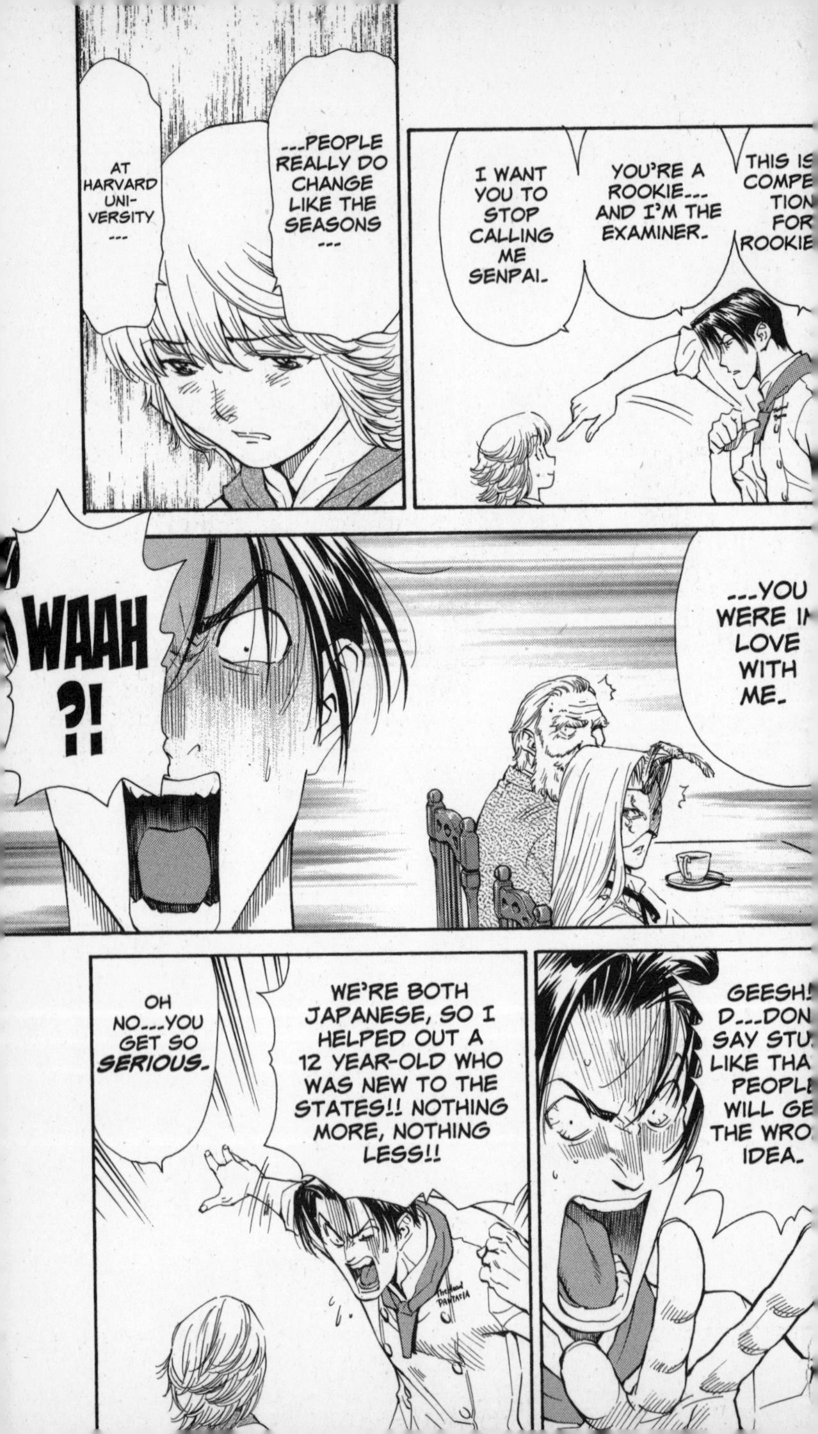
THIS IS COMPE TION FOR ROOKIE
YOU'RE A ROOKIE... AND I'M THE EXAMINER.
I WANT YOU TO STOP CALLING ME SENPAI.
...PEOPLE REALLY DO CHANGE LIKE THE SEASONS...
AT HARVARD UNIVERSITY...
...YOU WERE I LOVE WITH ME.
WAAH ?!
GEESH! D...DON SAY STU LIKE THA PEOPLE WILL GE THE WRO IDEA.
WE'RE BOTH JAPANESE, SO I HELPED OUT A 12 YEAR-OLD WHO WAS NEW TO THE STATES!! NOTHING MORE, NOTHING LESS!!
OH NO...YOU GET SO *SERIOUS*.

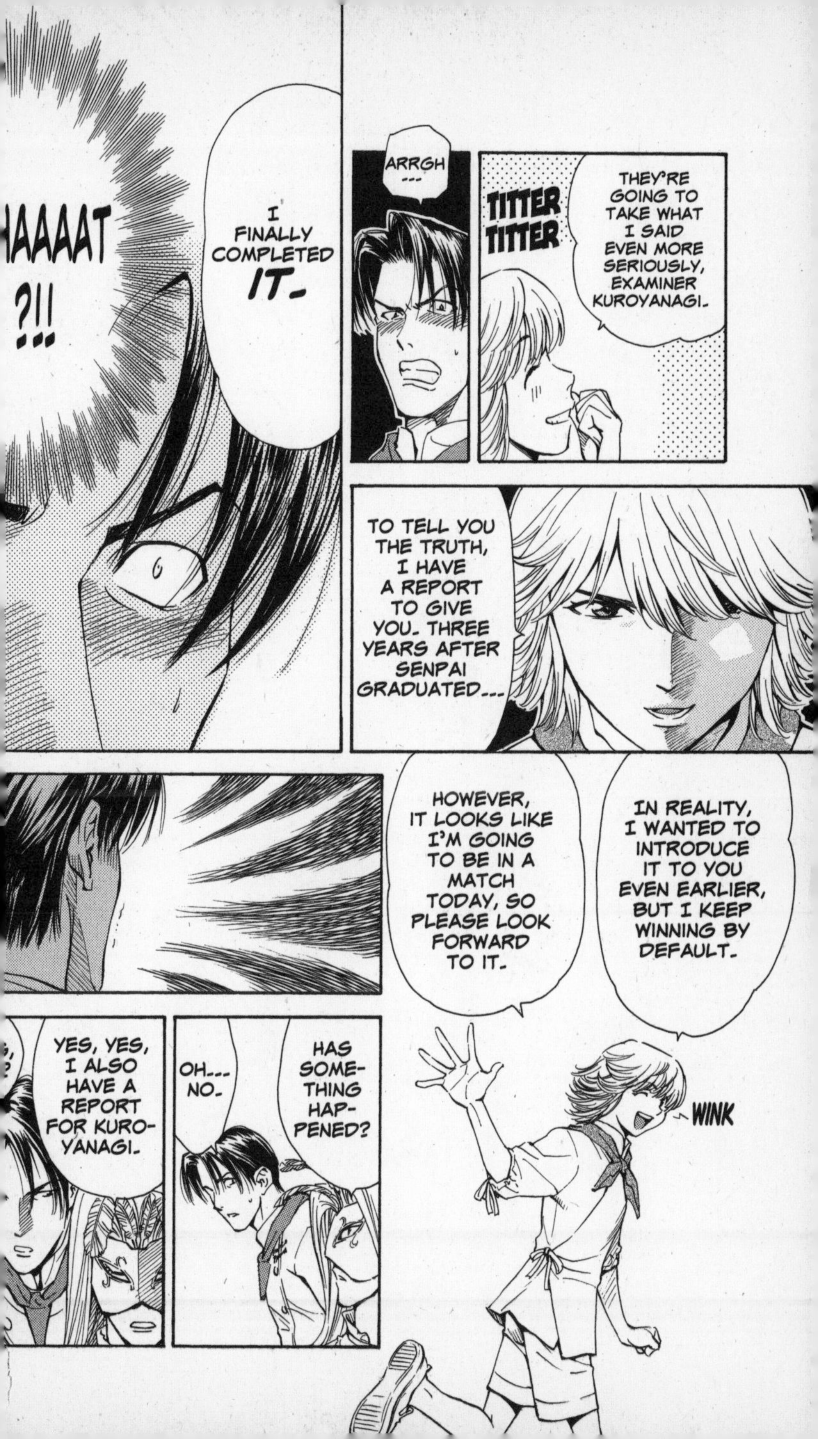

THEY'RE GOING TO TAKE WHAT I SAID EVEN MORE SERIOUSLY, EXAMINER KUROYANAGI.
TITTER TITTER
ARRGH ---
TO TELL YOU THE TRUTH, I HAVE A REPORT TO GIVE YOU. THREE YEARS AFTER SENPAI GRADUATED...
I FINALLY COMPLETED IT.
?!!
IN REALITY, I WANTED TO INTRODUCE IT TO YOU EVEN EARLIER, BUT I KEEP WINNING BY DEFAULT.
HOWEVER, IT LOOKS LIKE I'M GOING TO BE IN A MATCH TODAY, SO PLEASE LOOK FORWARD TO IT.
WINK
HAS SOMETHING HAPPENED?
OH... NO.
YES, YES, I ALSO HAVE A REPORT FOR KURO-YANAGI.

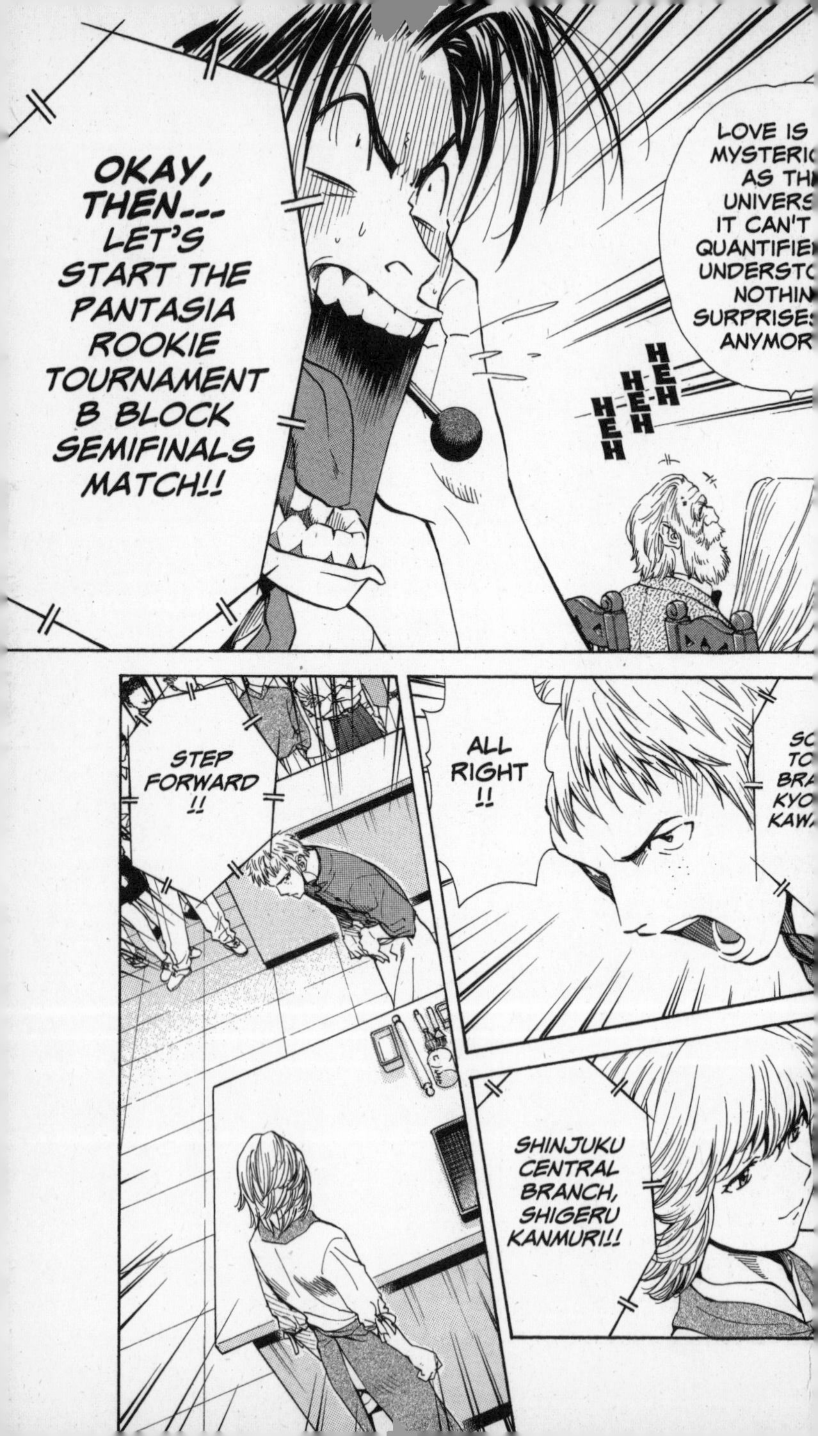
LOVE IS MYSTERIO AS TH UNIVERS IT CAN'T QUANTIFIE UNDERSTO NOTHIN SURPRISES ANYMOR
HEH HEH HEH
HEH HEH HEH
OKAY, THEN... LET'S START THE PANTASIA ROOKIE TOURNAMENT B BLOCK SEMIFINALS MATCH!!
SO TO BRA KYO KAWA
ALL RIGHT!!
SHINJUKU CENTRAL BRANCH, SHIGERU KANMURI!!
STEP FORWARD!!

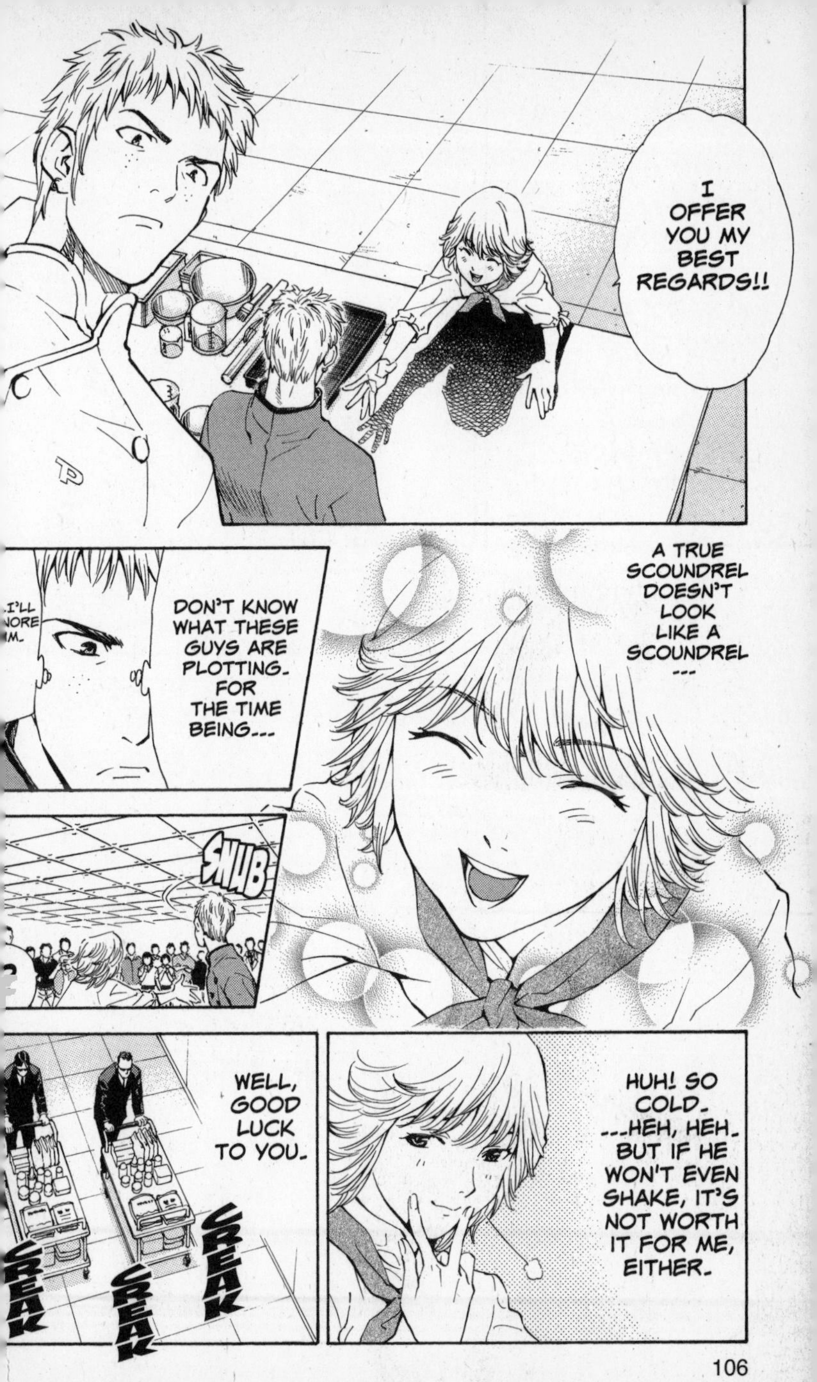
I OFFER YOU MY BEST REGARDS!!
A TRUE SCOUNDREL DOESN'T LOOK LIKE A SCOUNDREL...
DON'T KNOW WHAT THESE GUYS ARE PLOTTING. FOR THE TIME BEING...
.I'LL NORE M.
SNUB
HUH! SO COLD. ...HEH, HEH. BUT IF HE WON'T EVEN SHAKE, IT'S NOT WORTH IT FOR ME, EITHER.
WELL, GOOD LUCK TO YOU.
CREAK
CREAK
CREAK

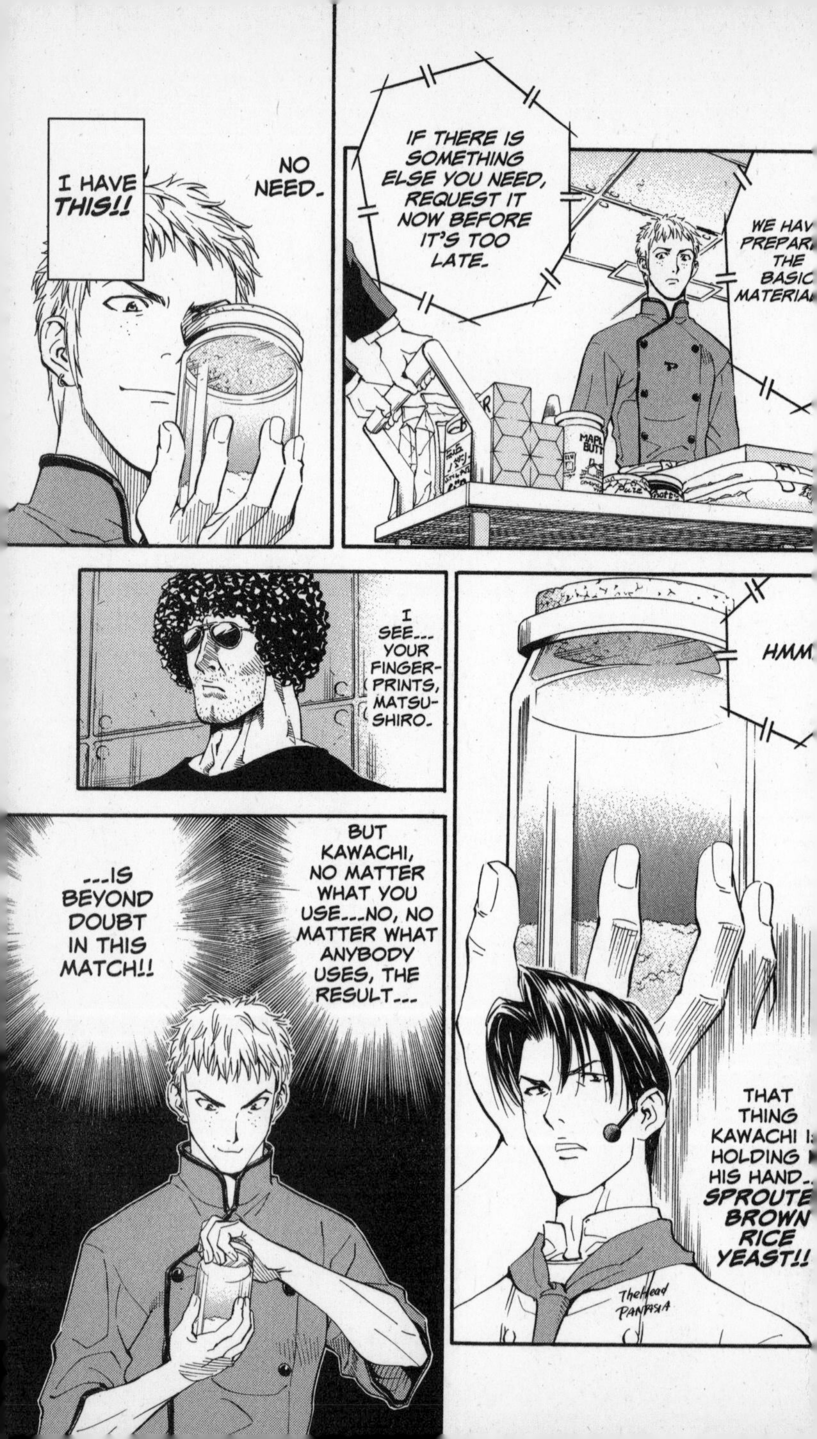
WE HAV PREPAR THE BASIC MATERIA
IF THERE IS SOMETHING ELSE YOU NEED, REQUEST IT NOW BEFORE IT'S TOO LATE.
NO NEED.
I HAVE **THIS!!**
HMM
THAT THING KAWACHI I HOLDING HIS HAND... **SPROUTE BROWN RICE YEAST!!**
TheHead PANTASIA
I SEE... YOUR FINGER-PRINTS, MATSU-SHIRO.
BUT KAWACHI, NO MATTER WHAT YOU USE...NO, NO MATTER WHAT ANYBODY USES, THE RESULT...
...IS BEYOND DOUBT IN THIS MATCH!!

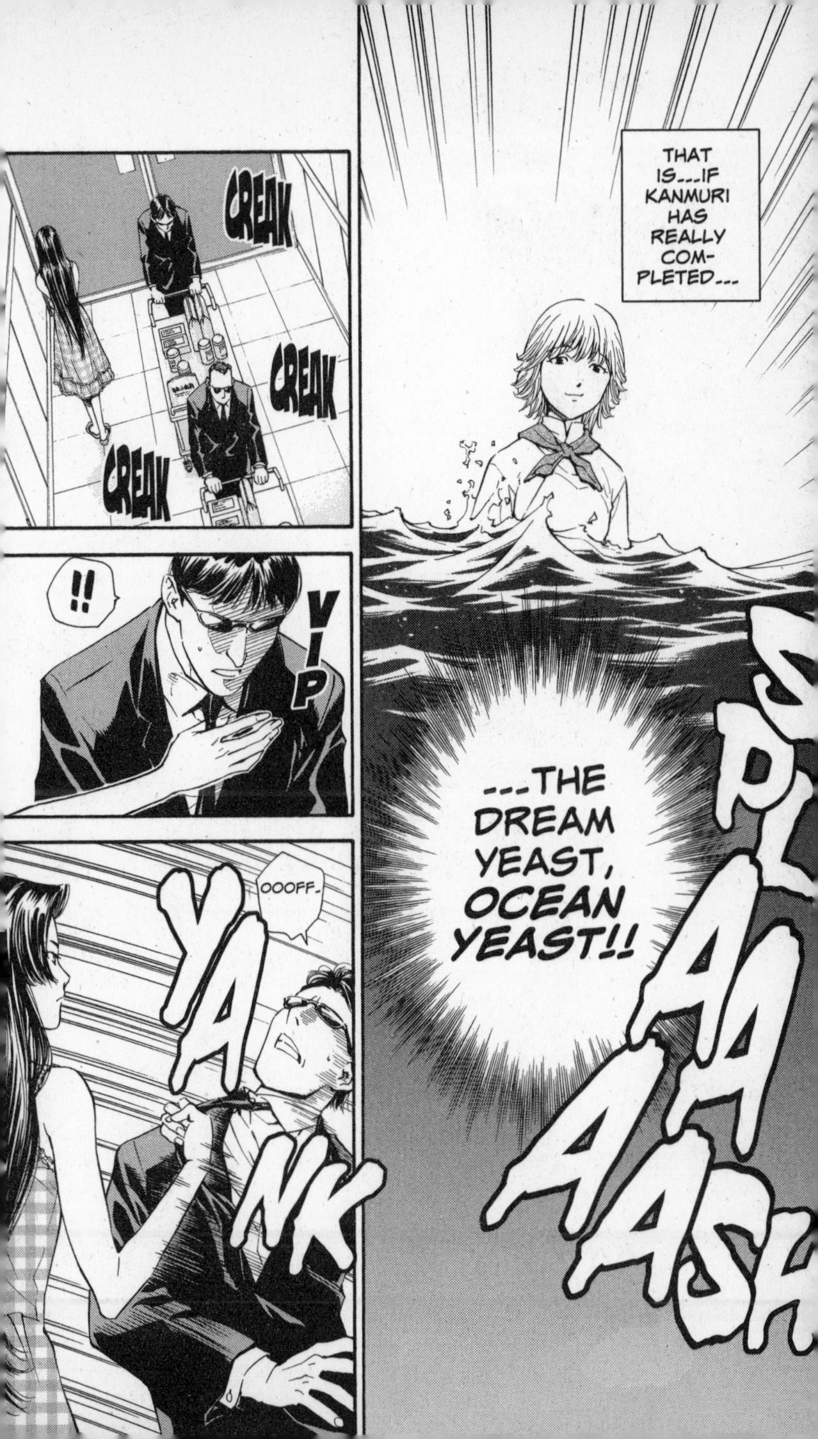
THAT IS...IF KANMURI HAS REALLY COM-PLETED...
...THE DREAM YEAST, OCEAN YEAST!!
SPLAAAAASH
CREAK
CREAK
CREAK
!!
VIP
YANK
OOOFF

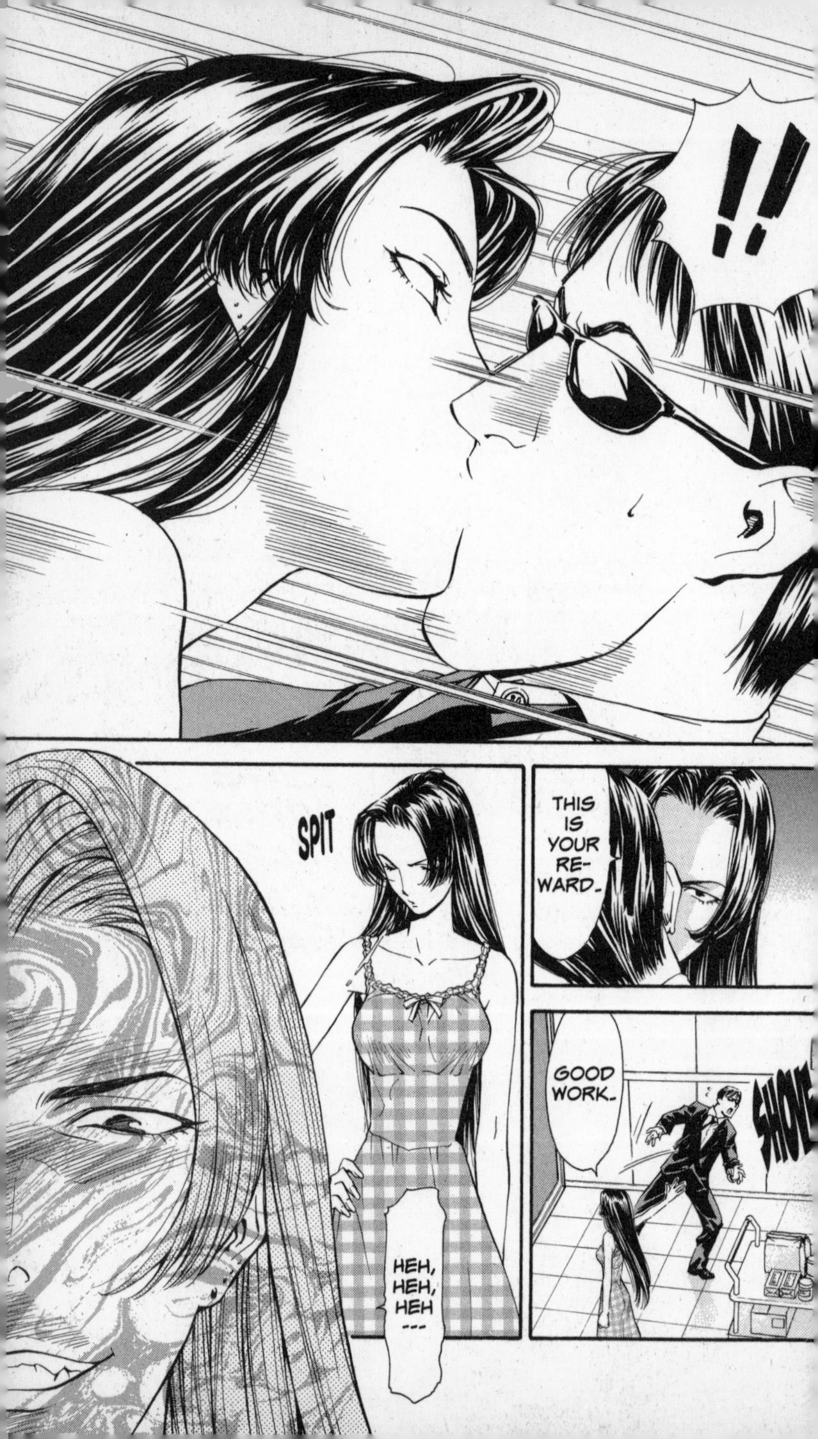
!!
THIS IS YOUR RE-WARD.
GOOD WORK.
SHOVE
SPIT
HEH, HEH, HEH ---

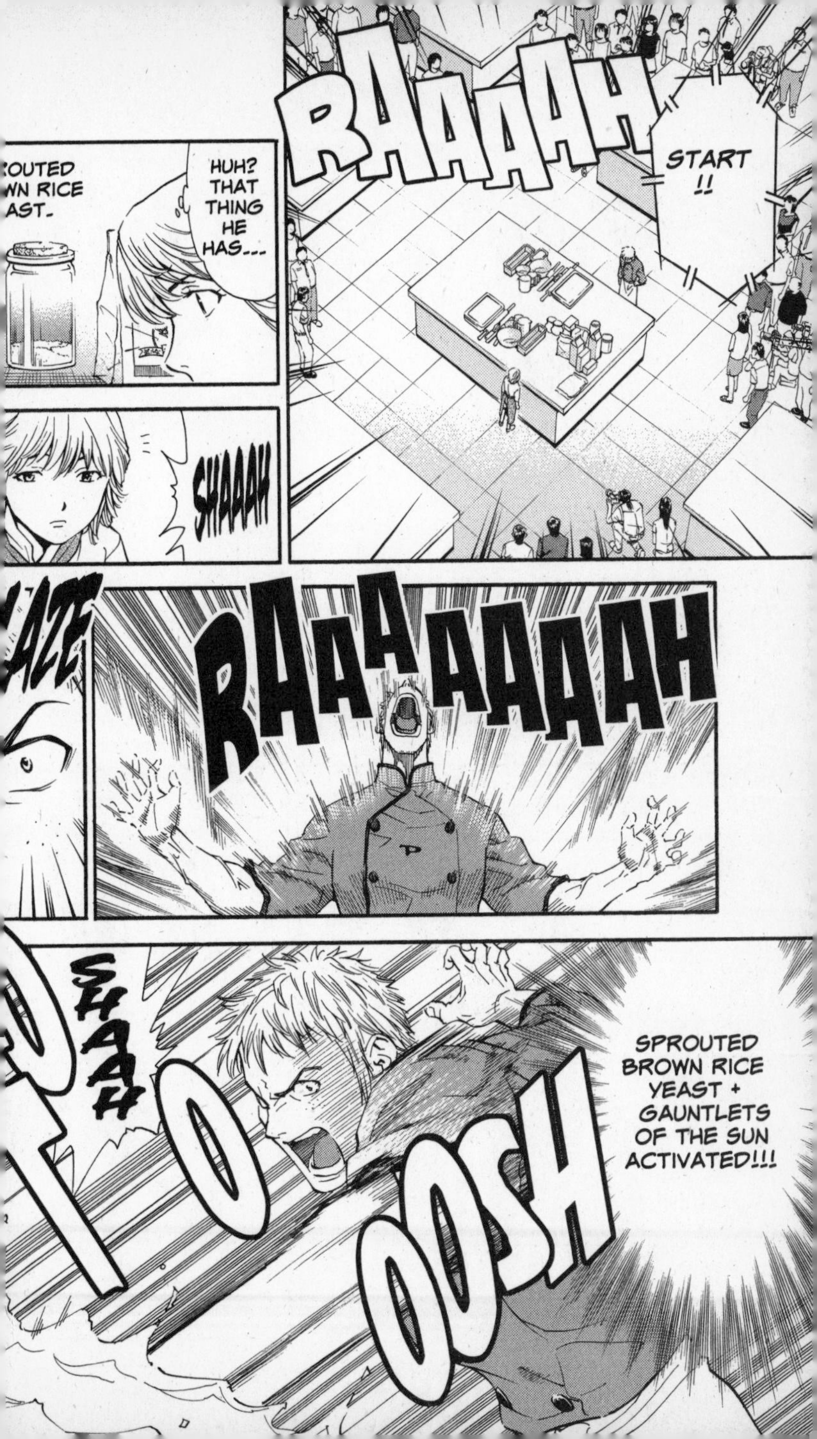
RAAAAH
START !!
HUH? THAT THING HE HAS...
ROUTED
WN RICE
AST.
SHAAAH
RAAAAAAAH
AZE
SPROUTED BROWN RICE YEAST + GAUNTLETS OF THE SUN ACTIVATED!!!
SHAAAH
OOSH

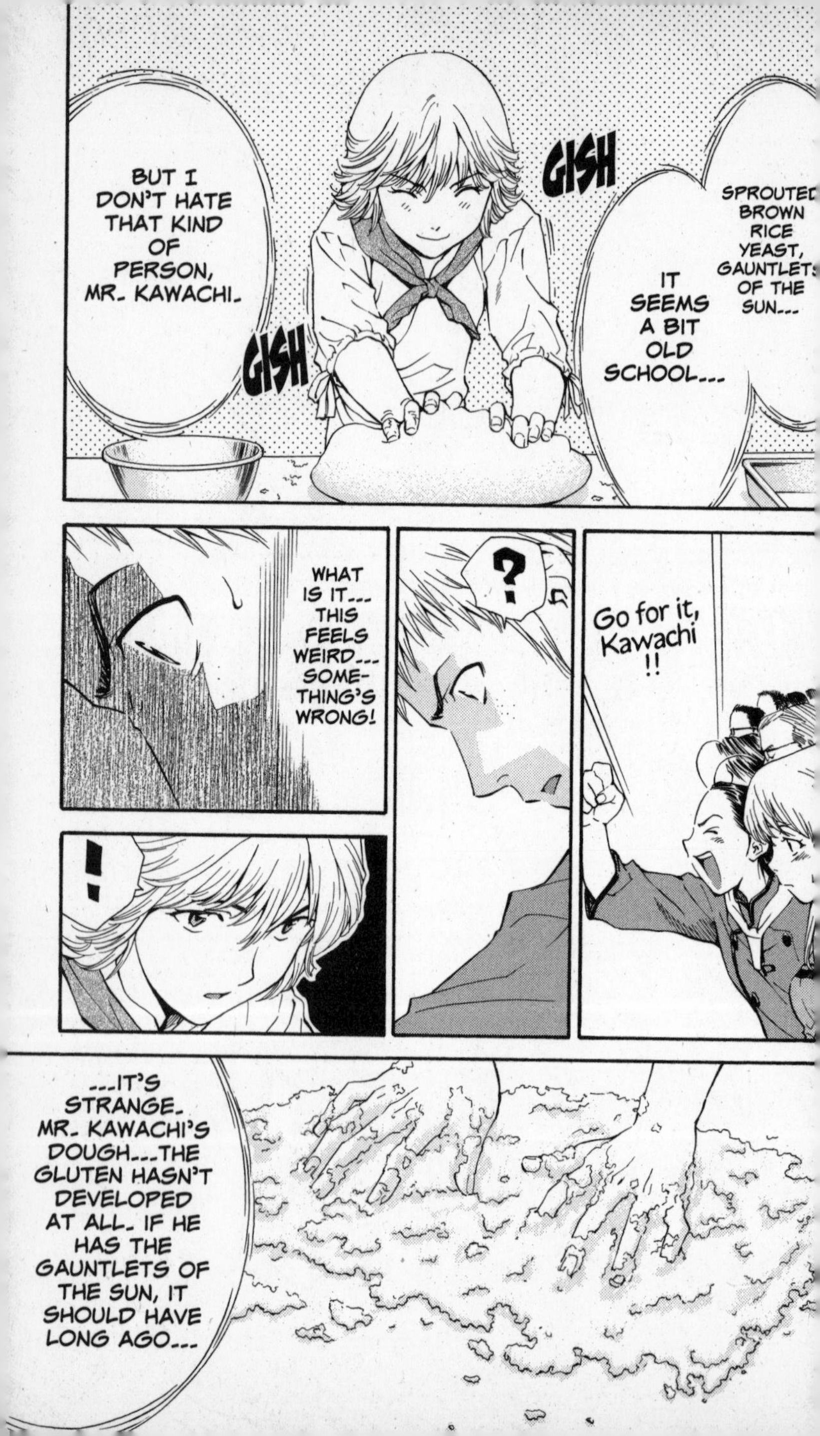
SPROUTED BROWN RICE YEAST, GAUNTLETS OF THE SUN...
IT SEEMS A BIT OLD SCHOOL...
GISH
BUT I DON'T HATE THAT KIND OF PERSON, MR. KAWACHI.
GISH
Go for it, Kawachi !!
?
WHAT IS IT... THIS FEELS WEIRD... SOMETHING'S WRONG!
!
...IT'S STRANGE. MR. KAWACHI'S DOUGH...THE GLUTEN HASN'T DEVELOPED AT ALL. IF HE HAS THE GAUNTLETS OF THE SUN, IT SHOULD HAVE LONG AGO...

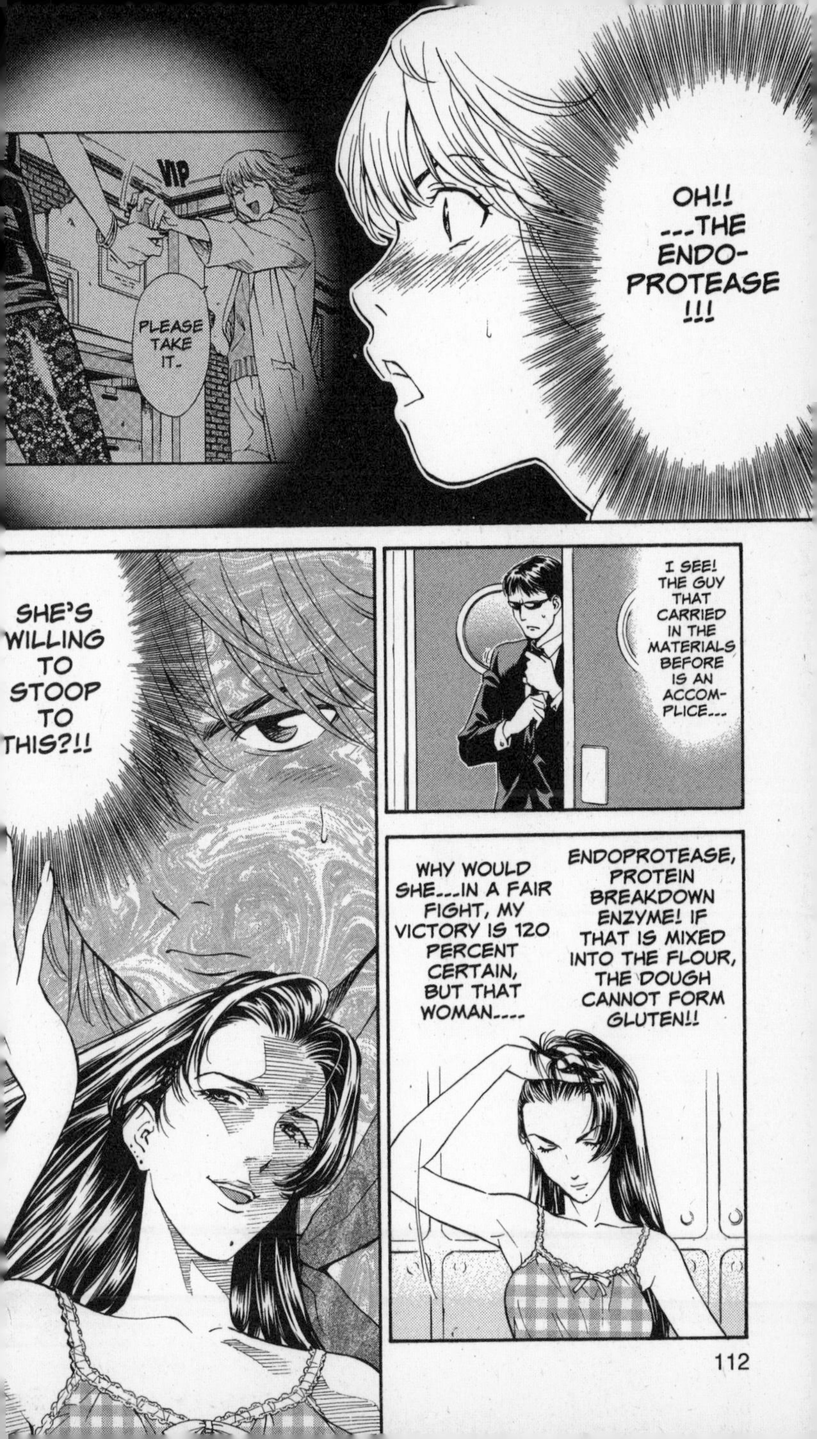
OH!! ---THE ENDO-PROTEASE !!!
PLEASE TAKE IT..
I SEE! THE GUY THAT CARRIED IN THE MATERIALS BEFORE IS AN ACCOM-PLICE---
ENDOPROTEASE, PROTEIN BREAKDOWN ENZYME! IF THAT IS MIXED INTO THE FLOUR, THE DOUGH CANNOT FORM GLUTEN!!
WHY WOULD SHE---IN A FAIR FIGHT, MY VICTORY IS 120 PERCENT CERTAIN, BUT THAT WOMAN----
SHE'S WILLING TO STOOP TO THIS?!!
VIP

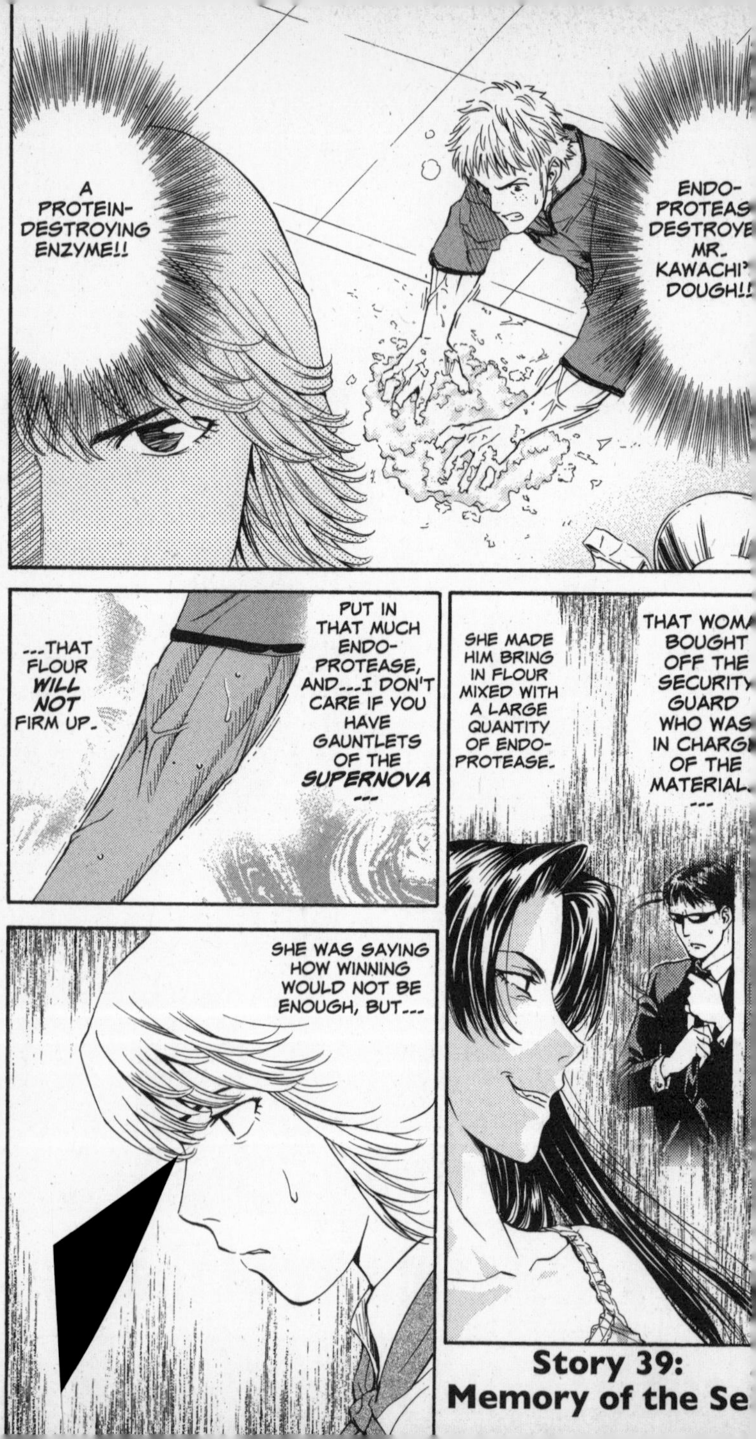
ENDO-PROTEAS DESTROYE MR. KAWACHI' DOUGH!!
A PROTEIN-DESTROYING ENZYME!!
THAT WOMA BOUGHT OFF THE SECURITY GUARD WHO WAS IN CHARG OF THE MATERIAL. ...
SHE MADE HIM BRING IN FLOUR MIXED WITH A LARGE QUANTITY OF ENDO-PROTEASE.
PUT IN THAT MUCH ENDO-PROTEASE, AND... I DON'T CARE IF YOU HAVE GAUNTLETS OF THE SUPERNOVA ...
...THAT FLOUR WILL NOT FIRM UP.
SHE WAS SAYING HOW WINNING WOULD NOT BE ENOUGH, BUT...

Story 39: Memory of the Se

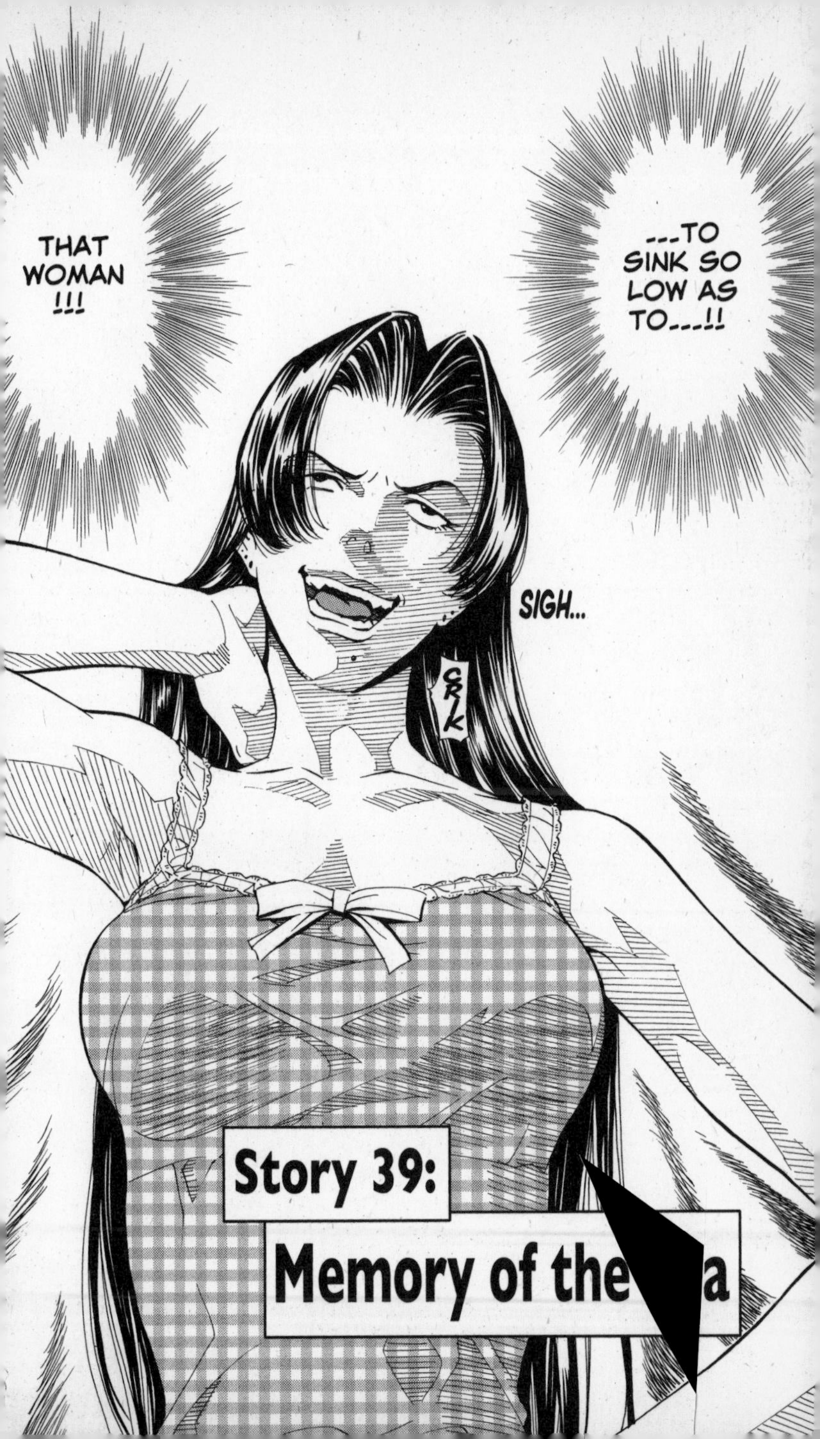
---TO SINK SO LOW AS TO---!!
THAT WOMAN !!!
SIGH...
CRK
Story 39:
Memory of the [redacted]

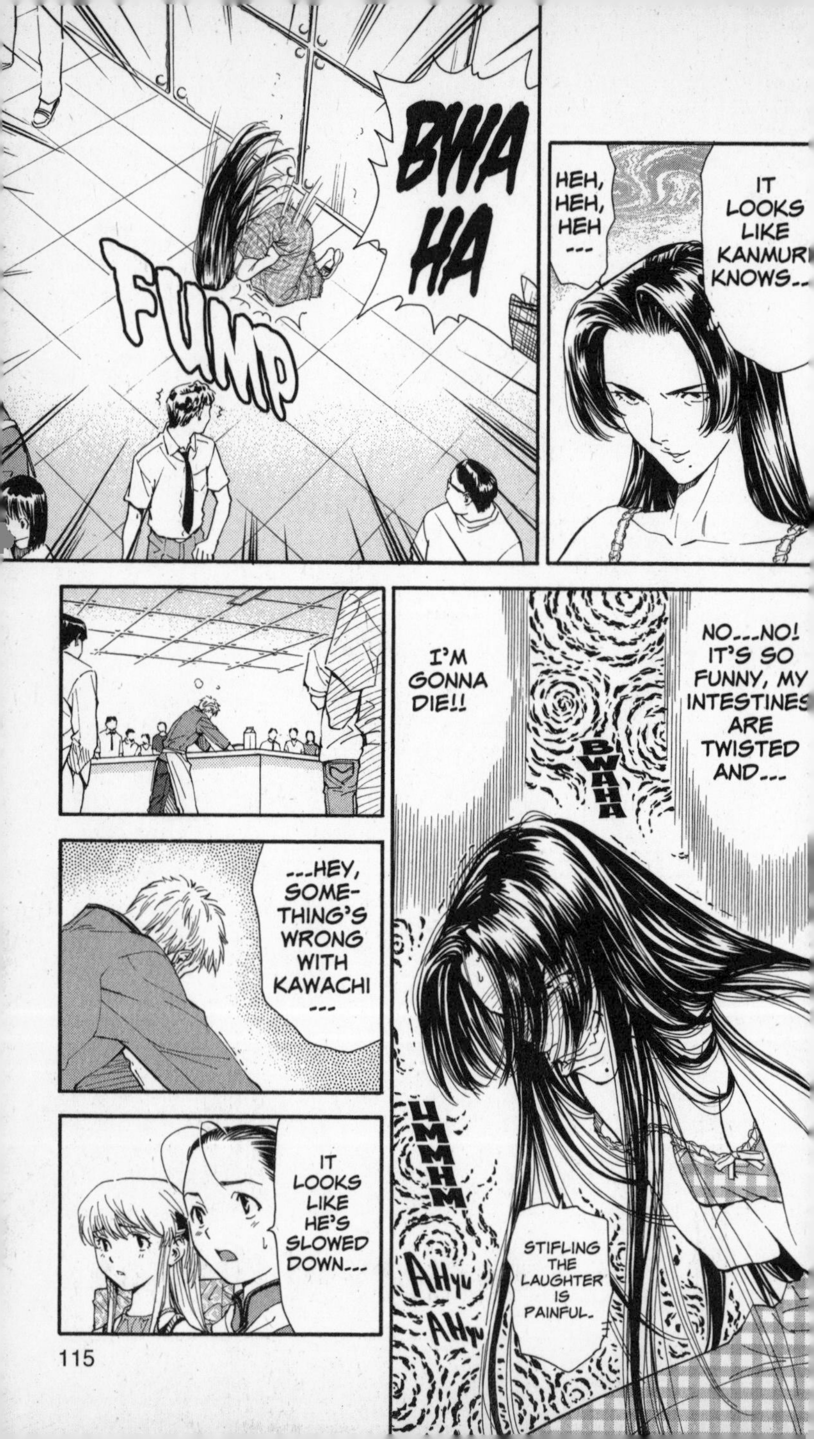
IT LOOKS LIKE KANMURI KNOWS...
HEH, HEH, HEH ...
BWA HA
FUMP
NO...NO! IT'S SO FUNNY, MY INTESTINES ARE TWISTED AND...
BWAHA
I'M GONNA DIE!!
UMMHM
STIFLING THE LAUGHTER IS PAINFUL.
AHyu AHyu
...HEY, SOMETHING'S WRONG WITH KAWACHI ...
IT LOOKS LIKE HE'S SLOWED DOWN...

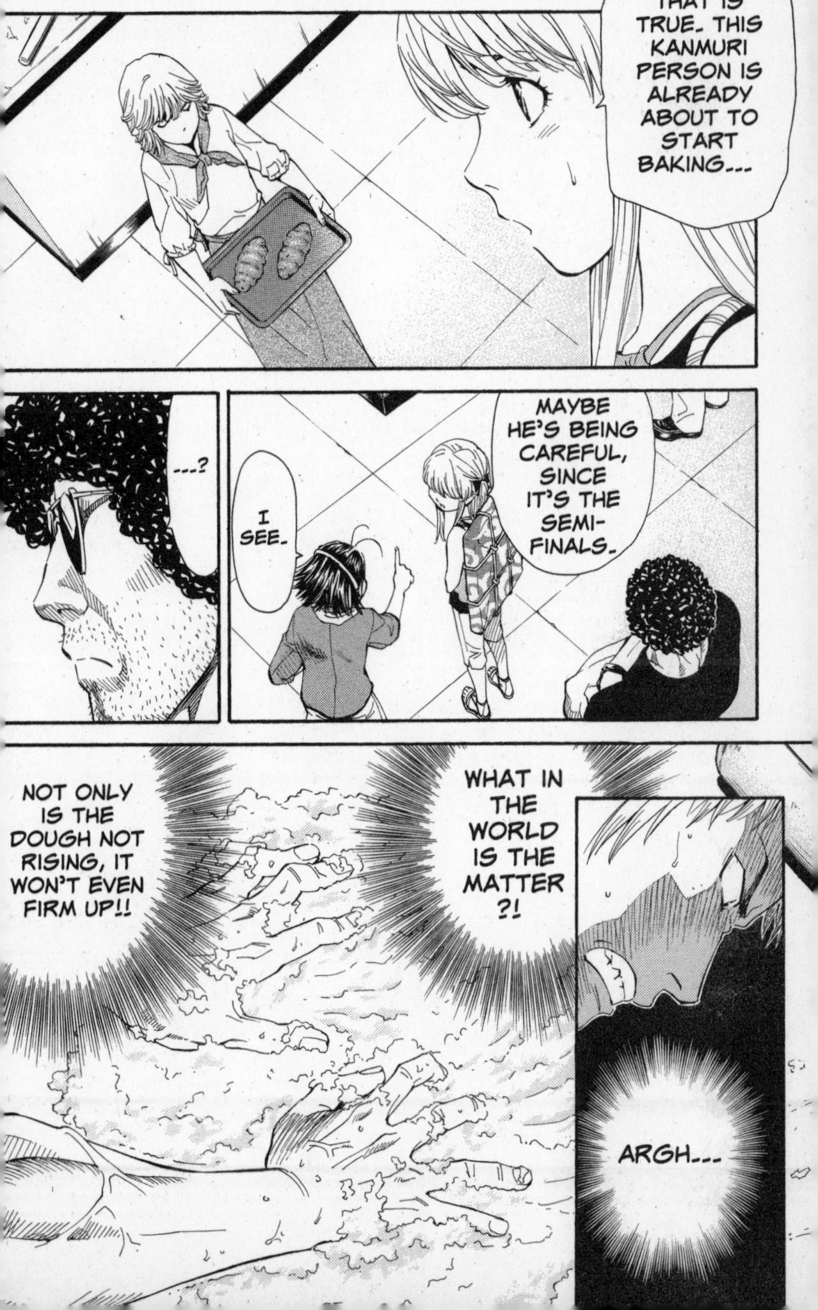
THAT IS TRUE. THIS KANMURI PERSON IS ALREADY ABOUT TO START BAKING...
MAYBE HE'S BEING CAREFUL, SINCE IT'S THE SEMI-FINALS.
I SEE.
...?
ARGH...
WHAT IN THE WORLD IS THE MATTER ?!
NOT ONLY IS THE DOUGH NOT RISING, IT WON'T EVEN FIRM UP!!

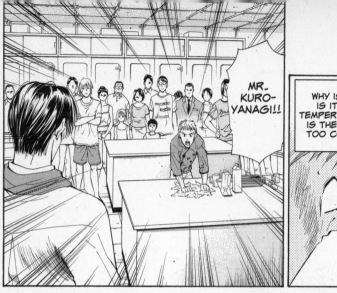

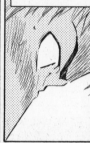

WHY IS IT?! IS IT THE TEMPERATURE?! IS THE ROOM TOO COLD?!
MR. KURO-YANAGI!!
WHA IS IT
THE FERMENTA-TION OF THE DOUGH IS NOT GOING THE WAY I WANT IT TO...
IT MIGHT BE THAT THE TEMPERATURE IS TOO LOW, SO CAN YOU CUT OFF THE AIR CONDITIONING FOR A WHILE?
THE AIR CONDITION-ING?!
The Head PANTASIA
HMM ...
ALL RIGHT, YOU GUYS ARE THE STARS. IF THAT'S WHAT IT TAKES TO MAKE DELICIOUS BREADS...

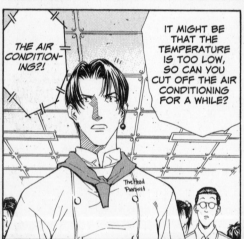

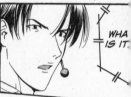

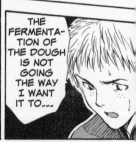

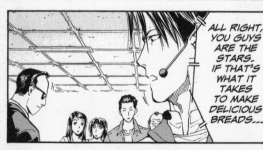

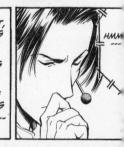

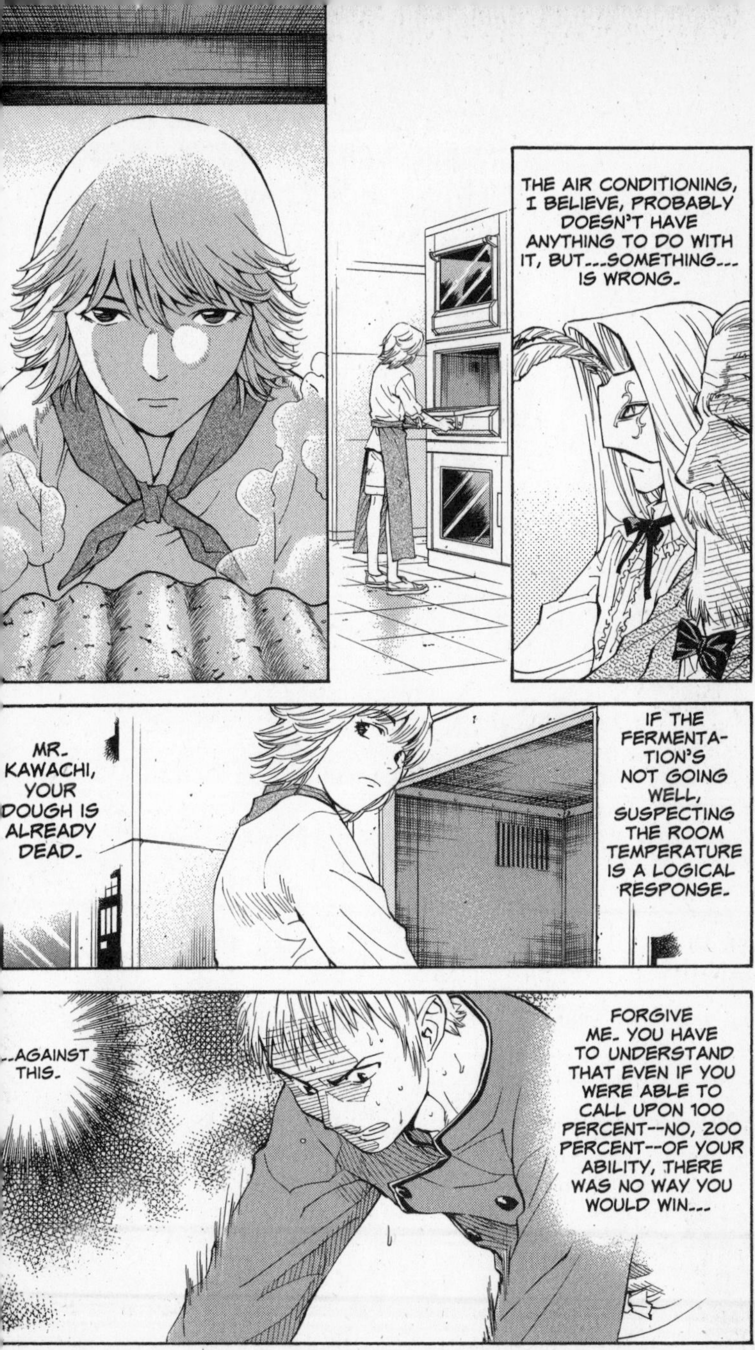
THE AIR CONDITIONING, I BELIEVE, PROBABLY DOESN'T HAVE ANYTHING TO DO WITH IT, BUT... SOMETHING... IS WRONG.
IF THE FERMENTATION'S NOT GOING WELL, SUSPECTING THE ROOM TEMPERATURE IS A LOGICAL RESPONSE.
MR. KAWACHI, YOUR DOUGH IS ALREADY DEAD.
FORGIVE ME. YOU HAVE TO UNDERSTAND THAT EVEN IF YOU WERE ABLE TO CALL UPON 100 PERCENT--NO, 200 PERCENT--OF YOUR ABILITY, THERE WAS NO WAY YOU WOULD WIN...
...AGAINST THIS.

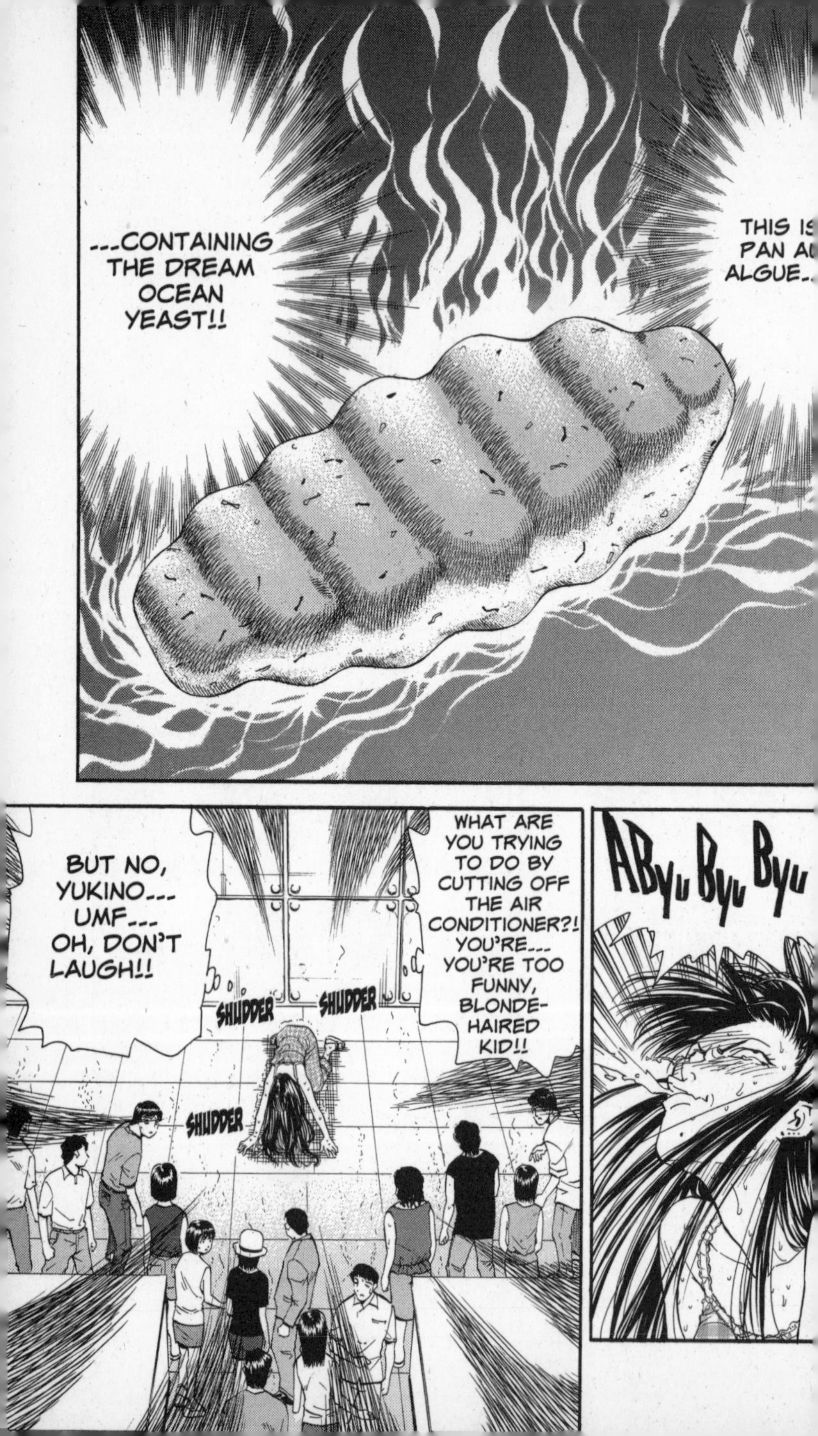
THIS IS PAN AL ALGUE..
...CONTAINING THE DREAM OCEAN YEAST!!
ABYu Byu Byu
WHAT ARE YOU TRYING TO DO BY CUTTING OFF THE AIR CONDITIONER?! YOU'RE... YOU'RE TOO FUNNY, BLONDE-HAIRED KID!!
SHUDDER
SHUDDER
SHUDDER
BUT NO, YUKINO... UMF... OH, DON'T LAUGH!!

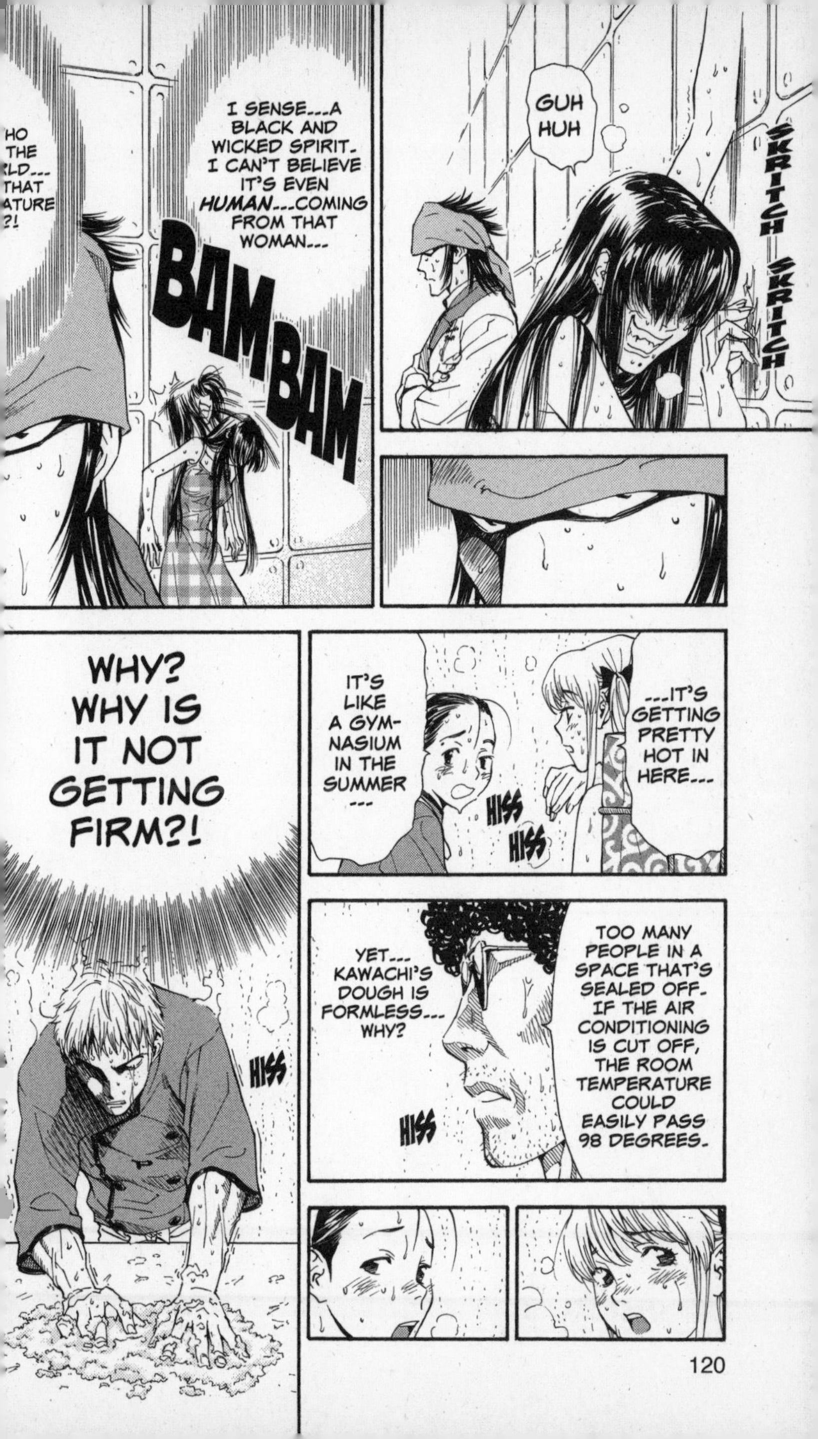
GUH HUH
SKRITCH SKRITCH
I SENSE...A BLACK AND WICKED SPIRIT. I CAN'T BELIEVE IT'S EVEN *HUMAN*...COMING FROM THAT WOMAN...
HO THE RLD... THAT ATURE ?!
BAM BAM
...IT'S GETTING PRETTY HOT IN HERE...
IT'S LIKE A GYM-NASIUM IN THE SUMMER ...
HISS
HISS
TOO MANY PEOPLE IN A SPACE THAT'S SEALED OFF. IF THE AIR CONDITIONING IS CUT OFF, THE ROOM TEMPERATURE COULD EASILY PASS 98 DEGREES.
YET... KAWACHI'S DOUGH IS FORMLESS... WHY?
HISS
WHY? WHY IS IT NOT GETTING FIRM?!
HISS

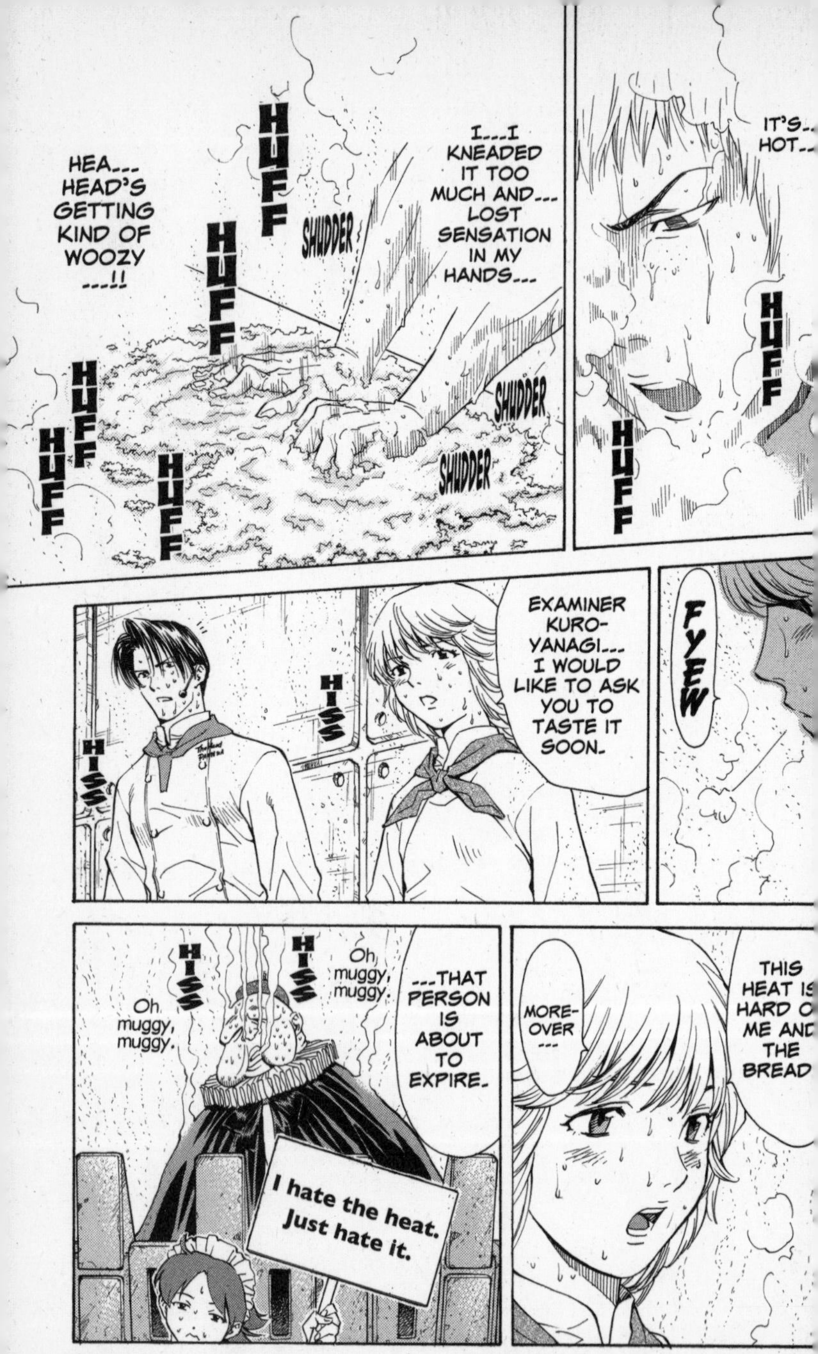
IT'S... HOT...
HUFF
HUFF
I...I KNEADED IT TOO MUCH AND... LOST SENSATION IN MY HANDS...
SHUDDER
SHUDDER
SHUDDER
HUFF
HUFF
HEA... HEAD'S GETTING KIND OF WOOZY ...!!
HUFF
HUFF
HUFF
FYEW
EXAMINER KURO-YANAGI... I WOULD LIKE TO ASK YOU TO TASTE IT SOON.
HISS
HISS
THIS HEAT IS HARD O ME AN THE BREAD
MORE-OVER ...
...THAT PERSON IS ABOUT TO EXPIRE.
Oh muggy, muggy.
HISS
HISS
Oh muggy, muggy.
I hate the heat. Just hate it.

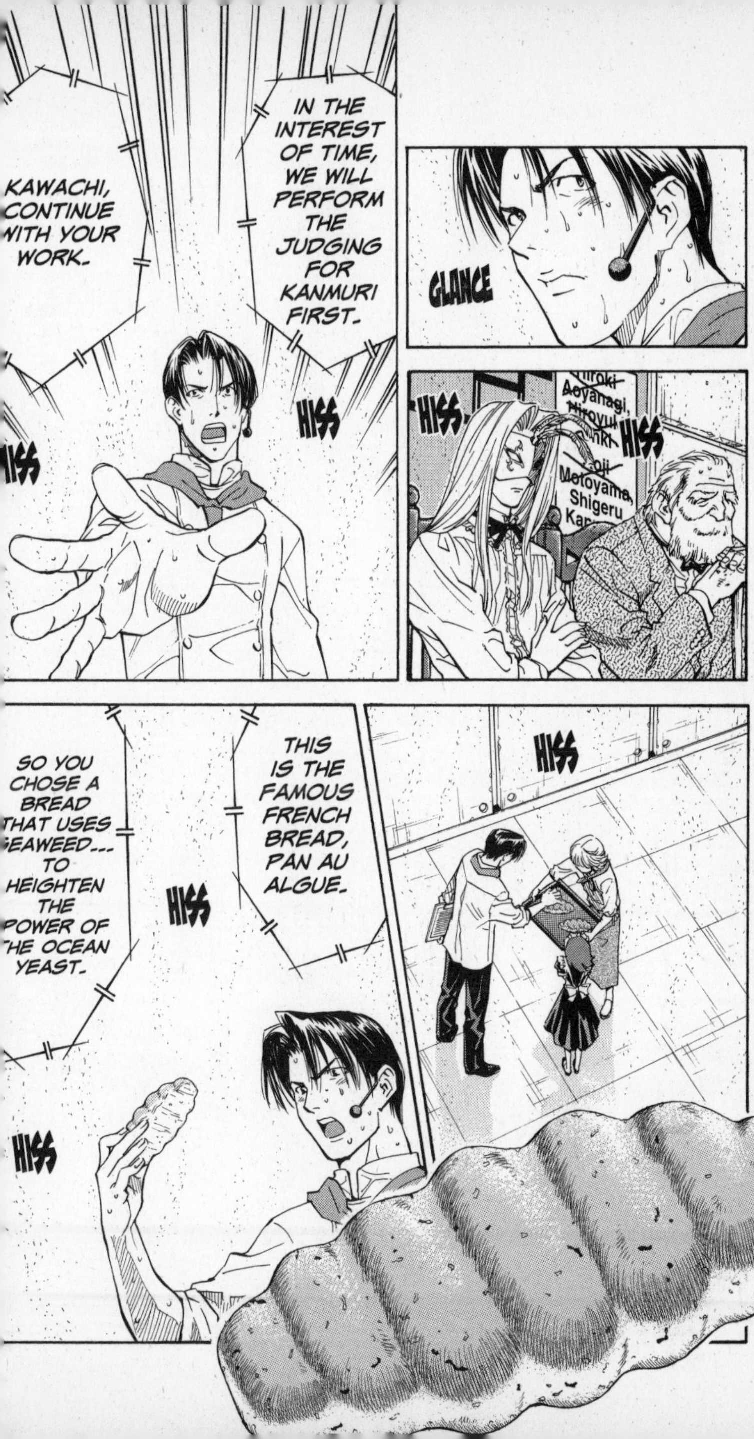
GLANCE
HISS
HISS
IN THE INTEREST OF TIME, WE WILL PERFORM THE JUDGING FOR KANMURI FIRST.
KAWACHI, CONTINUE WITH YOUR WORK.
HISS
HISS
HISS
THIS IS THE FAMOUS FRENCH BREAD, PAN AU ALGUE.
SO YOU CHOSE A BREAD THAT USES SEAWEED... TO HEIGHTEN THE POWER OF THE OCEAN YEAST.
HISS
HISS

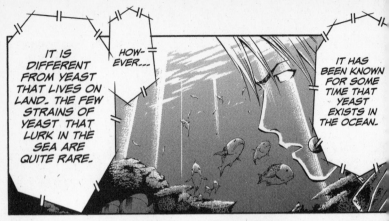

IT HAS BEEN KNOWN FOR SOME TIME THAT YEAST EXISTS IN THE OCEAN.
HOW-EVER...
IT IS DIFFERENT FROM YEAST THAT LIVES ON LAND. THE FEW STRAINS OF YEAST THAT LURK IN THE SEA ARE QUITE RARE.
MANY RESEARCHERS HAVE TRIED TO CULTIVATE YEAST IN SEAWATER... AND FAILED.
I WAS NO EXCEPTION...
CHOMP
I REGRET THAT YOU BEAT ME TO IT, BUT I THANK YOU FOR GIVING ME THE JOY OF BEING ABLE TO APPRECIATE *OCEAN YEAST WITH THIS TONGUE.
SPLAASH

* SANKYO (JOINT STOCK COMPANY) WAS FIRST IN THE WORLD TO SUCCEED IN CULTIVATING OCEAN YEAST. THEY DEVELOPED IT AS A BREAD YEAST.

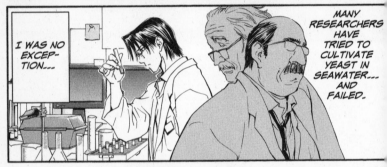

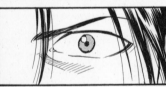

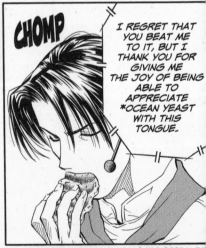

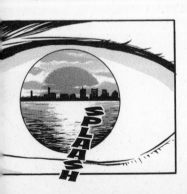

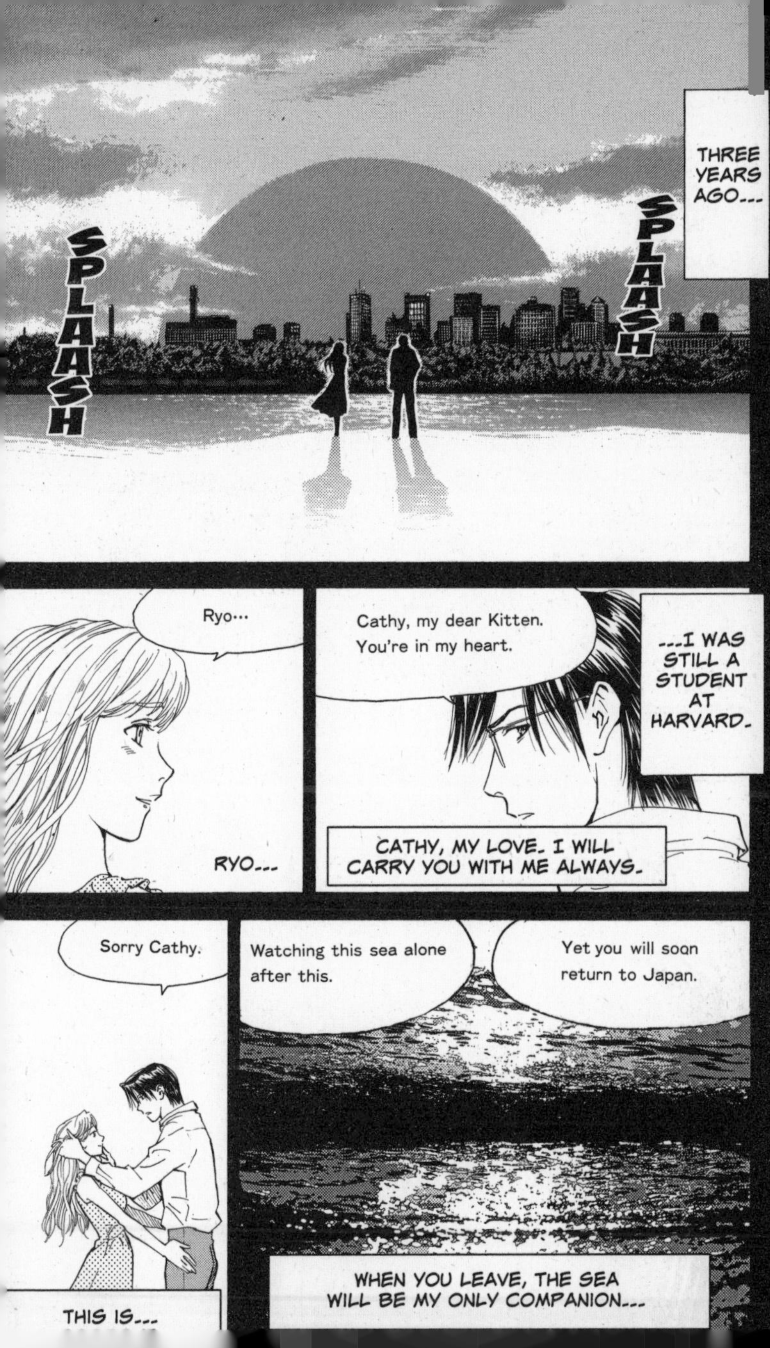
THREE YEARS AGO...
SPLAASH
SPLAASH
...I WAS STILL A STUDENT AT HARVARD.
Cathy, my dear Kitten. You're in my heart.
CATHY, MY LOVE. I WILL CARRY YOU WITH ME ALWAYS.
Ryo...
RYO...
Yet you will soon return to Japan.
Watching this sea alone after this.
WHEN YOU LEAVE, THE SEA WILL BE MY ONLY COMPANION...
Sorry Cathy.
THIS IS...

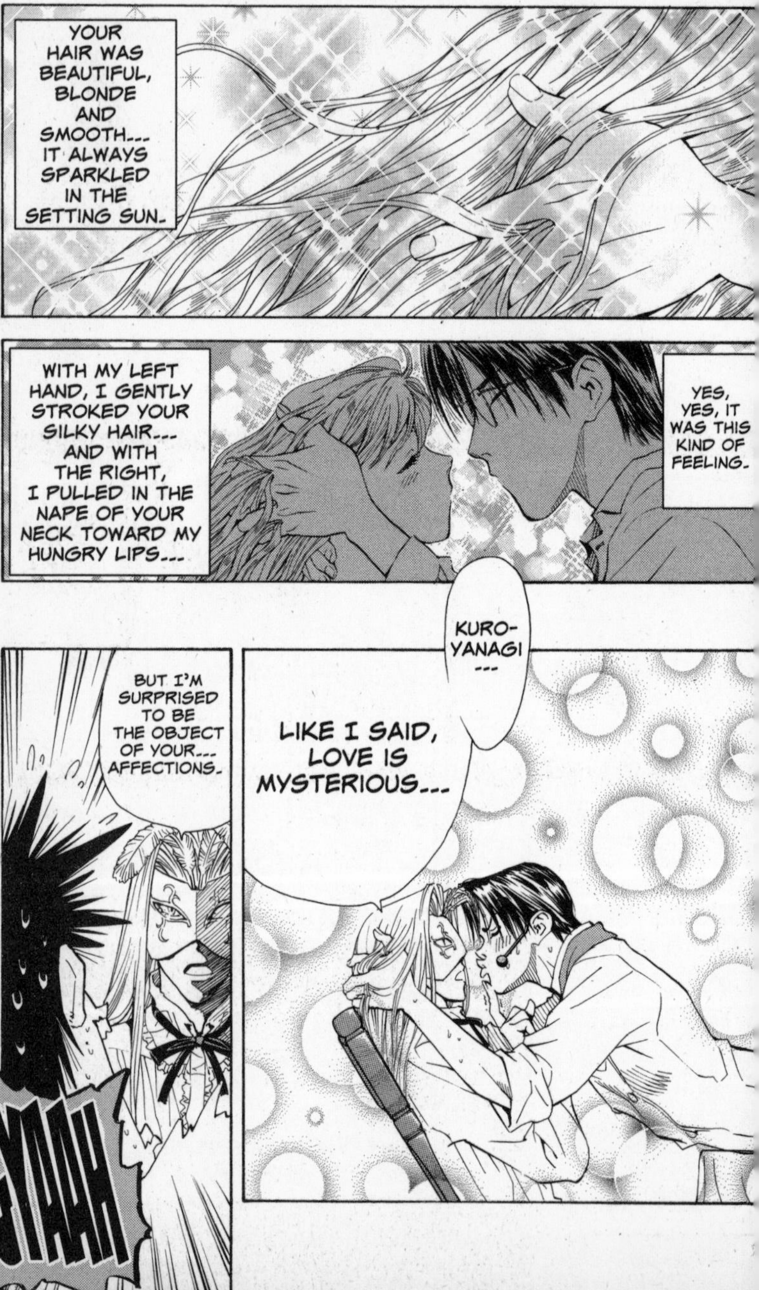
YOUR HAIR WAS BEAUTIFUL, BLONDE AND SMOOTH... IT ALWAYS SPARKLED IN THE SETTING SUN.
YES, YES, IT WAS THIS KIND OF FEELING.
WITH MY LEFT HAND, I GENTLY STROKED YOUR SILKY HAIR... AND WITH THE RIGHT, I PULLED IN THE NAPE OF YOUR NECK TOWARD MY HUNGRY LIPS...
KURO-YANAGI...
LIKE I SAID, LOVE IS MYSTERIOUS...
BUT I'M SURPRISED TO BE THE OBJECT OF YOUR... AFFECTIONS.
GYAAH

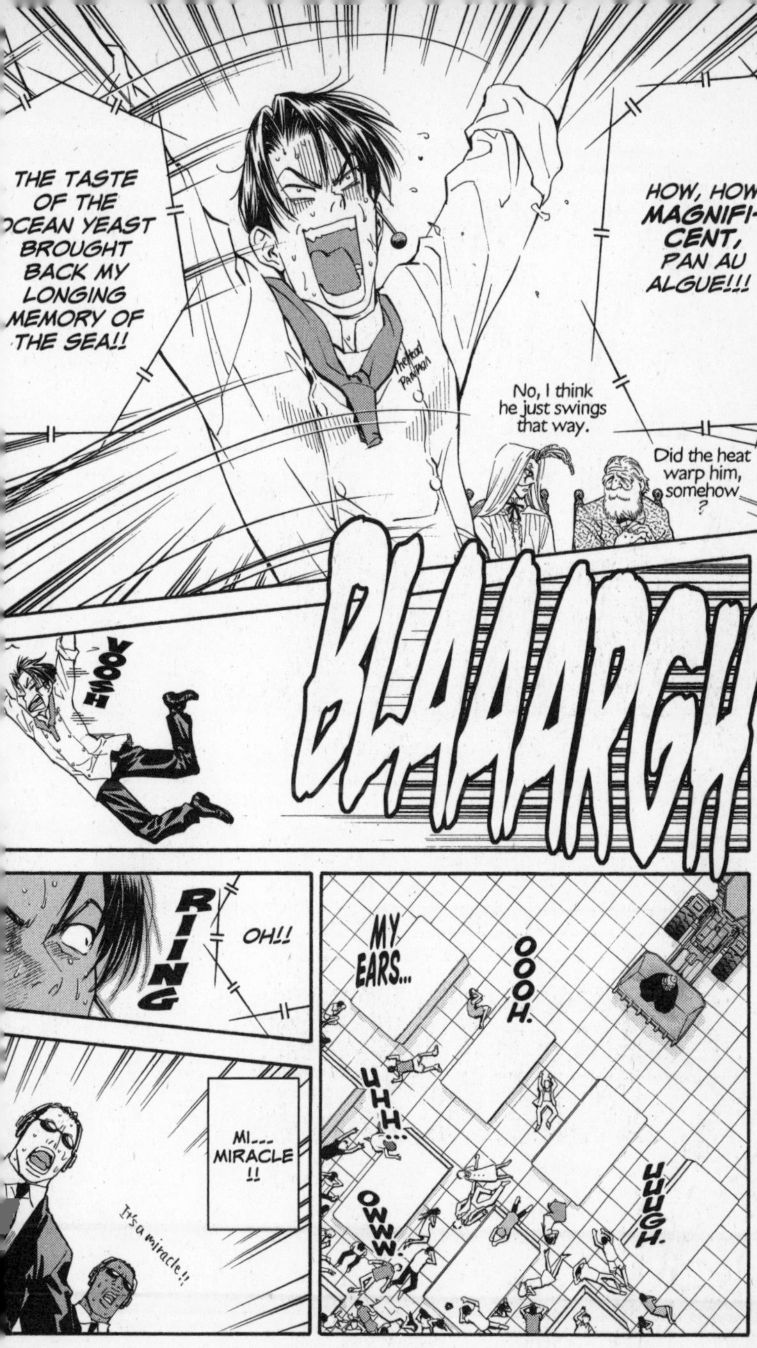
HOW, HOW MAGNIFICENT, PAN AU ALGUE!!!
THE TASTE OF THE OCEAN YEAST BROUGHT BACK MY LONGING MEMORY OF THE SEA!!
Did the heat warp him, somehow?
No, I think he just swings that way.
BLAAARGH
VOOSH
MY EARS...
OOOH.
UHHH...
UUUGH.
OWWW.
RIIING
OH!!
MI... MIRACLE!!
It's a miracle!!

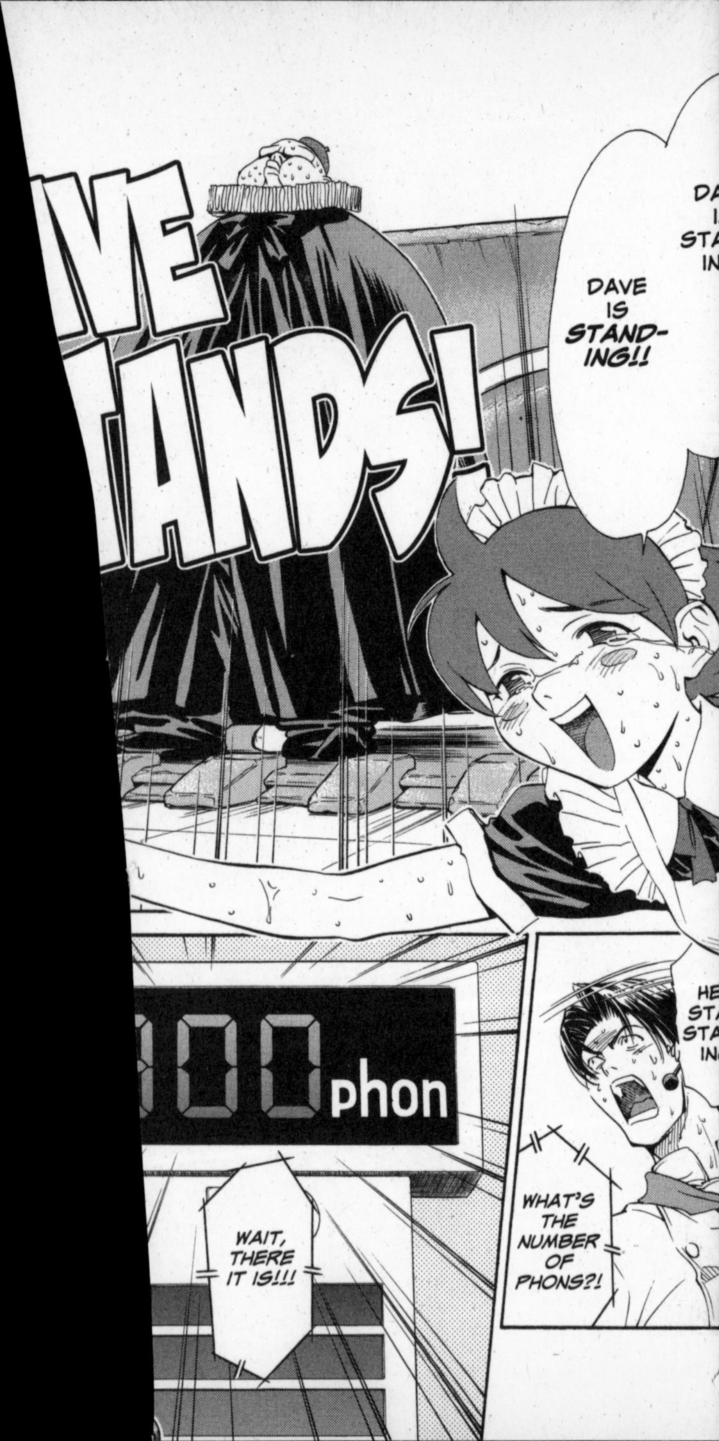
DAVE IS STANDING!!
WHAT'S THE NUMBER OF PHONS?!
phon
WAIT, THERE IT IS!!!

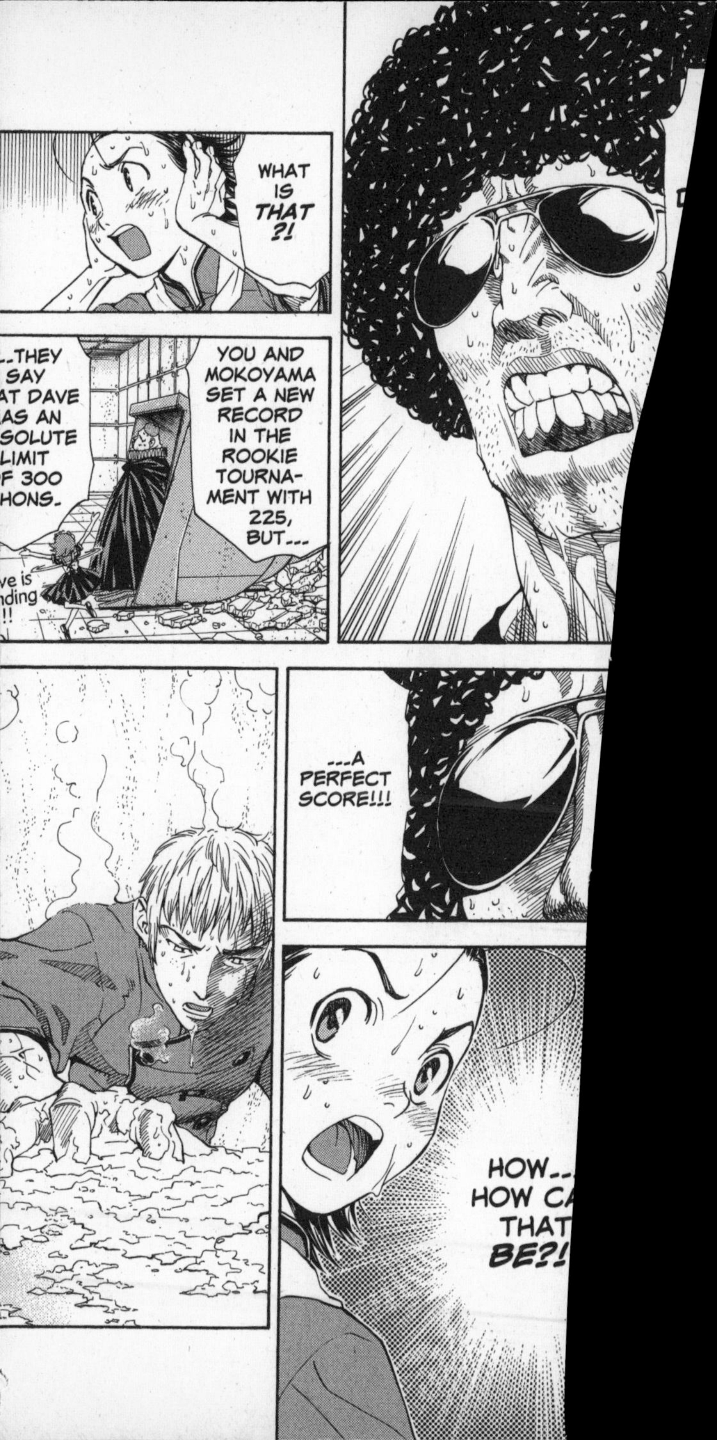

WHAT IS THAT ?!
YOU AND MOKOYAMA SET A NEW RECORD IN THE ROOKIE TOURNA-MENT WITH 225, BUT...
...THEY SAY AT DAVE AS AN SOLUTE LIMIT F 300 HONS.
ve is nding !!
...A PERFECT SCORE!!!
HOW... HOW CA THAT BE?!

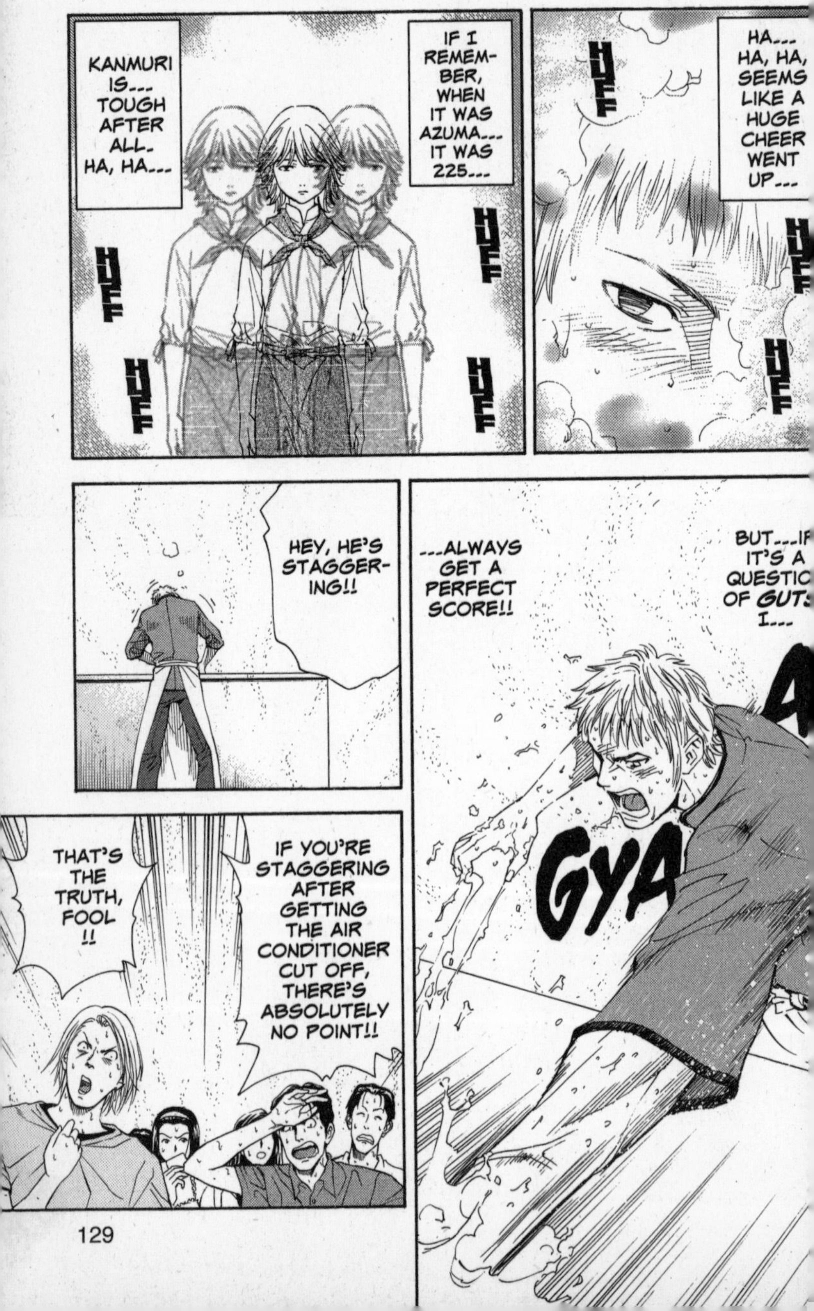
HA... HA, HA, SEEMS LIKE A HUGE CHEER WENT UP...
HUFF
HUFF
HUFF
IF I REMEMBER, WHEN IT WAS AZUMA... IT WAS 225...
KANMURI IS... TOUGH AFTER ALL. HA, HA...
HUFF
HUFF
HUFF
HUFF
BUT...IF IT'S A QUESTIO OF GUTS I...
...ALWAYS GET A PERFECT SCORE!!
GYA
A
HEY, HE'S STAGGERING!!
IF YOU'RE STAGGERING AFTER GETTING THE AIR CONDITIONER CUT OFF, THERE'S ABSOLUTELY NO POINT!!
THAT'S THE TRUTH, FOOL!!

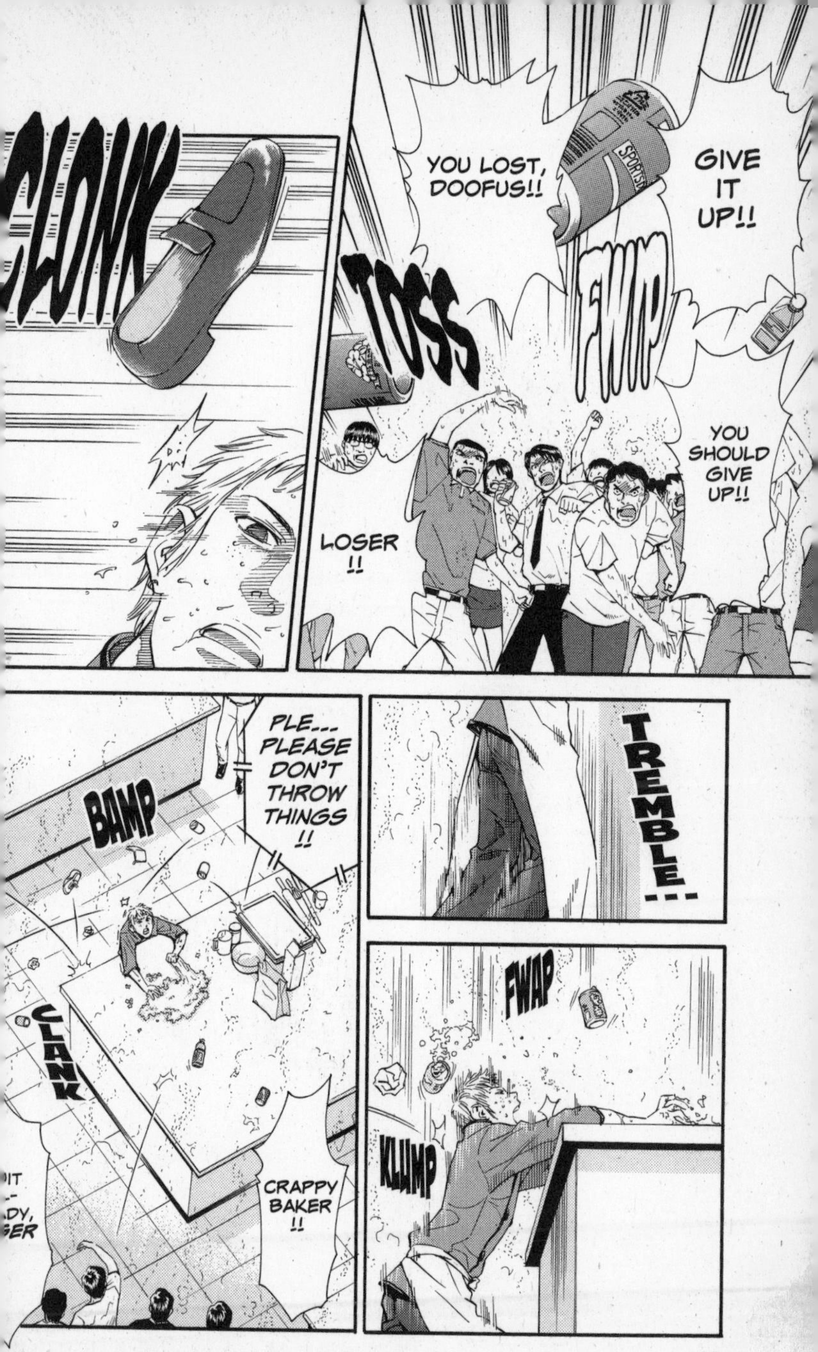
GIVE IT UP!!
YOU LOST, DOOFUS!!
FWIP
TOSS
YOU SHOULD GIVE UP!!
LOSER !!
CLONK
TREMBLE...
FWAP
KLUMP
PLE... PLEASE DON'T THROW THINGS !!
BAMP
CLANK
CRAPPY BAKER !!

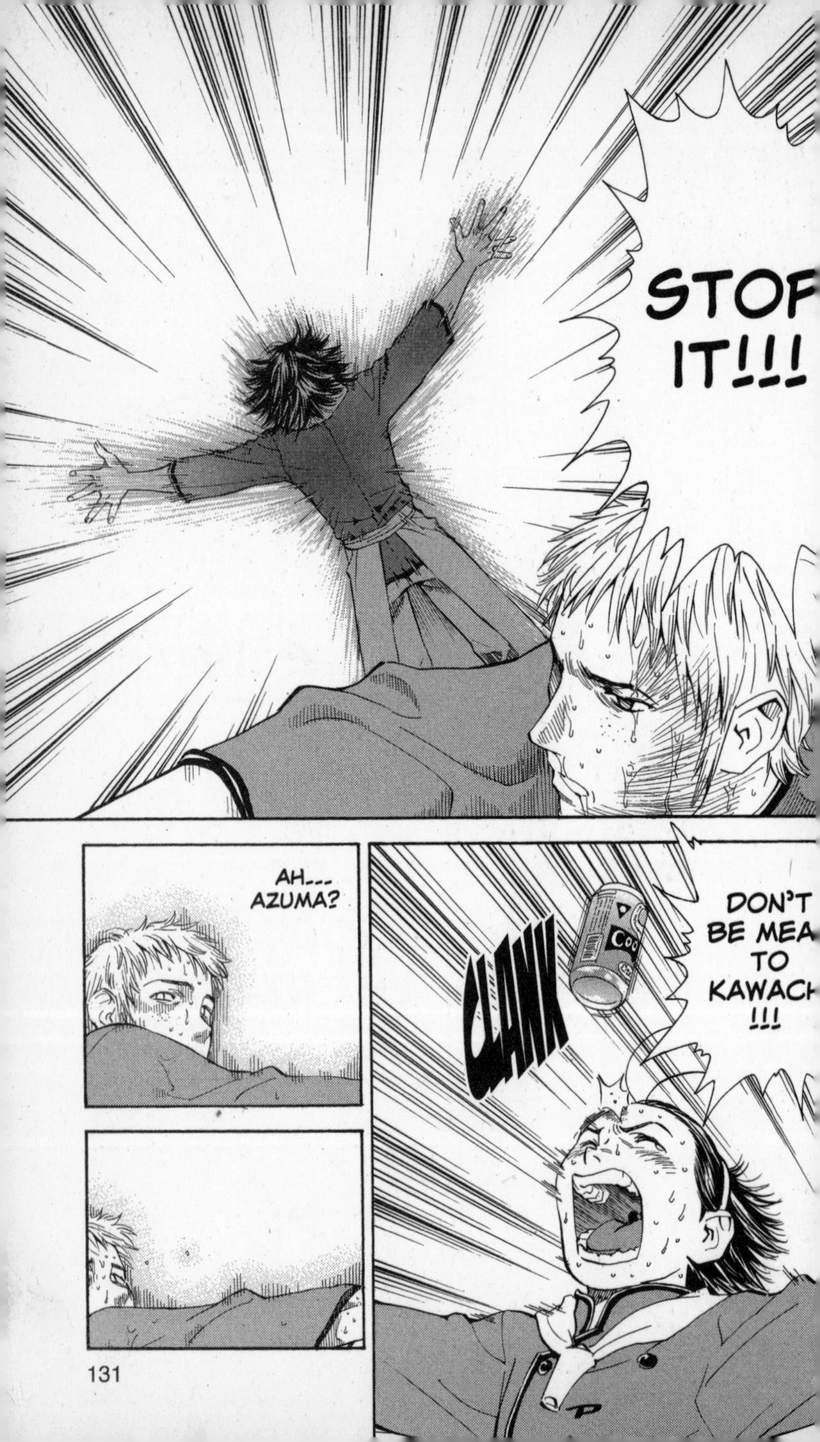
STOF IT!!!
DON'T BE MEA TO KAWACH !!!
CLANK
AH... AZUMA?

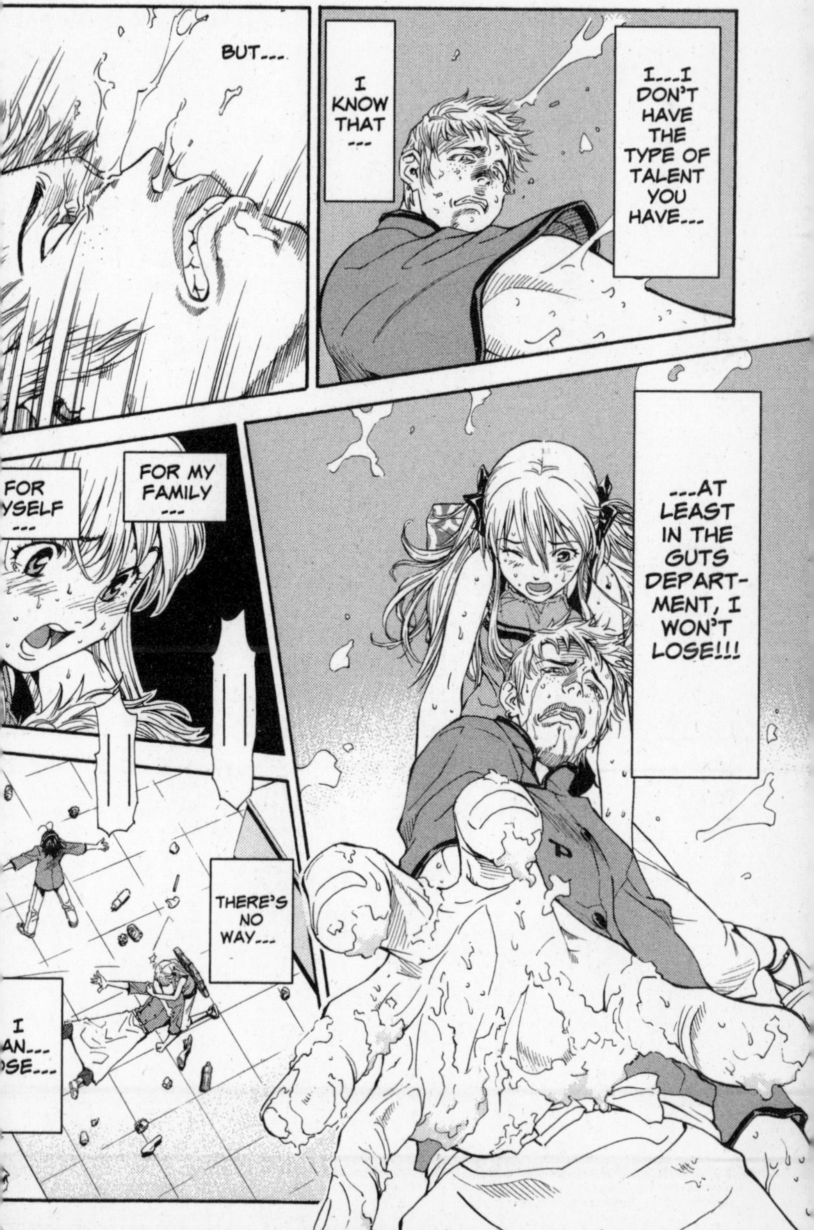
I...I DON'T HAVE THE TYPE OF TALENT YOU HAVE...
I KNOW THAT...
BUT...
...AT LEAST IN THE GUTS DEPARTMENT, I WON'T LOSE!!!
FOR MY FAMILY...
FOR YSELF...
THERE'S NO WAY...
I AN... OSE...

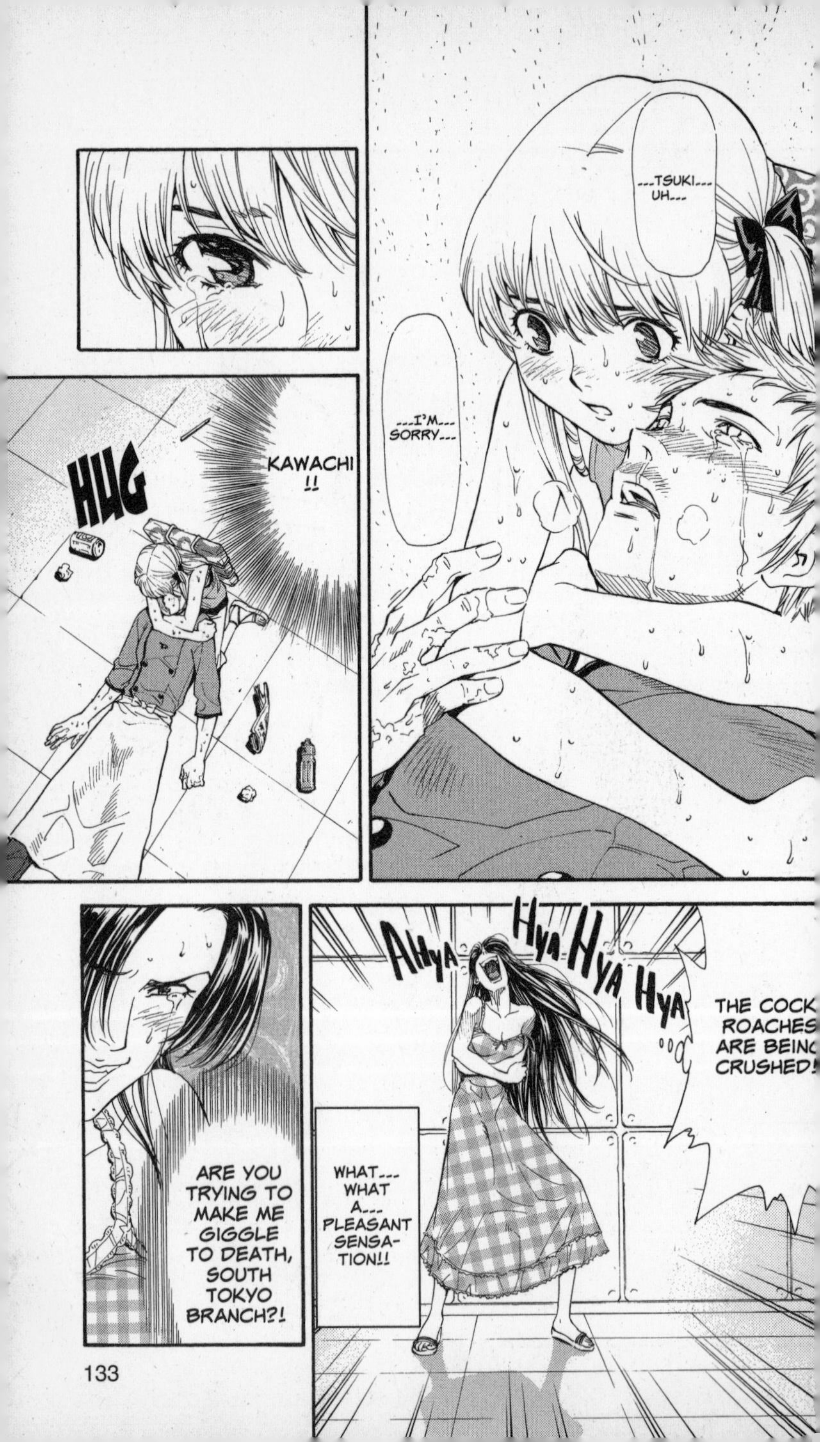
...TSUKI... UH...
...I'M... SORRY...
KAWACHI !!
HUG
THE COCK ROACHES ARE BEING CRUSHED!
AHYA HYA HYA HYA HYA
WHAT... WHAT A... PLEASANT SENSA-TION!!
ARE YOU TRYING TO MAKE ME GIGGLE TO DEATH, SOUTH TOKYO BRANCH?!

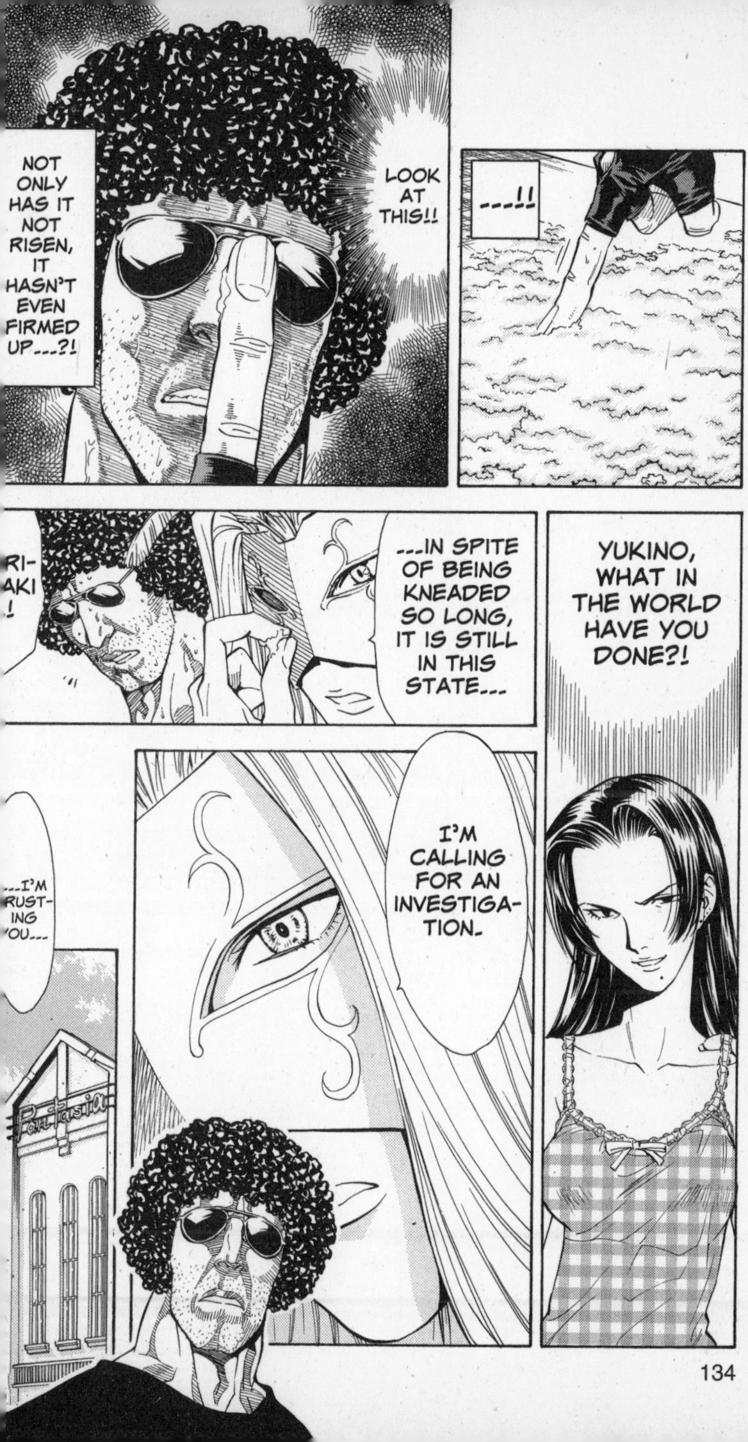
---!!
LOOK AT THIS!!
NOT ONLY HAS IT NOT RISEN, IT HASN'T EVEN FIRMED UP---?!
YUKINO, WHAT IN THE WORLD HAVE YOU DONE?!
---IN SPITE OF BEING KNEADED SO LONG, IT IS STILL IN THIS STATE---
RI-
AKI
!
I'M CALLING FOR AN INVESTIGA-TION.
---I'M
RUST-
ING
OU---

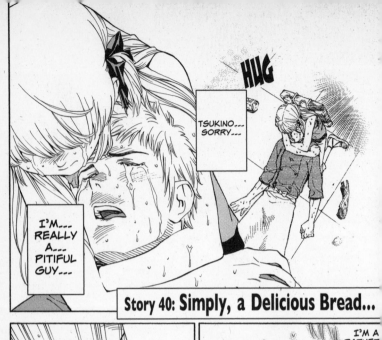

HUG
TSUKINO... SORRY...
I'M... REALLY A... PITIFUL GUY...
Story 40: Simply, a Delicious Bread...
I'M A PATHET HUMAN BEING...
NO...I'M BELOW A MEDIOCRE HUMAN BEING...
I COULDN' PROTEC A SINGLE WOMAN
I'M REALLY SORRY...
SORRY... TSUKINO !!!
GRIPP

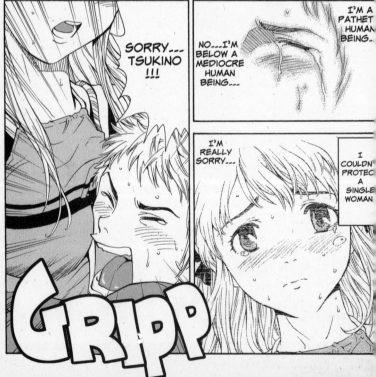

Story 40: Simply, a Delicious Bread...

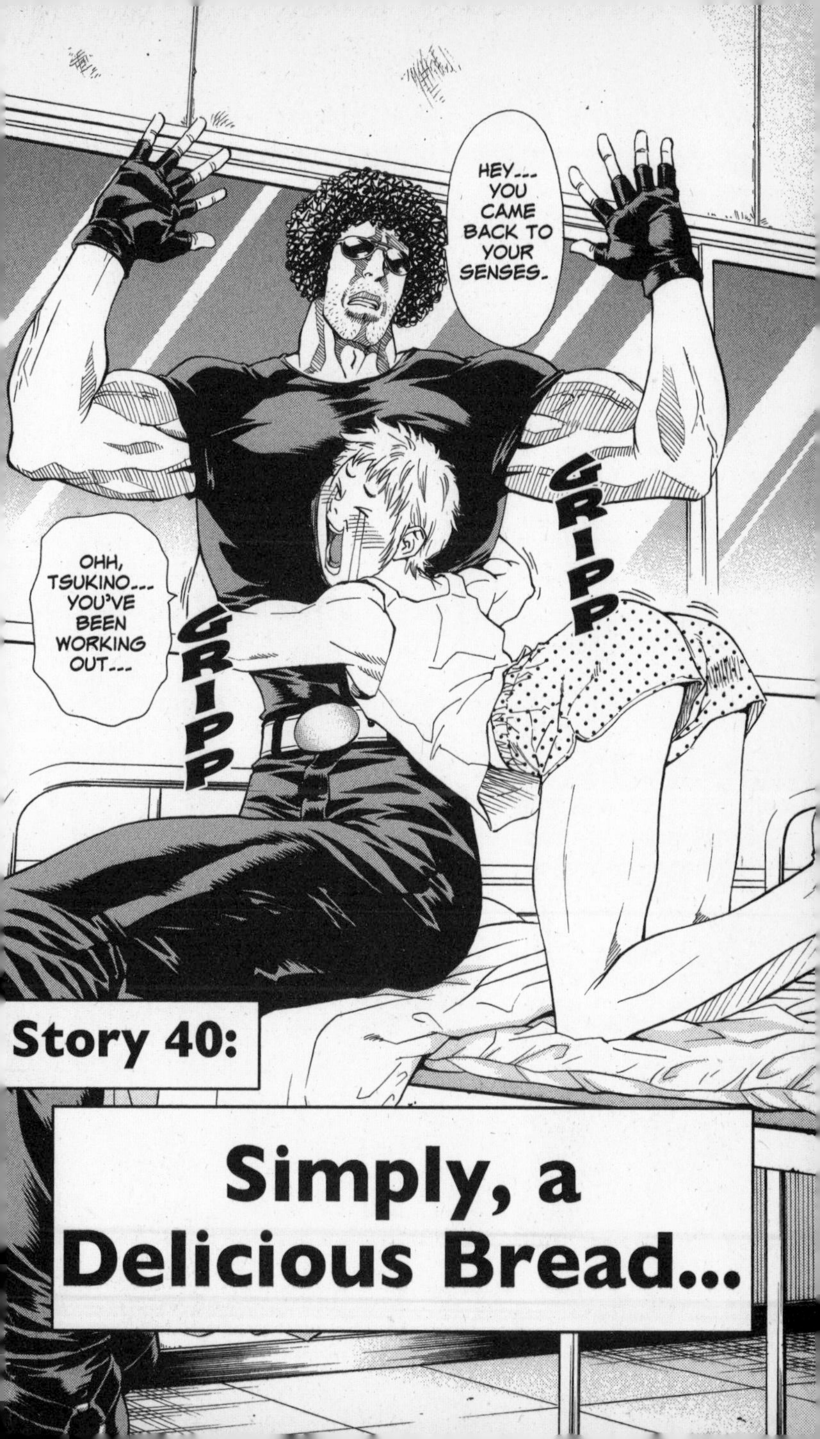
HEY... YOU CAME BACK TO YOUR SENSES.
GRIPP
OHH, TSUKINO... YOU'VE BEEN WORKING OUT...
GRIPP

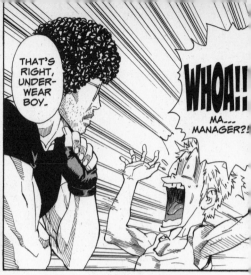

WHOA!!
MA... MANAGER?!
THAT'S RIGHT, UNDER-WEAR BOY.
WHE... WHERE ARE WE?
THE MEDICAL OFFICE.
OH YEAH... I...PASSED OUT DURING THE MATCH...
HOW ABOUT THE OTHERS?
AZUMA'S MATCH IS STARTING SOON. I SENT THEM BAC TO THE KITCHEN.
I SEE.
...ACCORD-ING TO THE DOCTOR, IT SEEMS TO HAVE BEEN A MILD HEAT STROKE.

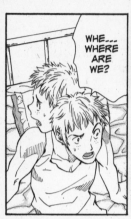

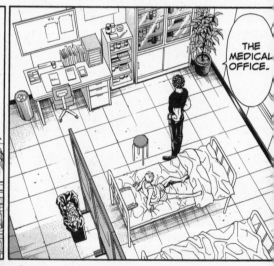

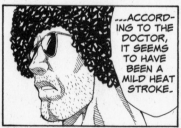

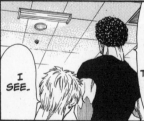

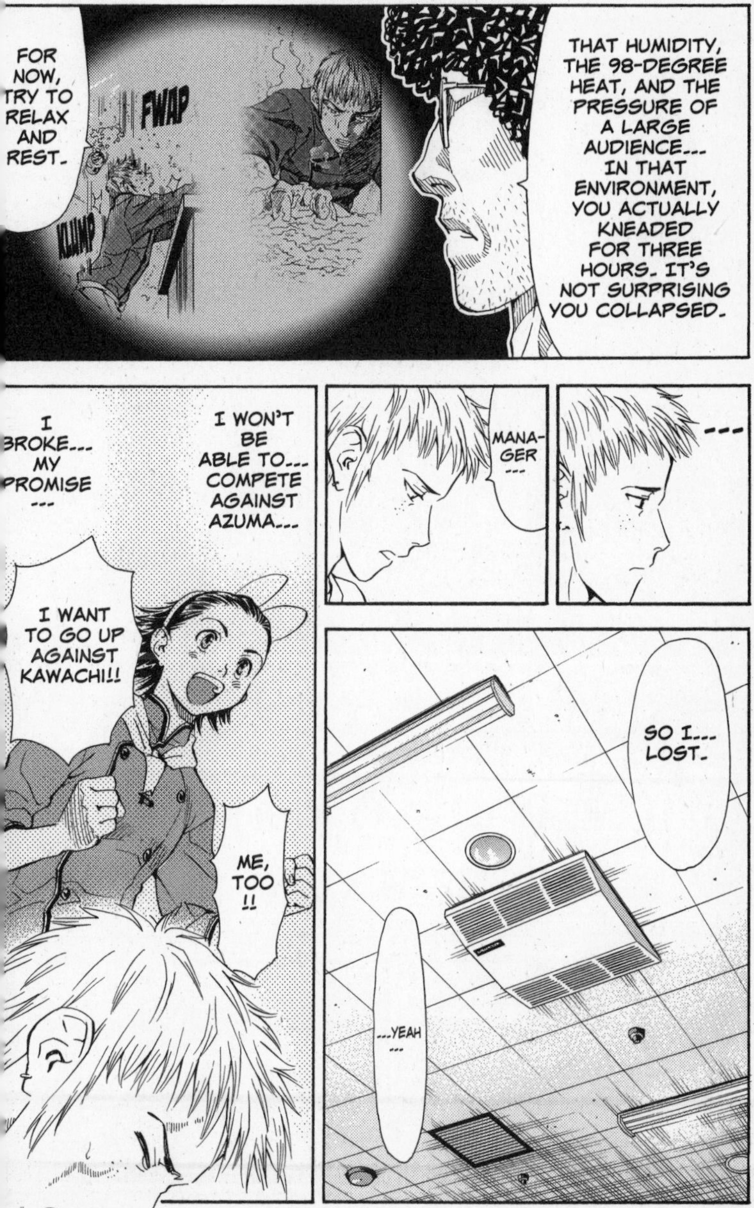
THAT HUMIDITY, THE 98-DEGREE HEAT, AND THE PRESSURE OF A LARGE AUDIENCE... IN THAT ENVIRONMENT, YOU ACTUALLY KNEADED FOR THREE HOURS. IT'S NOT SURPRISING YOU COLLAPSED.
FWAP
KLUMP
FOR NOW, TRY TO RELAX AND REST.
...
MANAGER...
SO I... LOST.
...YEAH...
I WON'T BE ABLE TO... COMPETE AGAINST AZUMA...
I BROKE... MY PROMISE...
I WANT TO GO UP AGAINST KAWACHI!!
ME, TOO!!

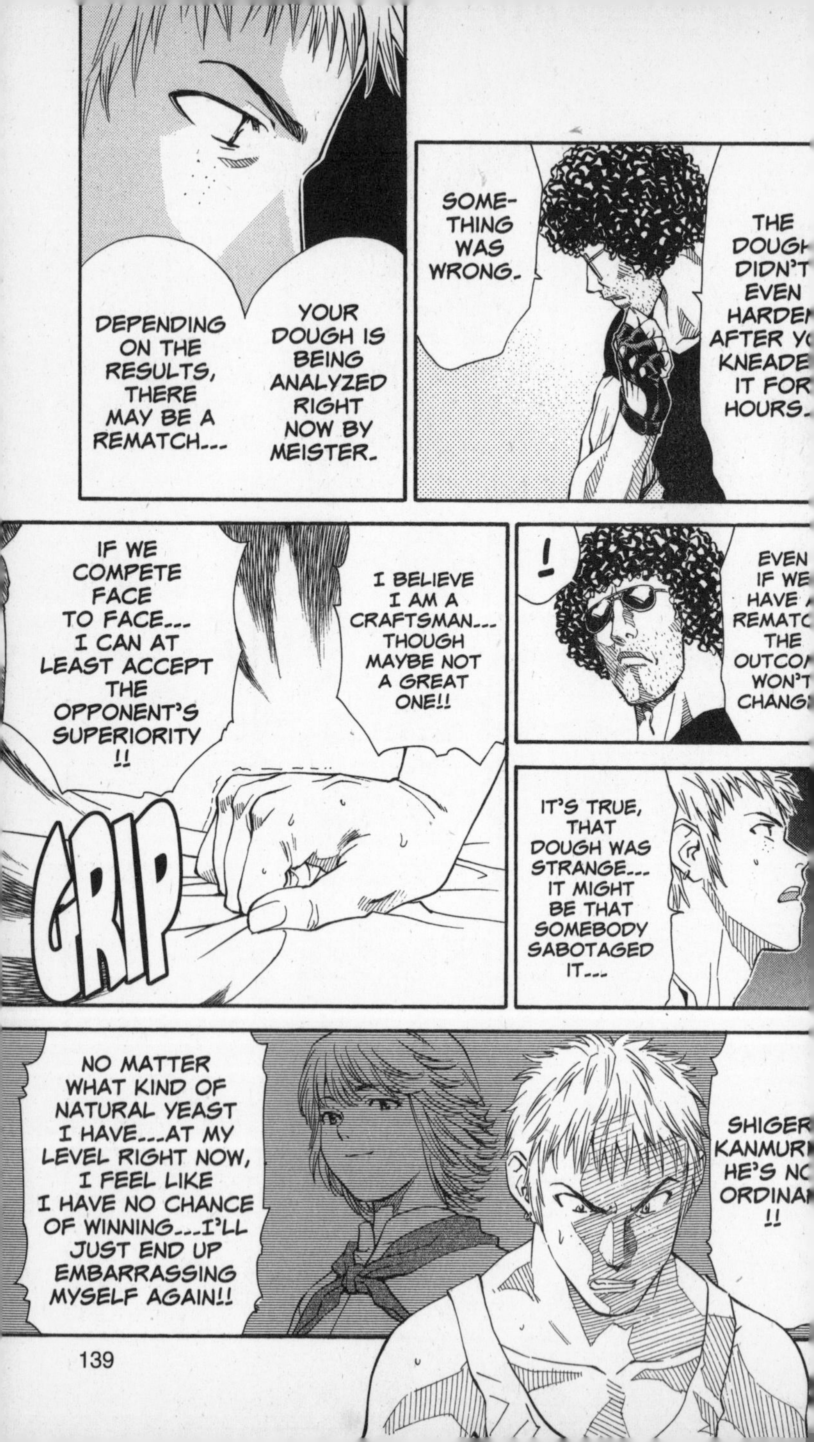

THE DOUGH DIDN'T EVEN HARDEN AFTER YO KNEADE IT FOR HOURS.
SOME-THING WAS WRONG.
YOUR DOUGH IS BEING ANALYZED RIGHT NOW BY MEISTER.
DEPENDING ON THE RESULTS, THERE MAY BE A REMATCH...
EVEN IF WE HAVE REMATC THE OUTCO WON'T CHANG
!
IT'S TRUE, THAT DOUGH WAS STRANGE... IT MIGHT BE THAT SOMEBODY SABOTAGED IT...
I BELIEVE I AM A CRAFTSMAN... THOUGH MAYBE NOT A GREAT ONE!!
IF WE COMPETE FACE TO FACE... I CAN AT LEAST ACCEPT THE OPPONENT'S SUPERIORITY !!
GRIP
SHIGER KANMUR HE'S NO ORDINA !!
NO MATTER WHAT KIND OF NATURAL YEAST I HAVE...AT MY LEVEL RIGHT NOW, I FEEL LIKE I HAVE NO CHANCE OF WINNING...I'LL JUST END UP EMBARRASSING MYSELF AGAIN!!

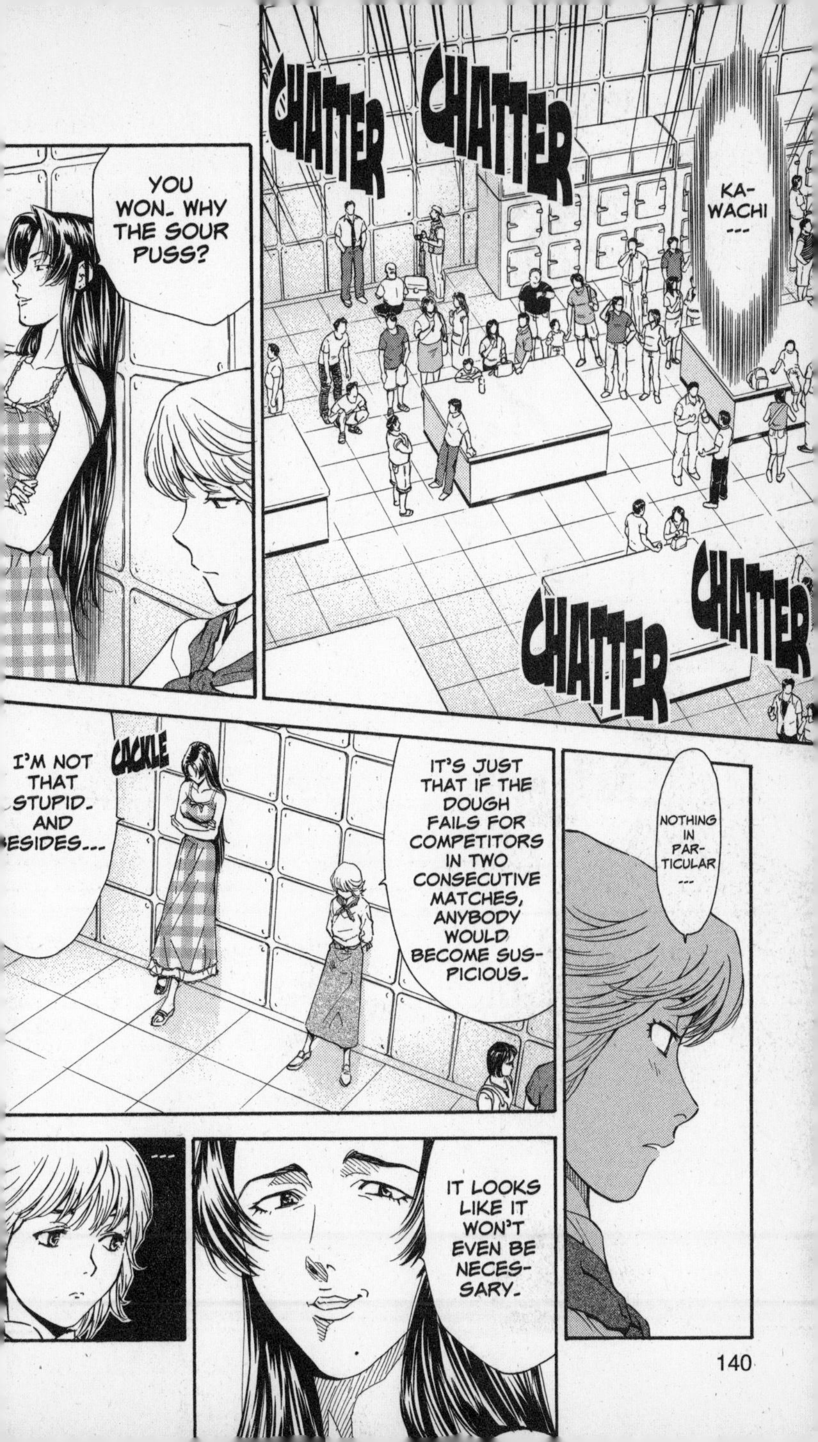
CHATTER CHATTER
KA-WACHI...
CHATTER CHATTER
YOU WON. WHY THE SOUR PUSS?
NOTHING IN PARTICULAR...
IT'S JUST THAT IF THE DOUGH FAILS FOR COMPETITORS IN TWO CONSECUTIVE MATCHES, ANYBODY WOULD BECOME SUSPICIOUS.
CACKLE
I'M NOT THAT STUPID. AND BESIDES...
IT LOOKS LIKE IT WON'T EVEN BE NECESSARY.
...

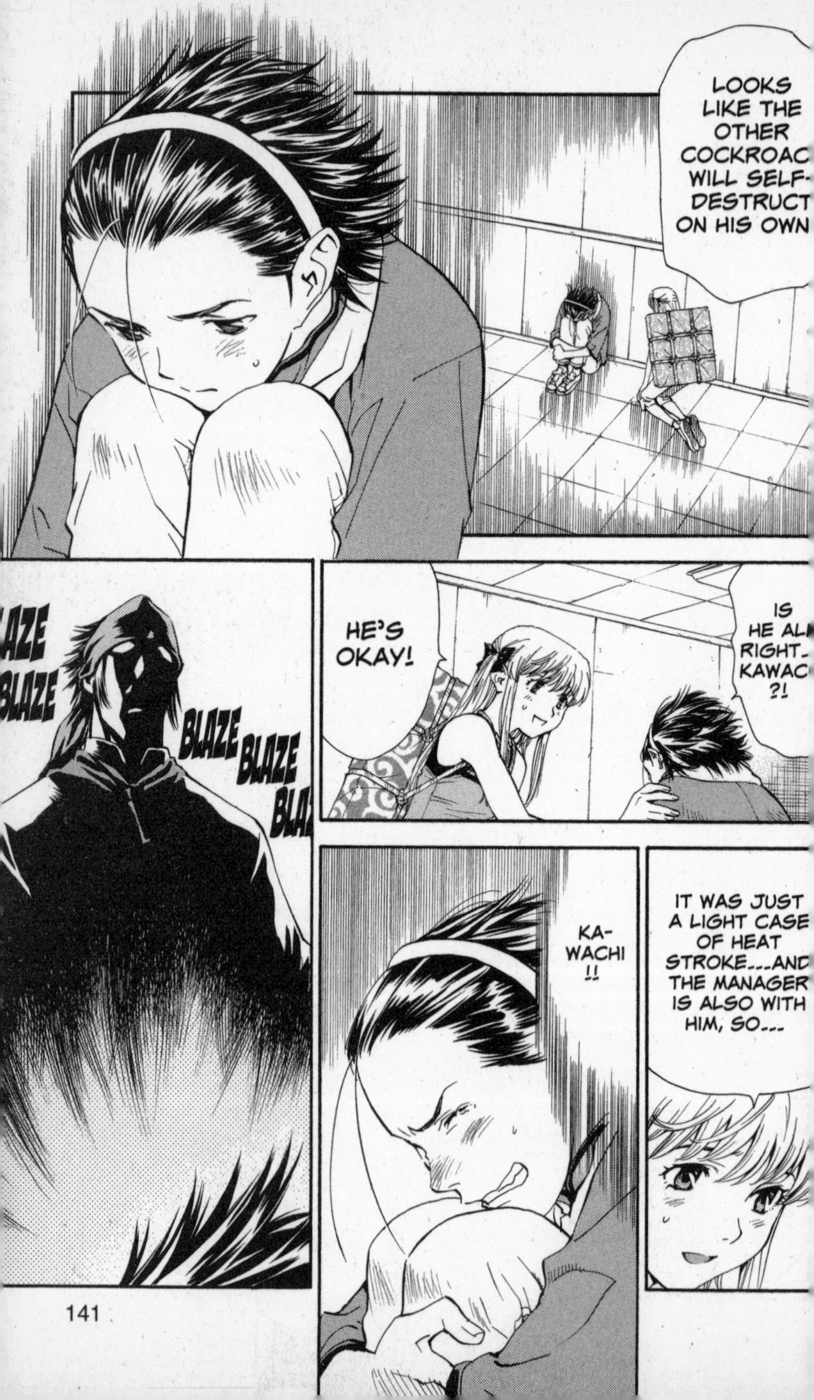
LOOKS LIKE THE OTHER COCKROAC WILL SELF-DESTRUCT ON HIS OWN
IS HE AL RIGHT_ KAWAC ?!
HE'S OKAY!
IT WAS JUST A LIGHT CASE OF HEAT STROKE...AND THE MANAGER IS ALSO WITH HIM, SO...
KA-WACHI !!
AZE BLAZE
BLAZE BLAZE BLA

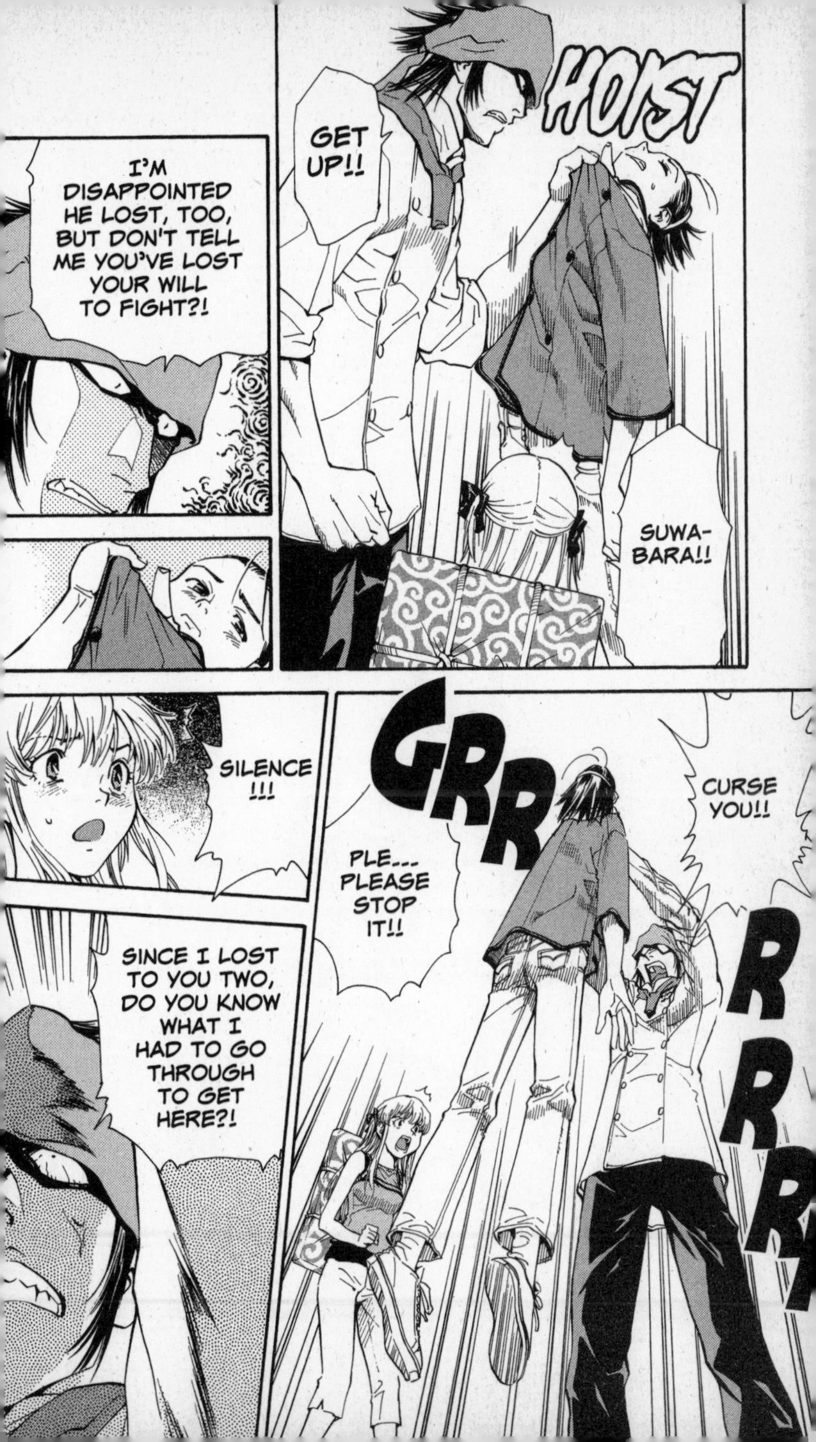
HOIST
GET UP!!
SUWA-BARA!!
I'M DISAPPOINTED HE LOST, TOO, BUT DON'T TELL ME YOU'VE LOST YOUR WILL TO FIGHT?!
CURSE YOU!!
GRR
PLE... PLEASE STOP IT!!
RRRR
SILENCE !!!
SINCE I LOST TO YOU TWO, DO YOU KNOW WHAT I HAD TO GO THROUGH TO GET HERE?!

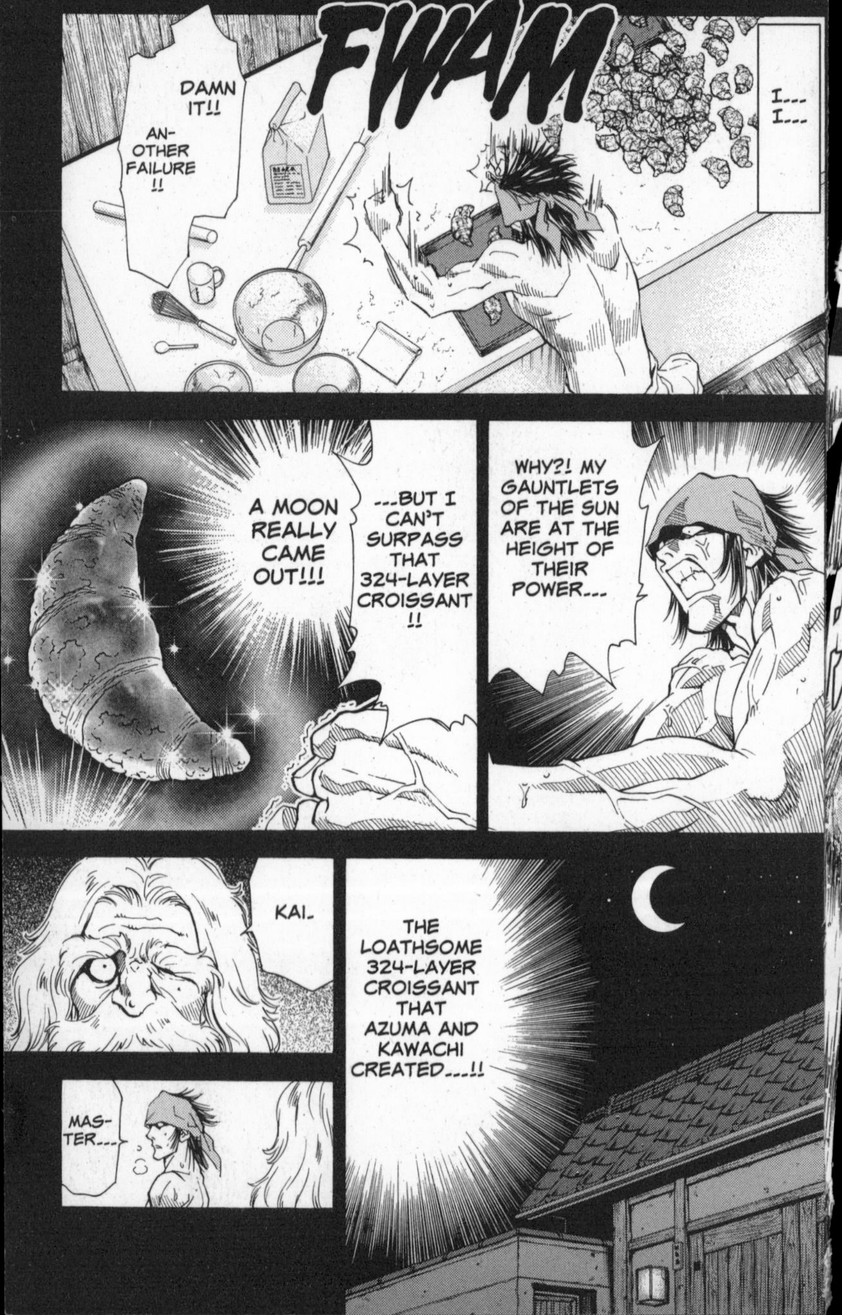
I... I...
FWAM
DAMN IT!!
AN-OTHER FAILURE!!
WHY?! MY GAUNTLETS OF THE SUN ARE AT THE HEIGHT OF THEIR POWER...
...BUT I CAN'T SURPASS THAT 324-LAYER CROISSANT!!
A MOON REALLY CAME OUT!!!
THE LOATHSOME 324-LAYER CROISSANT THAT AZUMA AND KAWACHI CREATED...!!
KAI.
MAS-TER...

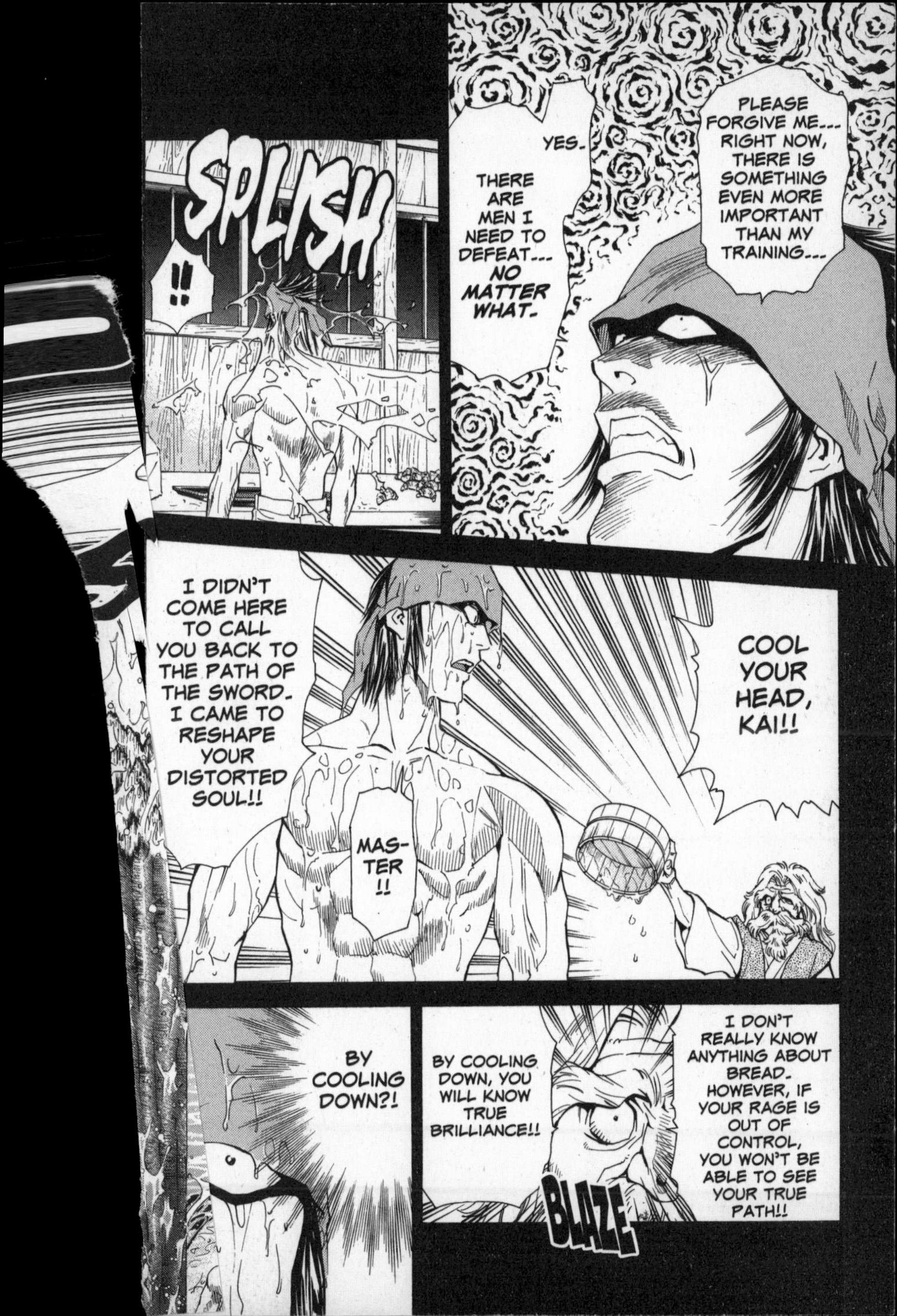
PLEASE FORGIVE ME... RIGHT NOW, THERE IS SOMETHING EVEN MORE IMPORTANT THAN MY TRAINING...
YES.
THERE ARE MEN I NEED TO DEFEAT... NO MATTER WHAT.
SPLISH
!!
COOL YOUR HEAD, KAI!!
I DIDN'T COME HERE TO CALL YOU BACK TO THE PATH OF THE SWORD. I CAME TO RESHAPE YOUR DISTORTED SOUL!!
MAS-TER!!
I DON'T REALLY KNOW ANYTHING ABOUT BREAD. HOWEVER, IF YOUR RAGE IS OUT OF CONTROL, YOU WON'T BE ABLE TO SEE YOUR TRUE PATH!!
BY COOLING DOWN, YOU WILL KNOW TRUE BRILLIANCE!!
BLAZE
BY COOLING DOWN?!

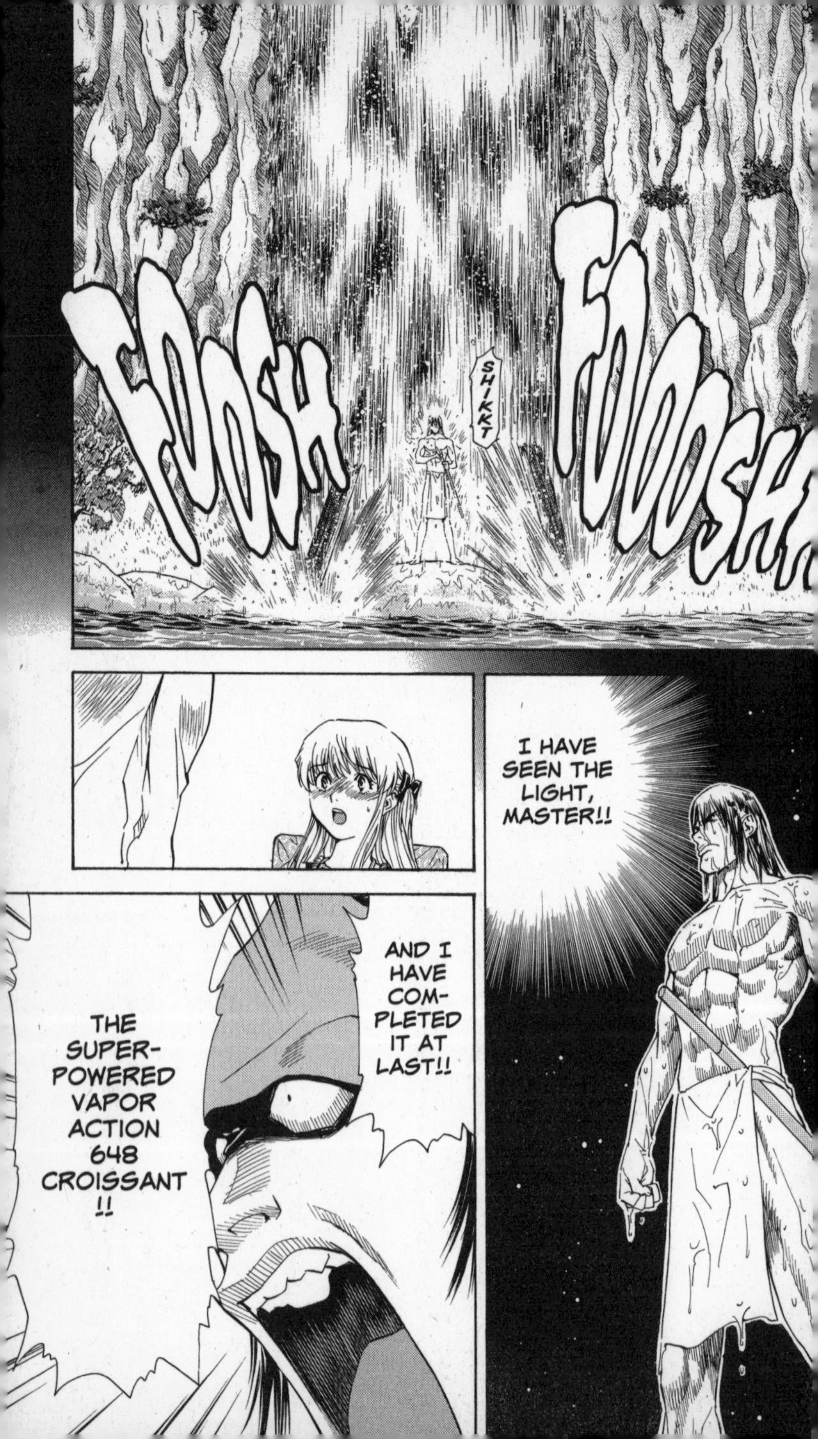

FOOOSH...
SHIKKT
FOOSH
I HAVE SEEN THE LIGHT, MASTER!!
AND I HAVE COM-PLETED IT AT LAST!!
THE SUPER-POWERED VAPOR ACTION 648 CROISSANT!!

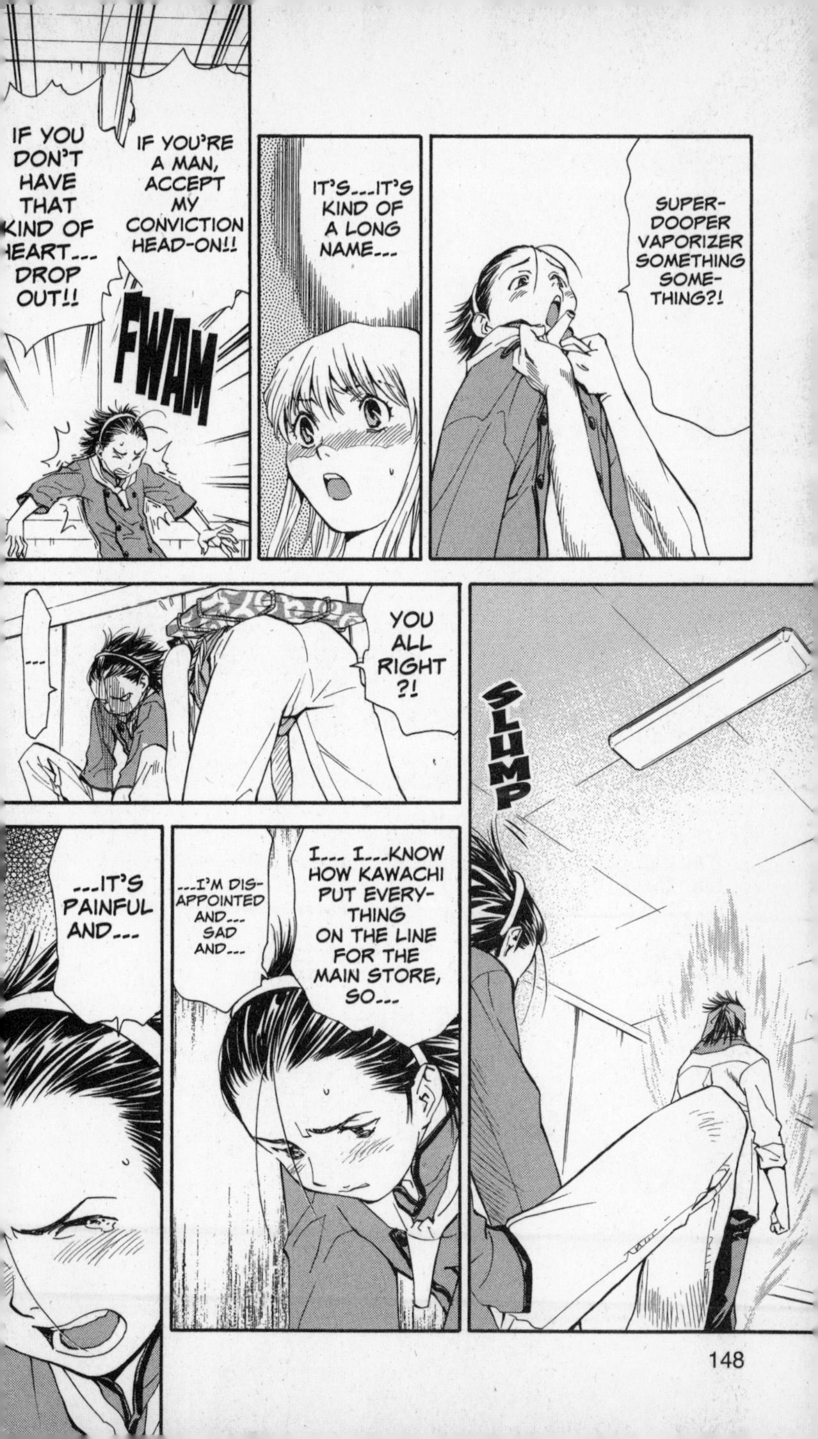
SUPER-DOOPER VAPORIZER SOMETHING SOME-THING?!
IT'S... IT'S KIND OF A LONG NAME...
IF YOU'RE A MAN, ACCEPT MY CONVICTION HEAD-ON!!
IF YOU DON'T HAVE THAT KIND OF HEART... DROP OUT!!
FWAM
SLUMP
YOU ALL RIGHT?!
...
I... I...KNOW HOW KAWACHI PUT EVERY-THING ON THE LINE FOR THE MAIN STORE, SO...
...I'M DIS-APPOINTED AND... SAD AND...
...IT'S PAINFUL AND...

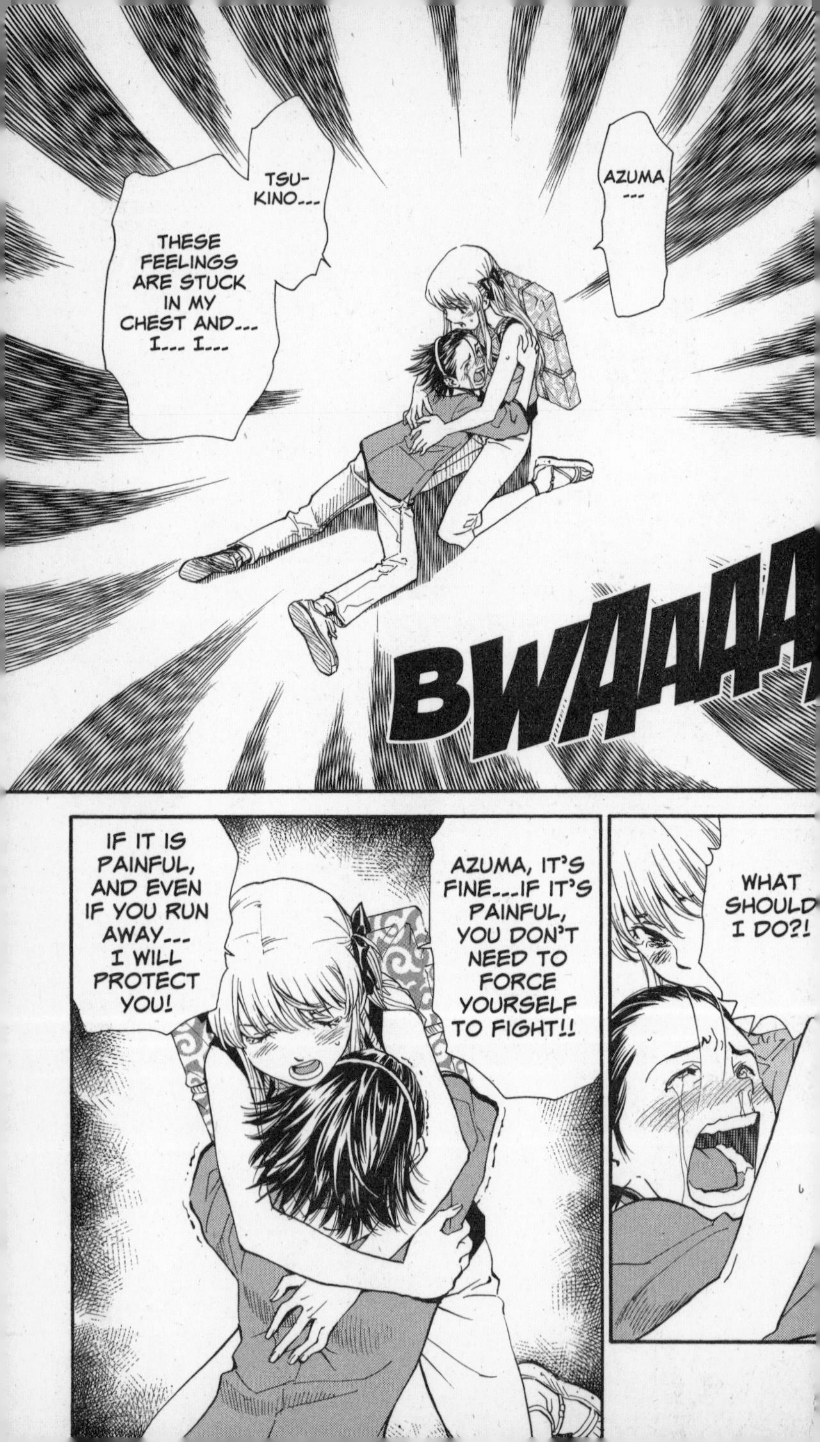
AZUMA ---
TSU-KINO...
THESE FEELINGS ARE STUCK IN MY CHEST AND... I... I...
BWAAAA
WHAT SHOULD I DO?!
AZUMA, IT'S FINE...IF IT'S PAINFUL, YOU DON'T NEED TO FORCE YOURSELF TO FIGHT!!
IF IT IS PAINFUL, AND EVEN IF YOU RUN AWAY... I WILL PROTECT YOU!

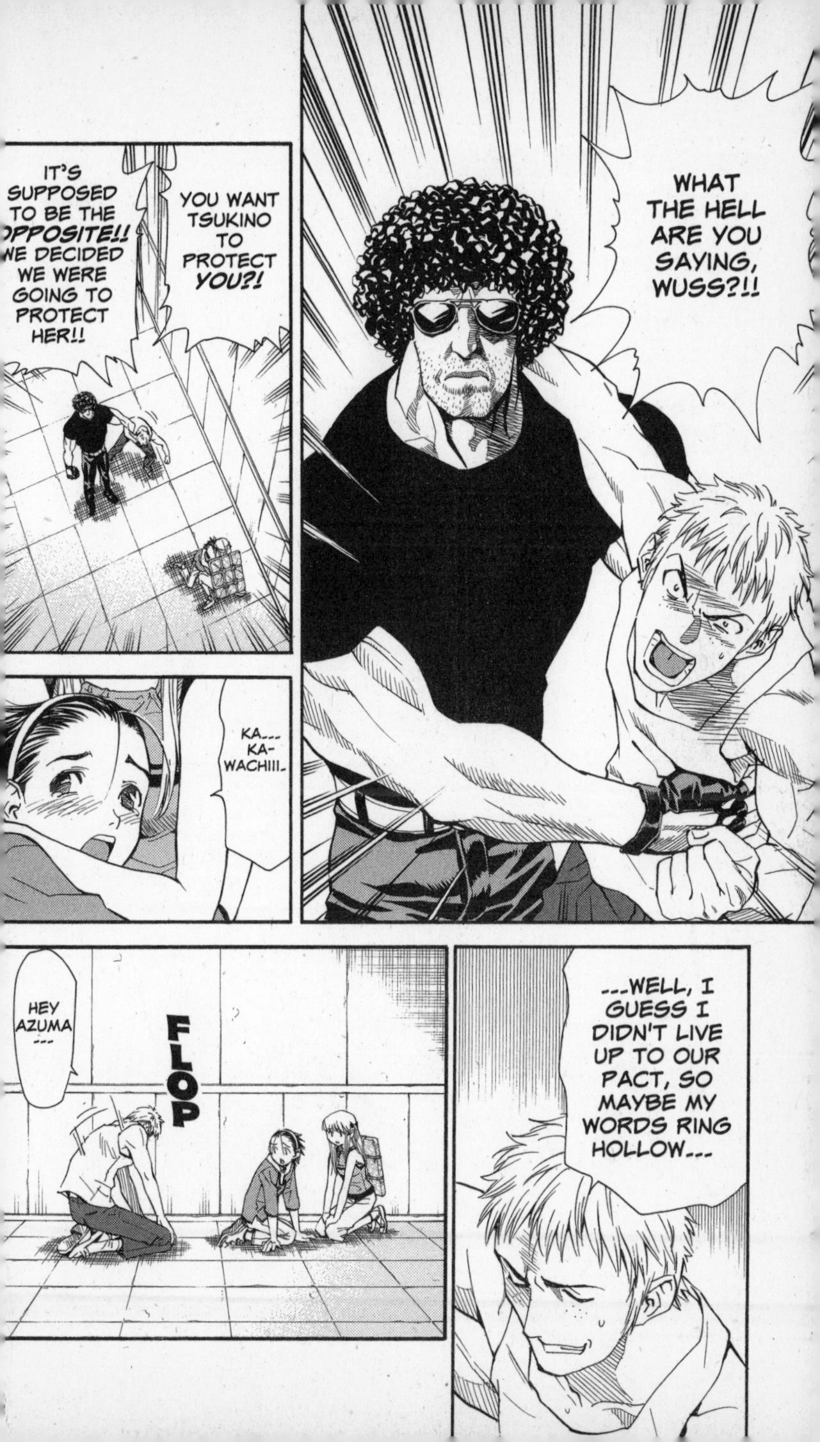
WHAT THE HELL ARE YOU SAYING, WUSS?!!
YOU WANT TSUKINO TO PROTECT YOU?!
IT'S SUPPOSED TO BE THE OPPOSITE!! WE DECIDED WE WERE GOING TO PROTECT HER!!
KA... KA-WACHIII.
...WELL, I GUESS I DIDN'T LIVE UP TO OUR PACT, SO MAYBE MY WORDS RING HOLLOW...
FLOP
HEY AZUMA...

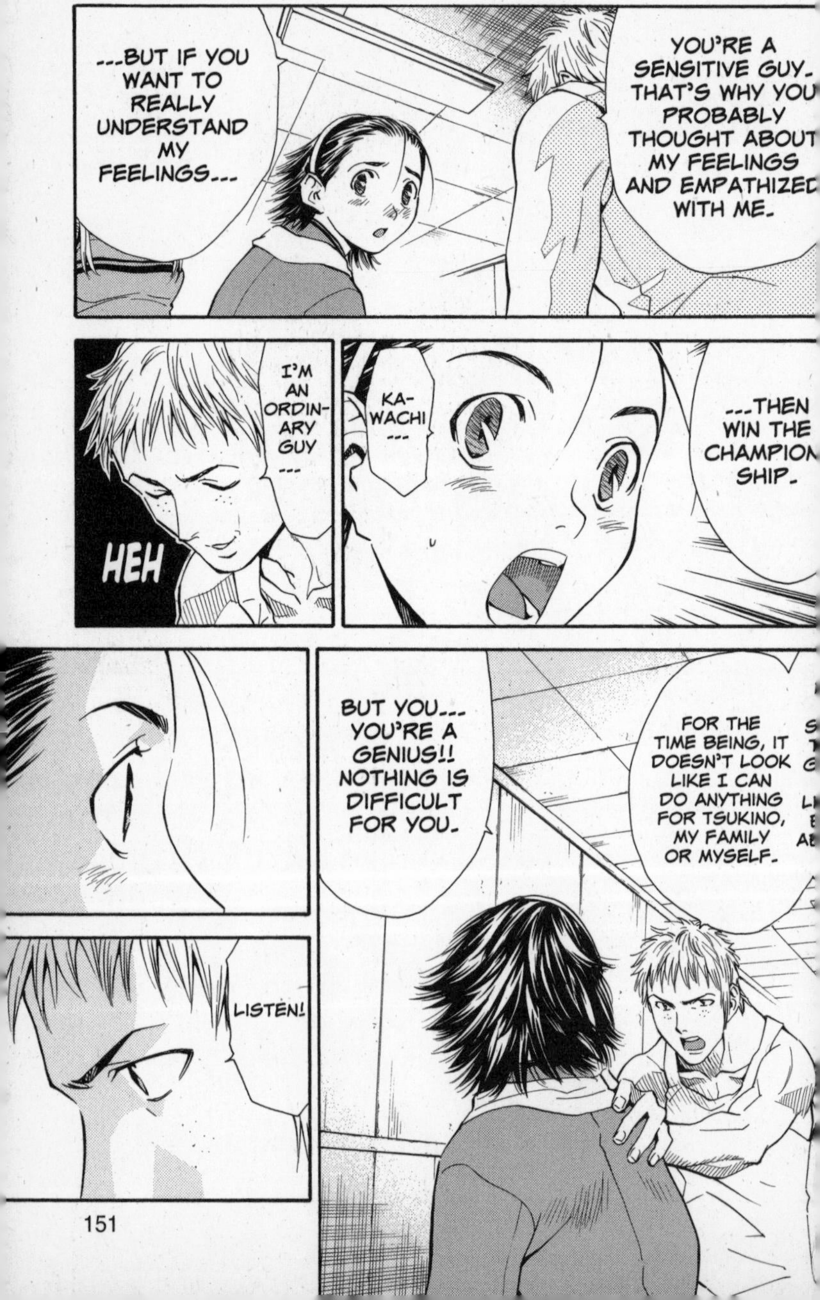

YOU'RE A SENSITIVE GUY. THAT'S WHY YOU PROBABLY THOUGHT ABOUT MY FEELINGS AND EMPATHIZED WITH ME.
...BUT IF YOU WANT TO REALLY UNDERSTAND MY FEELINGS...
...THEN WIN THE CHAMPIONSHIP.
KA-WACHI...
I'M AN ORDINARY GUY...
HEH
FOR THE TIME BEING, IT DOESN'T LOOK LIKE I CAN DO ANYTHING FOR TSUKINO, MY FAMILY OR MYSELF.
BUT YOU... YOU'RE A GENIUS!! NOTHING IS DIFFICULT FOR YOU.
LISTEN!

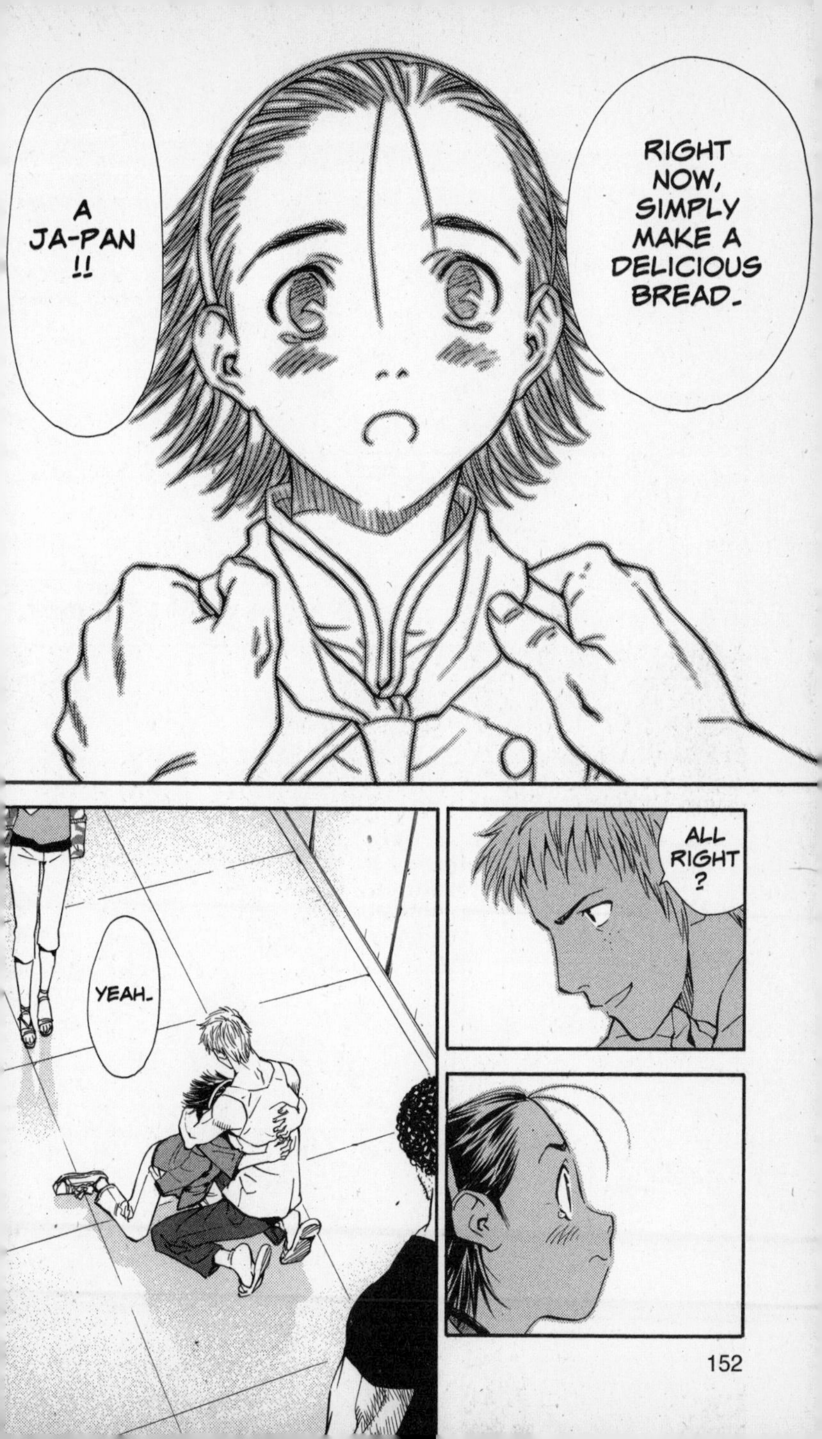
RIGHT NOW, SIMPLY MAKE A DELICIOUS BREAD.
A JA-PAN!!
ALL RIGHT?
YEAH.

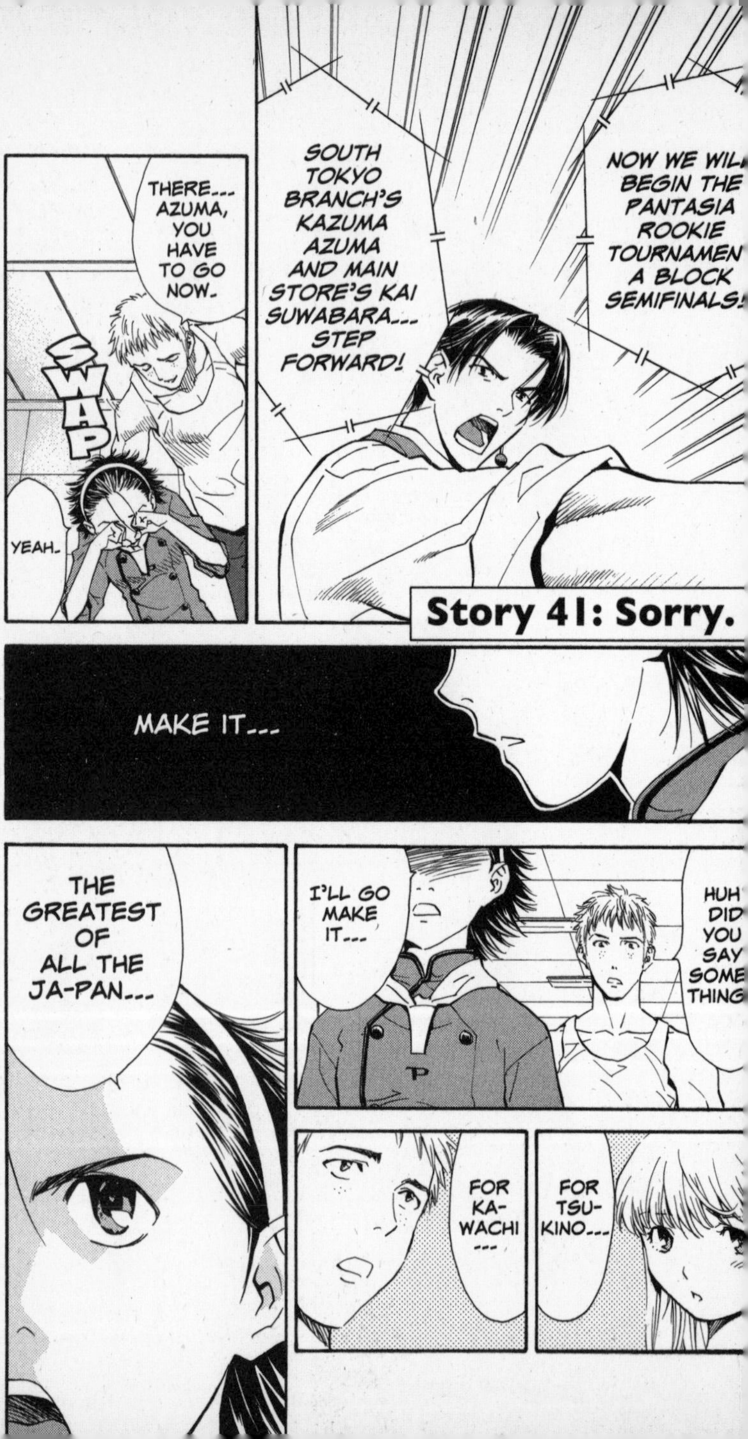
NOW WE WIL BEGIN THE PANTASIA ROOKIE TOURNAMEN A BLOCK SEMIFINALS!
SOUTH TOKYO BRANCH'S KAZUMA AZUMA AND MAIN STORE'S KAI SUWABARA... STEP FORWARD!
Story 41: Sorry.
THERE... AZUMA, YOU HAVE TO GO NOW.
SWAP
YEAH.
MAKE IT...
HUH DID YOU SAY SOME THING
I'LL GO MAKE IT...
FOR TSU-KINO...
FOR KA-WACHI...
THE GREATEST OF ALL THE JA-PAN...

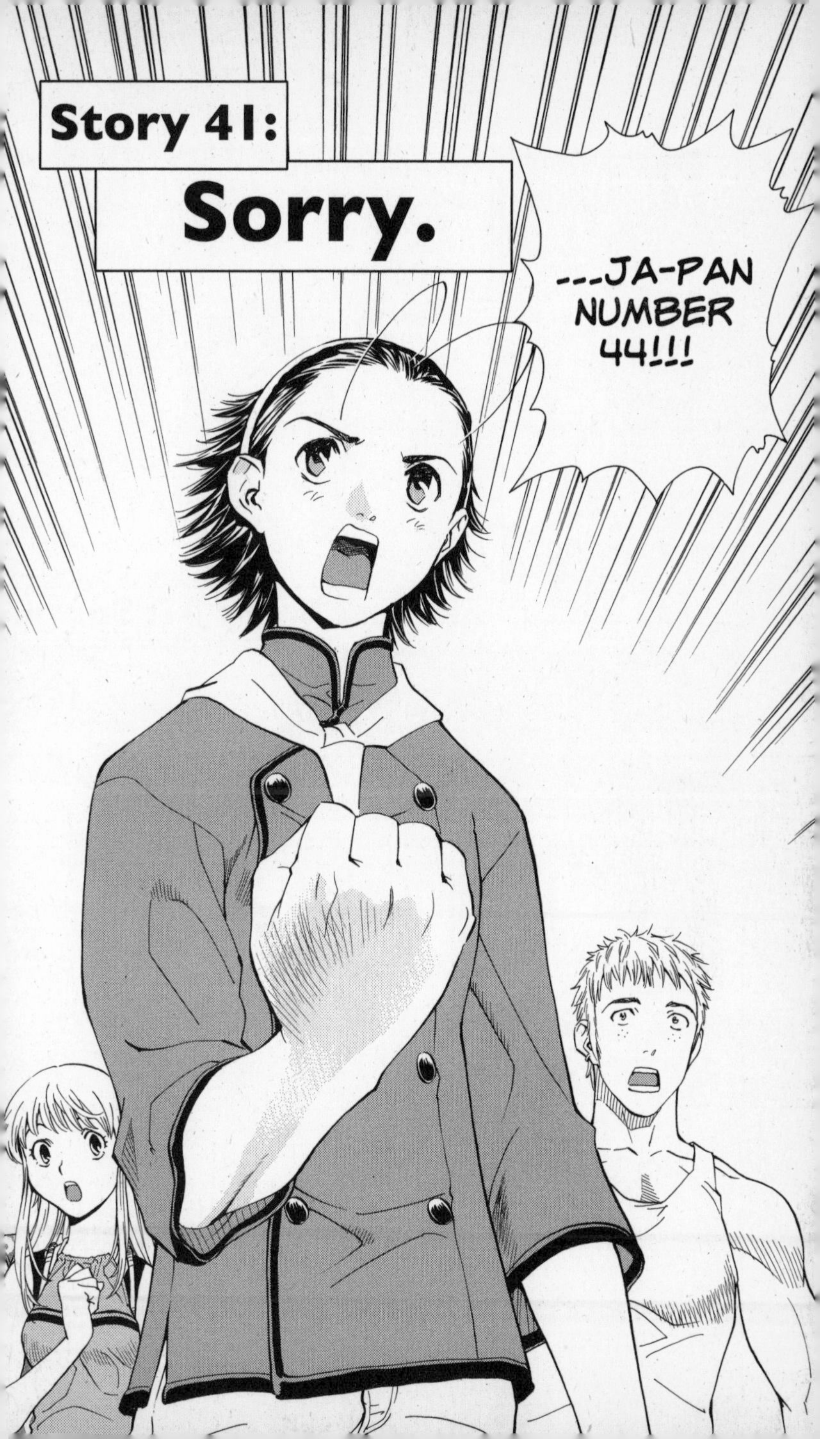
Story 41:
Sorry.
---JA-PAN NUMBER 44!!!

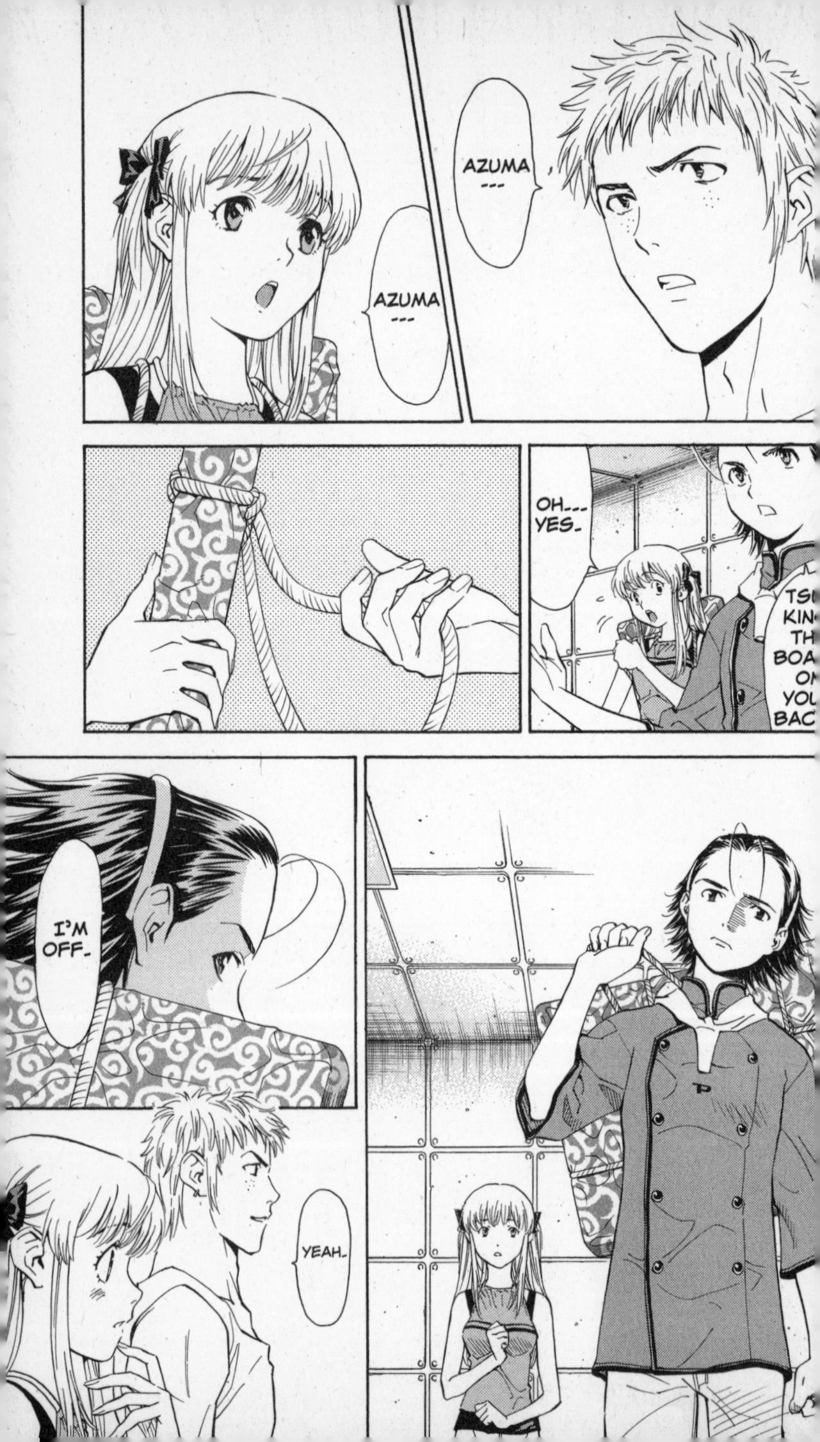
AZUMA ---
AZUMA ---
TS KIN TH BOA O YO BAC
OH... YES.
I'M OFF.
YEAH.

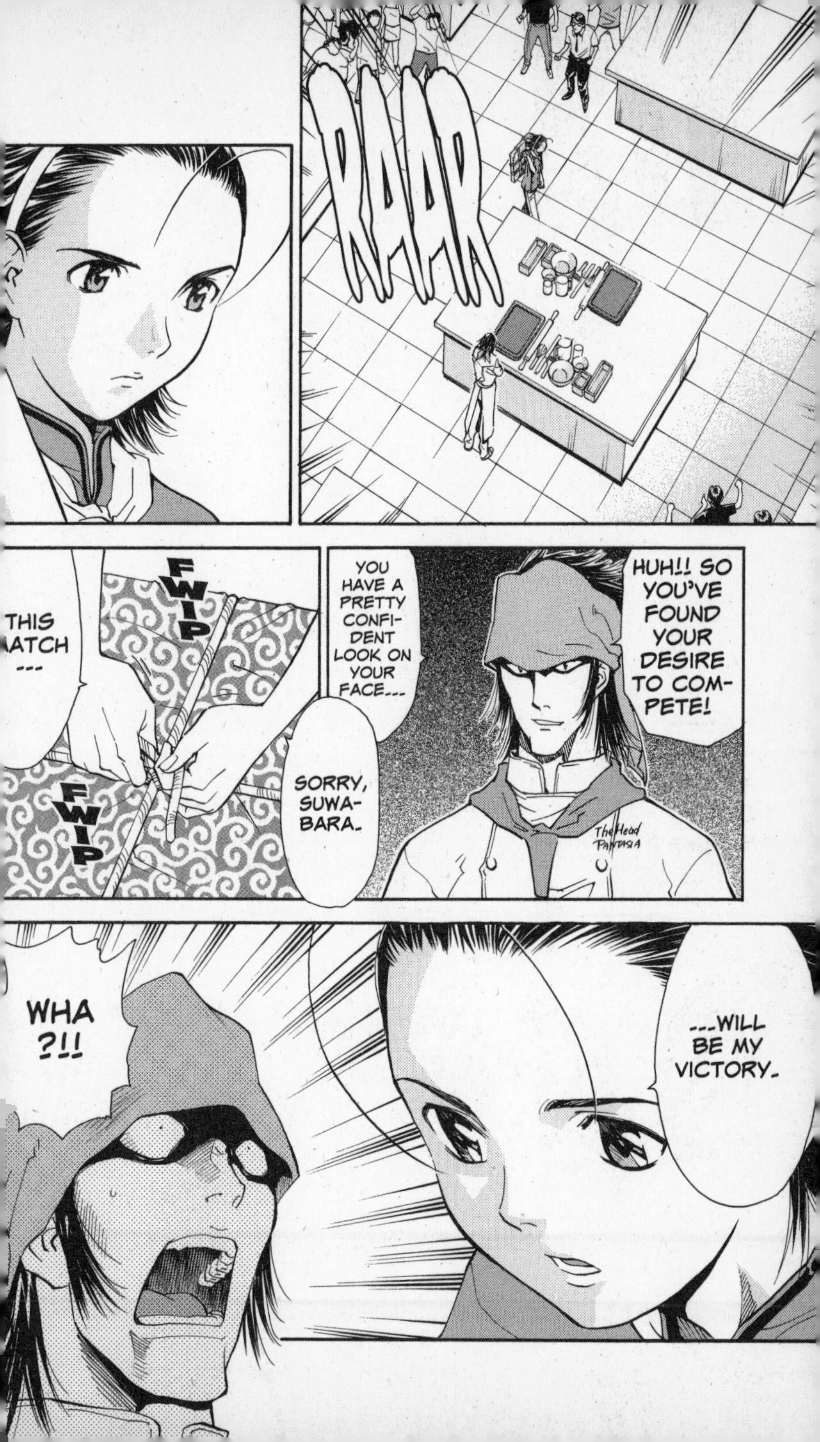
RAAR
HUH!! SO YOU'VE FOUND YOUR DESIRE TO COMPETE!
YOU HAVE A PRETTY CONFIDENT LOOK ON YOUR FACE...
SORRY, SUWABARA.
The Head PANTASIA
FWIP
FWIP
THIS ATCH ---
---WILL BE MY VICTORY.
WHA ?!!

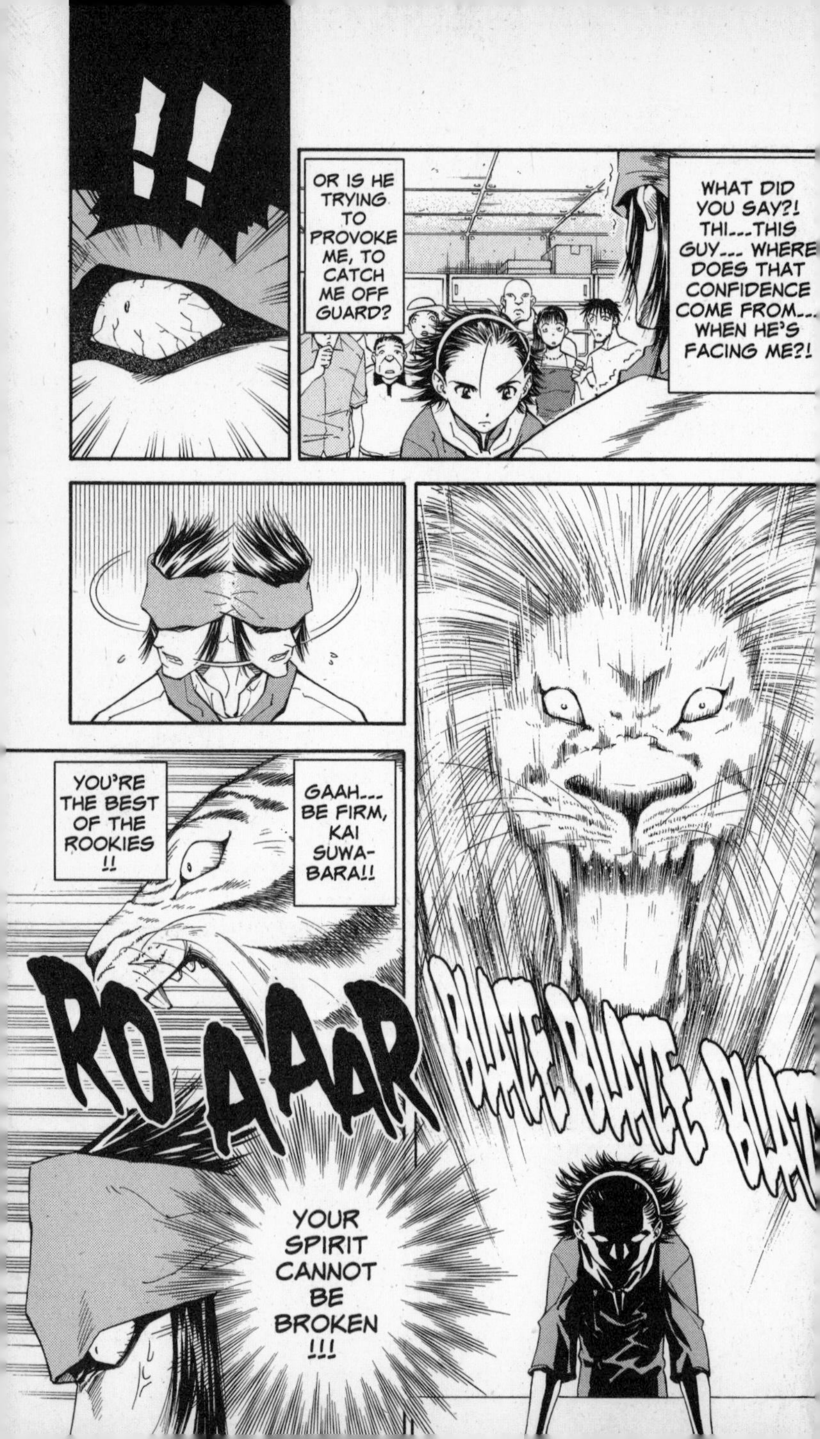
WHAT DID YOU SAY?! THI...THIS GUY... WHERE DOES THAT CONFIDENCE COME FROM... WHEN HE'S FACING ME?!
OR IS HE TRYING TO PROVOKE ME, TO CATCH ME OFF GUARD?
!!
BLAZE BLAZE BLAZ
GAAH... BE FIRM, KAI SUWA-BARA!!
YOU'RE THE BEST OF THE ROOKIES !!
RO AAAR
YOUR SPIRIT CANNOT BE BROKEN !!!

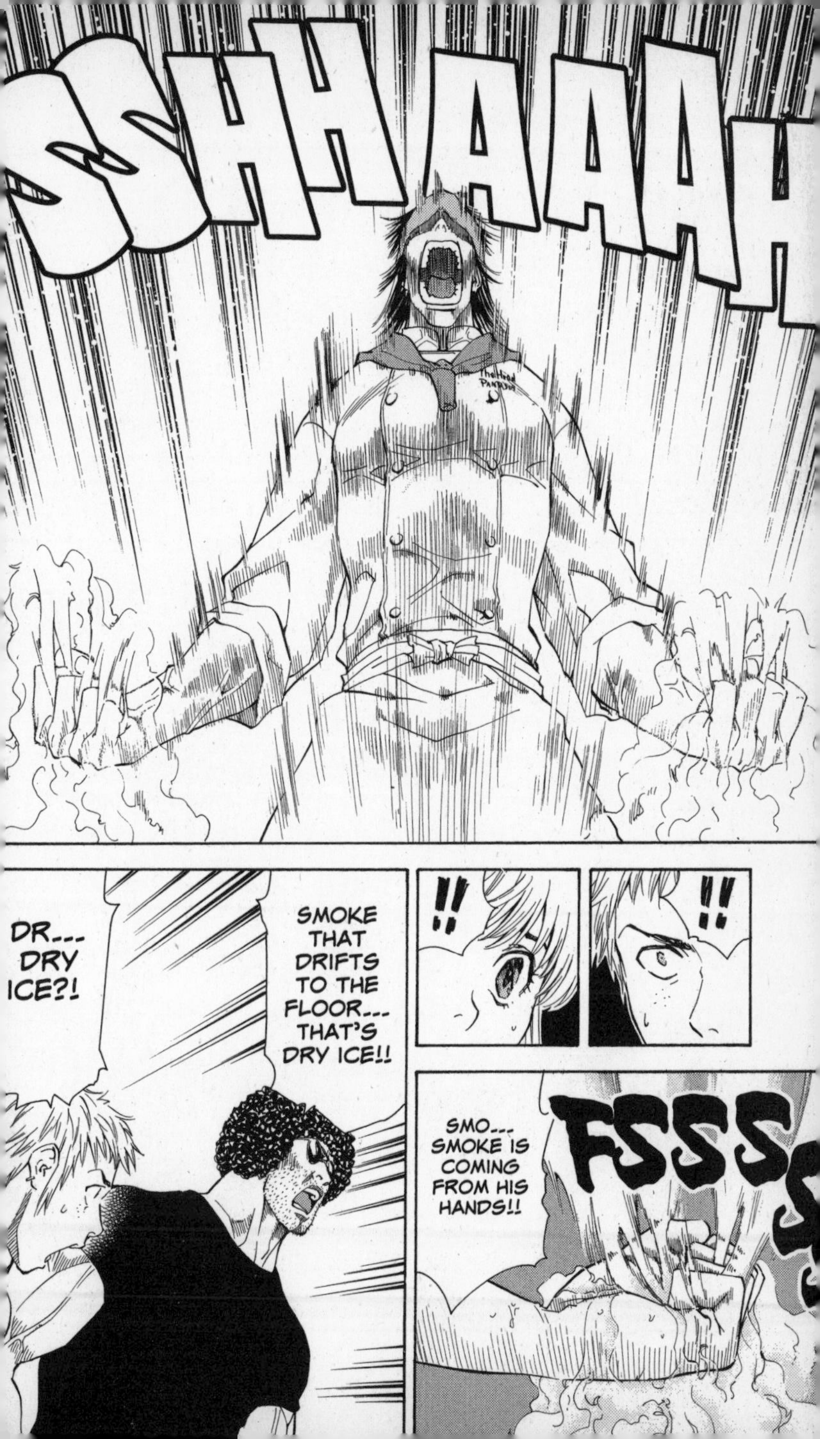
SHAAAAH
!!
!!
FSSSS
SMO... SMOKE IS COMING FROM HIS HANDS!!
SMOKE THAT DRIFTS TO THE FLOOR... THAT'S DRY ICE!!
DR... DRY ICE?!

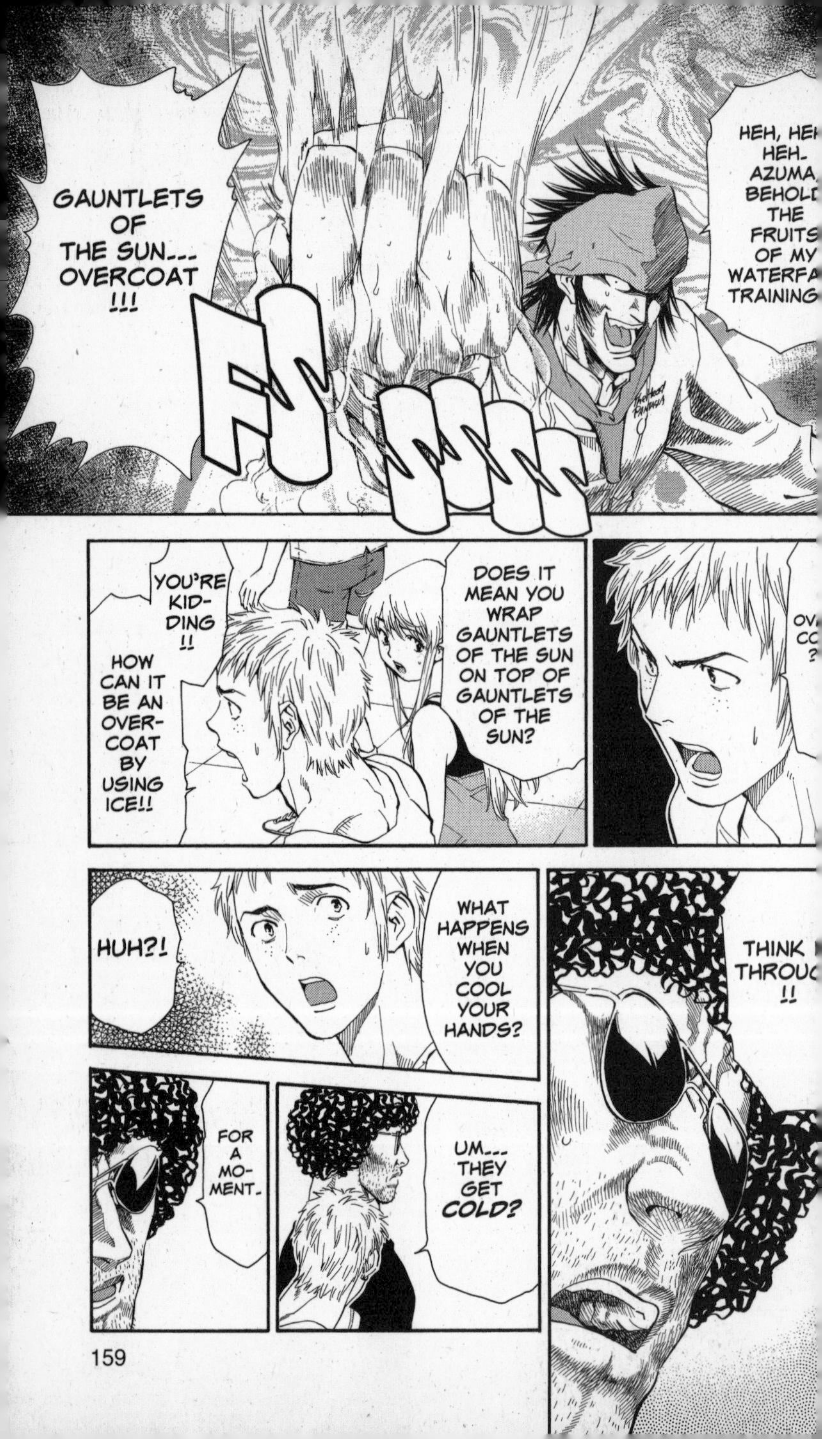
HEH, HEH HEH. AZUMA, BEHOLD THE FRUITS OF MY WATERFA TRAINING
GAUNTLETS OF THE SUN... OVERCOAT !!!
FSSSS
OV CO ?
DOES IT MEAN YOU WRAP GAUNTLETS OF THE SUN ON TOP OF GAUNTLETS OF THE SUN?
YOU'RE KID-DING !!
HOW CAN IT BE AN OVER-COAT BY USING ICE!!
THINK THROU !!
WHAT HAPPENS WHEN YOU COOL YOUR HANDS?
HUH?!
UM... THEY GET COLD?
FOR A MO-MENT.

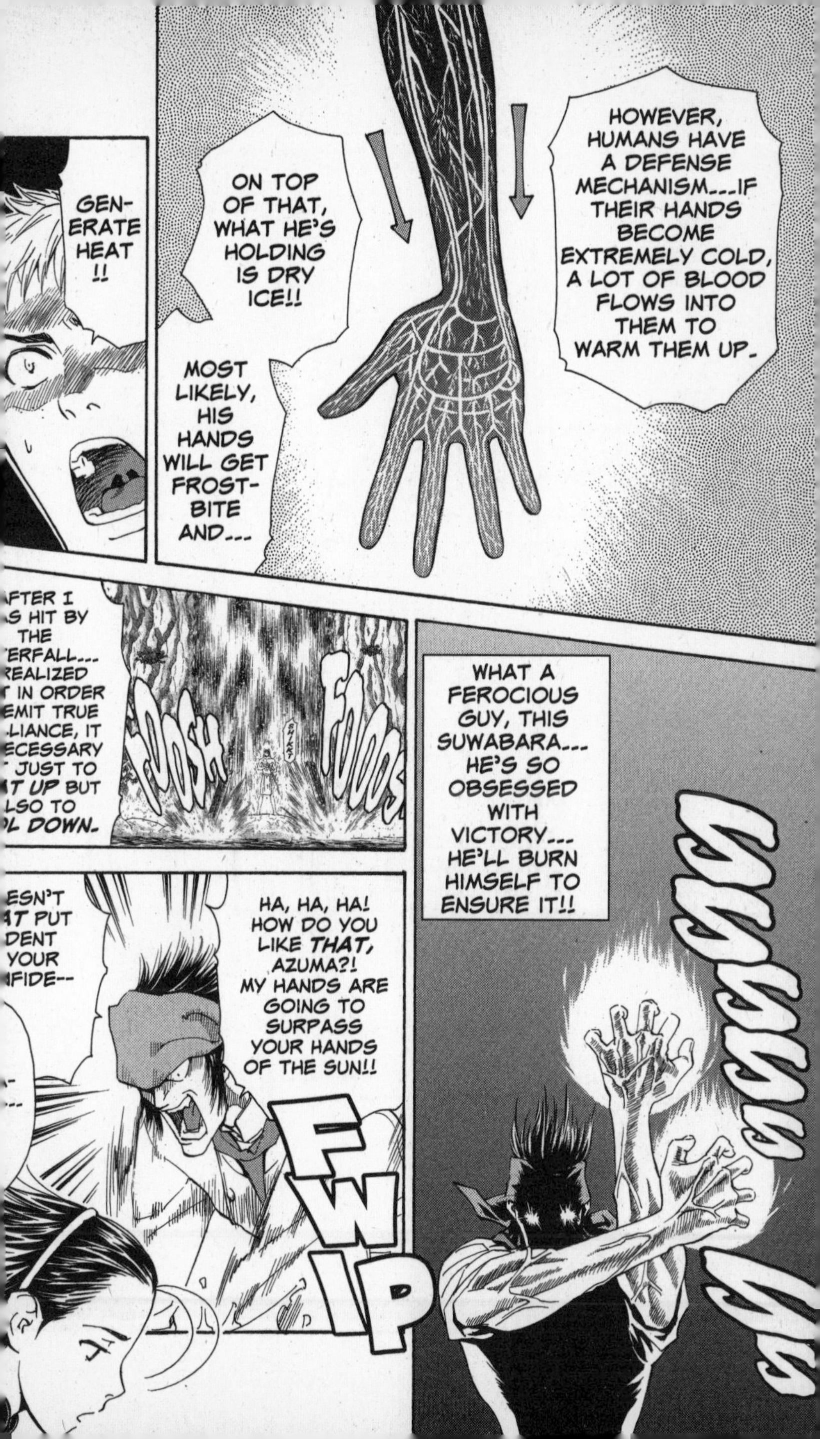
HOWEVER, HUMANS HAVE A DEFENSE MECHANISM...IF THEIR HANDS BECOME EXTREMELY COLD, A LOT OF BLOOD FLOWS INTO THEM TO WARM THEM UP.
ON TOP OF THAT, WHAT HE'S HOLDING IS DRY ICE!!
MOST LIKELY, HIS HANDS WILL GET FROST-BITE AND...
GEN-ERATE HEAT!!
WHAT A FEROCIOUS GUY, THIS SUWABARA... HE'S SO OBSESSED WITH VICTORY... HE'LL BURN HIMSELF TO ENSURE IT!!
FTER I
S HIT BY
THE
ERFALL...
REALIZED
T IN ORDER
EMIT TRUE
LIANCE, IT
ECESSARY
T JUST TO
T UP BUT
LSO TO
L DOWN.
FOOSH
SHIKT
HA, HA, HA! HOW DO YOU LIKE *THAT,* AZUMA?! MY HANDS ARE GOING TO SURPASS YOUR HANDS OF THE SUN!!
ESN'T
AT PUT
DENT
YOUR
NFIDE--
FWIP

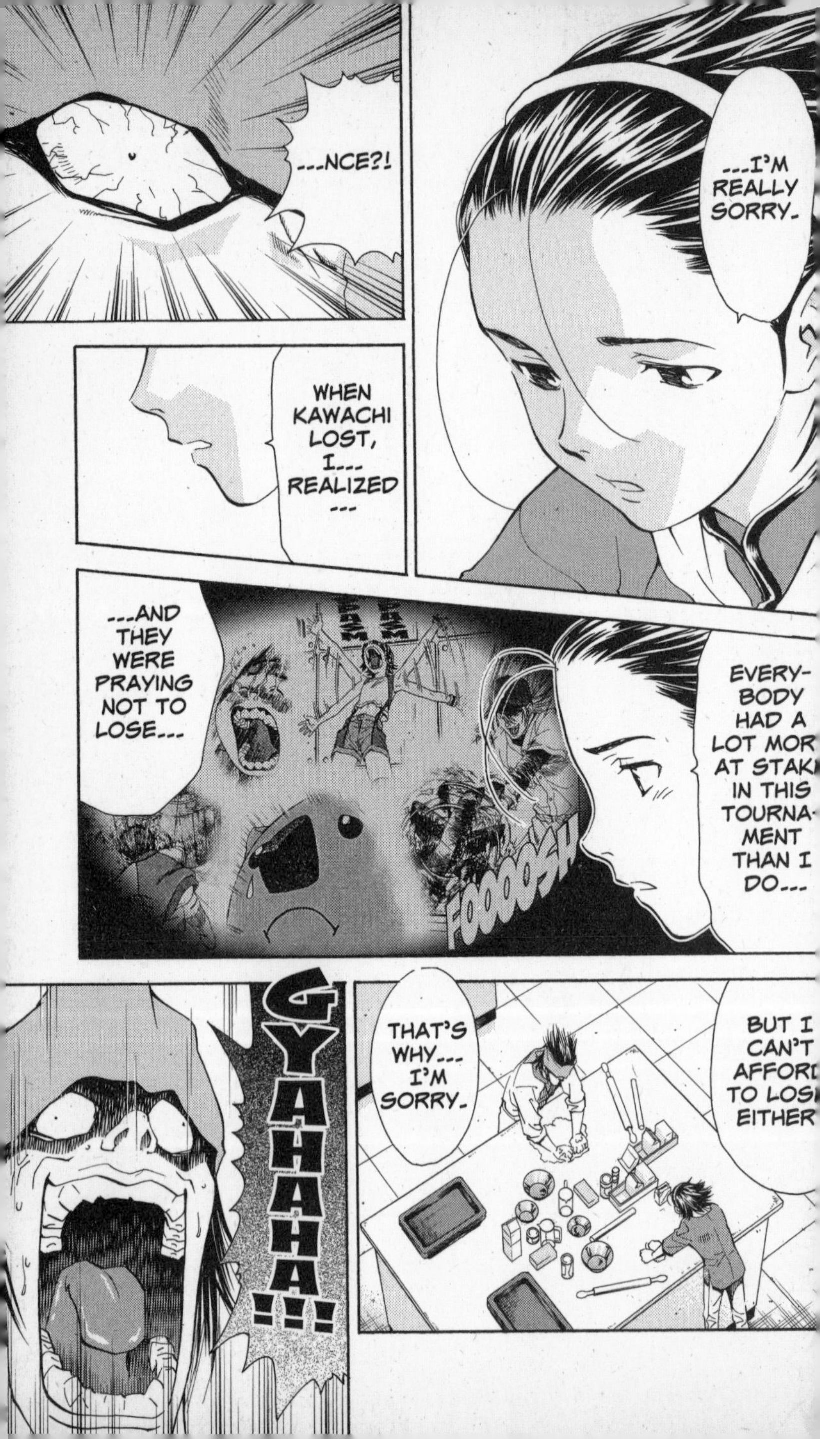
---I'M REALLY SORRY.
---NCE?!
WHEN KAWACHI LOST, I--- REALIZED ---
EVERY-BODY HAD A LOT MOR AT STAK IN THIS TOURNA-MENT THAN I DO---
---AND THEY WERE PRAYING NOT TO LOSE---
FOOOOSH
BUT I CAN'T AFFORD TO LOS EITHER
THAT'S WHY--- I'M SORRY.
GYAHAHAHA!!!

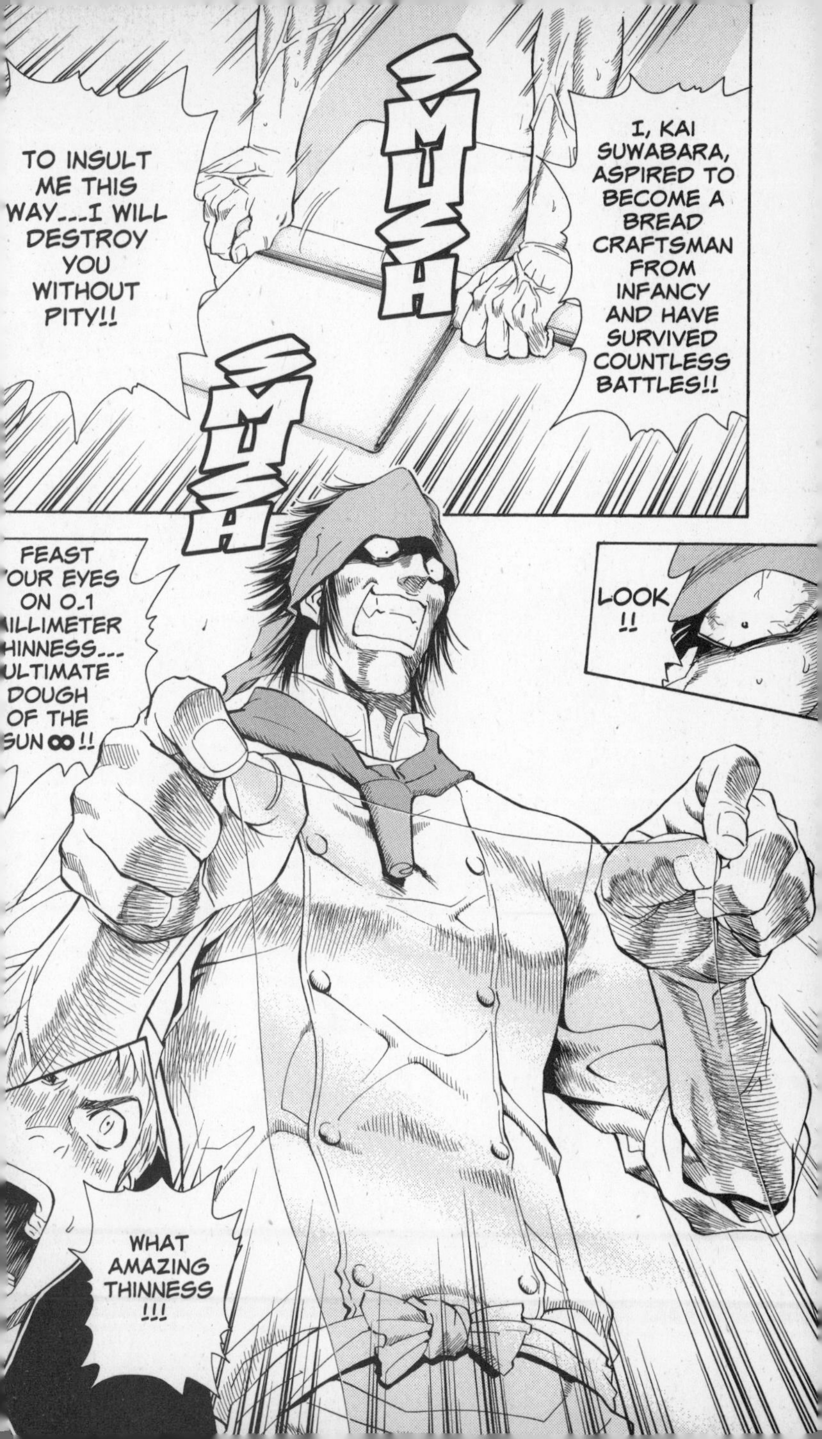
I, KAI SUWABARA, ASPIRED TO BECOME A BREAD CRAFTSMAN FROM INFANCY AND HAVE SURVIVED COUNTLESS BATTLES!!
TO INSULT ME THIS WAY...I WILL DESTROY YOU WITHOUT PITY!!
SMUSH
SMUSH
LOOK!!
FEAST OUR EYES ON 0.1 ILLIMETER HINNESS... ULTIMATE DOUGH OF THE SUN∞!!
WHAT AMAZING THINNESS!!!

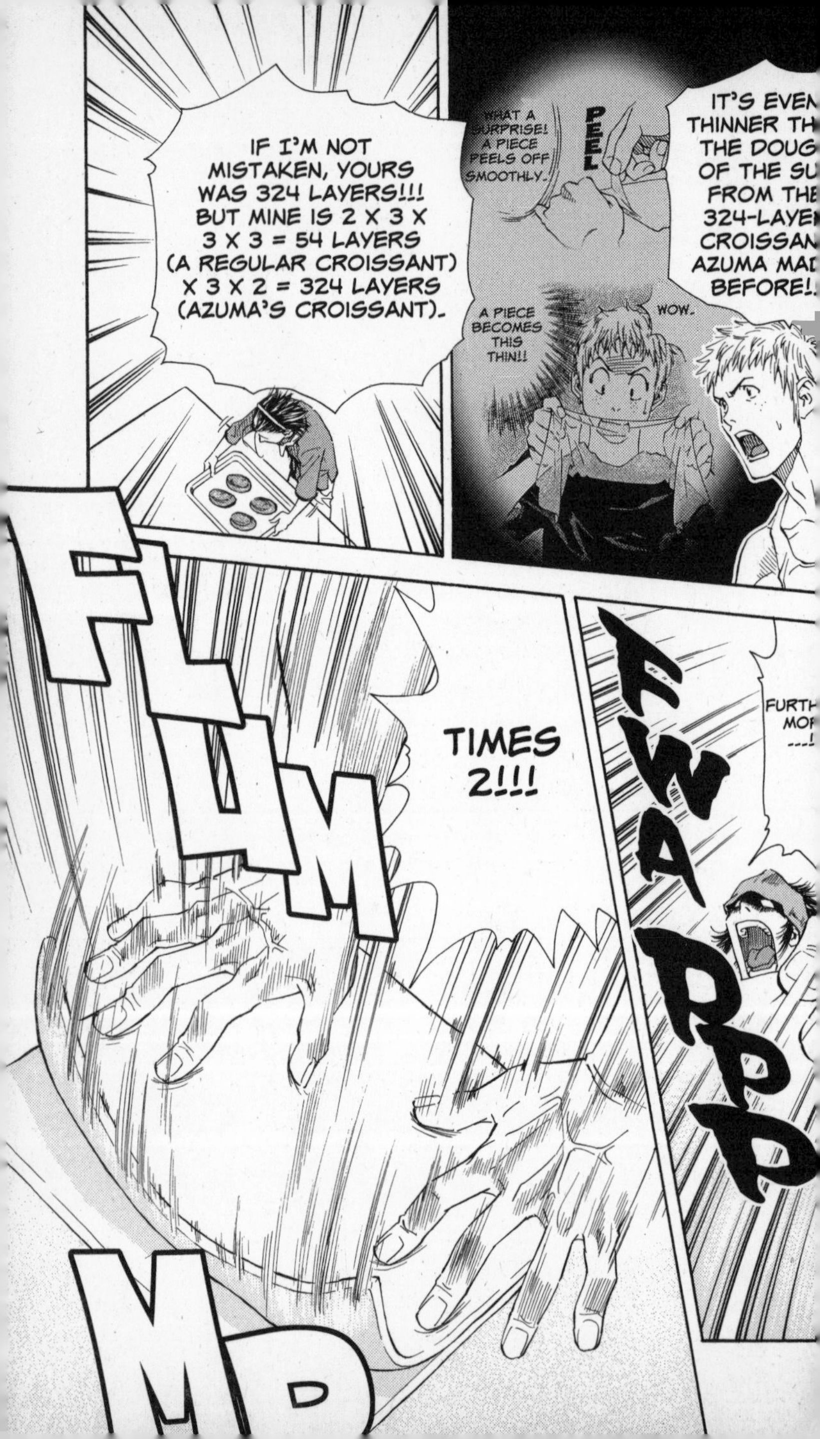

IT'S EVEN THINNER TH THE DOUG OF THE SU FROM THE 324-LAYE CROISSAN AZUMA MAD BEFORE!!
PEEL
WHAT A SURPRISE! A PIECE PEELS OFF SMOOTHLY...
A PIECE BECOMES THIS THIN!!
WOW...
IF I'M NOT MISTAKEN, YOURS WAS 324 LAYERS!!! BUT MINE IS 2 X 3 X 3 X 3 = 54 LAYERS (A REGULAR CROISSANT) X 3 X 2 = 324 LAYERS (AZUMA'S CROISSANT)...
FURTH MOR ---!
FWARPP
TIMES 2!!!
FLUMMP

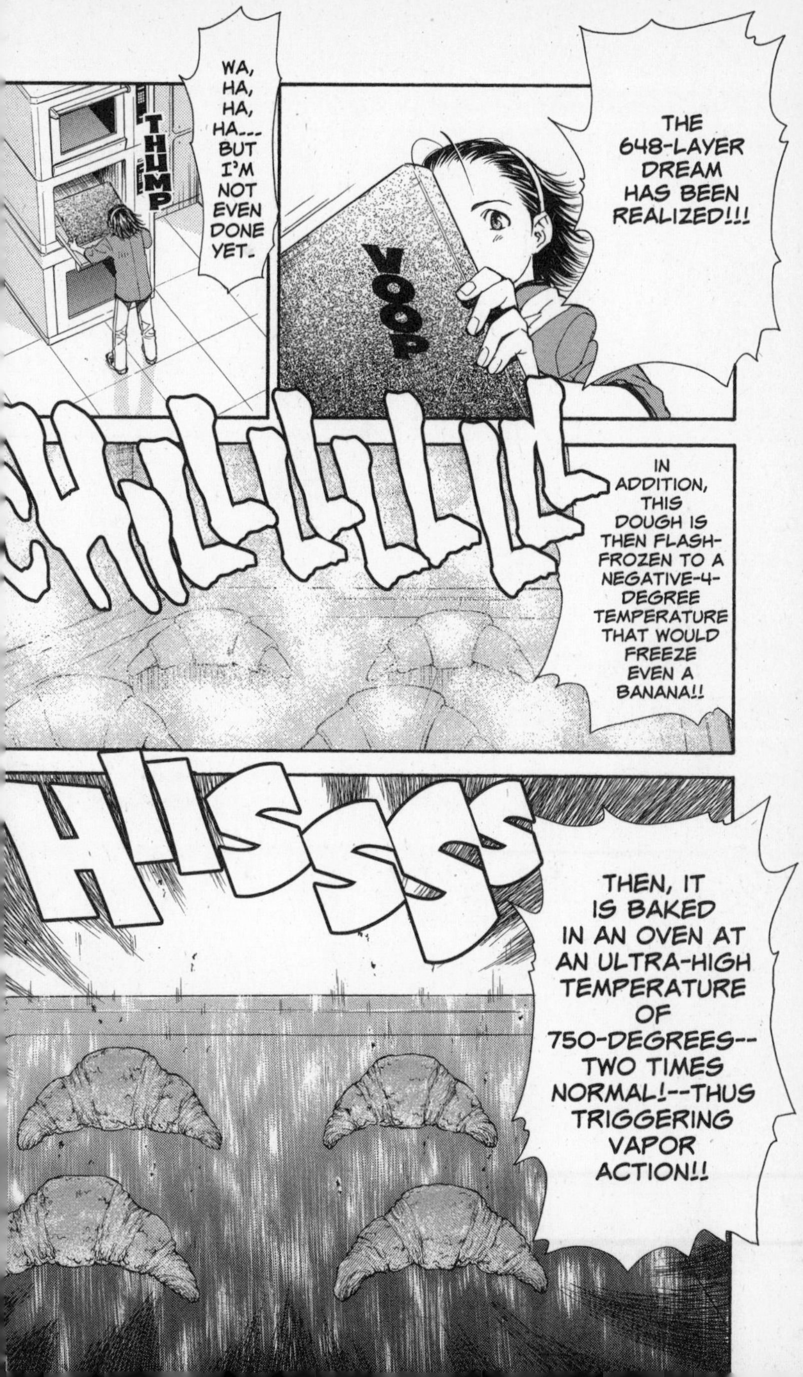

THE 648-LAYER DREAM HAS BEEN REALIZED!!!
VOOP
WA, HA, HA, HA... BUT I'M NOT EVEN DONE YET.
THUMP
CHILLLLL
IN ADDITION, THIS DOUGH IS THEN FLASH-FROZEN TO A NEGATIVE-4-DEGREE TEMPERATURE THAT WOULD FREEZE EVEN A BANANA!!
HISSSS
THEN, IT IS BAKED IN AN OVEN AT AN ULTRA-HIGH TEMPERATURE OF 750-DEGREES--TWO TIMES NORMAL!--THUS TRIGGERING VAPOR ACTION!!

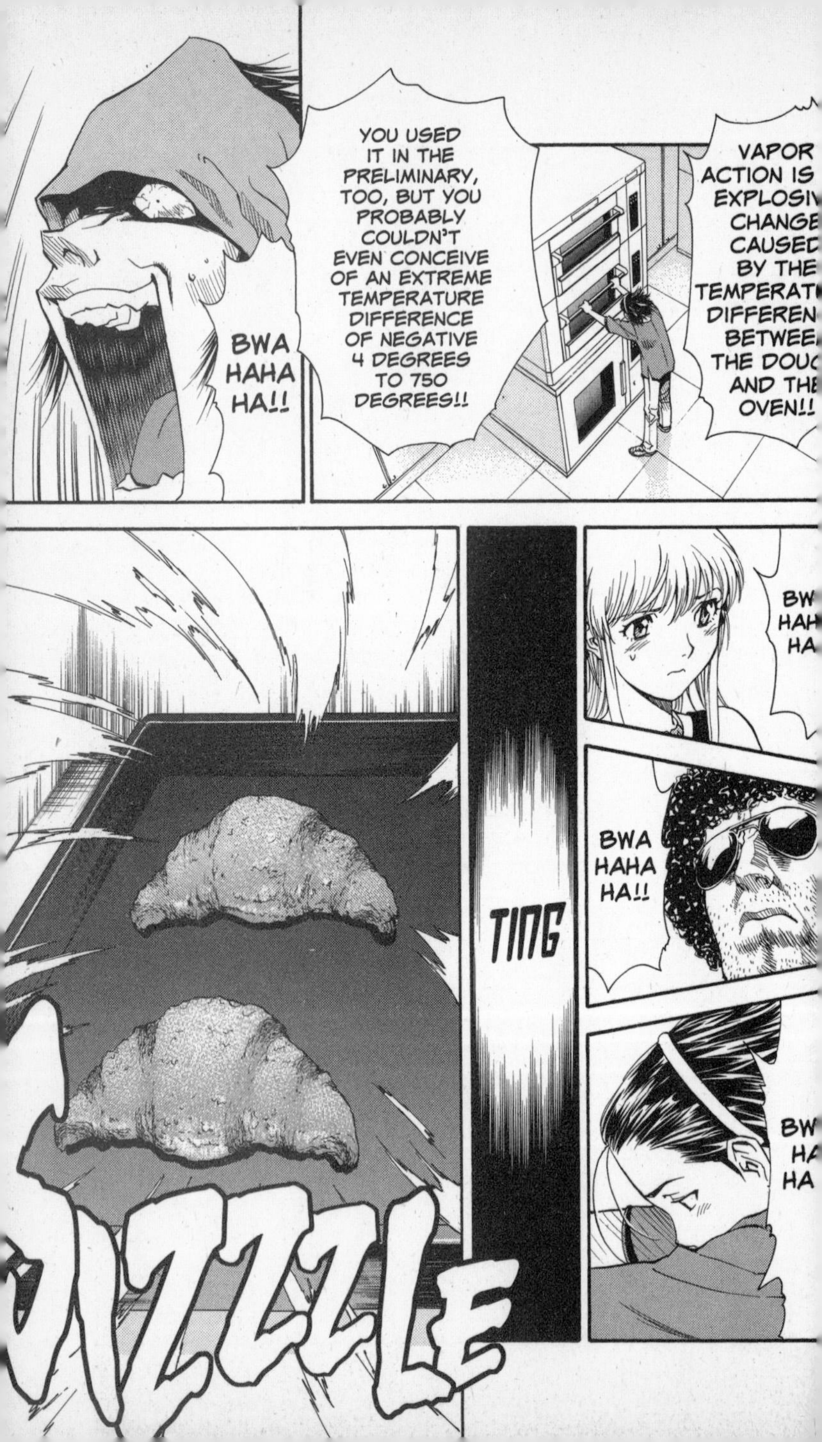
VAPOR ACTION IS EXPLOSIV CHANGE CAUSED BY THE TEMPERAT DIFFEREN BETWEE THE DOUG AND THE OVEN!!
YOU USED IT IN THE PRELIMINARY, TOO, BUT YOU PROBABLY COULDN'T EVEN CONCEIVE OF AN EXTREME TEMPERATURE DIFFERENCE OF NEGATIVE 4 DEGREES TO 750 DEGREES!!
BWA HAHA HA!!
BW HAH HA
BWA HAHA HA!!
BW HA HA
TING
ZZLE

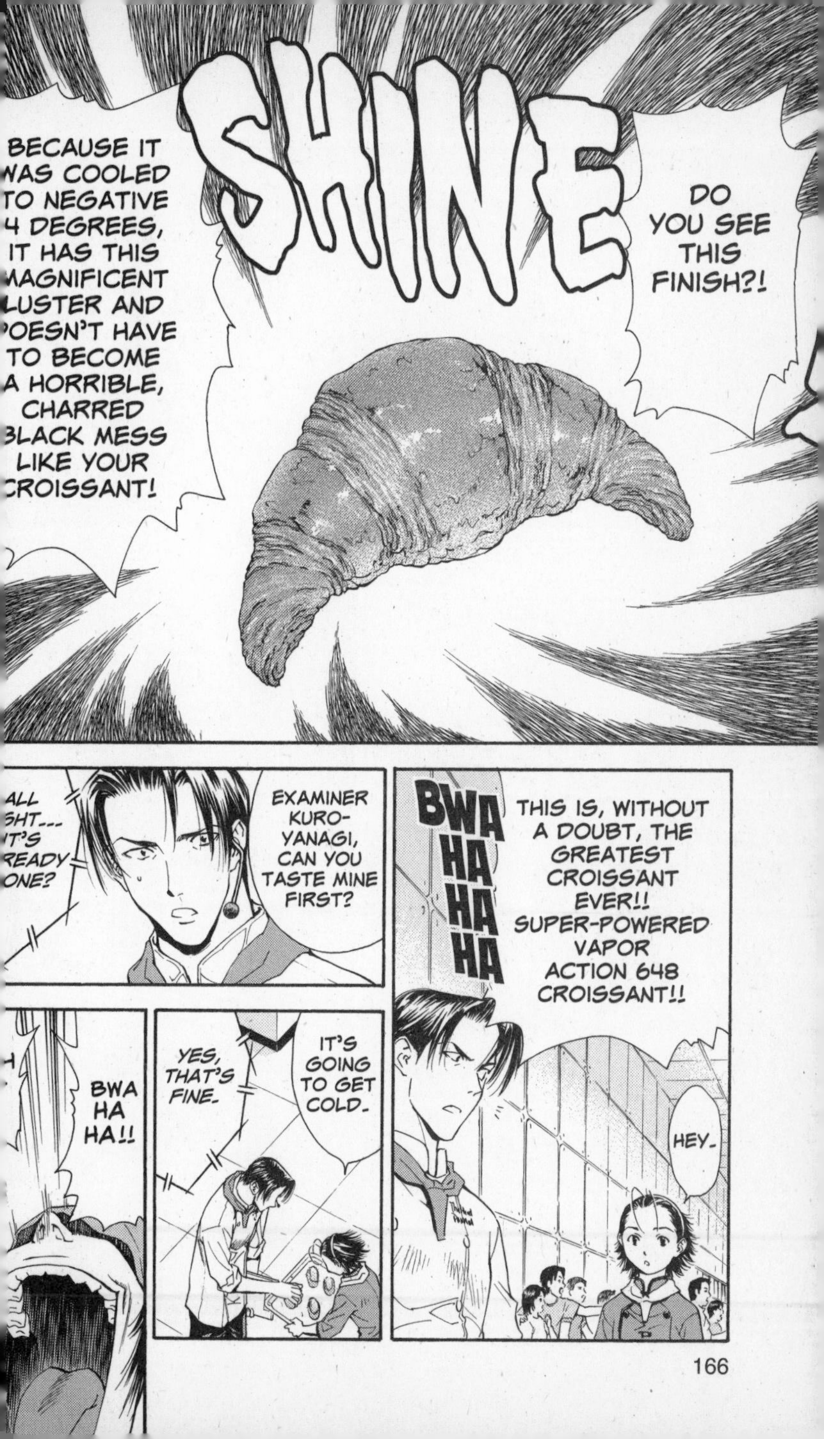
DO YOU SEE THIS FINISH?!
SHINE
BECAUSE IT WAS COOLED TO NEGATIVE 4 DEGREES, IT HAS THIS MAGNIFICENT LUSTER AND DOESN'T HAVE TO BECOME A HORRIBLE, CHARRED BLACK MESS LIKE YOUR CROISSANT!
BWA HA HA HA HA
THIS IS, WITHOUT A DOUBT, THE GREATEST CROISSANT EVER!! SUPER-POWERED VAPOR ACTION 648 CROISSANT!!
HEY.
EXAMINER KURO-YANAGI, CAN YOU TASTE MINE FIRST?
ALL ...GHT... IT'S READY ...ONE?
IT'S GOING TO GET COLD.
YES, THAT'S FINE.
BWA HA HA!!

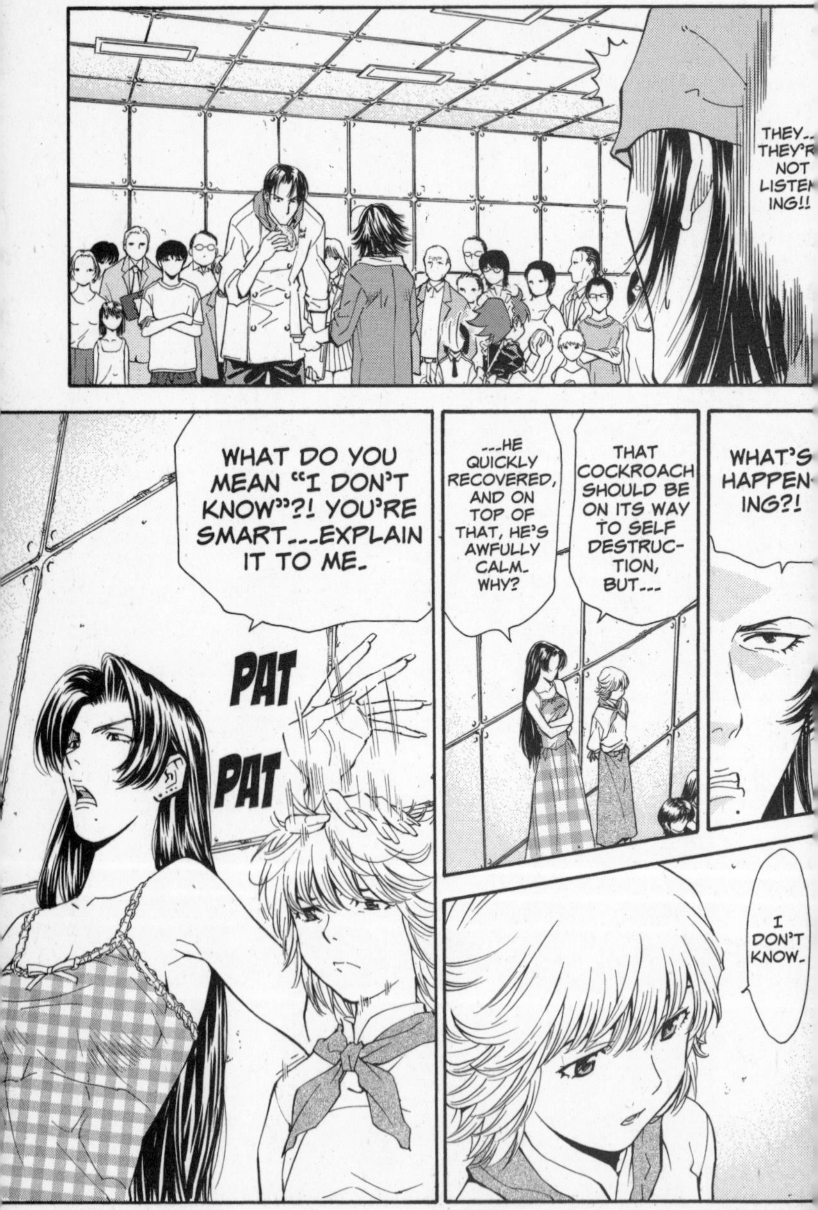
THEY... THEY'R NOT LISTEN ING!!
WHAT'S HAPPENING?!
THAT COCKROACH SHOULD BE ON ITS WAY TO SELF DESTRUCTION, BUT...
...HE QUICKLY RECOVERED, AND ON TOP OF THAT, HE'S AWFULLY CALM. WHY?
I DON'T KNOW.
WHAT DO YOU MEAN "I DON'T KNOW"?! YOU'RE SMART...EXPLAIN IT TO ME.
PAT
PAT

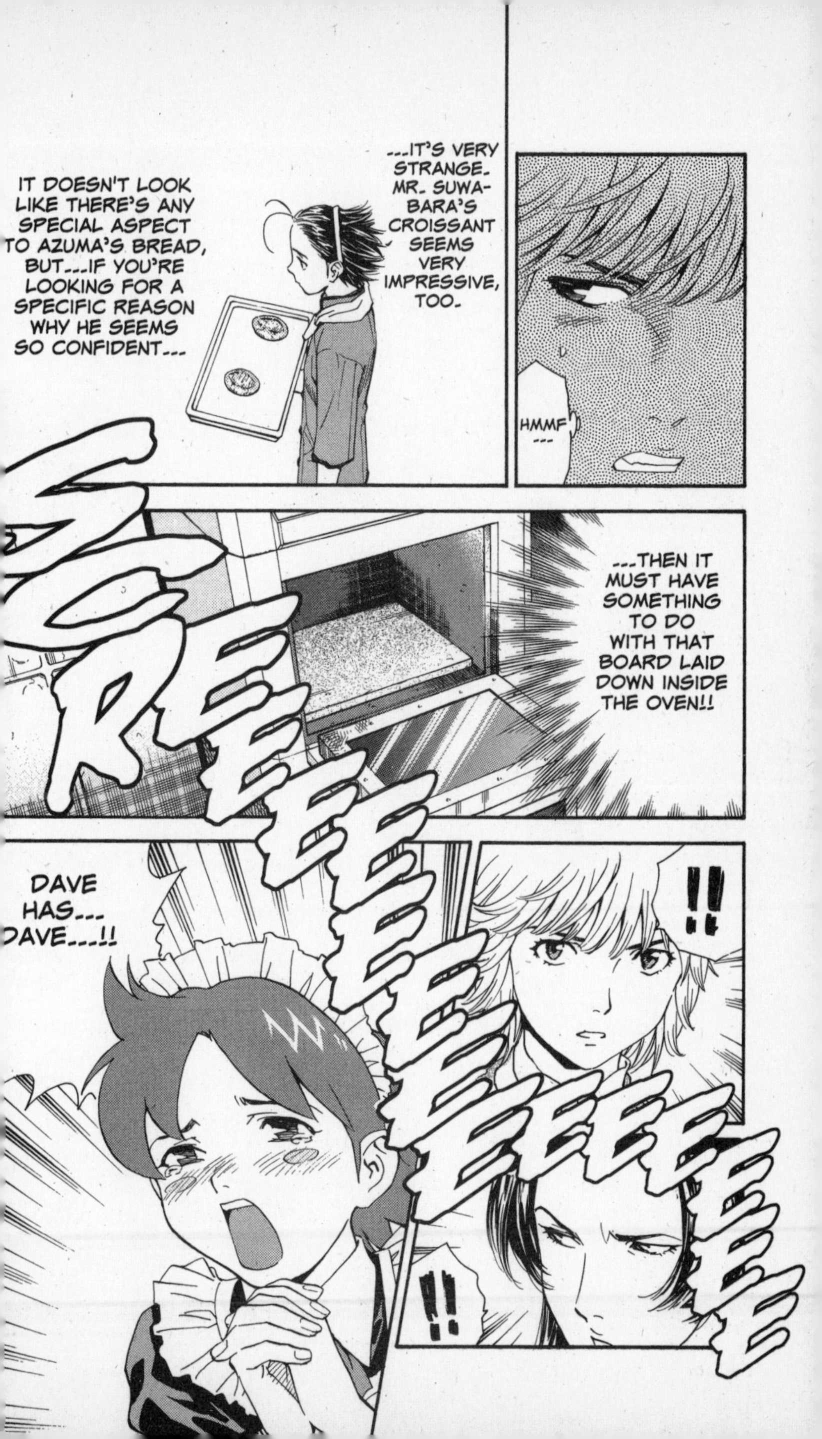
...IT'S VERY STRANGE. MR. SUWABARA'S CROISSANT SEEMS VERY IMPRESSIVE, TOO.
HMMF...
IT DOESN'T LOOK LIKE THERE'S ANY SPECIAL ASPECT TO AZUMA'S BREAD, BUT...IF YOU'RE LOOKING FOR A SPECIFIC REASON WHY HE SEEMS SO CONFIDENT...
...THEN IT MUST HAVE SOMETHING TO DO WITH THAT BOARD LAID DOWN INSIDE THE OVEN!!
!!
DAVE HAS... DAVE...!!
!!
SKREEEEEEEEEEEEEEEEE

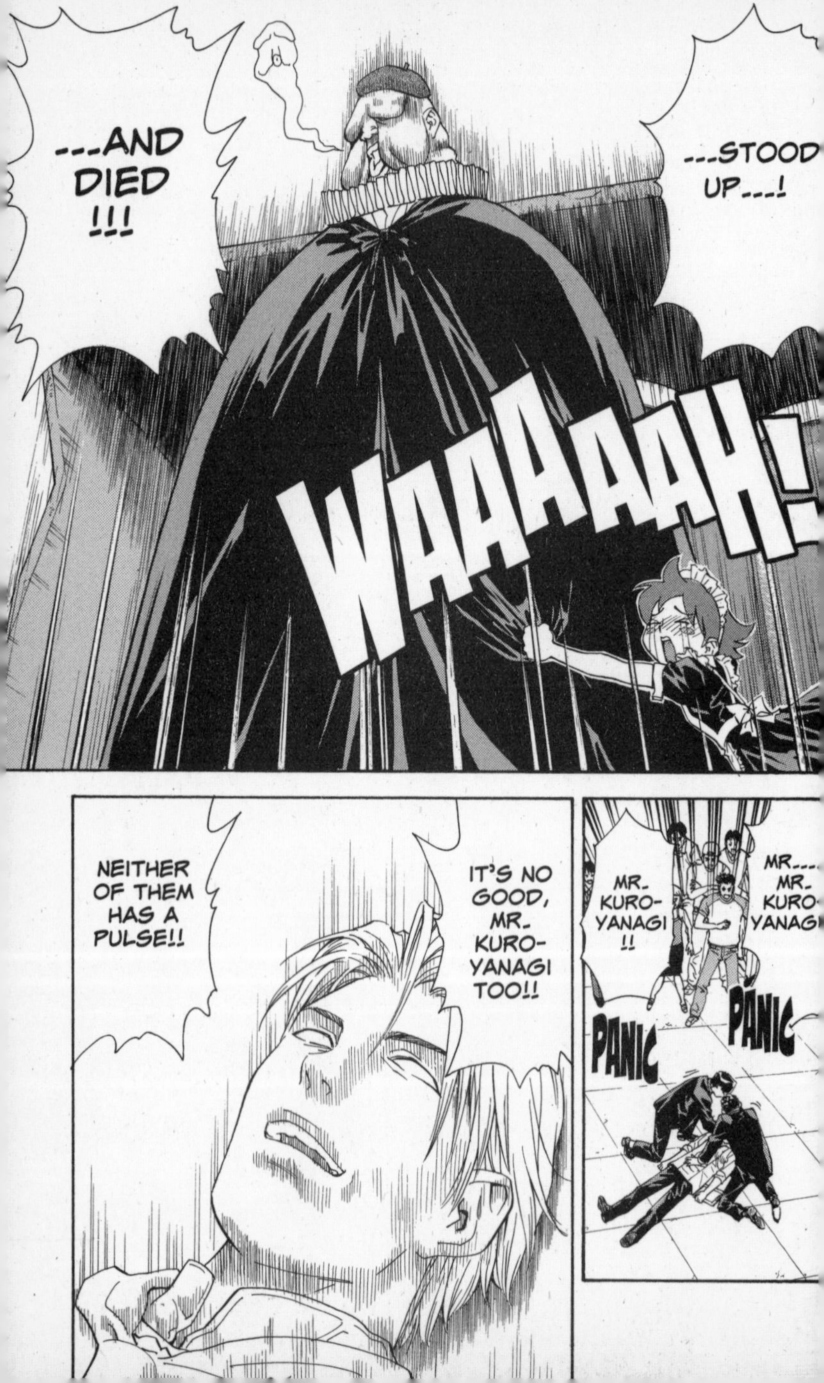
---STOOD UP---!
---AND DIED !!!
WAAAAAH!!
MR.--- MR. KURO-YANAG
MR. KURO-YANAGI !!
PANIC
PANIC
IT'S NO GOOD, MR. KURO-YANAGI TOO!!
NEITHER OF THEM HAS A PULSE!!

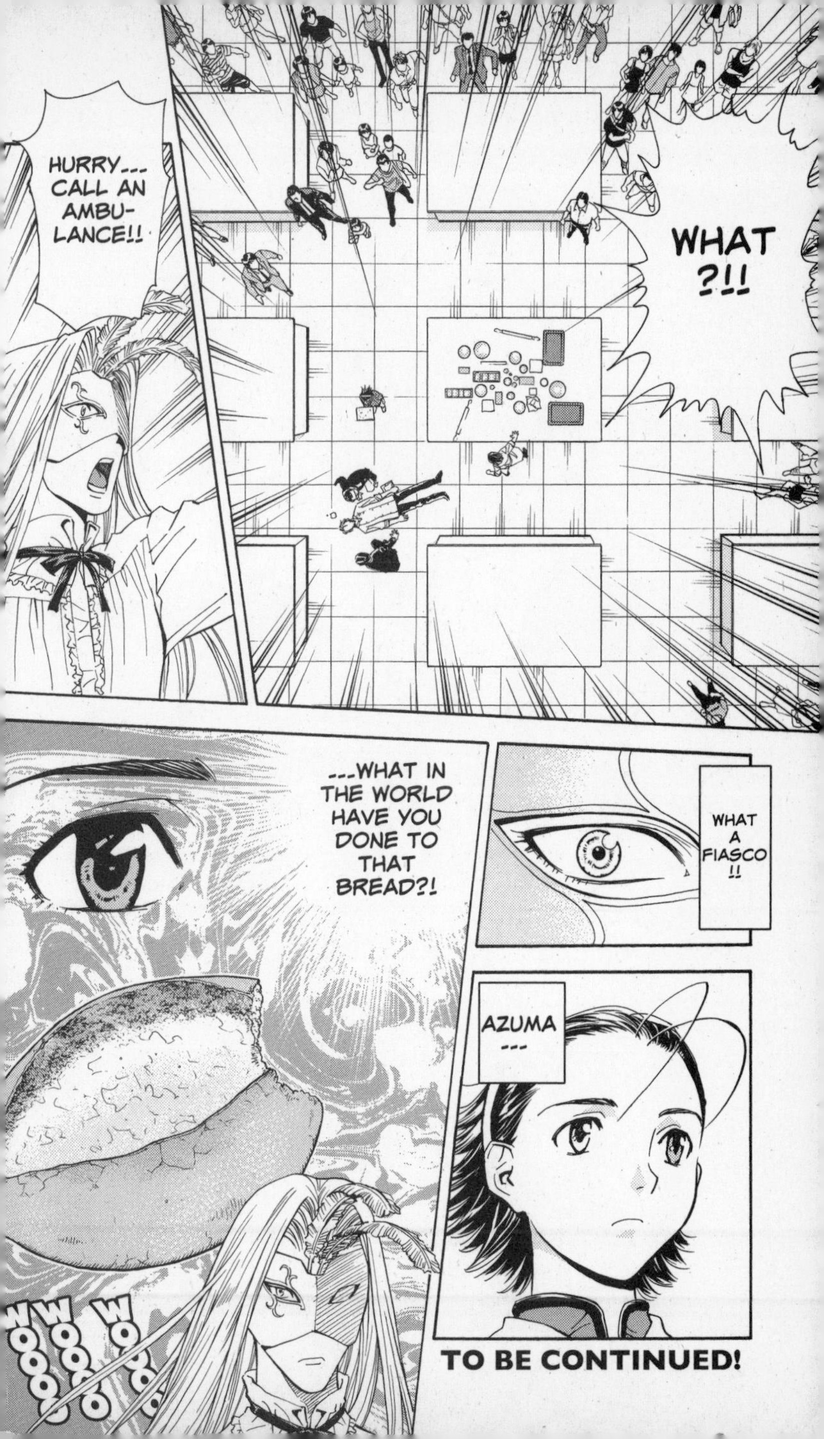
WHAT ?!!
HURRY... CALL AN AMBULANCE!!
WHAT A FIASCO !!
AZUMA ---
TO BE CONTINUED!
...WHAT IN THE WORLD HAVE YOU DONE TO THAT BREAD?!

BONUS♥

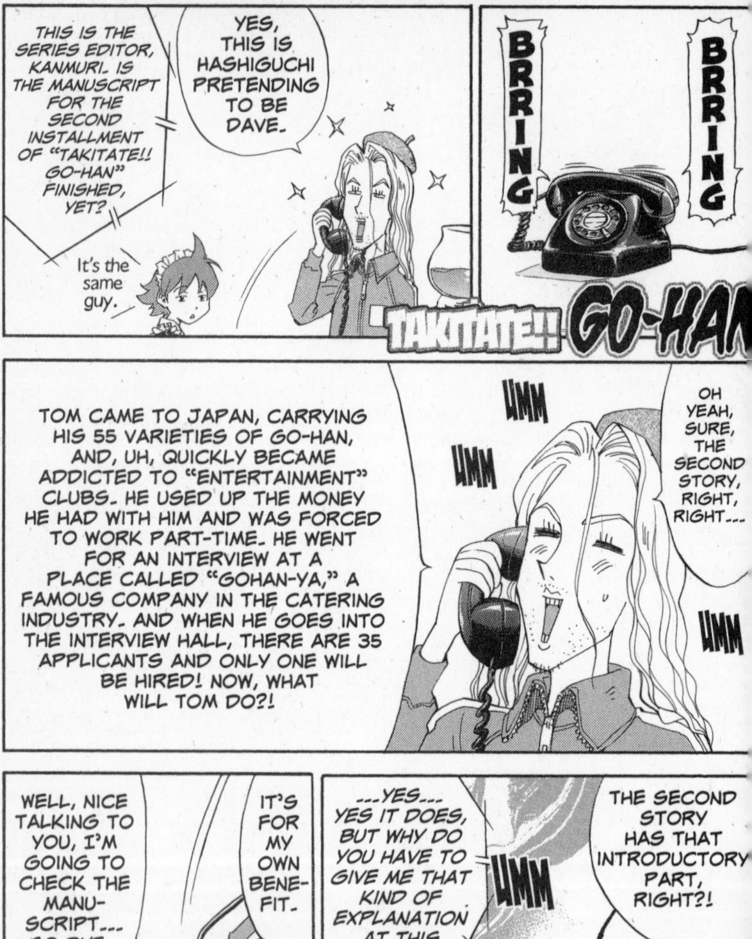
BRRING
BRRING
TAKITATE!! GO-HAN
YES, THIS IS HASHIGUCHI PRETENDING TO BE DAVE.
THIS IS THE SERIES EDITOR, KANMURI. IS THE MANUSCRIPT FOR THE SECOND INSTALLMENT OF "TAKITATE!! GO-HAN" FINISHED, YET?
It's the same guy.
OH YEAH, SURE, THE SECOND STORY, RIGHT, RIGHT...
UMM
UMM
UMM
UMM
TOM CAME TO JAPAN, CARRYING HIS 55 VARIETIES OF GO-HAN, AND, UH, QUICKLY BECAME ADDICTED TO "ENTERTAINMENT" CLUBS. HE USED UP THE MONEY HE HAD WITH HIM AND WAS FORCED TO WORK PART-TIME. HE WENT FOR AN INTERVIEW AT A PLACE CALLED "GOHAN-YA," A FAMOUS COMPANY IN THE CATERING INDUSTRY. AND WHEN HE GOES INTO THE INTERVIEW HALL, THERE ARE 35 APPLICANTS AND ONLY ONE WILL BE HIRED! NOW, WHAT WILL TOM DO?!
THE SECOND STORY HAS THAT INTRODUCTORY PART, RIGHT?!
...YES... YES IT DOES, BUT WHY DO YOU HAVE TO GIVE ME THAT KIND OF EXPLANATION AT THIS POINT...
UMM
HEH
HEH
HEH
HEH
IT'S FOR MY OWN BENE-FIT.
WELL, NICE TALKING TO YOU, I'M GOING TO CHECK THE MANU-SCRIPT... SO BYE.
CLOMP

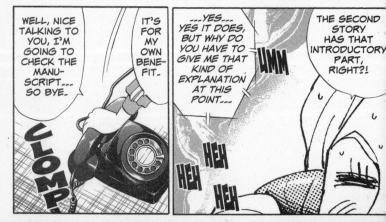

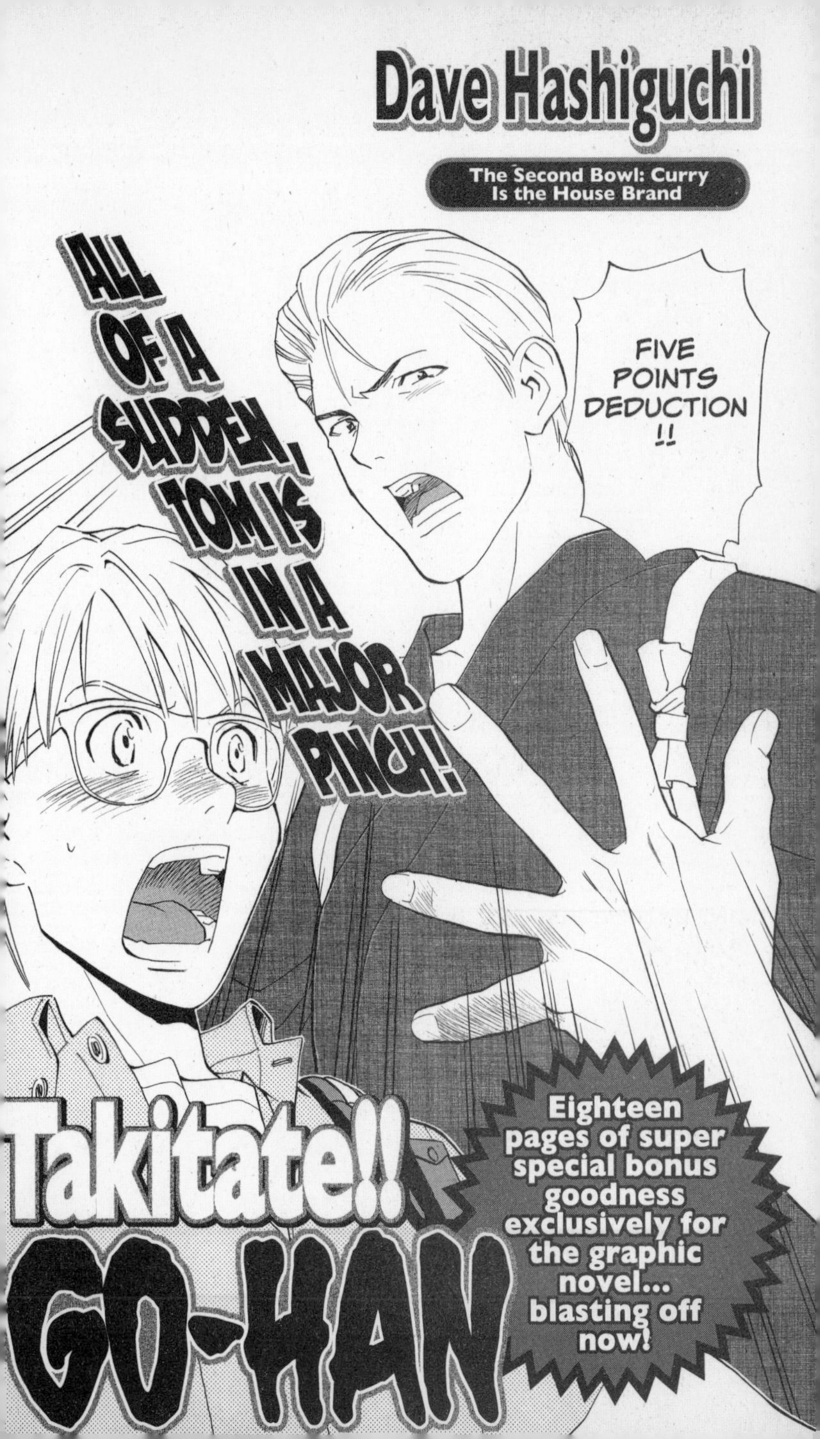
Dave Hashiguchi
The Second Bowl: Curry Is the House Brand
FIVE POINTS DEDUCTION !!
ALL OF A SUDDEN, TOM IS IN A MAJOR PINCH!
Takitate!! GO-HAN
Eighteen pages of super special bonus goodness exclusively for the graphic novel... blasting off now!

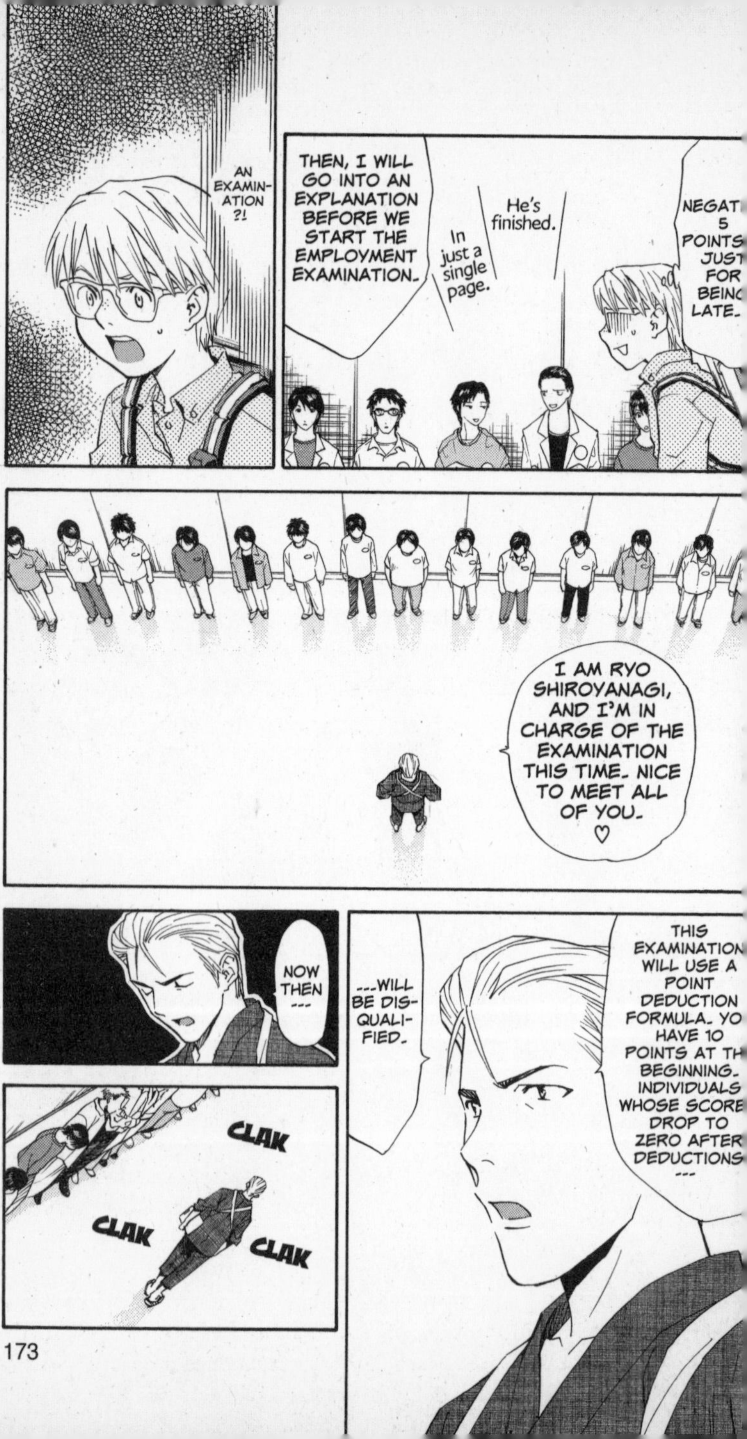
NEGAT 5 POINTS JUST FOR BEING LATE…
He's finished.
In just a single page.
THEN, I WILL GO INTO AN EXPLANATION BEFORE WE START THE EMPLOYMENT EXAMINATION…
AN EXAMINATION?!
I AM RYO SHIROYANAGI, AND I'M IN CHARGE OF THE EXAMINATION THIS TIME. NICE TO MEET ALL OF YOU. ♡
THIS EXAMINATION WILL USE A POINT DEDUCTION FORMULA. YO HAVE 10 POINTS AT TH BEGINNING. INDIVIDUALS WHOSE SCORE DROP TO ZERO AFTER DEDUCTIONS ---
---WILL BE DISQUALIFIED.
NOW THEN ---
CLAK
CLAK
CLAK

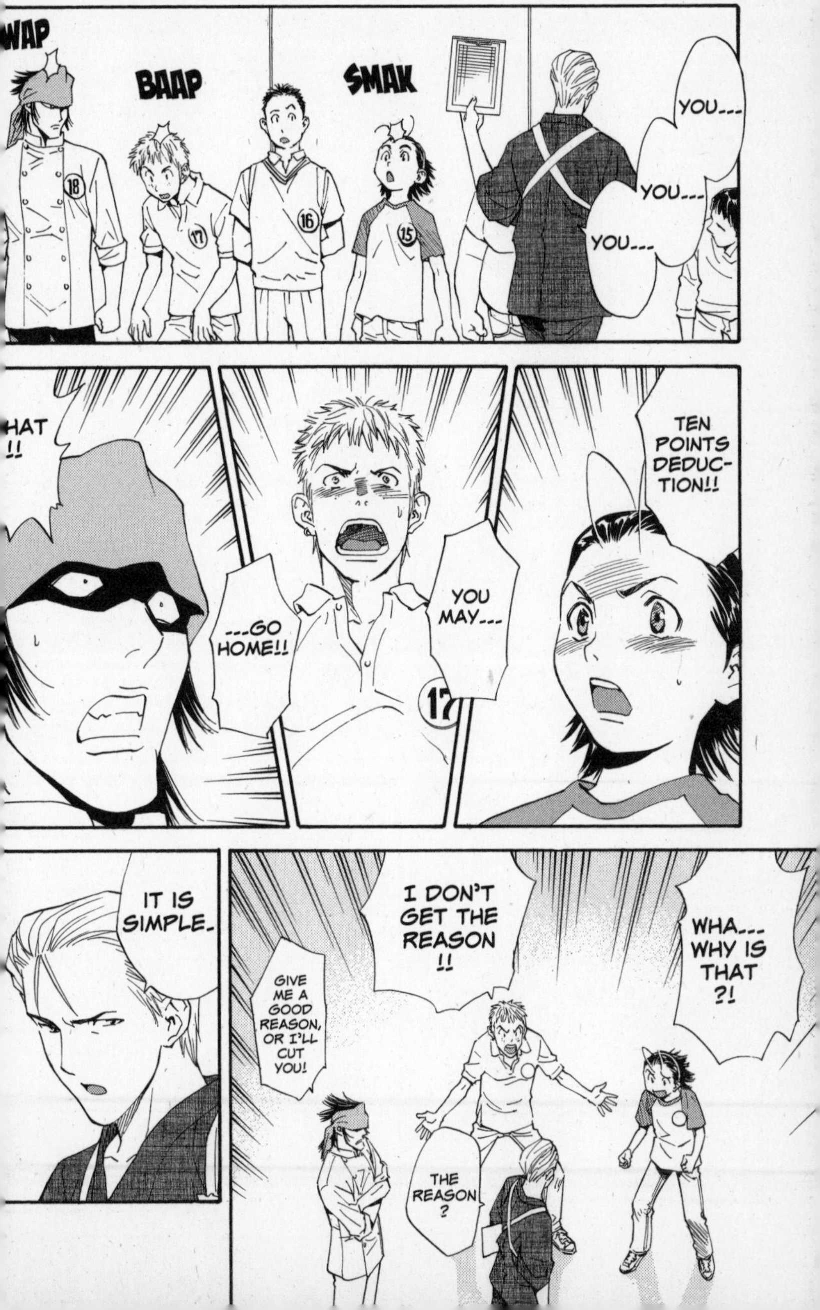
YOU...
YOU...
YOU...
SMAK
BAAP
WAP
TEN POINTS DEDUC-TION!!
YOU MAY...
...GO HOME!!
HAT !!
WHA... WHY IS THAT ?!
I DON'T GET THE REASON !!
GIVE ME A GOOD REASON, OR I'LL CUT YOU!
THE REASON ?
IT IS SIMPLE.

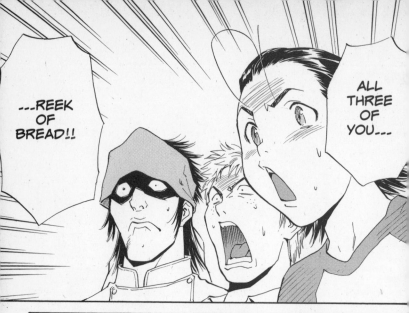

ALL THREE OF YOU...
---REEK OF BREAD!!
WE'RE A "GOHAN STORE," FOR RICE PEOPLE ONLY--WE DON'T HIRE BREAD LOVERS!
WHY DON'T YOU GO TO A BAKERY?
WAAAH
PFFT...
NOW... THE ASSIGNMENT FOR THOSE WHO REMAIN...
MAKE AN ONIGIRI !!

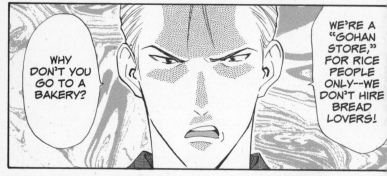

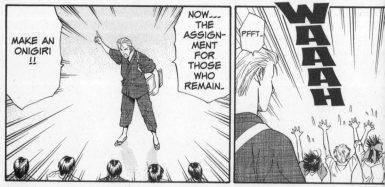

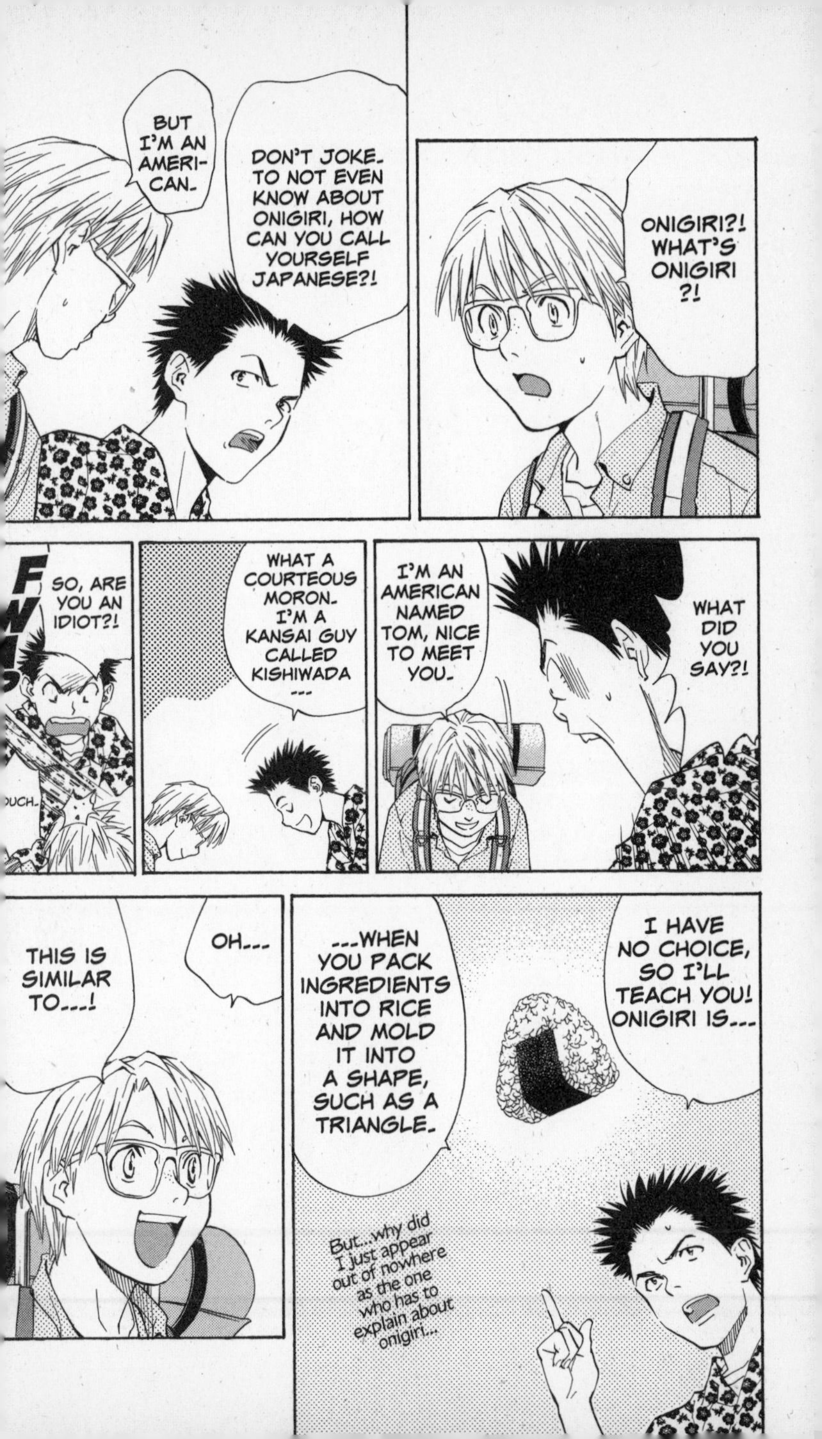
ONIGIRI?! WHAT'S ONIGIRI ?!
DON'T JOKE. TO NOT EVEN KNOW ABOUT ONIGIRI, HOW CAN YOU CALL YOURSELF JAPANESE?!
BUT I'M AN AMERI-CAN.
WHAT DID YOU SAY?!
I'M AN AMERICAN NAMED TOM, NICE TO MEET YOU.
WHAT A COURTEOUS MORON. I'M A KANSAI GUY CALLED KISHIWADA ...
SO, ARE YOU AN IDIOT?!
OUCH.
I HAVE NO CHOICE, SO I'LL TEACH YOU! ONIGIRI IS...
...WHEN YOU PACK INGREDIENTS INTO RICE AND MOLD IT INTO A SHAPE, SUCH AS A TRIANGLE.
But...why did I just appear out of nowhere as the one who has to explain about onigiri...
OH...
THIS IS SIMILAR TO...!

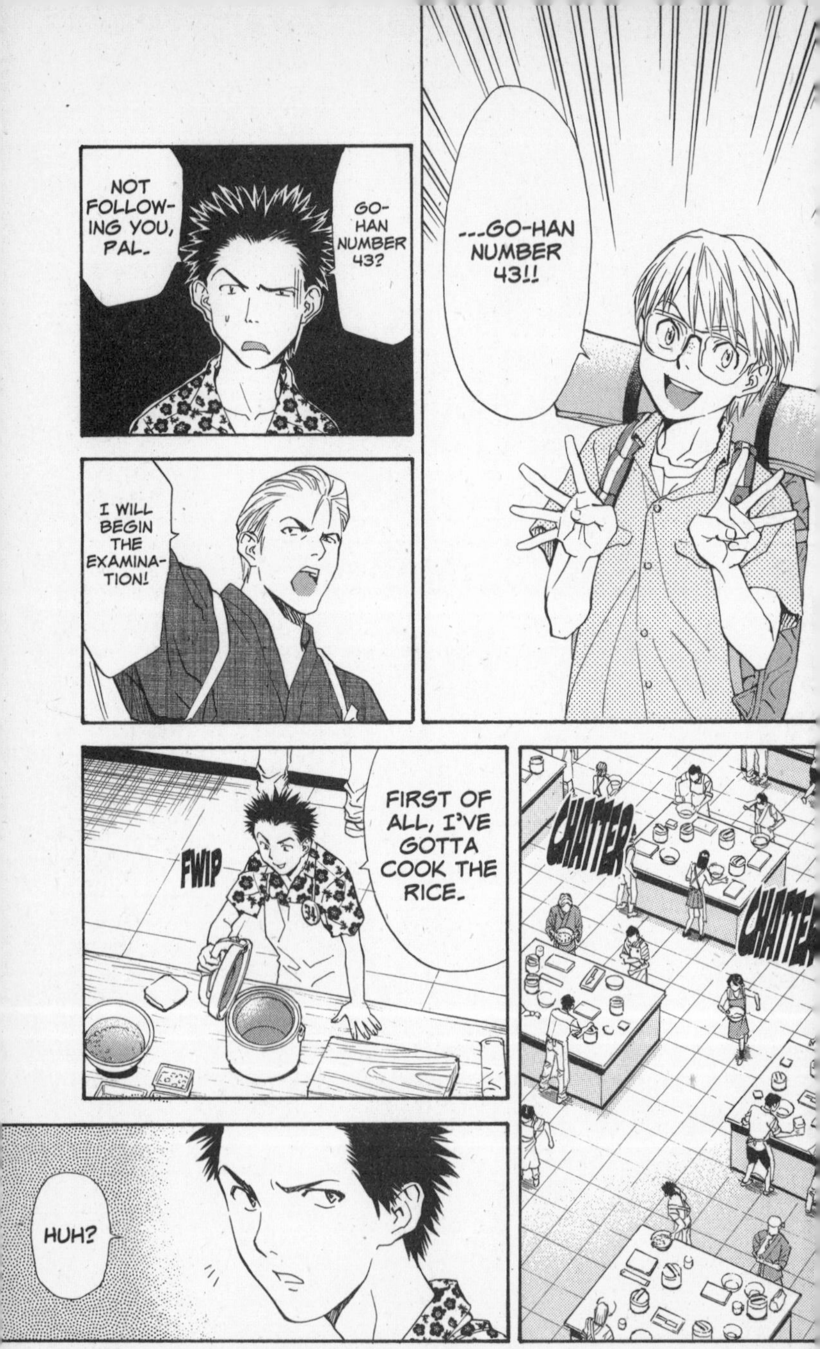
...GO-HAN NUMBER 43!!
GO-HAN NUMBER 43?
NOT FOLLOWING YOU, PAL.
I WILL BEGIN THE EXAMINATION!
CHATTER
CHATTER
FIRST OF ALL, I'VE GOTTA COOK THE RICE.
FWIP
HUH?

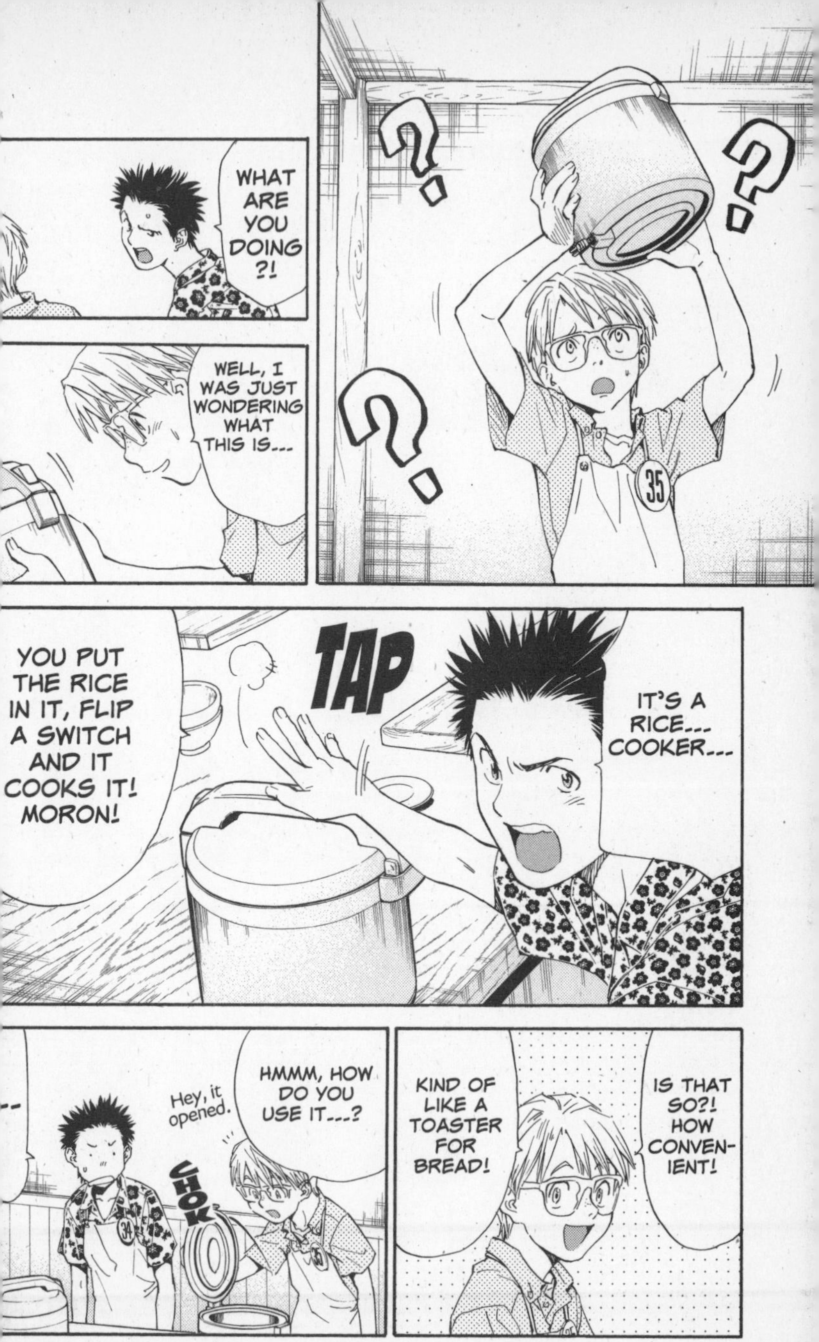

?
?
?
WHAT ARE YOU DOING?!
WELL, I WAS JUST WONDERING WHAT THIS IS...
IT'S A RICE... COOKER...
TAP
YOU PUT THE RICE IN IT, FLIP A SWITCH AND IT COOKS IT! MORON!
IS THAT SO?! HOW CONVEN-IENT!
KIND OF LIKE A TOASTER FOR BREAD!
HMMM, HOW DO YOU USE IT...?
Hey, it opened.
CHOK

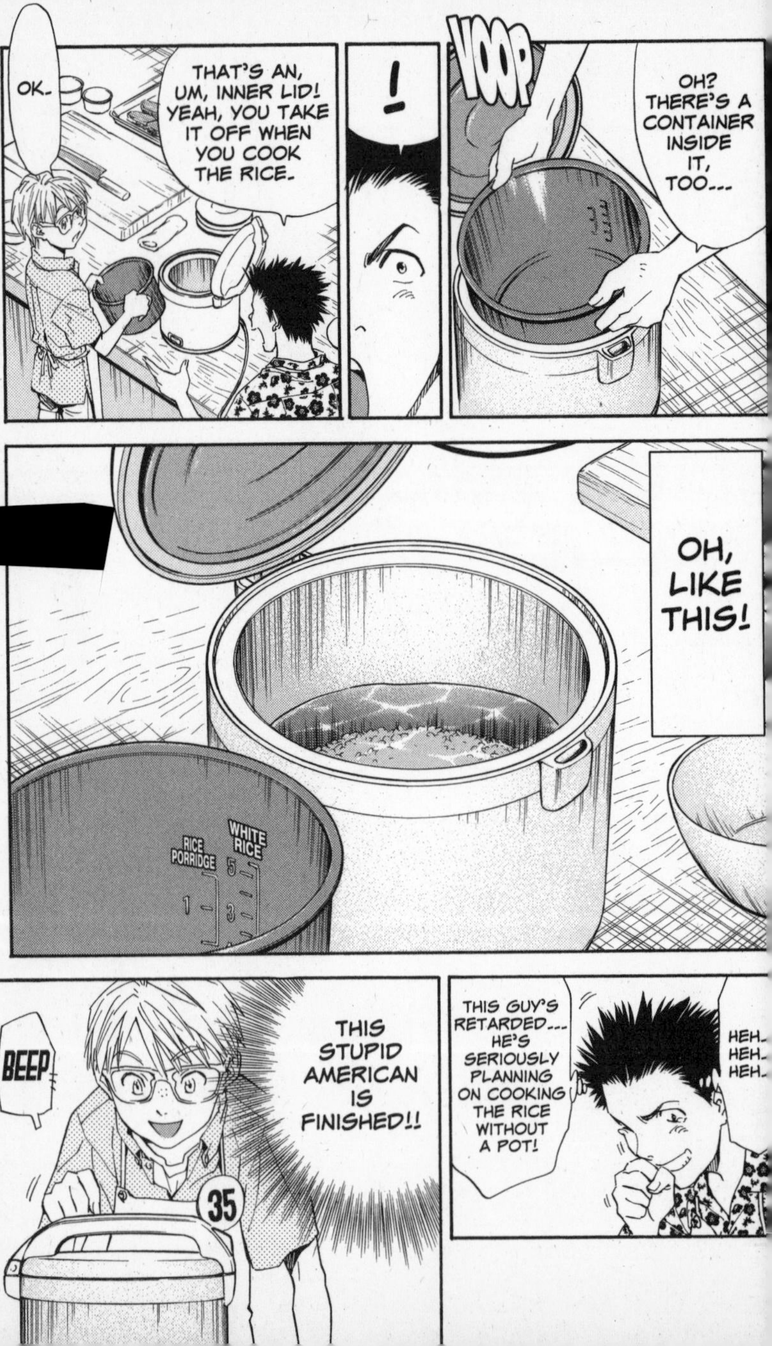
VOOP
OH? THERE'S A CONTAINER INSIDE IT, TOO...
!
THAT'S AN, UM, INNER LID! YEAH, YOU TAKE IT OFF WHEN YOU COOK THE RICE.
OK.
OH, LIKE THIS!
WHITE RICE
RICE PORRIDGE
HEH. HEH. HEH.
THIS GUY'S RETARDED... HE'S SERIOUSLY PLANNING ON COOKING THE RICE WITHOUT A POT!
THIS STUPID AMERICAN IS FINISHED!!
BEEP
35

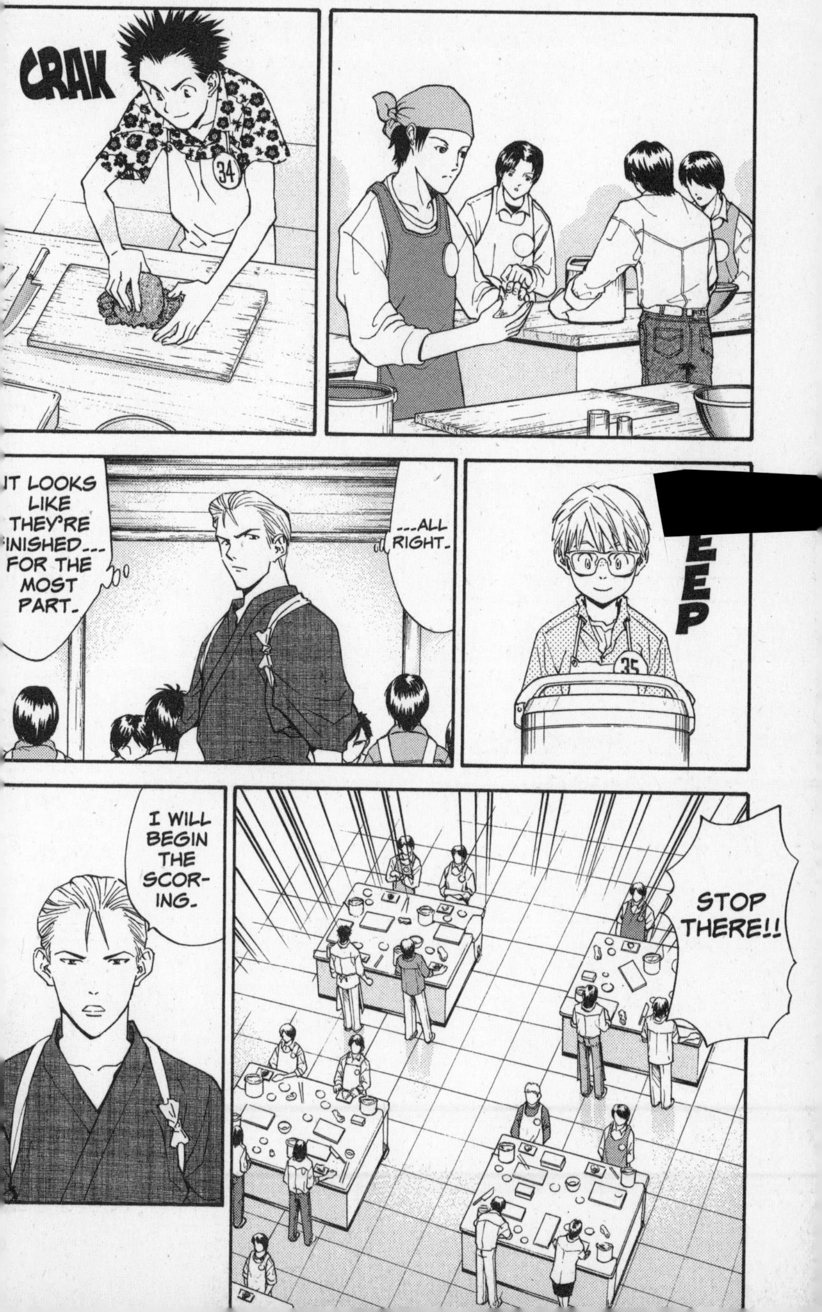
CRAK
[redacted]EEP
IT LOOKS LIKE THEY'RE FINISHED... FOR THE MOST PART.
...ALL RIGHT.
STOP THERE!!
I WILL BEGIN THE SCOR-ING.

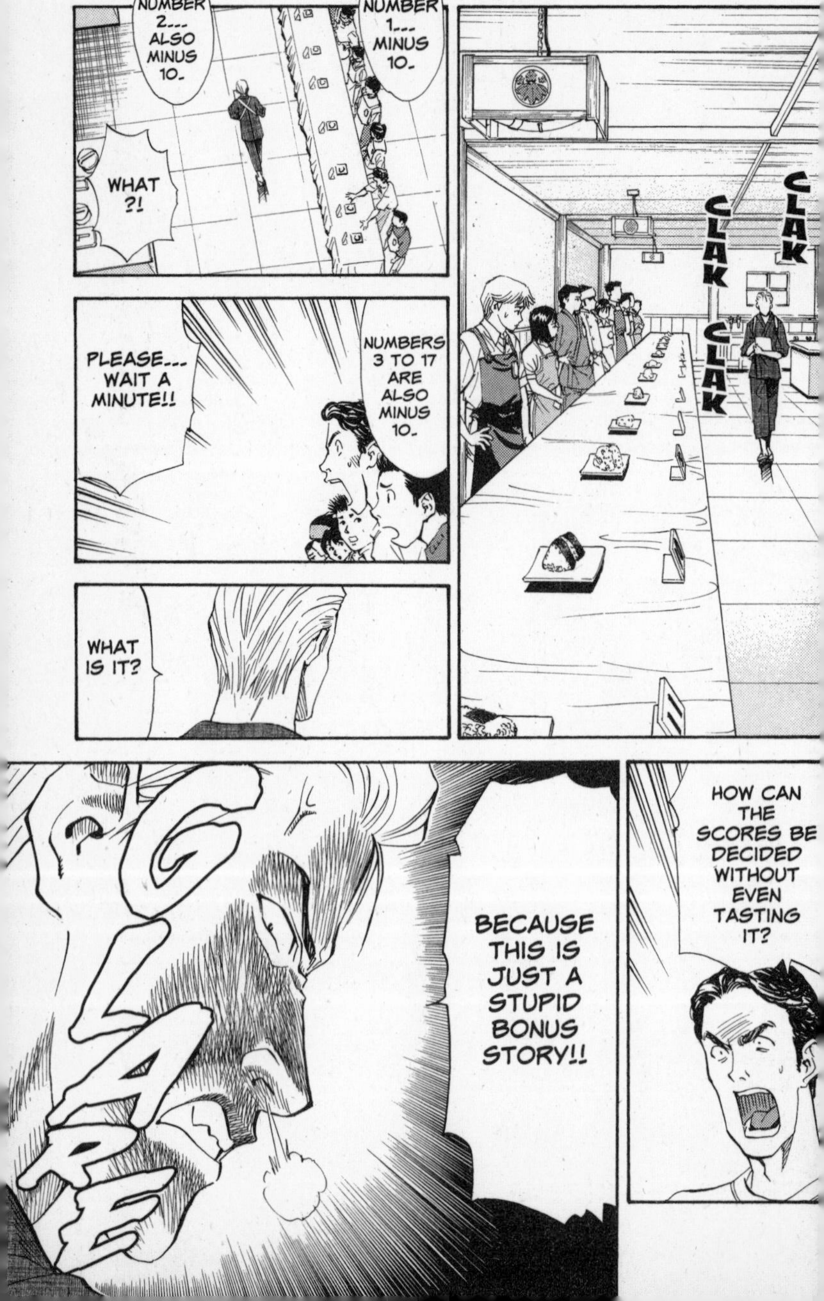
CLAK CLAK
CLAK CLAK
NUMBER 1... MINUS 10.
NUMBER 2... ALSO MINUS 10.
WHAT?!
NUMBERS 3 TO 17 ARE ALSO MINUS 10.
PLEASE... WAIT A MINUTE!!
WHAT IS IT?
HOW CAN THE SCORES BE DECIDED WITHOUT EVEN TASTING IT?
BECAUSE THIS IS JUST A STUPID BONUS STORY!!

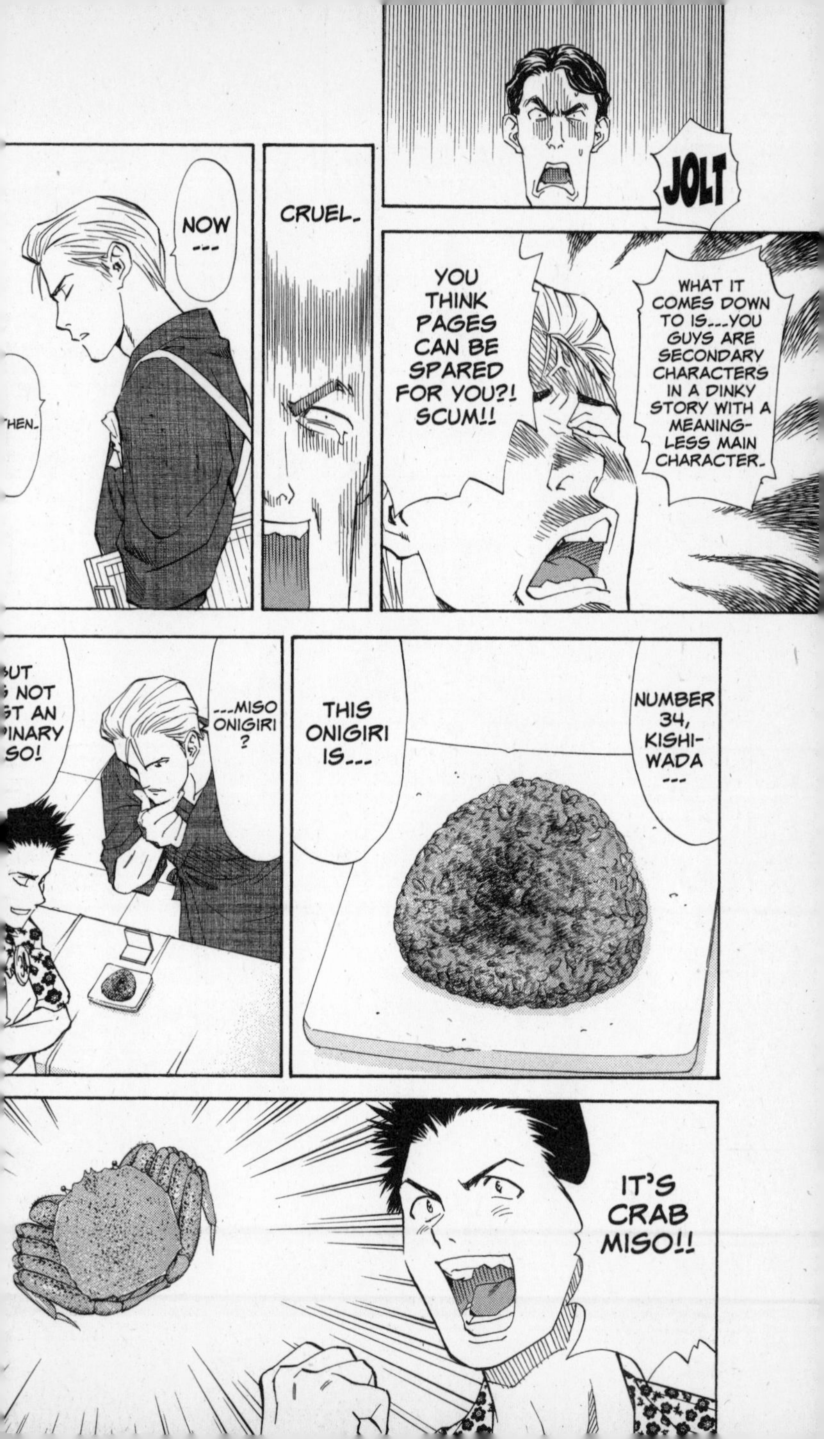

JOLT
WHAT IT COMES DOWN TO IS...YOU GUYS ARE SECONDARY CHARACTERS IN A DINKY STORY WITH A MEANING-LESS MAIN CHARACTER.
YOU THINK PAGES CAN BE SPARED FOR YOU?! SCUM!!
CRUEL.
NOW ---
THEN.
NUMBER 34, KISHI-WADA ---
THIS ONIGIRI IS---
---MISO ONIGIRI ?
UT NOT T AN INARY SO!
IT'S CRAB MISO!!

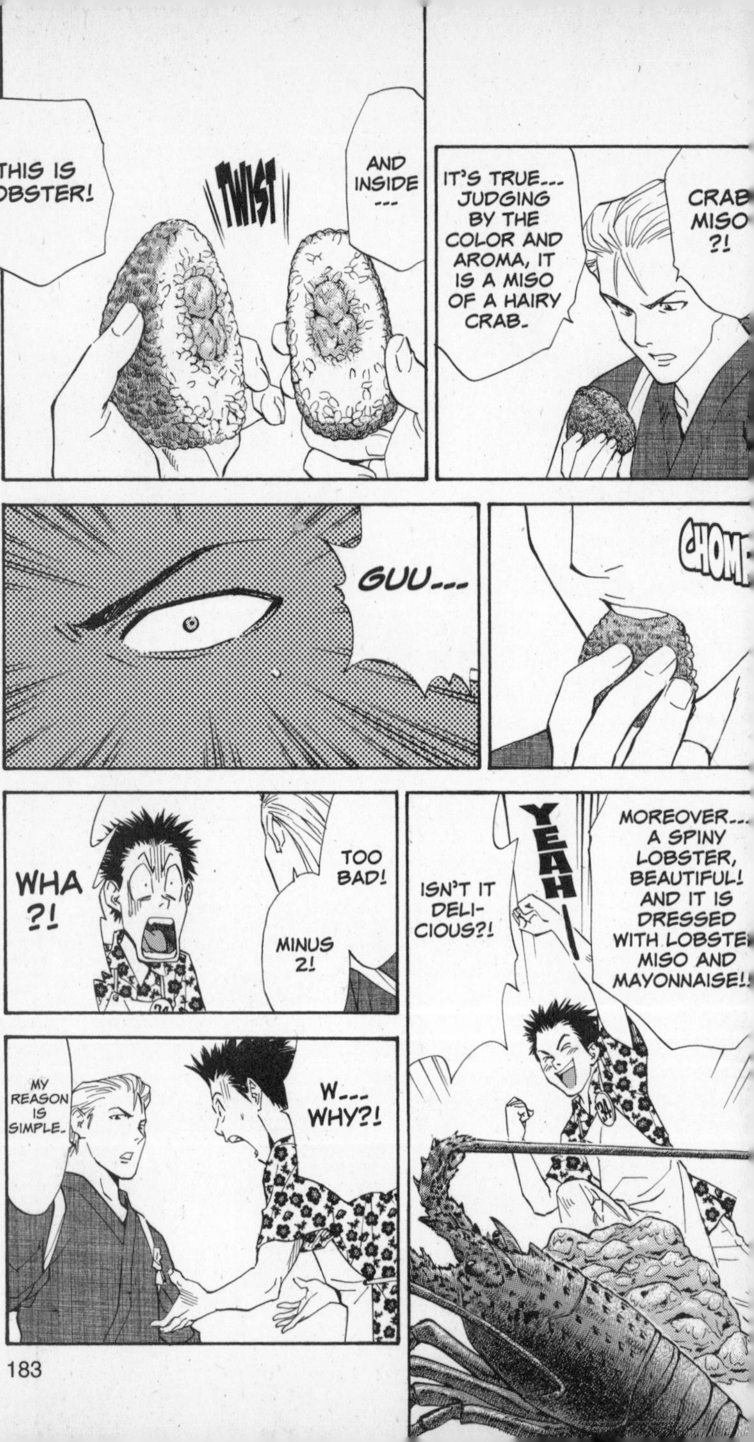
CRAB MISO ?!
IT'S TRUE--- JUDGING BY THE COLOR AND AROMA, IT IS A MISO OF A HAIRY CRAB.
AND INSIDE ---
TWIST
THIS IS LOBSTER!
CHOM
GUU---
MOREOVER--- A SPINY LOBSTER, BEAUTIFUL! AND IT IS DRESSED WITH LOBSTE MISO AND MAYONNAISE!!
YEAH
ISN'T IT DELI-CIOUS?!
TOO BAD!
MINUS 2!
WHA ?!
W--- WHY?!
MY REASON IS SIMPLE.

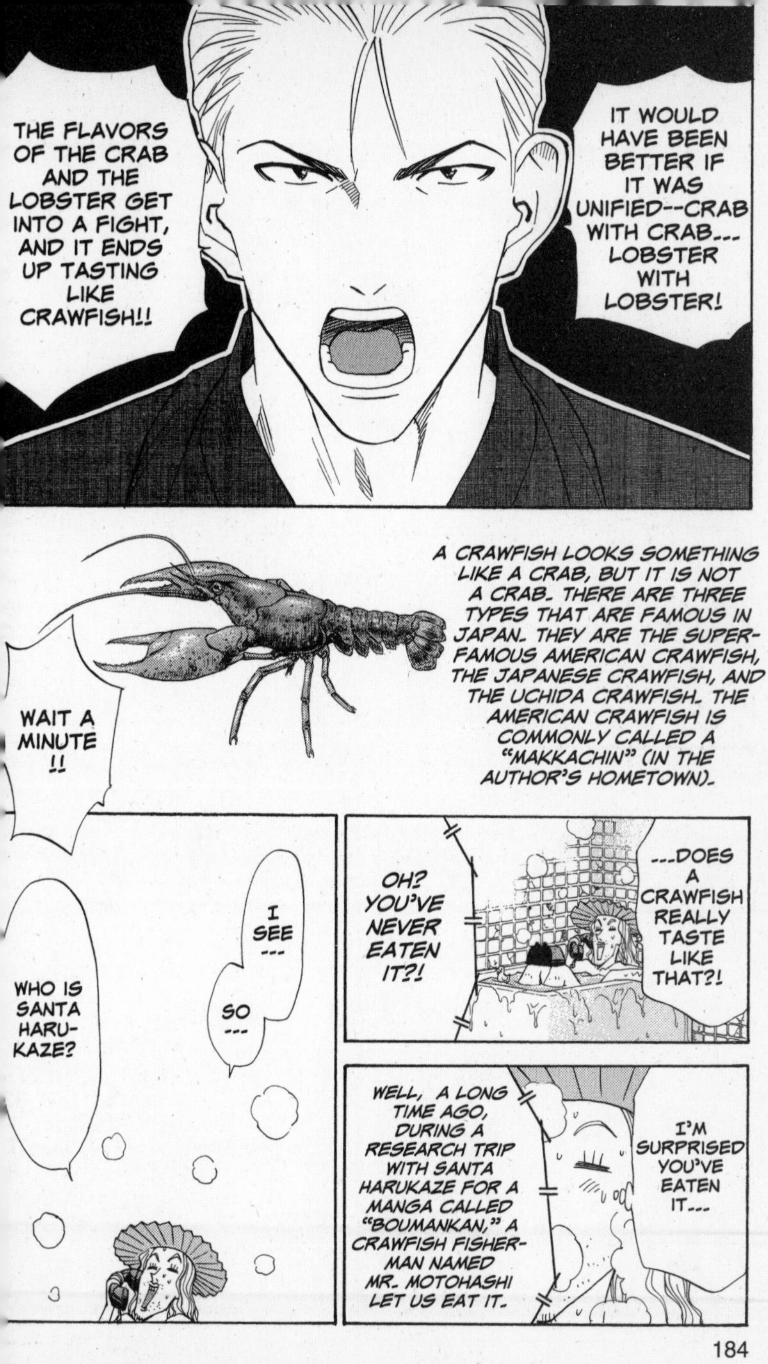
IT WOULD HAVE BEEN BETTER IF IT WAS UNIFIED--CRAB WITH CRAB... LOBSTER WITH LOBSTER!
THE FLAVORS OF THE CRAB AND THE LOBSTER GET INTO A FIGHT, AND IT ENDS UP TASTING LIKE CRAWFISH!!
A CRAWFISH LOOKS SOMETHING LIKE A CRAB, BUT IT IS NOT A CRAB. THERE ARE THREE TYPES THAT ARE FAMOUS IN JAPAN. THEY ARE THE SUPER-FAMOUS AMERICAN CRAWFISH, THE JAPANESE CRAWFISH, AND THE UCHIDA CRAWFISH. THE AMERICAN CRAWFISH IS COMMONLY CALLED A "MAKKACHIN" (IN THE AUTHOR'S HOMETOWN).
WAIT A MINUTE !!
...DOES A CRAWFISH REALLY TASTE LIKE THAT?!
OH? YOU'VE NEVER EATEN IT?!
I'M SURPRISED YOU'VE EATEN IT...
WELL, A LONG TIME AGO, DURING A RESEARCH TRIP WITH SANTA HARUKAZE FOR A MANGA CALLED "BOUMANKAN," A CRAWFISH FISHERMAN NAMED MR. MOTOHASHI LET US EAT IT.
I SEE ...
SO ...
WHO IS SANTA HARUKAZE?

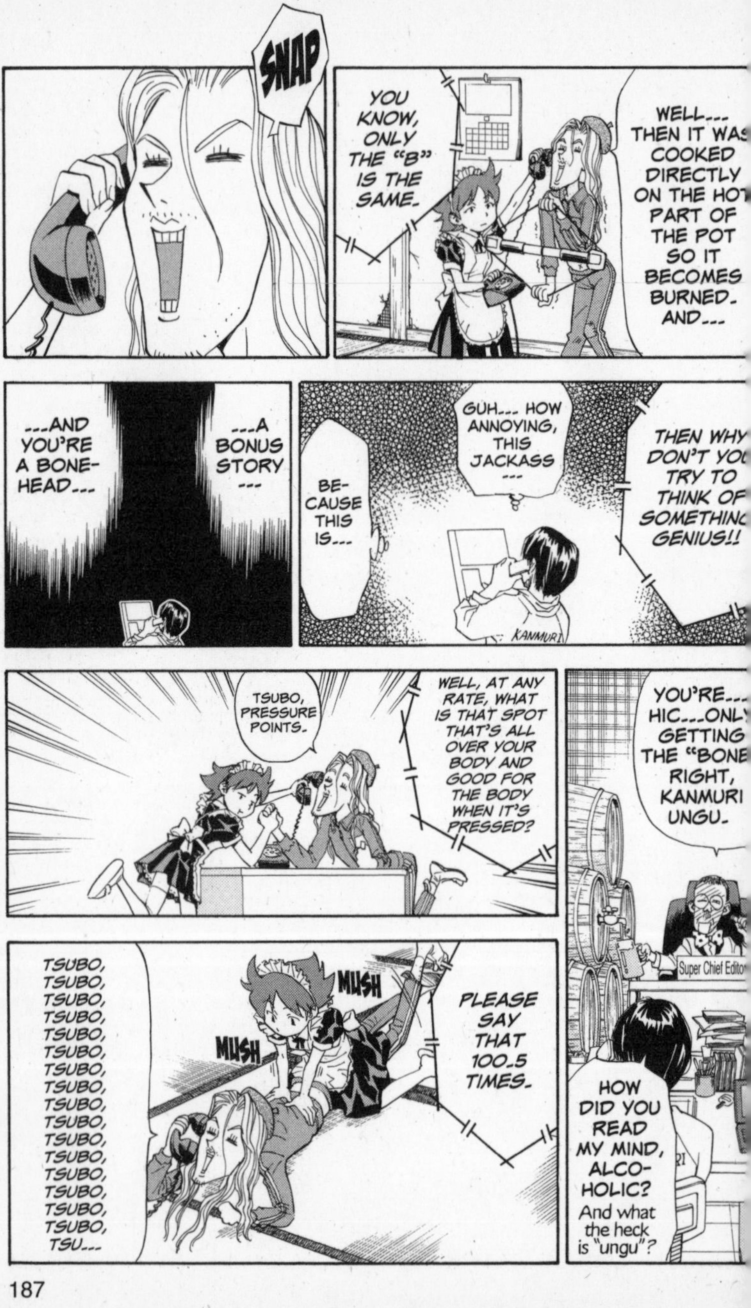
WELL... THEN IT WAS COOKED DIRECTLY ON THE HOT PART OF THE POT SO IT BECOMES BURNED. AND...
YOU KNOW, ONLY THE "B" IS THE SAME.
SNAP
THEN WHY DON'T YOU TRY TO THINK OF SOMETHING GENIUS!!
GUH... HOW ANNOYING, THIS JACKASS...
BE-CAUSE THIS IS...
KANMURI
...A BONUS STORY...
...AND YOU'RE A BONE-HEAD...
YOU'RE... HIC...ONLY GETTING THE "BONE" RIGHT, KANMURI UNGU.
Super Chief Editor
HOW DID YOU READ MY MIND, ALCO-HOLIC?
And what the heck is "ungu"?
WELL, AT ANY RATE, WHAT IS THAT SPOT THAT'S ALL OVER YOUR BODY AND GOOD FOR THE BODY WHEN IT'S PRESSED?
TSUBO, PRESSURE POINTS.
PLEASE SAY THAT 100.5 TIMES.
MUSH
MUSH
TSUBO, TSUBO, TSUBO, TSUBO, TSUBO, TSUBO, TSUBO, TSUBO, TSUBO, TSUBO, TSUBO, TSUBO, TSUBO, TSUBO, TSUBO, TSU...

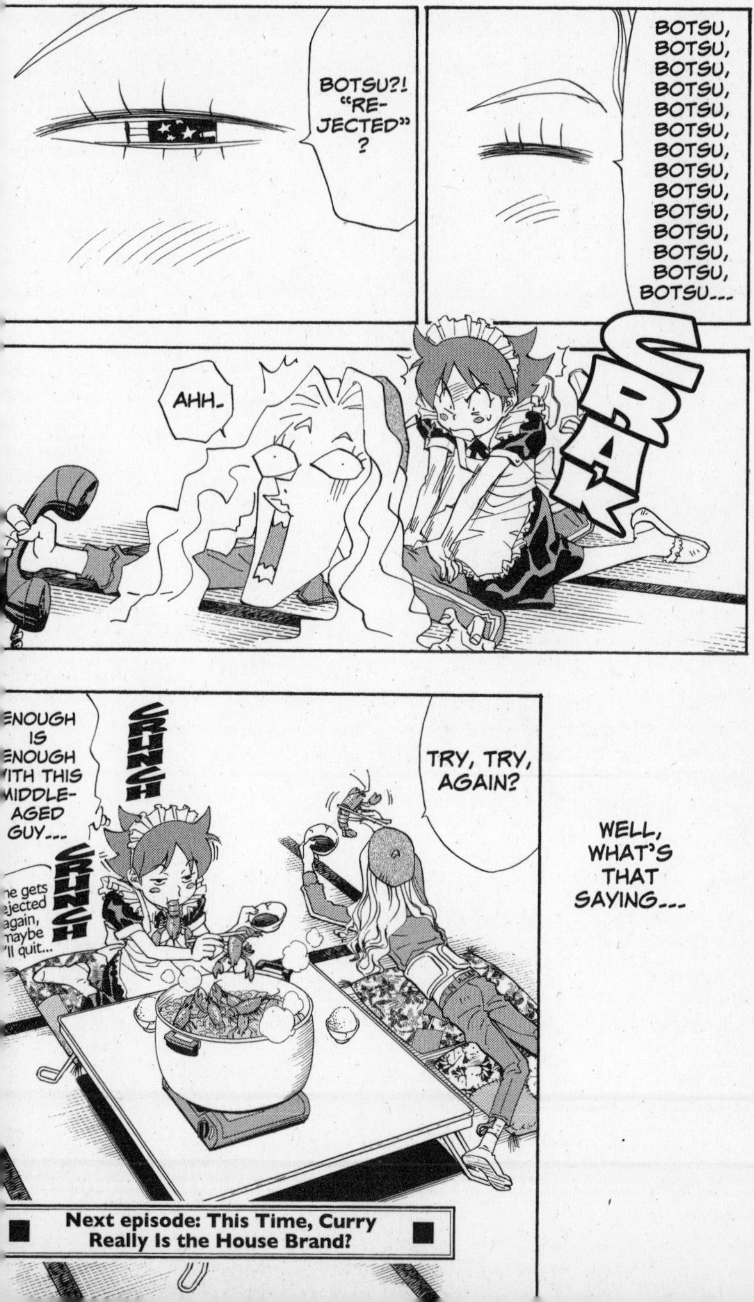
BOTSU, BOTSU, BOTSU, BOTSU, BOTSU, BOTSU, BOTSU, BOTSU, BOTSU, BOTSU, BOTSU, BOTSU, BOTSU, BOTSU...
BOTSU?! "RE-JECTED"?
AHH.
WELL, WHAT'S THAT SAYING...
TRY, TRY, AGAIN?
CRUNCH
ENOUGH IS ENOUGH ITH THIS MIDDLE-AGED GUY...
CRUNCH
he gets ejected again, maybe 'll quit...
Next episode: This Time, Curry Really Is the House Brand?

Freshly Baked!!
Mini Information

——— Croissant ———

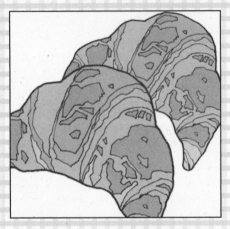

In the manga, Azuma and Suwabara make croissants with an incredible number of layers—like, several hundred and something layers—but in the world record for breads, there seems to have been a person who made one that went beyond 8,000 layers. But if you take that goal to the extreme (it becomes charred black because it's flavored with butter, sugar and so forth), it becomes a bread with no flavor. The moral of the story: in anything, moderation is the best.

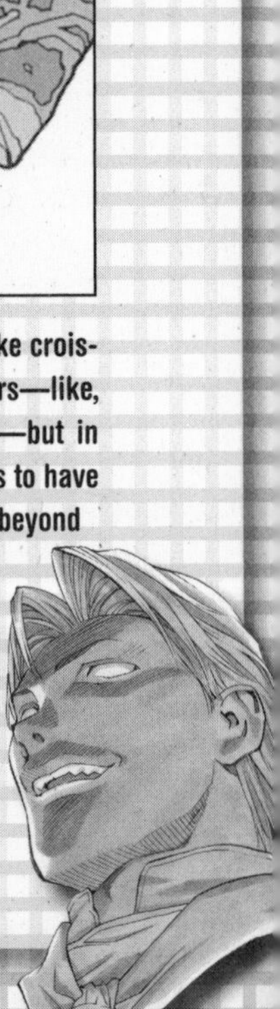

YAKITATE!! JAPAN
VOL. 5

STORY AND ART BY
TAKASHI HASHIGUCHI

English Adaptation/Drew Williams
Translation/Noritaka Minami
Touch-up Art & Lettering/Steve Dutro
Cover Design/Yukiko Whitley
Editor/Kit Fox

Managing Editor/Annette Roman
Editorial Director/Elizabeth Kawasaki
Editor in Chief, Books/Alvin Lu
Editor in Chief, Magazines/Marc Weidenbaum
Sr. Director of Acquisitions/Rika Inouye
Sr. VP of Marketing/Liza Coppola
Exec. VP of Sales & Marketing/John Easum
Publisher/Hyoe Narita

Published by VIZ Media, LLC
P.O. Box 77010
San Francisco, CA 94107

10 9 8 7 6 5 4 3 2 1
First printing, May 2007

www.viz.com   store.viz.com